Public Relations Techniques

D0503320

Books by the same author

Advertising
Advertising Made Simple
Advertising Today
Communication in Industrialising Countries
Dictionary of Marketing, Advertising and Public Relations
Effective Marketing Strategy
Effective Press Relations and House Journal Editing
Effective PR Planning
Effective Publicity Writing
First Course in Marketing
International Dictionary of Marketing and Communication
Introduction to Marketing, Advertising and Public Relations
Modern Marketing
Modern Marketing Communications
Planned Press and Public Relations
Public Relations
Public Relations for Management Success
Public Relations for Marketing Management
Public Relations for Your Business
Secrets of Successful Direct Response Marketing

Contents

Part Four Special Areas of Public Relations

Preface to the first edition

Managing public relations is rather different from creating public relations. It involves management responsibilities of control and direction. Many public relations consultancies have come and gone simply because their principals were merely creative, and had no idea how to run a business. Running a business means making a profit. Similarly, in-house PROs have sometimes lacked status and respect from top management because they have not behaved in a businesslike fashion. They have lacked the ability to plan objectively, and to operate with viable budgeting. Again, they were mainly creative, able to organize events, write news releases or edit a house journal.

Public relations management, whether in-house or consultancy, calls for skills in planning, budgeting, direction and evaluation. At the same time it calls for the widest knowledge of all the media and techniques available. Only thus can public relations attain such a professional standing that it deserves the respect of both top management and the media.

We live in a world peculiarly hostile to public relations. The public relations manager or consultant has a great responsibility to achieve a more harmonious situation. Both sides are at fault. Both sides need to understand each other and each other's motivation better. Journalists may be jealous of the higher salaries earned in public relations, but better management and staff training and supervision could avoid criticism from the media of the shoddy workmanship of public relations staff.

Some newspapers, like *The Financial Times*, admit their debt to public relations and welcome its services. Others adopt a cynical intellectual attitude. As an example, the following description of public relations appeared in the *Guardian's* back page People Diary on 28 August 1986: 'massaging the public face of the RAF'. In the same piece the RAF director of public relations 'purrs . . . tongue in cheek' which is a rather odd mixture of metaphors.

Within business, we also have to contend with the antagonism of marketing people. Some of this has been inspired by Philip Kotler's definition which refers to 'planting commercially significant news'. When I asked the head of a marketing department at a British college why he objected to public relations he retorted 'It has taken us a long time to make marketing respectable without getting involved in public relations'. So the public relations professional is the victim of assaults from all sides.

This book aims to help the public relations manager or consultant to operate in such a way that by his skills and integrity, both as a practitioner and as a manager, he can earn the respect of others, and provide public relations services which achieve their objectives cost-effectively. To do so he must have the active support, understanding and appreciation of top management, marketing personnel and representatives of the media.

Frank Jefkins

Preface to the second edition

Since the first edition of this book was published in 1988 there have been great changes in both the world of public relations, and in education and training for public relations. This new edition aims to address both sets of changes.

The media of public relations have seen remarkable developments in the past few years. The old 'street of ink', Fleet Street, has vanished. The old letterpress newspaper works have been replaced by new offset-litho or flexographic plants in East London and Docklands, while some newspapers are printed by contract printers around the country. Magazines are mostly printed by offset-litho. The magazine world has seen French, German and Spanish publishers challenging the domain of the old big circulation photogravure-printed journals.

The Independent Broadcasting Authority has been replaced by the Independent Television Commission and the Radio Authority. Each has its crazy system, introduced by Mrs Thatcher via the Broadcasting Act 1990, of auctioning station franchises. We now have a number of new companies, such as Carlton in London, Meridian in the South and Good Morning TV at breakfast time. The first national independent radio licences have been awarded to Classic FM and Virgin. Both commercial radio and television programmes can now be sponsored by advertisers.

Video has become a major private public relations medium, the videotape being more versatile and convenient than the old 16 mm film, and we now see the video news release growing in popularity for reasons explained in this book. Business or corporate television has also taken off in the UK, thanks to satellite facilities. Both have a big place in international public relations.

Sponsorship has seen many developments, and a completely re-written and up-to-date chapter deals with this subject in some detail.

The CAM examinations have become increasingly popular, partly because of the need for training and for the security offered by qualifications, and partly because the Institute of Public Relations requires applicants for membership to hold the CAM Diploma or its equivalent. Meanwhile, the Institute's membership topped 5000 in 1993, and Charter status has become less of a dream.

This book has been revised for the benefit of not only CAM Diploma students, but also as essential reading for those taking first and second degree courses at a number of universities, both in the UK and overseas.

Frank Jefkins

Acknowledgements

I would like to express my gratitude to all those who have generously supplied me with information, examples and illustrations for this book, including my fellow members in the IPR, IPRA, BAIE and IABC. A number of quotations have been taken from the press and other publications, and these have been acknowledged in the references at the end of relevant chapters.

My thanks are also expressed to British Telecommunications plc, Fairways Communications and Fuji Film (UK) Ltd, Texaco Ltd, Rentokil Ltd and Jim Macnamara of Macra Communication, Australia, for special material. Since the book is of particular interest to CAM Diploma students I am grateful to the CAM Education Foundation for permission to reproduce syllabuses and past examination papers. My thanks are also due to the Institute of Public Relations for permission to print the Code of Professional Conduct in its latest version, complete with interpretation.

PART ONE

Planning and Management

1

Introduction

The current situation

Public relations is often referred to as a new or a young profession or business, but this is not really so. This supposed newness is sometimes given as an excuse for misunderstandings about public relations. Partly this is voiced by management whose training has often never touched the subject, or by new recruits who are bewildered by its breadth. Between them they often create a mystique which is unnecessary. They often fail to recognize the very simple purpose of public relations which is to create *understanding*. They try to pretend that public relations is something more complex or devious, like advertising or propaganda, and they go on to confuse it with those two very different promotional forms of communication. We shall return to this theme when discussing definitions.

It is, however, true to say that public relations has developed very rapidly in recent years, partly because the managements of various commercial and non-commercial organizations have discovered a need for public relations activities, and again because throughout the world there has been a huge increase in the means by which public relations messages can be conveyed. It may also be true that the terms 'public relations' and 'public affairs' have been given to communications, implying something unduly special, but organizations of all kinds have been communicating for centuries. All that modern public relations has done has been to refine the techniques and integrate the action so that we have a distinct discipline.

To explain this briefly: many governments have been using public relations techniques for at least the past seventy years; house journals have been published for more than 150 years; documentary films have been produced for the past fifty years; and public relations has been organized professionally by the Institute of Public Relations in Britain

and the Public Relations Society of America in the USA since 1948.
Where does its history begin? Probably as soon as people found it
necessary to communicate in order to make themselves understood. It
exists whether we like it or not. It would not be improper to suggest
the Bible is full of examples, with tablets of stone and scrolls of
papyrus as early media.

Little has been published on the history of public relations but one
record was produced in 1977 by Freddie Gillman, who was president
of the IPR in 1961. A condensed version was published in the fortieth
anniversary issue of *Public Relations*.[1] The present author produced a
history of public relations as a keynote address at a Summer School,
and this was reproduced in another of the author's books.[2]

Among the earliest examples of public relations were forms of
corporate identity, as in transportation, beginning with the bird or
animal symbols on the sails of Phoenician and Viking ships. Over the
centuries the funnels of steamships, together with stage-coaches, trains,
trams, taxis and buses have been painted in identifying colours.
Emblems on shields and the uniforms of armed and other uniformed
services were similar forms of corporate identity. This kind of identification and distinction has grown up into systems of logotypes,
typography, uniforms, dress and badges, colours and the liveries of
transportation, of which the modern airline is a prime example.

Government and public services have been among the leading users
of public relations techniques. The British Treasury had its spokesman
in 1809, Lloyd George as Chanceller of the Exchequer used public
relations to explain the new old age pension scheme in 1912, and the
first president of the IPR, Sir Stephen Tallents, used public relations to
promote the Empire Marketing Board between 1926 and 1933.

In many parts of the developing world, public relations techniques
have been adopted because of the urgent need to educate people about
new public services, and in order to introduce new lifestyles. In such
countries, this need to communicate in ways quite different from
advertising and propaganda, has demanded the use of new methods.
This need has aroused great interest in the subject in countries throughout Africa, Asia, the Caribbean and, more recently, in the Middle East.
Better education, greater literacy and the use of both mass media and
traditional folk media known as oramedia, have made possible the
application of public relations techniques. People in industrialized
countries of the North are often surprised by the extent of public
relations in countries like Nigeria and Malaysia.

Meanwhile, British public relations has seen a boom in demand for
consultancy services, some of which trebled their billings in the mid-
1980s, although some suffered loss of business during the recession of

the 1990s. New industries, services and technologies, and new kinds of media with all their additional opportunities for the communicator, have seen an upsurge in the fortunes and the application of the practice. As evidence of this we have seen the success of *PR Week* with a circulation of 15,000 copies, something which would have been impossible only a few years ago when earlier publications failed.

This has created a demand for not only more staff but more able and versatile personnel in spite of virtually no pre-entry training system, and very meagre training facilities for those employed. However, realization that one cannot just train on the job, and that training is vital to the healthy growth of the profession, and to its ability to provide efficient, cost-effective services, has exercised the urgent attention of the professional bodies. In 1992, an IPR survey revealed that there were at least 28,500 people employed in some public relations capacity.

The Communication, Advertising and Marketing Education Foundation (CAM) has been re-organized; the Institute of Public Relations has succeeded in gaining control of the public relations side of CAM; a number of degree courses have been launched at Bournemouth, Leeds, Manchester, Plymouth and elsewhere; the London Chamber of Commerce and Industry has won greatly increased interest in its examinations in public relations; and the International Association of Business Communicators has been developing its accreditation by examination programme. There is also the international public relations diploma course at the West Herts College, Watford, and an MSc in Public Relations at Stirling University.

We have also moved from the minor role of the press officer to the senior managerial one of the practitioner in charge of a separate department, and for management to recognize the need to be involved in communications instead of regarding it as the lonely function of some tame underling. The range and responsibilities of the practitioner will be seen later in the Mexican Statement definition of public relations.

Much of modern public relations calls for mature people with some experience of business who are able to advise management on a great variety of issues. Consequently, recruits are often second or third career people and this poses a dilemma for young would-be entrants even if they are graduates, but it is significant that a large proportion of CAM students are graduates. Few professions have such high calibre personnel. Now that the IPR requires membership applicants to hold the CAM Diploma (or its equivalent), the number of registered CAM students grew in the 1990s in spite of recession. The compromise is probably to define the qualities required of any person likely to succeed in public relations whatever his or her age, experience, academic or vocational qualifications.

Broadly, the public relations practitioner needs to have the following attributes:

1 Ability to communicate.
2 Ability to organize.
3 Ability to get on with people.
4 Personal integrity.
5 Imagination.
6 Willingness to learn.

It is also necessary to be something of a jack-of-all-trades (unlike advertising agency personnel who are mostly specialists) with a knowledge of many ancillary subjects. Some of these may be listed as:

1 Media, both existing mass and created private.
2 Printing.
3 Photography, video and other audio visuals and visual aids.
4 Exhibitions.
5 Marketing research.
6 Sponsorships.

In addition, the ability to plan, budget and direct programmes is necessary. The old 'gin and tonic' idea of a PRO hardly fits into this.

All this is very different from the elementary abilities to write news releases and entertain journalists, especially when the experience of the media people is that very few practitioners are capable of writing a publishable news release! This abysmal state of the art has resulted in the 'adversarial situation' between the media and public relations. At least 70 per cent of the news releases received by editors are unusable, and they flood in from famous sources. However, this is not a British phenomenon but is common worldwide.

This situation is worsened by the exploitation of editorial fax machines to receive unsolicited releases of no possible editorial value. Editors will welcome the faxing of urgent material which they have invited, but the general distribution of releases by fax has become an abuse of the privilege. Why should editors have to pay to receive rubbish?

The adversarial situation is demonstrated by the glee with which the following was printed in bold type in *The Independent* Diary:[3]

SEVEN identical press releases, all in separate envelopes but sent to the same addressee, have just arrived at this newspaper; it's the kind of crass wastage of trees, fuel and money that happens from time to time. The press release alerts us to a forthcoming and fat report on how well the sender is keeping its green promises. And who might that sender be? The Department of The Environment.

Untypical? Not unlikely!

Or walk round the despatch department of that excellent firm Two-Ten Communications and see the junk mail being sent out to the press. Some of it is even in boxed sets like boxed Christmas cards. You only have to *look* at many of these releases to see that they are advertisements tarted up with all the tricks of word processors to pretend they are news stories. Clients are actually paying so-called consultants to send out this stuff. Obviously, neither clients nor consultants ever read newspapers.

The adversarial situation is created by public relations practitioners, not the media. There is often a cry for 'PR for PR' but it has got to start with the workmanship of the practitioners themselves in what may well be called 'the most untrained profession'. Until things change the Privy Council is unlikely to welcome the IPR's bid for charter status.

Public relations defined

Having set the scene, let us now establish a clear understanding of what public relations is all about. This will be done with two definitions followed by an explanation of the Public Relations Transfer Process.

Public relations practice is the planned and sustained effort to establish and maintain goodwill and mutual understanding between an organization and its publics.

This is the revised IPR definition. Its importance lies in emphasizing the need for *planning, sustained effort* and *mutual* understanding. A lot of public relations is ineffective, and not cost-effective, because it is haphazard instead of being planned. This is where the managerial aspect becomes apparent. Bad public relations results from this and that being done, as and when someone wants it done. There is no management in that dogsbody situation, but it happens all too often. In the end, public relations is criticized as being intangible and a waste of money. Of course it is as if fire-fighting exercises are engaged in, instead of conducting a planned programme with clear objectives so that results can be assessed. Also, unlike advertising which may have short-term campaigns, public relations needs to be a sustained day-in day-out activity. Finally, and again unlike advertising, there must be *mutual* understanding. In public relations we receive as well as transmit information, we listen as well as speak. This may require research and the use of various feedback techniques. Even a press cutting can reveal what and how the media are reporting about the organization, which is very different from counting column inches or centimetres.

Public relations practice is the art and social science of analysing trends, predicting their consequences, counselling organization leaders, and implementing planned programmes of action which will serve both the organization's and the public interest.

Known as the Mexican Statement because it resulted from an international conference of public relations organizations held in Mexico City in 1978, this is a more comprehensive definition. It is worth careful analysis because it does spell out the full role, nature and responsibilities of public relations. Moreover, it closely resembles the Six Point Public Relations Planning Model which will be discussed in Chapter 4, and it also calls for application of the attributes of a practitioner set out earlier in this chapter.

First, the Mexican Statement refers to *analysing trends*. Before we can begin the planning emphasized in the IPR definition it is necessary to discover the present situation or the current image. What opinions or attitudes exist, what is the extent and accuracy of awareness, is there understanding or misunderstanding and does a good, bad or false image exist? Those concerned may consist of the community, employees, suppliers, distributors, consumers, financial institutions, politicians, civil servants, academics and a whole host of influential opinion leaders. No campaign can be planned until we have studied the trends which influence the organization's future. Until we know the communication problems we cannot plan the communication solutions. Much of public relations work is about effecting change.

This is basic to the management of public relations. No public relations departmental manager or consultant can recommend a programme and expect money to be funded for its execution unless this foundation has been laid. Yet it is not uncommon for practitioners, in-house and in consultancies, to be presented with the management's concept of the situation which is no more than an optimistic belief. This wishful thinking is known as the mirror image. It is a trap which can only lead to ineffective public relations. A great deal of public relations is conducted in this casual and futile fashion. The management factor arises here: the efficient public relations manager or consultant will insist on an initial study of the situation. This happens in marketing and advertising, so why not in public relations? It may cost money, but it is an insurance against wasting money on bad practice.

Second, once the situation has been studied the consequences can be predicted. Usually, unless remedies are applied, a bad situation can only get worse. As we shall see from the Public Relations Transfer Process discussed next in this chapter, most public relations is about converting negative situations into positive ones.

Third, we have the important advisory role of public relations. Much of public relations work is involved in advising management and that is why maturity is so often required of the in-house manager or outside consultant.

There are two aspects of public relations management – management of the in-house department or the consultancy, and client services and working with top management of the organization. Giving advice to management can range from personal advice on a day-to-day basis to attending committees consisting of other managers or even as a board director. In many of our most successful companies there is a one-to-one relationship between the chief executive officer and the public relations director. This is where the positioning of the PRO is important, as is the budgeting of public relations funds. A proper relationship is impossible if the PRO is placed in the marketing department, public relations is regarded as 'below-the-line', and its funds come within the advertising budget. The absurdity of that situation is apparent if one accepts that public relations should service the entire organization.

Having conducted the research and assessed the findings it is now the practitioner's task to advise management on what needs to be done. The plan of campaign complete with ideas, methods and budget has to be presented. This calls for diligent planning of the workload in terms of manhours and use of materials, resources and expenses.

This leads to the *fourth* part of the definition, implementation of the planned programme, including opportunities to report progress, and to be flexible if circumstances change. This programme should have objectives, and the extent to which these objectives are eventually achieved should be either obvious or measurable. The programme should be conducted in such a way that it serves the organization's interests.

Finally, there is a *fifth* consideration. The programme should also serve the public interest. In other words, it should be responsible and in no way be unethical or anti-social, nor should it exploit or corrupt the integrity of the media. If the practitioner is a member of his professional body (e.g. the IPR) he will be expected to uphold a code of professional conduct. As a manager this relates not only to his external relations but to his refusal to accept instructions to behave unethically.

This is not being purist, but very practical. It is amazing how some employers and clients take it for granted that the public relations man or woman can be used to manipulate the media, and can be expected to serve as a confidence trickster, a fixer and a face saver. Armed with the code of conduct, a professional practitioner can withstand these abuses. The supposedly dubious role of the PRO is frequently depicted in novels, plays and on TV as some sort of big business hit man, an expert in dirty tricks. Such a situation cannot of course happen when the practitioner is in a senior position, respected as a professional adviser, nor when top management has a proper under-standing of public relations and recognizes the importance of integrity and credibility. Public relations cannot perform unless it is believed.

We said earlier that the bad practitioner was responsible for the conflict involved in the adversarial situation, but it is also true that journalists create a false idea of public relations when they refer sarcas-tically to 'PR exercises'. These are usually political initiatives which they consider to be insincere. An example of this was a leader in *The Independent on Sunday*[4] which commented on how the tabloids had tricked David Mellor before his resignation. The leader concluded by saying 'Thus newspapers created an image of Mr Mellor quite different from the one he wished as the "official" image. But a respectable press, of which everyone approves, is a press not worth having; better a pack of dogs than a flock of sheep grazing on PR handouts.' Thus, the newspaper expressed its contempt, rightly or wrongly, for public relations. But sometimes the press dislike of public relations is attached to things that have nothing to do with public relations, such as a presidential visit to a disaster area where even a sincere action is mocked. Very sagely, Herb Schmertz, in his book *Goodbye to the Low Profile*,[5] warned that friendship with journalists was inadvisable.

Once again, the comparison can be made between public relations and those other two forms of communication, advertising and propa-ganda, with which it is sometimes confused. To succeed — and this may be hard to swallow because wishes and intentions may be differ-ent — public relations should be unbiased. It should deal in facts, not fancies. But to succeed, both advertising and propaganda must be biased because they must say only good about their subjects. In con-trast, public relation may be required to explain the bad. It has to climb right down the greasy pole, not make excuses and pretend bad things have never happened. The public relations man or woman cannot afford to be an apologist or a trouble-shooter, no matter how much some managements would like this, or how they may be portrayed in fiction. In fact, crisis management has become a major area of public relations. On the other hand, the humble news release becomes a puff if it presents biased information, and is scorned by the editor.

Credibility is vital in public relations, and this is really the answer to the unfortunate adversarial situation. Obviously, it is easy for the practitioner to feel sincerely biased towards his or her company or client. That's only natural. We have to believe in the product or service, and we may honestly believe it is superior to any other. But it is advertising to say so, and in public relations we must avoid self-praise. For example, when a news release is published it becomes the message from the media and it will be expressed objectively. We cannot put nice words in the editor's mouth.

The primary objective of public relations

Here we touch on yet another misconception about our subject. The object of public relations is frequently though to be the achievement of a favourable image, a favourable climate of opinion, or favourable mention by the media. That is an unfavourable fallacy. How does it maintain all these favourable aspects for most of our public service organizations − the police, Post Office, water, gas and electricity authorities, public transport and so on − which are bound to have to deal with numerous unfavourable situations? Since they serve the multitude they can seldom please most of the people most of the time. All they can achieve is *understanding* which is very different from blanket approval. A classic case is the nuclear fuel industry, which is also under attack from propagandists like Greenpeace, however sincere.

Let us look more closely at this primary objective − *understanding* − by means of the Public Relations Transfer Process, which makes non-sense of the favourable fallacy.

With this model we have another example of the need to *analyse*

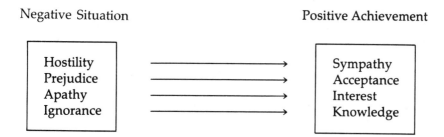

Negative Situation		Positive Achievement
Hostility Prejudice Apathy Ignorance	⟶ ⟶ ⟶ ⟶	Sympathy Acceptance Interest Knowledge

When the negative situation is converted into positive achievement − through knowledge − the result is the primary objective of public relations, **understanding.**

Figure 1.1 *The Public Relations Transfer Process*

trends in order to plan an objective programme. It indicates both the scope and the limitations of public relations. The responsibilities of public relations management are also highlighted. Moreover, it demonstrates the true nature of the subject and shows how it differs from persuasive, promotional activities such as selling, advertising, sales promotion and marketing. It also demonstrates how it can contribute to the success of every function of a business whether it be staff relations, marketing or finance. No activity conducted by any organization can succeed if understanding is lacking, which is why public relations relates to the total communications of any organization, inside and outside. That takes some expert managing.

Hostility   What is the extent of nature of hostility towards the organization, its people, activities, products or services? It is no use pretending hostility does not exist. It may be irrational, based on fear, misunderstanding or false information. Certain people may not like big companies or foreign ones. In some way, people may feel threatened by an organization or by what it does, yet no genuine threat may exist. It may be that dislike could remain − after all, some people like bitter or dry drinks, some prefer them sweet − but it is possible to achieve at least a sympathetic attitude, one of tolerance and understanding. In recent times many ideas which were once hated have now won sympathy if not support. In developing countries new lifestyles have been adopted which were once resisted, while in the industrialized world new technologies have won, or are winning, approval. There was at one time hatred towards Japanese products, the computer and the use of motorcar seat belts, just as centuries ago there was hatred towards machinery and workers threw their boots (*sabots*) into machines − hence the word sabotage!

Prejudice   Can we convert prejudice into acceptance? This task is not unlike changing hatred into sympathy, except that it is more difficult. Prejudice has usually endured longer, and is derived from upbringing, environment, education and other very powerful and usually very early influences. For instance, success and affluence seldom change the working class attitudes of a person and vice versa, as we see in election voting patterns. Prejudices can survive a lifetime. We see it in the religious and tribal disputes all over the world. Even in London, those who live South or North of the Thames regard each other as foreigners, while short stretches of water between Britain and the continent have deterred the British from regarding themselves as Europeans. They still talk of 'going to Europe' or having 'a holiday in Europe'. The saying, 'old habits die hard' is very true. Maybe the Channel Tunnel and the Single European Market will bring about changes of attitude but it could be a slow process.

Yet this is a situation which confronts public relations. It may be very difficult to interest a young housewife in an electric cooker if her mother always used gas. There can be whole 'shut off' areas where communication is confronted by walls of prejudice. No amount of advertising will knock them down, but the informative, educational efforts of public relations could be more successful. We have seen this in the travel business with people now taking holidays in countries towards which they were once deeply prejudiced, to mention only Germany, Russia, China and Japan.

Apathy People are naturally conservative. They have a self-protective resistance to change. They are wrapped up in their own private affairs. If public relations is to achieve understanding, it has to break down this unwillingness to want to know. Somehow, Festinger's famous theory of cognitive dissonance needs to be effected: the apathy needs to be converted into interest. The apathetic recipient of public relations messages has to be prodded into taking an interest. That is still, of course, a long way from being persuaded to buy. For instance, advertising will have no effect unless the subject has moved from the negative attitude of apathy to the positive one of interest.

To take the example a step further: apathy may deter a person from considering taking a holiday, public relations may develop an interest in holiday-making, advertising may produce an application for a brochure about holidays in Israel, but the Palestinian situation may discourage an actual booking. The role of public relations is seen here as an important stage in the communication process, but it is not promotional, and persuasions one way or the other depend on entirely different forms of communication.

Ignorance Finally, we arrive at a condition from which we all suffer. Inevitably, people are ignorant about a great many things. The PRO of an organization will be thoroughly familiar with his or her subject, and it may be difficult to reconcile himself or herself to the extent of most other people's ignorance about the subject. But how can you market something of which people are ignorant? It's done all the time, of course, at great profit to the media and the advertising agencies, and at great cost but little, if any, profit to the promoters. Once again, we see the role of public relations in educating the market. Call it market education or pre-selling, the aim is to prepare the market so that it is more likely to respond to advertising. Such a process may occupy 18 months' to two years' work before advertising breaks. Many products have failed, costing their companies fortunes, because market education was not undertaken.

Probably the best example that can be quoted concerns woodworm. Few houses in Britain are without woodworm. Thirty years ago the average householder knew little about timber pests. Woodworm was considered a rarity, something you found in old property, or which existed only in dirty houses. All that has changed. No building society will agree a loan without checking for woodworm. Meanwhile, the leading company in the woodworm treatment business, Rentokil, is a successful growth company in spite of recession. During those 30 years Rentokil's public relations was ubiquitous, but its advertising was minimal. When Clive Thomson took over as chief executive (coming from Britain's largest advertiser Cadbury-Schweppes) he was surprised to find how little Rentokil spent on advertising. Rentokil's success owes much to the excellence of its products and service, and 60 per cent of its business is said to derive from recommendations. Nevertheless, financial growth would not have been possible if ignorance had not been removed. Significantly, Rentokil has used every technique in the public relations book, and during those thirty years it was blessed by top management which understood public relations, and knew what it wanted. Literally, during that period the company's communications developed from a duplicated bulletin for salesmen to a video studio. The full story is told in another book by the author.[6]

But public relations can be equally valuable in preparing the way for big spenders on advertising. When Philips launched its CDi system in 1992 it was well known by the trade, educationalists, company trainers and others. On the other hand, disaster hit Sinclair's C5 electric tricycle because the advance story had hinted at an electric car, and expectations were demolished when the roofless and hazardous C5 was advertised. This was a prime example of advertising being unable to sell not only a bad product but also an unknown one.

From these comments on the four negative states of hostility, prejudice, apathy and ignorance it should be clear that before planning, budgeting and recommending a public relations programme it is essential to find out the extent and nature of these four weaknesses. It is not unlike a SWOT analysis which looks at strengths, weaknesses, opportunities and threats. Some or all of these failings may exist. In contrast, there may also be strengths where the opposite situations are found to exist. There may be no hostility, only rapturous acclaim. No one may be prejudiced: everyone may have an utterly fair-minded attitude to our company or product. As for apathy, no, everyone is wildly enthusiastic. And instead of being ignorant, most people will be thoroughly knowledgeable. That ideal situation is unlikely. There are people who detest baked beans, are prejudiced about their name, shape, colour, taste or smell, are unable to work up any enthusiasm for them, or wouldn't know a baked bean even if a plateful was put in front of them.

All this adds up to the primary purpose of public relations, the creation of *understanding*.

Is understanding the primary purpose of public relations?

Many people, from top management to public relations practitioners themselves, and different associated outsiders from politicians to journalists, may not be content with the author's claim that the primary purpose of public relations is the creation and maintenance of understanding, no more, no less. That is a tremendous task in itself, and an extremely difficult one.

It has nothing to do with advertising and not always anything to do with marketing. If one is trying to create understanding of a hospital's work in heart transplant surgery, or the achievements of the police in multi-racial communications, the purposes of a micro-chip, the tenets of Islam, the geographical location of the Isle of Bute, or the nutritional value of a peanut one is not involved in advertising.

Yet there are those who insist that public relations is and should be a form of advertising, that it is certainly a cheap substitute for advertising, while the media tend to regard public relations stories as advertisements (which, unfortunately, too many of them are!). A problem which occurs in the consultancy world is that consultancy staff are often too junior to be able to resist the demand from clients to issue unpublishable puffs. Presumably clients employ consultants with juvenile staff because the fees are low, and they can get their own way. That sort of luxury is not serious public relations, and does media—public relations relations no good at all.

While it is true that most public relations people work in-house, and not in consultancies, which is the opposite of advertising practice, it is also true that the greater part of public relations activity is outside the business or commercial world. This also means that its users probably engage in little, if any, advertising or marketing. This huge area of public relations embraces central and local government, quangos, political parties, trade unions, professional institutes, voluntary bodies and trade associations, the police, the armed forces, the fire and ambulance brigades, the health and social services, charities, special interest societies and clubs, sports clubs and societies and so on.

There are also those who see public relations as a means of promoting, influencing, convincing, encouraging, persuading and so on which are the responsibilities of advertising, sales promotion and propaganda. Similarly, public relations is thought to be a kind of below-the-line activity. These are eminent people who claim that public relations is a form of propaganda, which is nonsense. There are others who argue that its aim is to persuade people to take certain action, but are we in the persuasion business? It is none of these things, any more than a cabbage rose is one you eat or a tea rose is one you drink: However, the perversion of public relations in these strange directions has resulted in:

1   Top management's misunderstanding of the purpose of public relations.
2   Cowboys and cowgirls who abuse and pervert the practice because of their ignorance of what it really is all about.
3   The adversarial situation between the media and public relations which has been created by organization leaders and their PROs abusing and perverting public relations, and by the media assuming that it is the system of manipulation, distortion and dishonesty which is their daily experience. The evidence lies in hundreds of editorial waste bins every day in every editorial office throughout the world. It is as if public relations possesses a death wish and is anxious to destroy itself by its own hand. Or, to take another analogy, it is like having a medical profession aimed at killing its patients. The absurdity of the situation is not even like old-fashioned quackery.

Fortunately, the reverse is also true resulting in:

1   Top management which understands public relations and knows exactly what it needs to communicate. The chief executive is literally the organization's first PRO. This is true of most of our very successful companies and is reflected in their share prices.
2   PROs who are answerable to their chief executives, and may be board directors. Consultants who serve appreciative top management.
3   Good media relationships based on mutual frankness and respect. Practitioners understand how, when and why editors need material, and editors know who they can rely on to supply what they want when and how they want it.

Positioning of in-house PRO

Many organizational charts of business do not show the PRO in an independent role. This can be seen in some of the best books on management. This may be because the PRO doubles as something else from appeals organizer to marketing services manager, while public relations may feature in the job specification of many directors, managers and executives. Figure 1.2 positions the PRO who has a full-time public relations job.

In other words, the PRO services all functions of the organization and reports directly to the chief executive. We call him or her PRO but the designation could be 'manager' or 'director'.

Public relations and public affairs

Some unnecessary confusion has been created by the use of these two expressions. Public affairs is an American expression which has been imported into Britain. The attempt is made to relegate the more commercial and perhaps marketing-orientated communications to public relations, and to create the new and maybe more respectable sounding title of 'public affairs' for corporate and financial communications. It is almost as if top management is ashamed of being associated with public relations.

There is no difference between public relations and public affairs, and the attempt to create such a division makes nonsense of the concept of public relations as the total communications of any organization. We do not have separate institutes, examinations, qualifications or journals. This is amplified by Figure 1.2 showing the positioning of the in-house PRO.

Public relations and marketing

This is a controversial topic. There are those who see public relations as part of marketing. It is often listed together with marketing, as in book catalogues or in programmes of courses, or as part of the job specification for a marketing person in a recruitment advertisement. These associations are misleading. It would be truer to say that there was a public relations element in every stage of the marketing mix, rather than that public relations was part of marketing − if only that public relations concerns the total organization and not merely marketing. Moreover, it concerns organizations which are not engaged in marketing.

Consequently, considerable antipathy exists between marketing and public relations. This is a pity because public relations can be a greater ally of marketing than most marketing people will admit. One of the problems is that some marketing people see public relations as a form

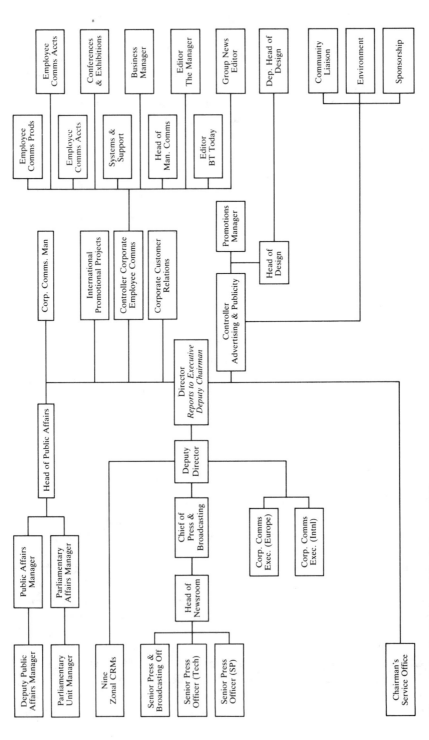

Figure 1.2 *Positioning of the in-house PRO*

of free advertising, and they destroy its credibility by, for instance, insisting that a news release should be more promotional.

A basic reason for this misunderstanding of public relations is the original definition expounded by Philip Kotler, whose books have had international influence in the marketing world. Unfortunately his idea of public relations has been largely responsible for the marketing person's misunderstanding of our subject. The Kotler perversion claims:

> Publicity is non-personal stimulation of demand for a product, service or business unit by planting commercially significant news about it in a published medium or obtaining favourable presentation of it upon radio, television, or stage that is not paid for by the sponsor.

Kotler even calls public relations 'publicity'. Is it any wonder that people in marketing have a jaundiced view of public relations, and also think that it starts and finishes with editorial publicity?

It is some years since Kotler sowed his bad seed, but the debate continues and a feature on Public Relations vs Marketing appeared in the IABC journal *Communication World* in 1993[7]. In this feature James E. Grunig, professor at the University of Maryland, was quoted as stressing the elementary difference between the two disciplines by saying:

> Marketing deals with markets and public relations with publics. Organisations can create a market by identifying a segment of the population for which a product is or could be in demand. Publics create themselves however, whenever organisations make decisions that affect a group of people adversely.

In the same feature another American academic, Martha Lauzen, assistant professor at San Diego State University, offered the following warning:

> Marketing imperialism is the intrusion of marketing into the activities traditionally within the domain of public relations.

This cautionary comment is relevant, and is equally true in the UK where we have seen the attempt by marketing people to usurp public relations, even going so far as to invent the concept of 'social marketing' for activities that were regarded as part of public relations.

Marketing was established many years ago in our universities, but degrees in public relations are very new. It is important that the two disciplines are clearly perceived, but it was not very encouraging that when degree courses were first created there were no academically qualified teachers of public relations, and teaching staff had to be recruited from other disciplines such as marketing.

Perhaps the last word rests with Philip Lesley,[8] who says:

> Public relations people have the role of being always in the middle – pivoted between their clients/employers and their publics. They must be attuned to the thinking and needs of the organization they serve or they cannot serve well. They must be attuned to the dynamics and needs of the publics so that they can interpret the publics to the clients, as well as interpret the clients to the publics.
>
> This role 'in the middle' does not apply to any other group that deals with the climate of attitudes. Experts in other fields – journalists, sociologists, psychologists, politicians, etc. – are oriented in the direction of their specialities.
>
> The role of the public relations professional is to apply this unique and increasingly crucial orientation – plus our special skills – to reading the trends in attitudes, assessing what the trends will mean for society and for various organizations, and recommending what to do to accommodate to these conditions and trends . . .

The last paragraph is reminiscent of the Mexican Statement definition quoted earlier in this chapter.

Public relations and advertising

We have already made several comparisons between public relations and advertising. To emphasize and distinguish the differences between the two let us consider four distinct areas in which these differences occur. They are:

1 The people addressed – the target audiences or publics.
2 The media through which these people are addressed.
3 The costs and methods of payment.
4 The purpose of the communication.

1 The people addressed

Advertising campaigns are usually concentrated on the largest number of potential buyers. Public relations programmes are dispersed to many different groups of people. Advertising addresses the target audience: public relations addresses many publics. While advertising is aimed mostly at distributors, users and consumers in order to sell, and to possible recruits and suppliers in order to buy, public relations publics – as we shall see – can include all kinds of people with whom the organization does or should communicate. But not all organizations are in industry, trade or commerce. We have already mentioned that most public relations exists outside the business world, and to substantiate this claim here, in greater detail, are some of the non-business organizations in which public relations is very important:

- The police, armed forces, prison service, fire brigade, ambulance services.
- Hospitals and other health services.
- Universities, schools and other educational establishments.
- Societies, institutes and associations representing special interests, including professional and trade bodies.
- Churches and various religious organizations such as missionary and denominational educational societies.
- Cultural organizations, e.g. libraries, museums, art galleries, symphony orchestras, and choirs and choral societies.
- Sports clubs representing every kind of amateur and professional sport.
- Political parties, political societies, trade unions.
- Central government, ministries and departments and the hundreds of quasi-autonomous national government organizations (quangos) set up by government.
- Local government authorities.
- Charities and voluntary bodies ranging from Barnardo's to the Royal National Lifeboat Institution.

From this brief list it will be realized that many thousands of organizations make up this vast world of non-commercial activity. Some of them, it is true, use advertising techniques to raise funds but even so they are usually non-profit-making and the funds derived from trade are required for administrative or charitable purposes. They are the very fabric of civilized society.

2 The media

If the lists below are compared side by side it will be found that there are differences in the use of some similar or identical media, while there are many media used only by advertising, and yet more which are specially created for public relations purposes. The latter may be called private or sponsored media and they are seldom mass media, whereas advertising exploits existing mass media which operate to make a profit. Advertising tends to be mean in its choice of the fewest possible economically effective media whereas public relations is greedy and almost profligate in its use and creation of media.

Media comparisons

Advertising media	Public relations media
(i) Display and classified ads in newspapers, consumer magazines, trade, technical and professional journals	(i) News stories, feature articles, pictures for the press. Internal and external journals
(ii) Commercials (film or video tape) and advertising films for showing on television and cinema screens. Sponsored TV/radio programmes	(ii) Videotapes, slides, cassettes, corporate video by satellite, video news releases
(iii) Radio commercials	(iii) Taped radio interviews, studio interviews, phone-ins, news
(iv) Posters, signs and other out-door and transportation advertising	(iv) Educational visual aid posters
(v) Public, trade, permanent, mobile exhibitions	(v) Public relations aspects of all exhibitions and private exhibitions for public relations purposes
(vi) Sales promotion schemes	(vi) Educational literature − printed information
(vii) Point-of-sale displays	(vii) Sponsored publications
(viii) Sales literature − leaflets, brochures, catalogues	(viii) Seminars, and conferences − spoken word sometimes combined with video shows, slide presentations, and exhibits.
(ix) Direct mail	(ix) Press facility visits, works visits, open days

Media comparisons — contd

Advertising media	*Public relations media*
(x) Door-to-door mail drops of sales literature, samples, cash vouchers	(x) Annual reports and accounts, company histories
(xi) Sponsorship with direct marketing and advertising purposes	(xi) Participation in events, e.g. floats at carnivals, awards of prizes, sponsorship of events and causes
(xii) Special forms of advertising: aerial, shopping bags, novelties, etc	(xii) Corporate identity: house style, livery of transportation, symbols (logos), colours, typography, uniforms, dress, badges

These lists are by no means complete but they help to show that advertising and public relations communicate differently by means of different communication media. The above comparison does not include corporate, issue and financial advertising which is used for public relations purposes. This is discussed in Chapter 36.

3 Costs and payment

The financial sides of advertising and public relations can be compared in a similar way. By costs we mean what has to be bought; by payment (or remuneration) how an advertising agent or a public relations consultant receives monies to recover what has been spent on a client's behalf and to make a profit.

In advertising it is usual to refer to **above-the-line** and **below-the-line** costs, the first covering the main five media of the press, television, radio, outdoor and cinema. All the other media – which do not usually pay the advertising agent a commission – are termed below-the-line. It is wrong to include public relations in this second category for it is not a part of advertising and needs its own budget. The mistake occurs perhaps when public relations is seen as a promotional tool (in the unfortunate Four Ps context), and consists of no more than product publicity to supplement advertising. But that does not take public relations seriously, and reflects the typical marketing person's narrow view of public relations.

To explain the advertising agency commission system more thoroughly, agencies may be 'recognized' (or 'accredited' as it is called in some countries) by bodies representing publishing houses and broadcasting stations or contractors. It is more convenient for the media to deal with a small number of space and airtime buyers (advertising agents) than with large numbers of advertisers, provided accounts are settled promptly, say, in thirty days. The media owners' bodies (e.g. Newspaper Publishers' Association and the Independent Television Association) grant these agents 'recognition' — on the basis that they have sufficient cash flow to pay their bills promptly — and invoice less the commission so that the agent can charge his client the full amount and gain the difference. The commission is seldom adequate and agents commonly charge their clients a supplementary percentage. Agents also earn commission on work which they put out in order to produce advertisements, e.g. typesetting and photography, but in some cases, e.g. printing, the supplier does not deduct a commission but adds a percentage which represents the agent's handling cost. Thus, it could be cheaper for the client to buy print direct, whereas it would not be cheaper for him to buy space or airtime direct. The agent's sources of income are therefore various and complicated. There are some agents who reject the commission system and work more professionally for fees which represent manhours and expertise, expenditures for clients being charged net. There are also media independents which only plan and buy media and *à la carte* agencies which only do creative work.

Public relations consultancies are not in the commission business; mainly they are selling time which is representative of manhours and expertise, plus materials and expenses. The hourly or daily rate for public relations services covers salaries, overheads and profits. We shall deal with this in the chapters on consultancy and budgeting, but here let us examine costs under sets of comparative lists.

Whereas the advertising agent's main cost is on space, airtime and the production of advertisements, the public relations consultant's main cost is on manhours to service the account. This leads to another difference: agency commission covers the cost of the account executive who services the account and acts as the liaison between the client and the agency. Commission also covers administrative costs such as media planning and buying. The consultant has to charge for every minute spent on servicing the account, including talking to the client. Quite simply, there are only two payers of the consultant's costs, 'them and us'. Anything not paid by the client has to come out of the consultant's pocket and is a loss.

Cost comparisons

Advertising costs	*Agency payment*
(i) Advertising space in the press	(i) Commission on space, airtime and screen bookings, poster site rentings
(ii) Airtime on television and radio	
(iii) Rent of poster sites	(ii) Charges for artwork and costs of production
(iv) Screen time on cinemas	
	(iii) On-costs on work farmed out to suppliers such as printers
(v) Stand space at exhibitions	
	(iv) Discounts from suppliers such as photographers, film and video-tape makers

(vi) Production costs of:
    (a) Press advertisements
    (b) Television commercials
    (c) Radio commercials
    (d) Cinema screen commercials
    (e) Exhibition stands
    (f) Print, display material
	(v) Fees for work which bears no commission

Public relations costs	*Consultancy payment*
(i) Time − salaries	(i) Fee based on hourly/daily rate
(ii) Materials − stationery, postage, photography	(ii) Recovery of cost of materials, usually at cost, but sometimes with handling charge
(iii) Expenses − travelling, hotels, hospitality	(iii) Recovery of expenses at cost

4 The purpose

The different purposes of advertising and public relations need to be distinguished very clearly. These purposes may be confused when the mistake is made of regarding public relations as a form of advertising, a substitute for it, 'unpaid or free advertising', or a soft sell. It is none of these things, however much some people would like it to be or, indeed, turn it into when they write so-called news releases which are really puffs. When the latter happens, as it so often does, it is to be expected that editors will regard public relations as camouflaged advertising. Another problem occurs when the in-house manager responsible for public relations is also responsible, or principally responsible, for advertising, and finds it difficult to understand the difference.

Put very simply, public relations aims to educate and inform in order to create knowledge and understanding, whereas advertising seeks to inform or remind in order to persuade and sell. The two may be related in the sense that it is difficult or excessively costly to persuade and sell if prospective buyers lack knowledge and understanding of what is being advertised. The success of the advertising may also depend on the corporate image and the reputation of the advertiser which also requires knowledge, understanding and perhaps previous experience. Thus public relations and advertising are very different forms of communication, with different objectives. Moreover, public relations may have nothing to do with the promotional side of the business, to mention only employee and financial relations, and is a much bigger subject than advertising.

Although the following is limited to written materials, it helps to clarify the purposes of the two forms of communication:

Item	Readers	Style
Press advertisement	Distributors – consumers – users	Informative – reminder – persuasive – action seeking
Sales letter	Distributors – consumers – users	Informative – persuasive – action seeking
News release	Editor – readers (distributors – consumers – users)	Factual – news – informative – educational
Feature article	Editor – readers (distributors – consumers – users)	Factual – creative – informative – educational

Public relations management

The management of public relations requires two forms of *control* and *direction* as already suggested by the chart of the positioning of the PRO. Having established the role of public relations, and how it differs from other forms of communication, let us conclude this chapter by examining this dual aspect of management.

First, there is the leadership function of managing a public relations department or a public relations consultancy or a section of it. Consultancies are nowadays adopting a greater division of labour, not unlike service advertising agencies except that the public relations services are things like types of client or kinds of public relations work rather than functions such as media buying and creativity.

Second, there is the direction of campaigns, whether in-house or by a consultancy. The positioning of the PRO within the organization is important to his or her managerial status, but ideally — as shown in Figure 1.2 — the PRO should report direct to the chief executive. In some large companies where public relations plays a significant role, the PRO is an adviser to the board or a board director. Even more significantly, this is often true of those companies which have successfully weathered the recession.

Thus, in addition to departmental management there is the managerial role of the PRO in relation to other directors, managers or executives. He or she is involved in policy decisions, will be privy to confidential information, and concerned at the earliest possible stage in new developments. He or she will attend meetings to discuss every aspect of the organization's affairs. More than anyone else in an organization, the PRO needs to know what is going on, and it may be his or her responsibility to give professional advice on every topic under discussion.

This is neither presumptuous nor an exaggerated view of the managerial role of the PRO. *Everything an organization does involves communication of some kind.* Even a price or an instruction on a label is a form of communication. But there are also major issues such as a change of company name, relocation of a factory, or a rights issue of shares which can involve the public relations manager, and it is necessary to be involved in the proceedings.

The responsibilities of the PRO are not always as clearly or as broadly defined as this, and the situation is not helped by the assortment of titles used ranging from information officer to external relations manager, with scores of variations in between. There is also an extraordinary array of people who combine public relations with press relations, advertising, sales promotion or marketing services, and their often curious and conflicting mixture of duties is reflected in their different titles or responsibilities. Unfortunately, 'marketing' has become a much abused job title for people as diverse as advertisement space salespeople and entertainments publicity officers. Looking at situations vacant advertisements in journals like *Marketing* one finds that a 'marketing executive' is supposed to be able to handle public relations!

One has only to look at the syllabus of the Chartered Institute of Marketing examination to see how little even trained and qualified marketers are expected to know about public relations. In fact, it is so little that while the holder of a CIM Diploma can get exemption from five out of six CAM Certificate subjects they are not exempt from the public relations paper.

The positioning of the PRO is also not very clear, and perhaps we have to blame some of our management consultancies who seem to have very obscure notions about public relations. When the PRO is mistakenly located in the marketing department, his or her responsibilities are likely to be limited and there is unlikely to be that essential access to top management.

It may be excellent that a company has recognized the value of public relations to the extent that it has at least allied public relations to marketing, or a marketing director has been sufficiently enlightened to appreciate the need for public relations. However, as we shall see in the next chapter it could be a serious handicap if public relations is buried in the marketing department.

Today, public relations concerns not only internal and external communications for the total organization and all its functions of management, finance, production, and staff relations but engages in many activities quite beyond the elementary ones of information services and product publicity. It is possible to conduct public relations without ever writing a news release or dealing with the mass media. The six attributes of a PRO should now make sense in relation to the job of a PRO capable of operating in the sphere of top level management.

Fairway's prize-winning Fuji Film airship campaign

In America, Europe and the Far East Fuji airships have become a familiar sight for some years. Painted in the well-known characteristic red and green colours, these airships make an imposing sight and immediately spell out Fuji even from a distance. It is by far the most successful use of airships for public relations purposes for the corporate identity is instantly recognizable.

Figure 1.3 *The Fuji Film airship,* Spirit of Fuji, *flying over Tower Bridge, London, during its visit to Britain in 1992. The public relations programme for the visit was organized by Fairway Communications of Bradford-on-Avon, who won the* PR Week *Best Promotional Campaign Award for its Fuji Film airship programme*

For its two week visit to Britain in 1992 (see Figure 1.3), the programme was arranged by a small West of England consultancy, Fairway Communications, which not only handled a complicated assignment very efficiently but carried off the Model Solutions Award (sponsored by Manning, Selvage and Lee) for the Best Promotional Campaign. Jackie Elliot, joint managing director of the award sponsors, said in *PR Week*[9] that this £12,000 project was 'An energetic campaign that delivered terrific value'.

Airships, for advertising and public relations purposes, have featured in a number of the author's books, the latest being *Advertising.*[10] In Fuji's case, the airship is 190 feet long, 54 feet wide, 62 feet high, uses helium gas, has two Continental 210 BHP engines, can fly at 30–50 knots per hour, operates at from 1000 to 6000 ft and carries a pilot and seven passengers. It was built in 1988. For night flights, screens either side of the envelope carry 10,000 different-coloured light bulbs which are controlled by a computer unit on board the airship. The builders are WDL Luftschiffgesellschaft MbH of Germany who have been building such airships for clients for nearly 20 years.

The *Spirit of Fuji*, with its total air and ground crew of 20, tours Europe each year, and in 1992 it flew for 76 hours in the UK. It landed at Manston and was then based for one week at Goodwood and for a second week at Fairoaks, the latter being a well-known airfield for hot air balloons and airships.

It was quite a difficult project to organize because the number of passengers the airship can carry is dependent on the weather, time of day (e.g. in the morning the envelope may be damp and the airship will not be able to take the extra weight of many passengers), and the weight of the passengers themselves. It is also dependent on the type of guest because TV camera crews would need to take a good deal of heavy equipment on board, as would some photographers.

It was found that guests had to be fairly agile in order to climb into the carousel. The airship is caught by ropes by a team of very strong Germans when it lands and is not able to be held for very long. Therefore the procedure for boarding has to be carried out very quickly, with guests being steered across the airfield in order not to disrupt other air traffic.

The procedure for boarding is that the airship has to be weighted with sandbags which have to be taken off one by one as each guest climbs on board. Where guests are taking over from a previous flight, one person climbs on board while one climbs out. The leader of the German crew estimates the weight of passengers before they board.

'It was found,' says Kim Cherry who handled the account, 'that a great deal of patience, tact and diplomacy was essential when dealing with this promotion.'

A tight schedule had to be kept and updated each day of the two-week visit. Weather reports had to be studied on a day-to-day basis so that guests who had some distance to travel could be informed in advance if it was not possible for their flight, and they then had to be rescheduled.

Trips were arranged for Fuji Photo Film (UK) Ltd's customers and staff, plus local press, trade press, local radio, television crews, photographers, politicians, celebrities such as David Bellamy, and others. Bad weather did mean that some guests were disappointed. However, during the first week at Goodwood perfect weather conditions prevailed and TVS Maidstone were able to fly the *Spirit of Fuji* in order to film the entrance to the Channel Tunnel, TVS Southampton came aboard to film the surrounding area of Goodwood, while BBC South and BBC

News Round were able to interview David Bellamy and his team from Population Concern while on board the airship.

Research discovered Mr Hunt, son of the R101 senior coxswain who died in the disaster, and who is fund-raising for an airship museum at Cardington, and he was given a flight and interviewed. A flight was also arranged for local schoolchildren at Fairoaks who were compiling a project on airships.

This was a modest programme which exercised the imagination and organizational ability of a small consultancy working over a short period. In particular, it was an example of the importance of timing.

References

1 Gillman, F.C., *UK Public Relations – The Early Days, Public Relations* 40th Anniversary Issue (Summer), Institute of Public Relations, London, 1988
2 Jefkins, Frank, *History of Public Relations*, Keynote address, 16th Anniversary Summer School, Frank Jefkins School of Public Relations, London, 1989; subsequently published in *Public Relations*, IPR, London, and reprinted in *Public Relations*, 4th edn, Pitman, London, 1992
3 *The Independent*, Diary, 8 October 1992
4 *The Independent on Sunday*, Leader, 27 September 1992
5 Schmertz, Herb and Novak, William, *Goodbye to the Low Profile*, Mercury Books, London, 1986
6 Jefkins, F., *Planned Press and Public Relations*, 3rd edn, Blackie, Glasgow, 1993
7 Briggs, William and Tucson, Marilen, PR vs marketing, *Communication World*, IABC, San Francisco, March 1993
8 Lesley, Philip, Part II of Report of the Advance Planning Committee of the Public Relations Society of America, reproduced in *Lesley's Handbook of Public Relations and Communications*, 4th edn, Amacon, Probus Publishing Co., New York, 1991
9 *PR Week*, PR Week Awards 1992, 29 October 1992
10 Jefkins, Frank, *Advertising*, Made Simple Series, Butterworth-Heinemann, Oxford, 1992

2

In-house public relations departments and public relations consultancies

Although the consultancy seems to be the most glamorous side of public relations, and to read *PR Week* you would think it represented the whole of public relations, only about one-third of public relations personnel work in consultancies. The in-house PRO, public relations manager or director is the predominant practitioner, especially if he or she services the communication needs of the total organization.

As we shall see later on, there are advantages and disadvantages in the internal and external roles, but the reason for the dominance of in-house personnel lies in the nature of the work. To do a proper public relations job it is necessary to have an intimate knowledge of an organization (and perhaps of the industry or business it is in), and to have well-established lines of communication within the organization. This is different from advertising which may concern only the marketing department, but needs expert outside services such as media buying and creative. The in-house public relations manager has to be a jack-of-all-trades, employing many personal skills.

This chapter will be devoted to a comparison between the strengths and weaknesses of the in-house public relations department and the consultancy. For the sake of the comparison the ideal will be assumed of an independent public relations department. It is not intended to say that one is better than the other. Let us begin with the in-house public relations department.

The BT public relations department

Probably the largest in-house public relations department is that of British Telecom (BT) which has a staff of 245, of whom 133 are based in the field staff located at regional offices throughout the UK. Their responsibilities are explained in Figure 2.1. Five UK public relations consultancies are used for special projects, as are seven located in Europe, Hong Kong, Japan and the USA.

The departmental chart shown here in Figure 2.1, and a description of each function, is given in a 24-page booklet *This is Corporate Relations*.[1] It describes the vision and mission of the corporate relations department, and its various services under the headings: planning and public relations support; external communications; public affairs; employee communications; advertising and publicity; corporate customer relations; marketing public relations; international promotional projects; chairman's service office; and senior managers in the corporate relations department.

Advantages of an in-house public relations department

1 A full-time service

The in-house PRO, and his or her staff, can provide a full-time service, and this may not be limited to office hours, nor will he or she be subject to the limitations of a consultancy fee which is based on manhours. Time has still to be planned, but does not have to be shared between different clients according to the size of fee in each case. Moreover, the in-house PRO tends to be permanent, and less likely to change jobs like consultancy staff. The nature of the job is different, and the PRO may have grown up in the organization or the industry.

2 Good communication

Whereas creative work and media planning/buying can be put outside to an advertising agency, and the advertising manager can supervise

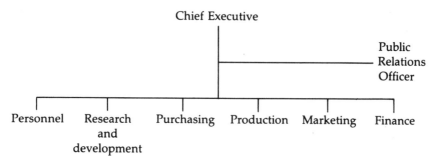

Figure 2.1 *BT Corporate Relations Department*

this as may be necessary, public relations calls for a more intimate set-up internally. The PRO needs to have good lines of communication throughout the organization, and this could be on a national or international basis. He or she is an integral part of the organization who needs to know people and to be known to people. This is far less necessary in advertising. The PRO must have these well-defined lines of communication so that information can be obtained quickly, or the PRO can be informed when something occurs of public relations significance. It will be very helpful if he or she is the internal house journal editor, or the editor is in the department, because this will provide continual access to people throughout every division, department and location.

To maintain these intimate contacts the in-house PRO should pay visits to the organization's locations, attend conferences and meetings, visit exhibitions and other events in which the company is engaged, and generally become immersed in company affairs. Some of this may occupy leisure hours. The consultant is unlikely to get so closely involved, if only that the fee will not permit that sort of expenditure of time.

3 Continuity

As we have already said, company personnel tend to stay in their jobs longer, perhaps growing up with the company. The PRO may have transferred from another sector of the company. He or she may have been trained in the industry. This continuity gives them greater knowledge of the subject, and greater familiarity with the company. It will help to give others confidence in him or her, especially when information is needed from them. This will also give the PRO more authority when dealing with the media because he or she will be recognized as being more of an expert in the subject than the consultant can ever be. This can be a serious problem when a consultant takes on a new account, even if the principles are the same. This permanency can also mean that in-house practitioner is often older, more mature and experienced than the average consultancy executive.

4 Value for money

Being on the spot, knowing people and able to move about easily and confidently within the organization, the PRO can often work very economically. Jobs can be dovetailed, such as researching material for feature articles while working on the house journal, or finding material for the house journal, video, the photographic library and so on while engaged in other activities. Mixing with so many people, and knowing what is going on, the PRO can cut a lot of corners. In fact, although it may cost a lot more to staff, equip and finance a public relations department than a consultancy fee, there is likely to be greater value for money for the reasons outlined here.

5 *Immediate access to information and decision makers*

The PRO is on the spot when the organization is in the news, often able to act spontaneously because the facts are known, or can be obtained quickly because the PRO has immediate access to those with the information or who make the decisions. This can be important in crises or controversial situations. Moreover, the PRO is in a position to put the media in touch with his or her seniors and not act as a buffer between them.

6 *Proximity*

Working closely with management the in-house PRO is in a strong position to demonstrate the value of public relations. Thus management is more likely to understand and appreciate public relations than is possible when dealing with a remote outsider.

From the above six advantages it is pre-supposed that the PRO is an independent department manager with direct access to the chief executive. These advantages depend very much on his status within the organization, remembering that status is seldom given but has to be earned. Experience, training, qualifications, success, personality and grade or salary bracket (where known) will all contribute to status and acceptability. The person who complains about his lack of status is usually in the wrong job, or has yet to establish himself fully in it.

Disadvantages of an in-house public relations department

1 *Lack of impartiality*

A serious disadvantage can be the tendency for the PRO to be uncritical and biased, partly out of loyalty or zeal, partly because of pressure from management (especially if the PRO is located in the marketing department where there is bound to be a promotional attitude to public relations). It may be that he or she honestly feels enthusiasm about the organization and what it makes or does. Yet to achieve credibility and acceptance by the media, this tendency to be less than impartial has to be curbed. It is not easy, but the penalty is the derisive editorial comment 'You only say that because you work for them'. Nothing could be more destructive of good media relations.

It depends on the professional status which the PRO has achieved. The PRO who is merely management's dogsbody is in a hopeless position. So much stems from how much management needs and respects the PRO's expertise. After all, management does not tell the architect to put the roof in the cellar, and the cellar on the roof.

2 Narrow range of experience

An inherent weakness may be the narrowness of the industry or business the PRO is in so that the broad span of public relations activity and experience is not enjoyed which is characteristic of the consultancy. The PRO may be in, say, food or textiles or engineering which require contact with a limited section of the media, or confine him or her to only certain kinds of public relations activity. The in-house practitioner may never edit a house journal, make a video, deal with television, organize seminars or write feature articles, and could be out of his or her depth if the company diversified or acquired other interests.

3 Lack of training

The in-house person may have been transferred to public relations from another job in the company and have received no training in public relations, and being perhaps a senior person may be reluctant to attend professional courses. Some very odd appointments are made by management which does not appreciate that much has to be learned before one can practise public relations. Sometimes a sideways promotion can put a poor communicator into the hot seat of public relations. The profession is not helped by such dubious appointments which encourage the cynicism of the media. It is astonishing how people will admit that they have been put into a public relations job, but know nothing about it. This farcical situation is all too common. It is like asking a plumber to perform as a doctor.

As research has shown,[2] there are probably some 20,000 people who are employed in some public relations capacity but who have no training or qualifications. At the time of writing CAM has just over 4000 registered students, a fraction of the potential number.

4 Public relations responsibilities assigned to inappropriate personnel

Similarly, public relations duties may be assigned to an existing executive such as a marketing, product, personnel or commercial manager who knows nothing about the subject, may well treat it as some form of free advertising or an excuse for expense account high living, and probably do untold harm. Even if such a person is aided by a consultant, he or she will not be speaking the same language, and could be a liability. These are the sort of people who flood editors with news releases which are pure advertisements. They help to create the adversarial situation between the media and public relations.

5 Responsibility for public relations assigned to potential top management executives

In some large organizations − multinationals, for example − an executive who is being groomed for top management may be put in charge of public relations for perhaps three years. While it shows recognition of the need for top management to understand public relations and to be good communicators, it may be unwise to place such an unskilled and unqualified person in *control* of the public relations function. The place for this executive's training is in a postgraduate course such as that at Stiring University. One wonders what the media think of these high-powered birds of passage.

6 PRO employed for wrong reasons

He or she may be employed for the wrong reasons. Management may misunderstand public relations to the extent that it employs a PRO for protective reasons, either to shield top management from the media, or to act as an apologist for management inadequacies. This is an abuse of public relations but has been known where management is nervous of criticism. Unhappily it is a view of public relations almost universally held by writers of novels, plays and films. It also happens in developing countries where management of parastatals is inexperienced and frightened by criticism.

In the above two sections on strengths and weaknesses we have described a blend of in-house situations which suggest that while the in-house PRO has many advantages over the consultant, and can perform a valuable function, it is necessary for the job specification to be right. But what is the job specification? Does one exist? Sometimes the employer has no idea, and very often the PRO − once in the job −

has to prepare and present a job specification in his or her own interests. The job specifications produced by management consultants are ludicrous, especially when they locate the PRO in the marketing department.

In some developing countries the job specification is so vague that the PRO is little more than an odd-job person, fulfilling a sort of social function as required, buying airline tickets, meeting guests at the airport, undertaking protocol arrangements and organizing social functions. In certain Third World countries this has occurred because a foreign management consultant has included PRO in the list of executives to be appointed. No one knows his duties, and the only requirement set out in the recruitment advertisement was that he or she should have a degree! Fortunately, there are PROs throughout the developing world who are doing a perfectly professional and conscientious public relations job. –

Let us now consider the opposite side of the coin: what are the advantages and disadvantages of the public relations consultancy? How does the consultancy compare with the in-house PRO? Why employ a consultancy, whether or not there is also an in-house PRO?

A public relations consultancy is not a public relations agency. The misleading and incorrect term 'public relation agency' is borrowed from advertising, and is another example of the confusion that exists about the two. It does not help that the misnomer is perpetuated by *PR Week*, a journal that dwells on the minority world of the consultancy. It is like the journalist's use of the term 'PR' for PRO. How can a person be a PR? So let's get our meanings clear, and refer to the public relations *consultancy*.

Historically and strictly speaking, an advertising agent is an agent of the media from which he or she gains most of their income in the form of commission on the space or airtime they buy for clients. They are 'recognized' or 'accredited' for the purpose by the organizations which represent the owners of the newspapers and magazines, commercial television and radio stations. They are a kind of commission agent: the *public relations consultant is not,* because, like most professionals, he or she sells their time and expertise. There are today, however, some creative or *à la carte* advertising agencies which buy no media, do not require recognition, and charge fees for their creative services. There are also some advertising agencies which have renounced the commission system in favour of charging fees representing manhours and skills. This is more professional than the anomalous commission system.

Another interesting difference between advertising agencies and public relations consultancies concerns how, why and when each is appointed. When a company reaches a certain level of expenditure on advertising it will be an economic proposition to appoint an advertising agency, and the company will seek higher creative and media buying skills than it can provide itself. In contrast, a company is likely to employ a public relations consultancy when the volume of work does not justify having a full-time public relations department. When the client can justify a full-time department it will cease to use the consultancy. But it may also use a consultancy either to augment its busy department, or to handle specialized or *ad hoc* public relations work. This will be explained later in the chapter.

There are some 1200 consultancies in the UK. Many are small, but the larger ones have their own trade association, the Public Relations Consultants Association. The members of the PRCA are company or corporate members. The Institute of Public Relations has individual elected members. The names and addresses of consultants, often with client lists, will be found in the *Advertiser's Annual*[3] and the *Hollis Press and Public Relations Annual*.[4] The latest information can be obtained on-line from the Hollis PR database.

While it is clear that clients will use an advertising agency for its variety of creative, media and other services, enjoying a share of a team of high-standard personnel which it would be uneconomic to employ in-house on a full-time basis, a very different situation may occur in public relations. A company may employ its own team of personnel permanently. Why is this? Is it better to employ a full-time PRO or a consultant?

One argument needs to be settled right away. The consultant is not necessarily more expensive than an in-house PRO. Like must be compared with like. It is no use comparing the consultancy fee with the salary of an in-house PRO, unless one also calculates the cost of providing the staff man or woman with an office, secretary and essential equipment, resources and expenses.

Reasons for appointing a public relations consultancy

1 Because the organization has not reached a level of expenditure on public relations which justifies the cost of setting up its own public relations department.
2 Because management needs counselling services on communication problems. These might be short term, calling for a report and recommendations.
3 To provide a press relations service.
4 To provide a central information service. A number of consultancies offer press bureau services.

5 To plan and execute a complete public relations programme.

6 If the organization is out of town, to use a city-based or media-centre-based consultancy for organizing press functions such as press conferences, press receptions and facility visits.

7 To handle *ad hoc* assignments such as public relations in connection with participation in an exhibition.

8 For export purposes, as when public relations consultancies may be engaged overseas.

9 To provide specialist services, often augmenting the work of the in-house public relations department. These services may be:

(a) House journal editing, design and production.

(b) Corporate and financial public relations including special work during take-over bids or privatization of state enterprises, for which a large number of specialist consultancies are located in the City of London.

(c) Print design, e.g. educational literature, annual reports.

(d) Parliamentary liaison, such as advising clients on Parliamentary procedures concerning committee stages of bills, White Papers, Green Papers, and Select Committees, plus lobbying of Ministers, MPs and civil servants, both at Westminster and in Brussels, Luxembourg and Strasbourg, and interpreting EC directives.

(e) Fund raising. Certain consultancies specialize in this work.

(f) Sponsorship. Again, there are specialist consultancies which can bring together potential sponsors and interests seeking sponsorhip, and then organize and handle the entire sponsorship.

(g) Special interest. There are consultancies which handle public relations in particular fields such as motoring, entertainments, food, fashion, travel, electronics and so on.

(h) Crisis management, including training.

Kinds of consultancy

There may be special reasons for appointing a certain type of consultancy such as:

Public relations department of an advertising agency

Because of the boom in public relations or a fall in advertising income, a number of advertising agencies, especially in the provinces, now offer public relations services. Overseas, where demand may be less than it is in Britain or the USA, it is not uncommon for advertising agencies to offer public relations services. A thoroughly good service may be provided, but it all depends on whether the agency is merely trying to augment advertising campaigns with some press relations, or whether the public relations department is headed by an able practitioner who undertakes a comprehensive service.

Generally speaking, advertising agencies seldom understand public relations. They may attempt to offer a one-stop package without realizing that the bulk of public relations has nothing to do with advertising.

Public relations subsidiary of an advertising agency

Here we have a separate sister organization operating in its own right, having its own clients (which may not be agency clients) and being responsible for its own profitability. There will be linking directorships, chairmanships or partnerships with the advertising agency. It may operate under a name distinctly different from that of the advertising agency. An advantage of this type of consultancy is that it can draw on the back-up services of the agency's studio, print production, library and other facilities.

An occasional problem, however, is that clients do not always appreciate why they have to deal with two executives from what, to them, is the same firm. In addition, clients may be confused if one operates the commission system and the other charges fees. There can also be problems in the two account executives' attitudes to the same client: the advertising agency executive will tend to be flattering while the public relations consultancy executive is likely to be more candid.

Independent public relations consultancy

The majority of consultancies are of this kind, that is they are free of parental advertising agency ties. The consultancy may, however, have a working arrangement with an advertising agency, or with clients' agencies, and − like Burson-Marsteller − it may operate the other way round and provide its own advertising service. Some of its clients may not be involved in advertising at all and require only public relations services, while public relations programmes (e.g. corporate and financial) may not be related to advertising campaigns.

Specialist public relations consultancies

As already described under *Reasons for appointing a public relations consultancy*, there are consultancies which specialize in particular classes of public relations work.

Freelance consultants
In recent years we have seen the prevalence of the freelance consultant who handles *ad hoc* assignments. Anyone can call themselves a freelance consultant, so it may be difficult for a potential client to assess their ability. If they possess the right experience, training and qualifications, their service could be ideal when short-term service is required. They could augment the in-house department from time to time. Their fees could be modest because of their low overheads. Probably the best way to judge their proficiency is to check whether they are members of the IPR. Membership does require years of experience and qualifications such as the CAM Diploma. There is a Freelance Directory in *PR Week*.

Just as we listed and compared the advantages and disadvantages of the in-house public relations department now we shall examine the strengths and weaknesses of the consultancy. It is worth repeating that the in-house department and the outside consultancy each has its characteristic advantages and disadvantages. Neither is necessarily better than the other. Both may be employed, and when this happens the consultancy may be used to provide an outside opinion, to augment a busy in-house department, to undertake work for which it is specially qualified, or for occasional *ad hoc* assignments.

Advantages of the public relations consultancy

1 *Offers independent unbiased advice*

In this respect its advice can be very different from that of an advertising agency. While an advertising agency may seek to please a client, a consultancy may be paid to criticize. It may even be necessary for the consultancy to express opinions about the advertising, especially if it is considered to be in bad taste, in any way damaging to the client's image, or is likely to provoke ill-will. The agency may be the herald of a company's wares, but the consultancy is the guardian of its reputation. There is a marked difference in responsibility.

'Advice' can cover scores of communication topics concerning the entire range of a client's activities, internally and externally. A possible change of company name, how to deal with a proposed relocation, how to conduct public relations overseas, the effects of new legislation EC directives, or a Monopolies and Mergers Commission report, how to make representations to a Select Committee, what sort of video system to set up, how to distribute videos, how to deal with a take-over bid, these and countless other problems may be presented to the consultancy.

2   Long and varied experience

To a large extent this depends on how long the consultancy has been established, but since it services a number of accounts its experience will be spread over their different and special needs. Collectively, this experience is likely to be greater than that of any individual client. The spread of media will be greater, the problems dealt with will be more diverse, and the activities engaged in will be more varied. One client may require television coverage, another may be engaged in exhibitions, and yet another may make great use of video. Without divulging confidences, experience gained in servicing one client can be useful to another client. Over the years, the consultancy will have gained a rich store of experience, just as any professional service does. In fact, a consultancy is likely to be appointed according to its record of past work, possibly in the same or related field.

In buying consultancy services, the client should therefore examine qualifications, experience and record of past work, while these will be among the selling points which the consultancy will present to potential clients.

3   Experience in a wide range of media

Having worked for a number of clients over a period of years, the consultant is experienced in the use of all the media of communication, both existing like the commercial mass media (*macro-media*), and created like the private media of videos, house journals and private exhibitions (*micro-media*). The consultant will be aware of the opportunities offered by new media and technology, to mention only the constant changes in press and broadcasting media, but the use of new facilities such as video news releases and corporate video by satellite.

Knowing people in the media means knowing who they *are*, what they *want* and *when* they want it, not how to manipulate favours in a Fleet Street bar or West End club. This should not be misunderstood under that old misnomer of 'good Fleet Street contacts'.

4   Good location

Location can be an important asset of the consultancy. Many clients are outside the city centre and are located in remote parts of the country, whereas consultancies are usually located close to the media. This is a convenience which may be a consultancy strength. However, this situation is not always true. Consultancies are nowadays scattered throughout the country, while the press have been moving out of

London for years, the move out of Fleet Street beginning with Rupert Murdoch's newspapers in 1986. Central location will become less and less important as on-line computer facilities become commonplace.

5   Access to, and knowledge of, services

This again may result from a city location. Printers, photographers, video makers, exhibition designers, research units and other suppliers will be known to consultancies who will know how to buy all these services and how to work with suppliers. Usually, these suppliers will be independent of the consultancy, but if there are any financial associations (under the IPR and PRCA codes of conduct) they must be disclosed. Similarly, if suppliers give discounts or commission to consultancies, this source of income should be understood by consultancy clients. Because of years and variety of experience, the consultancy is likely to know the supply market very well — it is part of the consultant's expertise — so that the best suppliers can be selected and recommended to clients.

6   International services

If a client is interested in export public relations, whether in the Single European Market or elsewhere in the world, a consultancy with overseas branches or associates and 'networking' facilities could be very useful.

From the above six sections it will be seen that the competent consultancy has much to offer, and that these services have the special merits of independence, versatility and experience. Nevertheless, consultancies do represent a minority area of public relations.

Disadvantages of the public relations consultancy

In spite of the glamour that surrounds the consultancy world, with potential recruits to public relations tending to think first of getting a job in a consultancy, there are some disadvantages both from the client's and the consultancy's point of view. These weaknesses may stem from what may appear to be the strengths of being independent and proprietorial rather than being a big corporation. A consultancy can be a precarious business, accounts come and go, and so do consultancies.

If one does not have a good business head it is easy to lose money.

This is very easy if clients are given more service than they are paying for, and it is naturally in a client's interest to be an Oliver Twist, always asking for more. The creative mind is not always given to careful costings, careful keeping of daily timesheets, and strict budgetary control. The consultancy has only its time to sell at so much an hour or per day, and it has to be rationed among personnel in proportion to the varying fees paid by different clients. If there is no extra payment, extra work for one client can only be done by robbing another client. The disadvantages from the client's point of view are:

1 Provision of only a partial service

The client will receive only what he pays for — a certain number of hours' or days' work — but public relations is a relentless process and it is threaded into the whole fabric of an organization. It does not have office hours. Consequently, a consultancy can provide only a partial service.

The strict economics of consultancy finances need to be understood by clients. If £10,000 represents 100 hours at £100 per hour the client can expect no more, and neither dare the consultant give more. The arithmetic is as simple as that.

Clients are sometimes apt to think that because they have appointed a consultant they have hired that consultant's services full time. They have not. They have merely bought a share of the consultant's time along with a number of other clients. The only full-time service might occur if the consultancy seconded a member of its staff to a client to work in-house on a full-time basis.

The mistake is sometimes made of thinking that it is more expensive to hire a consultant than it is to employ a full-time PRO. This is clearly not so if it is realized that one buys only a portion of the consultant's time whereas the in-house PRO is not only employed on a full-time salary but has to be provided with an office, staff and equipment.

2 Lack of intimacy in client–consultancy relationship

Since public relations concerns the communications of the total organization, and lines of communication are needed with directors, managers, executives and others in responsible positions, there can be a lack of intimacy in the client–consultancy relationship. The consultancy, while on the one hand enjoying a city location, may also suffer from being remote from the client. Public relations is like an intelligence service with numerous scattered informants. Advertising is more like a flow chart.

3   Divided loyalties

The consultancy is able to offer only a share of its time and expertise, according to the fee, whereas the in-house PRO provides a full-time service and is loyal to only one employer. The divided loyalties of the consultancy may lead to misunderstandings when a client demands service and consultancy staff are busy servicing other clients.

4   Lack of specialized knowledge

Consultancies service clients in scores of trades and industries and cannot have expert knowledge of them all, although the principles of public relations are generally applicable to any client. Nevertheless, it does take time to acquire understanding of a client's business, and clients are apt to get impatient and critical. If the consultancy staff are new or young, the situation may be worsened.

5   Inexperienced junior staff

Recruits have little or no experience or training, and the quality of consultancy service may suffer because of low-grade junior staff. This is a problem which has resulted from the charging of low fees to cover inadequate programmes because:

(a)   Clients do not have the confidence to buy objectively planned schemes, and
(b)   Consultancies do not have the confidence to recommend them.

Thus occurs the dilemma that if the consultancy attracts only small budget accounts it has to rely on cheap labour. This is a vicious circle in which low-salary incompetent staff service low-fee accounts that produce highly critical media and very disappointed clients. However, it is encouraging that many consultants new sponsor employees to take the CAM examinations and so learn their trade.

The above remarks are made in fairness to consultancies rather than in criticism of them. Client attitudes to consultancies are often poor. This may − as we shall see later in this chapter − be the client's own fault, but it may be caused much more by unbusinesslike consultancy practices. Of these, failure to cost a scheme properly, or the attempt to get an account at any price, can lead to eventual criticism from clients. It is no use getting business by means of cut-price fees in the hope of raising them when the work proves to be successful. When clients decide to spend more they usually move on to a bigger consultancy, and the price-cutting optimist loses in both directions. The saying 'start as you mean to go on' is very apt, and the bold rather than the nervous consultancy is more likely to succeed in business. It may even pay to reject uneconomic accounts.

Perhaps the greatest weakness with some consultancies is that they aim to please the client instead of being candid about its shortcomings. The consultant needs to be a surgeon rather than a beautician. This weakness is most noticeable when consultancy executives allow themselves to be bullied into distributing news releases which please clients, not editors and readers.

How to appoint a consultancy

When choosing a consultancy, the client should look beyond the principal or managing director, and check out who will actually handle the account. Is the account executive well-trained, experienced and competent, possibly holding the CAM Diploma or being a member of the IPR? It is important to check the credentials of a consultant because the profession is not subject to registration, and anyone can call himself or herself a public relations consultant, perhaps transferring from some other calling such as journalism, advertising or something even less to do with communications. To ask such questions is a management responsibility on the client side where, unfortunately, skills in buying such services are too often poor.

A great problem when appointing either advertising agencies or public relations consultancies is that negotiations are usually conducted between the top people on either side, but once the contract has been signed the day-to-day liaison is usually passed down the line to executives who are strangers to each other. These executives should be present during the negotiations and presentations, otherwise they may fail to work together. Client–consultancy relations can be delicate, relying on the compatibility of personalities, and must be excellent if an account is to be serviced successfully. We shall return to this theme in more detail later in the chapter.

A consultancy should be able to offer experience in most of the areas already listed under the heading of *Reasons for appointing a public relations consultancy* earlier in this chapter, but some may be particularly knowledgeable in certain techniques or industries. For instance, financial consultancies, with their expert knowledge of corporate affairs and the workings of the money market, and probably having an economics or City Page background, may well have little understanding of any other side of public relations. Similarly, a house journal expert would be especially professional at journalism, page layout design, typography and printing, including the buying of print and working with printers and nowadays the use of desk top publishing.

The buying of consultancy services therefore calls for understanding of what is required and what can be supplied. Lack of this understanding may result in a client not appreciating the range of services available, nor their value and necessity. Too often, clients think only in terms of press relations aimed at winning favourable coverage, misunderstanding the role of public relations in the affairs of their organizations. The consultancy has to perform its own salesmanship by presenting its variety of services and abilities in the form of a planned and budgeted proposition. There are thus buying and selling skills on either side, which are not helped by the ironic contradiction that clients rarely know what and how to buy, and consultancies are poor at selling. One solution to this is adoption of objective planning and costing which will be discussed in Chapters 4–10.

Nevertheless, it was significant that in October 1992, the very successful consultancy Countrywide Communications[5] released a survey report which showed that 64 per cent of consultancy clients put most value on the implementation of instructions and only 29 per cent looked for strategic counselling. The survey covered 43 of Britain's top 150 companies, and 83 others.

When appointing an advertising agency it is common to invite a number of agencies to make competitive bids or presentations, paying for any creative work involved. This is natural and sensible because the client needs to judge original ideas and practical media proposals based on figures. Being familiar with this procedure, clients tend to approach the appointment of a public relations consultant in the same way. But would you ask a number of doctors to present competitive cures for an illness? Would you invite alternative diagnoses? Similarly, would you invite competitive prosecutions or defences before appointing a lawyer? The service provided by a public relations consultancy should be based on a preliminary study of the situation, which may require some degree of research. Unless it is merely a product publicity or press relations assignment, a public relations programme cannot be based on the client's view of the situation (the mirror image), nor is it like giving an advertising agency a product or service to promote. The consultancy also needs to have far more confidential information than is possible when rival firms are asked to make competitive presentations. Once again we see how advertising and public relations differ.

To achieve a practical proposition from a consultant it is therefore best for the client to draw up a short list of likely consultants. Some he may know, others he may see advertised in trade and business journals, and other names may be obtained from trade and professional bodies. Addresses (and client lists) can be obtained from the *Advertiser's Annual*[3] the *PRCA Public Relations Year Book*,[6] and the *Hollis Press and Public Relations Annual*[4] (including the Hollis on-line database service). This information will reveal whether a consultancy handles accounts in the same industry, or has accounts which would be conflicting.

There *may* be good reasons for appointing a consultancy which does service rival companies, provided this is agreed between the rivals, simply because the consultancy has the right experience. Confidentiality will be maintained. For instance, one London consultancy is famous for handling public relations for banks while others specialize in hi-tech accounts.

The selected firms can then be visited for initial discussions, until one is chosen and invited to put up a proposition. By such a process of 'shopping around' it is possible for the client to satisfy himself about such important matters as the quality, experience and compatibility of the consultancy staff. After all, an advertising agency can buy in creative work from unknown freelancers, but a public relations consultancy has to sell the abilities of its existing staff. The client—agency relationship is far more intimate and critical. Ideally, the consultancy — upon appointment — should conduct a survey of the situation (at the client's expense) before proposing a plan of action.

This professional approach to the engagement of a professional service is fair to both sides, and if it is not adopted often enough it is because of the confusion that still exists regarding advertising and public relations. Their nature, services, staffing, costing, and the systems of appointment, payment and assessment of results are wholly different. Moreover, under the competitive proposition method the consultancy is obliged to spend a large sum of money on the preparation of schemes, with no recompense if it does not win the contract. Consultancies are rarely large firms, nothing like advertising agencies in manpower, resources and income, so they can survive only if the maximum amount of their time is devoted to producing income. They exist by selling their time.

The consultancy hourly or daily rate may seem high, but a large proportion of consultancy working hours are spent on administering the business, and that includes looking for new business, recruiting and training staff, and dealing with suppliers, the landlord, the Inland Revenue and the Customs and Excise. Some consultancies sell only 40 per cent of their time.

When appointing a consultancy it is essential to understand how the work will be costed and charged out, what the hourly or daily rate is,

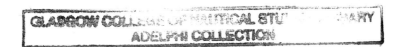

and whether fees will be charged monthly or quarterly in advance. A variety of methods are practised. The IPR publishes a practice paper on consultancy charges. Basically, fees are usually based on the system of hourly rates (or day rates) to cover manhours, office overheads and profit, plus materials (e.g news release headings, photography) and expenses (e.g. catering, fares). Consultancy budgeting will be dealt with thoroughly in Chapter 9, but here it is introduced as a serious consideration when appointing a consultancy. The client needs to be familiar with consultancy finances.

It is also necessary to be clear about whether a *retainer* or a *fee* is being charged. Sometimes the two expressions are used to mean the same thing, but strictly speaking they have very different meaning. A retainer merely retains a consultancy, and gives exclusivity to its services, but covers no work. A fee represents a volume of time expended on consultancy service, and is calculated on an hourly (but sometimes daily) rate, and this may vary according to the experience of the account executive. Different account executives may be charged out at different rates.

How public relations consultancies promote themselves

Unlike some professions, consultancies may advertise their services, but under their Code they must not poach clients from rival consultancies, although they may accept conflicting accounts if both clients agree to being serviced by the same consultancy. Within the confines of good practice, consultancies may promote their services through competitive advertising in the press and by direct mail. Advertisements are placed in trade journals, business newspapers and directories, stands are taken at appropriate exhibitions, and audio visual devices are used for presentations. Some consultancies issue newsletters and other publications for circulation to clients and prospects. In Britain, *PR Week*, with a circulation of some 15,000 copies, has greatly helped in making public relations services capable of being widely publicized.

Client–consultancy relations

How can the client work efficiently with the consultancy? How can an effective partnership be woven with an outside service, probably located some distance from the client's head office? While this may not be too difficult between an advertiser and an advertising agency (because the client has a good idea of what they want advertising for, and can see expenditure in the form of media and production), the circumstances can be very different with public relations. The client does not always know what they want or what can be done for them, often has a totally perverse idea of what public relations is all about, and is probably confused to find that it is costed rather like a taxi meter so that they have to pay every time they or the consultant opens their mouth.

Fortunately, the advertising world is changing over to the fee system, whether it be a large service agency which has renounced the old commission system, or an *à la carte* creative agency which buys no media, has no commission income and has to charge fees. The old idea of free account executive, copywriting and clerical services is disappearing in favour of the client having to pay for time and expertise. This is more professional. The public relations consultancy has to charge in these ways since it has no other source of income.

The financial side is stressed here because there is no easier way to suffer bad client relations than to have misunderstandings and arguments over money leading to disputed bills. The best way to avoid such conflicts is for the contract to be based on a fully budgeted proposition set out so precisely regarding jobs, workloads, manhours, fees and costs that no misunderstanding is possible as the work proceeds. At regular monthly contact meetings (with contact reports distributed afterwards to all concerned whether in attendance or not) the expenditure can be reviewed and agreed as necessary. If extra work is required, supplementary budgets can be approved.

In the event of a dispute over payment, an excellent way of resolving it is to show the client a copy of the timesheet. Clients do not always appreciate how much time has to be spent on different jobs. They are apt to judge the cost of press relations, for example, by the physical evidence of press cuttings. As we shall discuss in later chapters, press cuttings are not evaluated by their volume but by their quality and effect. But a client may compare, say, four press cuttings with the bill and think he has been overcharged, forgetting how much time was spent on researching and writing the story, getting it approved, maybe re-writing a final version, and then distributing it to carefully chosen media. All this could have added up to a day's work!

The regular monthly contact meeting, at either the client's or the consultancy office, is a very simple way of maintaining good relations. Some other methods of achieving good client–consultancy relations are:

1 Compatibility

In any relationship with an outside consultant (providing any sort of professional service) it is often true that the supplier of a service can only be as good as the client permits him to be. We shall return to this subject in other respects, but here let us consider this special problem of compatibility. This can also concern in-house relations between the PRO and others with whom he or she has to work.

At least two people have got to work together. One of the reasons why relations deteriorate to the extent that the contract is not renewed is that the representatives of the client and the consultancy are incompatible. The client representation can seldom be changed, and so it is vital that from the time of initial negotiations and presentation of proposals that the right account executive is assigned to the account.

It is surprising what can lead to friction. It may be that the account executive is too young, wears a beard or has a regional accent, even that he is too short or too tall! Vanity can provoke difficulties. Perhaps the account executive must not appear to be superior in some way to the client! It may be that a client may prefer to deal with either a man or a woman, perhaps because of the nature of the product or service. Women excel in public relations as they are often good organizers but sometimes they can be too feminist, or male management will not take them seriously.

The successful management of a consultancy may therefore depend on how carefully personnel are deployed to satisfy the quite irrational demands of clients. The account executive who is disliked by one client may be received warmly by another. This is a perennial problem in the management of consultancies, meanwhile the head of the consultancy somehow has to get on with every client!

2   Learning how each other works

Both representatives should get beyond each other's office or boardroom, and see behind the scenes in each other's organization. There may not be a lot to see in a consultancy for it is little more than a set of offices with office machines and equipment. But the client can get to know the rest of the staff, and discover what everyone does, especially if some perform special tasks, such as lobbying or dealing with take-over bids. For the account executive there is much more to see. He should visit offices, plants and various locations and learn what the client's organization does and how it does it. In this way, the account executive can develop lines of communication beyond the immediate client contact. Curiosity can be a consultancy asset.

Each should try to learn all they can about each other's business. If the client representation is not an in-house PRO but, say, the marketing services manager or a product manager, it will help the relationship if this executive takes the trouble to learn about public relations and how a consultancy operates. Conversely, the account executive should study the client's industry or business, so that he or she can read its literature intelligently, and talk about it with understanding. This can be no mean achievement since a client could come from any trade, industry or profession.

There are little things that matter. Does the account executive know a client's current share price? Has its latest product been sampled? Who is rumoured to be likely to make a takeover bid? How is the company affected by the latest draft EC directive? Does the account executive live in the client's world.

3 Augmenting the client's organization

The consultancy should not be seen as an isolated outsider, but as an extra arm, an extension of the existing organization. This encourages mutual confidence and the giving of confidences. When the client trusts the consultancy and shares secrets with it, the relationship is well cemented. Good relations can be developed if the client takes the consultancy account executive into their confidence, keeping him or her regularly up-dated on new product development and company policy. This can be further extended if the account executive is introduced to top management and invited to attend meetings so that he or she is accepted as a confidant. A good 'friend of the family' or 'father confessor' situation can enhance consultancy–client relations.

This aspect cannot be emphasized too strongly because some managements fear that confidences will go astray with account executives who tend to be less permanent than company staff. The ethics of the profession should be made known to a cautious and reticent client, and it could be very helpful if the client was given a copy of the PRCA or IPR Code of Professional Conduct. The client should know what membership of the PRCA or IPR entails.

In fact, when selecting a consultancy it would be pertinent to check whether the consultancy is a member of the PRCA, or at least whether the principal and especially the account executive are members of the IPR. If they are not in membership it would be a very sensible question to ask why not!

4 Punctuality

A frequent cause of criticism by clients is that account executives are late for appointments, and out-of-town clients often make early-morning demands. This problem surfaced once in a survey of advertising agency–client relations. It is a more important point than is always realized. Out-of-town people take punctuality for granted because they live close to their jobs, whereas city-based consultants are usually commuters who suffer from the vagaries of public transport and often arrive at their destinations by a process of luck. These contrary experiences have to be harmonized so that conflict does not occur. Perhaps the client should come to town occasionally, or the account executive should stay overnight in order to make that 8.30 a.m. appointment.

5   Prompt clearance

Another bone of contention is over the prompt approval of material submitted by the consultant, whether it be a news release, a speech, plans for a press reception, copy for a house journal, or proofs of printed material. Unless it is explained to them, and impressed upon them, that there are deadlines or that delay will incur extra costs (such as overtime at the printers), clients are apt to be casual. The author once resigned a client who never took news releases out of his in-tray. The success of much public relations work depends on timing, and can be destroyed by the whims of a client. Managing a client can often call for great tact and patience coupled with persistence. But a consultant should never be afraid to fire a bad client.

Sometimes, the consultant has to contend with the client who insists on a number of people vetting, approving and maybe rewriting a news release. While it is essential that facts be checked for accuracy, an 'approved' version can be rendered unpublishable. If the consultant is to be then accused of failing to obtain media coverage the only defence is attack in the sense that an 'approve it as it stands or fire me' attitude must be taken. One of the reasons why 70 per cent of news releases are rejected by editors is that they are 'approved versions' which the hapless account executive is weak enough or unprofessional enough to distribute. Unfortunately, this happens when the account executive is too junior to be able to convince the client that he or she does not know best. One of the lessons both clients and consultants have to learn is that the customer is seldom right. The ideal situation occurs when the client is willing to admit that the consultancy knows best, and that is why it has been hired. It may take time for this happy situation to develop, but that is what good client relations are all about. They depend on trust and frankness, not bullying and subservience.

6   Flow of information

A very important element in good relations is that both sides should keep the other well-informed. The consultant can keep his or her eyes open for things that may be valuable to the client such as White Papers, survey reports, articles in the press or programmes on radio or TV. The client should also feed relevant information to the consultancy and this may include:

- News about research and development work, information about prototypes of new products, and reports on tests (such as by independent laboratories).
- Details of supply or production problems, including trade and industrial disputes, import, political or legal difficulties.
- Relocation or new location plans, and any redundancy or recruitment problem.
- Company publications such as house journals, videos, annual reports and accounts, catalogues, price lists and sales literature.
- Advertising media schedules and pulls of advertisements.
- Samples of new products and their packaging.
- Details of changes in products, prices and packaging.
- Lists of stockists or agents.
- Information about changes in distribution methods.
- Information about new appointments and changes in key personnel.

At no time should the consultancy learn anything about the client from a third source, and be disadvantaged by ignorance which the client could have avoided. This can happen when a journalist rings the consultancy for a statement, but the consultant knows nothing about the subject.

These are management matters for which both sides are responsible. The client should be forthcoming and the consultancy should encourage this co-operation.

References

1 *This is Corporate Relations*, booklet, British Telecommunications plc, London, 1992
2 *Membership Survey*, Institute of Public Relations, 1992
3 *Advertiser's Annual*, IPC Media Publications, Windsor Court, East Grinstead, RH1G 1XA
4 *Hollis Press and Public Relations Annual*, Hollis Directories, Sunbury on Thames
5 Countrywide Communications report, Banbury, October 1992
6 *Public Relations Year Book*, FT Business Information Ltd with Public Relations Consultants Association

3

Writing reports and proposals

Why reports and propositions are necessary

Reports and propositions are necessary in order to spell out what the PRO or consultant recommends. Again, it is businesslike, and something management understands and appreciates. It shows logical, responsible thinking.

It is no use making suggestions or recommendations verbally. They will probably be met by a response of 'No!' or 'What will it cost?' Armed with a written scheme and calculated costs, the practitioner is in a strong position to argue a case. Never say, 'Wouldn't it be a good idea if . . .' *unless* you have done your homework first and can back up your proposal with facts and figures.

A written report or proposition needs to be set out in an acceptable and readily understood fashion. It should be written in an objective, factual style, the information should be presented in a logical sequence, and different kinds of information must be easily located. It should be comprehensible to anyone reading it at any time.

The report should be preceded by the *brief* – that is, a statement of the purpose, scope and limitations of the report. If initiated by someone other than the writer, it will be on instruction. In order to understand the report it is necessary for the reader to understand the brief. The reader will also require a *summary* which gives a quick, simple impression of the proposals.

The writer should consider how, when and by whom the report will be read. These considerations may be as follows:

1 The reader is likely to be busy and have to read many documents. The report has to be both concise and comprehensive.
2 It may have to be dealt with at a board or committee meeting, it may not have been studied beforehand, and so the *reader* needs

to be able to find his or her way about the report in the midst of a discussion.

3 The report should be capable of easy reference and understanding by anyone reading it in the future since reports are likely to be kept on file.
4 Those reading it may not have detailed knowledge of the subject. It should not be too jargonized and essential terms should be explained, if necessary in an appendix.

The above remarks should emphasize that writing a report or proposition is very different from writing advertisements, news releases or feature articles, all of which have their special literary styles. They are as different as a map, a poster, a telegram and a book. The skilled communicator has to be able to change writing styles according to the job. The proposition also has to sell.

Three things are therefore essential to the preparation of these documents:

1 Adequate research.
2 Concise, precise writing.
3 Methodical lay-out of the information.

Here, then, are the outlines for two reports, first an internal report to management, second a business proposition from a consultant (or any other outside service). While a good consultant should automatically produce such a report, the PRO should also expect one. Two extremes do occur: some consultants are poor businessmen and think a letter is sufficient, while others indulge in showmanship and dress up propositions in too-fancy binders.

The plan of an internal report could follow the following pattern:

Internal report

Title page − perhaps stating the purpose of the report and for whom it is intended.
List of contents, giving chapter or section headings and page numbers.
The brief − purpose, extent and limitations of the study.
Summary of findings or proposals.
Methodology − if there has been research, a statement of the methods used. If a questionnaire has been used, this should be reproduced in the appendices.
Appreciation of the situation.

Solution or recommendations.
Techniques or plan of action with perhaps a timetable.
Budget.
Appendices containing specific supporting items.

The plan of consultancy proposition will be slightly different because (*a*) the client has to be convinced of the consultant's ability to perform, and (*b*) the client has to understand how the costs are arrived at and how the consultant will be remunerated. This proposition may well have to compete with other propositions. The budgetary aspects will be dealt with in Chapter 9.

Consultancy proposition

Title page — stating for whom the document is prepared, and by whom.
List of contents, giving section headings, and page numbers.
The brief — as instructed by the client.
Summary of recommendations.
Statement of experience setting out consultant's relevant experience with other clients.
Personnel — identification of account executive who will handle the account, plus names of any specialists who may be used.
Appreciation of the situation as researched by the consultant, resulting in certain problems or needs which the recommendations will be designed to resolve.
Recommendations and programme — an outline of the consultant's plan of action.
Budget — allocation of manhours on an hourly or daily rate basis, arriving at the fee, plus estimates for materials and expenses.
Payment — method of payment, e.g. quarterly in advance.
'Brag list' — list of clients, past and present, serviced by the consultant.
Appendices — supporting material such as samples of work done.

The production of the report should be neat and orderly, but not flamboyant. All pages should be numbered and a contents list or index is essential. The document should be presented in a convenient form, say A4 size, printed on one side of the paper only, and bound in stiff covers with perhaps a slide, spiral or comb (wire or plastic) binding. Thus the report will be easy to read and easy to keep flat and clean.

The significance of certain items will be brought out in the chapters on planning and budgeting, but here it is apparent from these items that both the internal report and the consultancy proposition should be explicit. They imply preliminary research, analysis of the situation, and a logical plan with detailed costings. Between the lines one can see the Mexican Statement emerging! The reader of the proposals will be able to understand exactly what is being presented, and this can lead to the necessary considerations and discussions, resulting in rejection amendments or acceptance. After this, there should be no misunderstandings between management and PRO, or between client and consultancy. From a public relations point of view, it is an exercise in responsible, professional management.

If regular progress meetings are held at least monthly, when adjustment can be made as circumstances demand, proper control can be maintained. Any plan has to be flexible, and public relations is often confronted by the unexpected, but there must be a plan in the first place as represented by the report or proposition. Such reporting inspires the confidence of management, and status and respect for the PRO or consultancy will stem from this businesslike beginning.

In-house PROs who complain that they have to dance to the whims of management who want this and that done, and consultants who despair of the demands made by clients, are usually those who have failed to lay the foundations properly by setting out and gaining approval of basic proposals.

It is all the difference between tangible and intangible public relations. Written proposals, as demonstrated in both examples given above, represent solutions to problems. Being objective, they must lead to results which can be evaluated by observation, experience or research. In later chapters we shall examine all these aspects more clearly.

Fundamental to the report and the proposition is the budget made up of manhour costs, materials and expenses. The estimation of the workload necessary to carry out the programme establishes *time* as a primary factor which has to be agreed in terms of salaries and fees and what can be done best with the available quantity of time. Although this will be discussed more fully in Chapter 9, it is important to establish here that a major responsibility of public relations management, whether in-house or in the consultancy, is the assessment, allocation and control of labour for public relations is labour intensive. Thus, fees and salaries represent hours or days, and the programme will depend on how much time is available to allocate to various activities. This must be established first *before* any monies can be allocated to materials. It is pointless budgeting the cost of printing a house journal if there is no one with the time to edit it.

It is no different from calculating the quantity and use of bricks or blocks to build a house. The logic is the same. Take away some of the labour, or some of the bricks, for some other purpose and the original purpose cannot be achieved. In a consultancy this is especially critical because staff can be employed or newly hired only if the cost of their time is justified and met by fees. The point at which to recruit another executive is a delicate one bound up in the profitability of the firm.

As we shall see as we proceed, public relations management is to do with the acceptance of constraints and priorities. It is sometimes thought that this elementary discipline does not apply to public relations, although it does in every other kind of management. It is very much the art of the possible.

But of course it is not quite as simple as that. Time will be used most cost-effectively according to the extent to which the PRO or the consultant possesses the six attributes set out in Chapter 1.

4

Managing planned public relations programmes

Objective planning

Both the IPR definition of public relations and the Mexican Statement lay emphasis on planning public relations programmes, and the latter adds 'analysing trends' and 'predicting their consequences'. To these we can now add another definition which brings out 'objectives'.

Public relations consists of all forms of communication outwards and inwards, between an organization and its publics for the purpose of achieving specific objectives concerning mutual understanding.

The above is the author's definition, and the stress in this case is on 'specific objectives'. If there are specific objectives it now becomes possible to evaluate results. This makes public relations accountable, cost-effective and tangible, which are management responsibilities, whether the programme is conducted by an in-house public relations manager or by an outsider consultancy, and was introduced in the previous chapter on the writing of reports and propositions.

We are not concerned with haphazard 'off-the-cuff' efforts, 'playing it by ear', or short-term trouble-shooting or 'fire-fighting' exercises, or with vague, intangible public relations to achieve favourable this or that. To be successful, and that is to justify the effort and cost, a public relations programme has to be organized like a marketing strategy, an advertising campaign or a production schedule. The programme should be planned to cover a reasonable length of time such as a financial year. Some large organizations prepare three-year programmes. Like other programmes, it needs to be planned well in advance, probably co-incidentally. Thus, if the financial year begins on 1 January the time to plan the programme for the forthcoming year may be in August or September of the previous year.

It may be argued that public relations has to deal with the unpredictable. A few things may be unpredicted, such as a crisis situation, but no business can operate on a pragmatic day-to-day basis. For example, the British government sets out its plans in the Queen's Speech and the Budget Speech and knows what it wants to do, but in the course of the year all manner of unexpected issues will occur which will require attention and adjustments.

There are two ways of dealing with the unexpected. First, from experience and even anticipation it can be estimated that a certain volume of time will have to be allocated for such eventualities. A typical example is a press office facility to deal with enquiries whose nature cannot be known in advance. Second, there can be a contingency fund to allow for expenditures which cannot be forecast. Third, the programme can be reviewed and amended at monthly contact meetings.

But as we shall see in the next chapter, certain things will be known because they will be based on the declared objectives of the programme. If a house journal is to be published it has to be written, edited, designed, printed and distributed regularly. The launching of new products or services will be expected, and the public relations programme may include activities which will precede or run in parallel with these launches. The programme may have to be dovetailed with many already planned events such as participation in an exhibition, the announcement of company results, sponsorship of events, a relocation programme, an opening ceremony or the celebration of an anniversary.

If the year's work is not planned and costed the likelihood is that a muddle of unconnected things will be attempted so that in the end nothing is done properly and it is impossible to assess any results. This can only breed scepticism about the value of public relations. It can lead to budgets being cut, staff being reduced and consultancies losing contracts.

But if there is a definite, objective programme it is possible to tailor supply of manpower and resources, and to operate within constraints. Unless there are major costs such as producing videos, touring a mobile exhibition, publishing a large-circulation frequently published house journal, or large sponsorship expenses, material costs will be comparatively small. Similarly, hospitality and expenses should be a modest proportion of the budget. The primary cost will be time as expressed by either in-house salaries or consultancy fees.

Submission of a public relations programme

In an efficiently run organization, the staff PRO will be expected to present a recommended programme and budget for the forthcoming financial year.

When making a presentation to a client, a consultancy should present a detailed programme of proposals supported by a fully calculated budget so that the client knows what can be expected for the money and the consultancy knows what it may expect to be paid. The agreed proposals should form the basis of the contract of service.

Even when top management does not expect a programme and budget, it will enhance the professional status of the in-house PRO if a businesslike approach is initiated by volunteering a programme and budget. This will then enable allocation and control of expenditure of time and money and establish quite clearly the scope and limitations of resources. It will clarify priorities and establish what can or cannot be done, helping to deter higher management from imposing extra work on the PRO unless other work is cancelled, extra staff or funds are provided, or the department is augmented by the outside services of a consultancy.

These are public relations management responsibilities, and the style of reports and proposals can follow the pattern set out in the previous chapter.

Example of a day's work

A public relations programme, with its estimation of the workload, may look as if certain items which total so many hours are complete blocks of time. Of course, in reality this time will be scattered over days, weeks or months in small segments of time. This is where the keeping of daily timesheets is important for the consultancy where time will be spent on behalf of different clients in the course of a single day.

The complexity of a typical day's work might be something like this for an in-house PRO:

9.00 a.m.	Read incoming post, which includes a quotation for printing an educational booklet. Compare quotation with others received.
9.30 a.m.	Dictate letters in reply, including acceptance of quotation.
10.00 a.m.	Read draft of article typed the previous day. Give revised draft to secretary for retyping.
10.30 a.m.	Phone photographer and arrange photographic session for illustrating a forthcoming news release.
10.45 a.m.	Visit hotel and agree plans with banqueting manager for a press reception.
12.30 p.m.	Take lunch while out of office.

1.30 p.m.	On way back to office collect proofs of invitation cards from printer.
2.00 p.m.	Read and correct proofs and give to secretary to return to printer.
2.15 p.m.	Answer phone call from radio producer wanting information.
2.30 p.m.	Write speech for managing director at press reception.
3.30 p.m.	Give speech to secretary for typing.
3.45 p.m.	Phone printer to make sure of delivery date of invitation cards.
4.00 p.m.	Sign letters.
4.30 p.m.	Receive telephone call from editor requesting photographs.
4.45 p.m.	Select pictures, make sure captions are correct and give to secretary to despatch.
5.00 p.m.	End of day – but possibly take typed draft of speech home to read overnight.

This day in the life of a busy staff PRO shows that he or she deals with outgoing work in preparing for a press reception, receives unpredictable and time-consuming phone calls, relies very much on an efficient secretary, and that the work may not be confined to office hours. But many of these actions are slotted into an overall plan of operation, and unless these jobs are done on this particular day they will be too late on another day. Unless the flow of contributory actions is sustained, deadlines will not be met. It will be seen from the above day's work that three jobs are in progress, and two unexpected ones emerge for which the PRO must be prepared with the back-up of existing information and the resources of a well-stocked photographic library.

Critical path analysis

The overall plan may be presented by a critical path analysis chart displayed on the PRO's office wall. This may look something like Figure 4.1. The items set out in this example are irrelevant as they relate to a case study, and the chart is reproduced from the author's *Effective PR Planning*.[1] It demonstrates how each job has to start and finish on certain dates along the line (which may be vertical or horizontal) in order to arrive at the completion of the task or year's work. The line represents the start and finish of the work, and resembles that for the construction of a building as used on building sites. An active critical path analysis chart would have dates for each job, running from say 1 January to 31 December. But it could also be applied to a single assignment such as the organizing of a press reception.

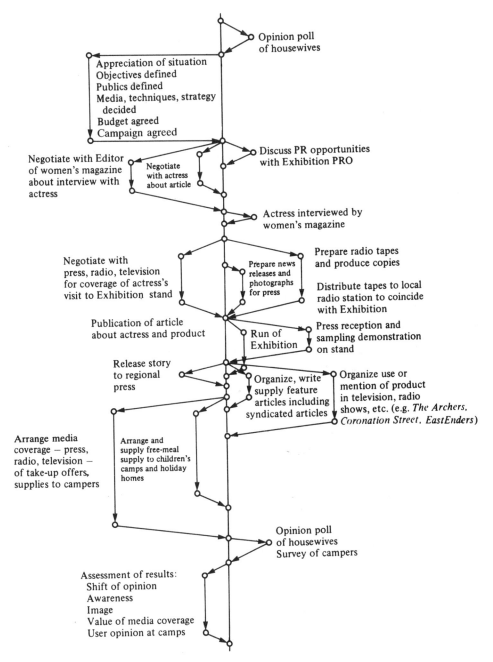

Figure 4.1 *Critical path analysis of a public relations programme. (Adapted from Jefkins,* Effective PR Planning, *where it relates to a case study)*

D-Day planning chart

For a separate job or event, such as a press reception where the preparation may be spread over three months, a D-Day planning timetable can be plotted, working back from the event to the first action. This diary of actions or responsibilities will help the organizer to plan the sequence of tasks which will lead up to the event which cannot occur unless this sequence has been followed. Once written down, the D-Day plan provides a checklist of things to do, and it can be associated with a budget of all the items which have to be ordered or bought. We shall return to this in Chapter 9 on budgeting. Figure 4.2 is an example taken from the author's *Effective Press Relations and House Journal Editing*.[2]

What will management ask?

Before approving a programme, management may ask the following questions, as set out in Robert D. Ross's book *The Management of Public Relations*:[3]

- Why are the objectives important to the organization?
- What will be the specific long- and short-range benefits in carrying out the plan?
- How much will it cost?
- What department will pay the bill?
- Why do the benefits warrant the cost?
- Will the plan really do effectively the job that it is intended to do?
- What will happen if it is not carried out?
- What departments will be involved?
- How will the plan affect their staff and their need for people?
- How will it affect the other jobs that they are charged with carrying out?
- Do the other groups and departments involved agree with the plan? Why?
- If some oppose the plan, why?
- How long will it take to carry out the plan?
- What are the alternatives to carrying out the plan?
- Have other plans with the same objectives been tried before?
- What were their results?

These questions could be asked of either the in-house PRO or the consultancy. As Robert D. Ross says 'Many excellent plans fail to get acceptance because those responsible for making them first fail to recognize the barriers to getting acceptance. It therefore pays to anticipate resistance and doubts, and to do more than that − understand the implications of the likely questions. If the above sixteen queries are reexamined it will be seen that management is concerned not only about

D-90	Decide date
D-85	Plan programme for press reception
D-85	Shortlist venues
D-85	Invite quotations, menus, from prospective venues
D-80	Complete compilation of invitation list: check names
D-75	Compare received hotel quotations and menus
D-70	Visit prospective venues
D-65	Select and appoint venue
D-50	Design invitation card: agree wording
D-50	Seek printer's quotation for card
D-42	Receive printer's quotation: order cards and envelopes
D-35	Photograph subject
D-32	Receive, check and return proof of invitation card
D-30	Write managing director's speech
D-30	Order self-adhesive lapel badges, press kit wallets, visitors' book
D-30	Book VCR, TV set, microphones
D-25	See contact prints: order photographs
D-24	Obtain approval of managing director's speech
D-22	Send special invitations to radio/television producers' news/ programmes
D-20	Write news release
D-14	Delivery of invitation cards and envelopes
D-13	Address envelopes and invitations
D-12	Despatch invitations; order studio artwork − tent cards for speakers, displays, directional signs
D-10	Record acceptances/refusals
D-9	Follow up non-replies, important refusals
D-8	Photographs supplied; items at D-30 delivered
D-4	Collect video
D-3	Give hotel numbers for catering, seating, together with plan of the room
D-2	Run off news releases, MD's speech
D-2	Assemble press kits
D-1	Deliver materials, equipment to venue
D-1	Prepare room
D-1	Rehearsal: run through video
D-Day	Press reception
D-Day +	Follow up enquiries, non-attenders

Figure 4.2 *D-Day planning timetable for a press reception*

what the PRO plans to do *himself* or *herself* but also how the scheme affects *other* people in the organization.

For instance, it is all very well proposing publication of a house journal but people in the organization will have to spend time writing for it. If a video is proposed, various people will have to give up their time for the shooting, and if a technical seminar or even a press reception is planned it will involve company speakers and spokespeople. A public relations programme is unlikely to be conducted without involving other company personnel, unlike an advertising campaign which is created and placed by outside people.

Management goes beyond telling people what to do and getting things done. It is also, as Robert D. Ross says:

1 Analysis and definition of opportunities and problems.
2 Making decisions as to what will be done.
3 Getting the decisions carried out.
4 Analysis of the other three steps and their results after the decisions are partly or fully carried out.

Two things are therefore necessary: (a) a practical plan has to be drawn up, and (b) it has to be capable of overcoming the objections of those who can give approval and authorize the expenditure.

It is no good saying 'Why don't we do this?' Top management will want to know why the proposals are being made, what they are likely to achieve and what they will cost. It is a selling proposition. This is clearly understood by a consultancy which is seeking business, but it may not always be seen like this by the salaried full-time staff PRO who already has a job with the organization.

Because he or she is already appointed, employed, salaried and maybe pensionable, it may not be recognized that this status and security relies on selling management a sound investment. He or she may – and quite a lot of in-house PROs do – simply carry out orders, little realizing how precarious is the yes-person's position. The PRO is never in a position to be irreplaceable or even appreciated. There is therefore a difference between a PRO who is not responsible for initiating and recommending what the in-house department shall do, and the PRO who is responsible for managing by objectives and is in control because proposals have been approved.

Controls – essential paperwork

The best way to control time is to use a simple daily or weekly *timesheet* on which the take-up of time is recorded. This discipline will provide a regular check on the amount of time spent on particular jobs, and it can be an early warning system if more time is being consumed on a job than was estimated in the agreed programme. In the case of first-time jobs, it will be a guide to future planning.

Timesheets are essential in the consultancy so that time may be rationed according to the different fees paid by different clients. This works both ways, helping to ensure that a client gets the time to which they are entitled, and warning the consultancy of excessive usage of time. As already explained, it is easy to allow a given amount of time to, say, the organizing of a press reception, but in practice it will be scattered in small portions over a period of perhaps three months as shown by the D-Day timetable and thrown up in the daily timesheets. If too

Week beginning . . . . Client								
	Mon	Tues	Wed	Thurs	Fri	Sat	Sun	Week's total
Daily totals								

Figure 4.3 *A weekly timesheet for a public relations consultancy client*

much time is spent on one job it means that less time can be given to another. The solution may not lie in working late, or taking work home, because some jobs can be done only when other people are available during their working hours. The effect of keeping timesheets can encourage an understanding of how much time ought to be spent on any given job, thus imposing a kind of productivity control.

When out of the office, time usage should be jotted down in a diary so that the timesheet can be completed when the office is revisited, although, if the absence exceeds a day, timesheets should be carried and completed while away from the office. It is fatal to get behind with timesheets, and to attempt to complete them from memory. Everything has to be put down, including telephone calls.

The public relations manager's or account executive's secretary should collect the timesheets at the end of the week, keep running totals of time expended, and compare them with target totals for the job. Without such control, a consultancy could go out of business. It is even possible for such a control system to reveal that a client is an uneconomic liability and that the account should be relinquished. There are clients whose fee represents only a day or two's work a week, but whose demands are for a full-time service which is far beyond the scope of the fee.

A second form of control is the use of *job numbers*. Each individual job such as a piece of print, a photographic session, or the production of a video is given a job number, prefixed with an identifying letter. Thus if a consultancy has twelve clients the job numbers can be coded A to L to identify each client. The in-house PRO can use one letter for the organization, or separate letters for different divisions, departments or subsidiaries. This job number is raised as soon as the job starts and goods or services are being ordered. Suppliers (e.g. photographers, printers) must be aware that they must not accept orders (verbally, on the telephone, in writing, by fax and so on) unless they are identified by a job number.

Suppliers can then put job numbers on their invoices, thus identifying work which has to be charged out to clients. The significance of this is apparent when a photographer invoices a client for a number of assignments, each of which may be on behalf of a different client. Without the job numbers it can be very difficult for consultancy staff to identify items and make sure that they are recovered. There is a serious cash flow situation here because it will be perfectly possible to pay the photographer's composite bill, and fail to collect monies due from individual clients. And if the job numbers are put on the invoice to the client the client can agree payment because the items will be in accordance with those on contact reports. The job number system is a form of accountancy communication which helps supplier, consultancy and client and so ensures a smooth flow of payments.

This is a very simple system which can save money and avoid disputes. The PRO or consultancy executive will rely on his or her secretary to keep a file of job numbers, and to issue new ones as required.

Instructions to secretaries

Good public relations management means teaching secretaries how to perform as public relations secretaries. Often, this means forgetting some of the things they were taught at secretarial college. Yet, to judge by what one receives from the majority of public relations offices, no special instructions are given to secretaries. This suggests that either the manager or account executive is dominated by his or her secretary, or fails to instruct the secretary properly. Some essential instructions are these:

1　All copy for printing, whether it be a news release, feature article or the text of a book or brochure, must follow the rules of presentation set out in Chapter 14. Among other things, this requires the work to be double-spaced, given good margins on either side, typed on one side of the sheet only, and all paragraphs but the first must be indented as in most newspapers, magazines and books. Secretaries mostly use block paragraphs as in business letters, with line spacing between them. This is wrong.
2　All pictures must bear a caption stating what the picture is about and identifying its public relations source. This rarely happens.
3　Pictures must not be sent out with a compliment slip attached by means of a paperclip, yet this is normal practice. Paperclips damage pictures.
4　Photographs must be protected by card, or packed in card-backed envelopes, and not put in large flimsy envelopes which mail delivery staff bend in half, either when bundling mail in rubber bands or when delivering through the letter box.

Contact reports

Good management requires that a contact report should be written and distributed after any meeting, whether it is a purely internal one or a meeting between the consultancy and the client. The account executive should write the latter and submit it as soon as possible after the meeting so that misunderstandings are avoided.

A contact report is a special form of *minutes*, being a brief account of decisions taken with individual responsibilities clearly stated. Verbatim reports are unnecessary, laborious and tedious.

At the top of the report there should be a description of the meeting followed by the distribution list, which may include people not present at the meeting. The items in the report should be brief statements of topics discussed and decisions taken. On the right-hand side of the sheet there should be a vertical line, and to the right of this may be entered the initials of the people who have to take some kind of action. If the agenda of the meeting quotes job numbers, these can be repeated on the left-hand side of the contact report.

If this report is submitted quickly any disagreements can be settled and the report can be revised. The reports can be filed in a facts book, providing a valuable record should any queries or problems arise. The collection of contact reports makes an excellent source of information when writing a report of the year's work, whether by the PRO or the consultancy account executive. Again, it is good management to produce an annual report, if only in one's own interest. If the public relations programme has followed an objective plan, the annual report can conclude with an assessment of the results of the year's work.

Six-point public relations planning model

So far we have discussed the wisdom of planning a public relations programme, and some of the ways of managing and controlling this programme. Now, and in the next six chapters, we will discuss and analyse the actual planning. The Six-Point Public Relations Planning Model was devised some years ago by the author, but it is interesting that the Mexican Statement resembles it closely. The six elements are:

1   Appreciation of the situation.
2   Definition of objectives.
3   Definition of publics.
4   Selection of media and techniques.
5   The budget.
6   Assessment of results.

Here we have an outline or synopsis of a public relations programme. Although listed like this it is not exactly a sequence of considerations as some of them will be considered in parallel while there may be a given budget. Nevertheless, taken in this sequence a series of constraints are in operation. The number of possible objectives may exceed the ability to meet them, perhaps through lack of media, but more likely because of the limitations of the budget. Again, there may be more publics than media to reach them. And when it comes to media a constraint may be the cost of creating media in the absence of existing commercial media. The practical and the possible replace the desirable and the idealistic. A problem in public relations is the temptation to attempt more than is feasible, but in the end it comes down to what can be done with the available time, money and resources. Even so, it is remarkable how little public relations costs and how much can be achieved and, as some very big spenders are finding, it can be more economical and effective than expensive forms of promotion.

I do not wish to imply that public relations is a cheap alternative to advertising, but there are times when public relations is more effective and more economical simply because advertising is the wrong medium. No one would buy Rentokil products and services unless they understood the problems they solved, and that calls for market education, not advertising.

As an introduction to the following chapters let us look briefly at the six elements of the Six-Point Public Relations Planning Model.

1 Appreciation of the situation

Sometimes called the *communication audit*, we are concerned here with determining the current image, that is, the sum total of how the organization and its products or services is perceived externally. Unless we know where we are now it is pointless planning a public relations programme: usually, the public relations evolves as a means of changing the situation.

For example, it may be found that there are unjustified negative situations of the kind expressed in the public relations transfer process described in Chapter 1, namely *hostility*, *prejudice*, *apathy* and *ignorance*. The *current image* may well be found to be at variance with the *mirror image*, fondly but unrealistically held by management. Nowadays it is popular to attack poor management as a cause of industrial ills, and one weakness has undoubtedly been management's false assumptions about the true external perceived image. What management thinks people think is seldom what people actually think about an organization.

Thus, the nature of public relations is seen to be about solving *problems* and changing *attitudes*, which is rather more complex than the bland one so often advanced of seeking favourable images, favourable coverage, favourable climates of opinion, and the rest of the favourable farrago. In this respect, we take issue with those who abuse public relations by seeking these simplistic aims. Life just isn't like that. Much of public relations has to deal with creating *understanding* of difficult, unpleasant and unpopular situations and issues. This is very true of organizations which serve or supply a large market, ranging from public authorities (including those like British Telecom and British Gas which have been privatized) to the manufacturers of Fast Moving Consumer Goods (FMCGs).

2   Definition of objectives

Elsewhere[4] the author has listed more than thirty possible objectives, but in Chapter 6 a different approach has been taken, and consideration of objectives has been taken from a public relations management point of view. This is not unlike a government or local authority considering departmental requirements when producing its budget. The ideal way to arrive at potential objectives is to discuss the future communication needs of the directors or managers in charge of the departments, divisions or subsidiary companies which the PRO has to serve. This would also be a practical approach for a public relations consultancy if it were called upon to serve the total organization, and was permitted to conduct such internal research.

The list is likely to be too long to be undertaken in its entirety, and priorities will have to be chosen to fit the budget. It is better to apply this restraint at the planning stage, otherwise the public relations effort will be spread too thinly over too many tasks and that can only invite failure to achieve worthwhile results. The simple logic here is that if the public relations programme has clearly defined objectives it is possible to assess results.

3   Definition of publics

Again, a long list can be assembled. It will be different from the target groups selected for advertising purposes, these usually being fewer and larger such as social grades, age or income groups, or a particular segment of the market. The public relations publics of an organization may range from school children to politicians, and not be limited to trade, consumer or user groups. We are not only concerned with marketing.

It is therefore very misleading to refer to 'target audiences' in public relations, although this frequently features as one of the ambiguities of CAM examination questions, which can only be blamed on lack of moderating of questions.

Not only will a budgetary constraint apply but also the ability to reach every public. Some may be reached accumulatively as when a television audience may comprise many publics. Other publics may have to be reached by private, created media, but will the budget permit this in every case?

4 Selection of media and techniques

This leads on from the definition of publics: is media available which will reach our various publics? In an industrialized country with a wealth of newspapers, magazines, radio and TV stations, the media may be ready-made, whereas in industrializing countries such media may be not only meagre but capable of reaching only a mainly urban, educated, literate, monied and elitist minority of the population. But in either kind of society, it may be necessary to create special media to reach certain publics. In the one it may be external house journals or videos, and in the other it may be mobile film units and the use of folk (oramedia) at village level.

Much of the PRO's or consultant's skill will be in using or devising the right media, and this calls for a much more extensive knowledge and understanding of media than is required in advertising where the fewest number of most effective media can be chosen statistically according to circulation, readership and audience figures plus comparative costs.

It is not always realized by public relations students that it is impossible to conduct a media relations programme unless one is familiar with all sections of the media. It is pointless to refer vaguely to 'the press', 'the nationals', 'the local press', 'the trade press', 'TV' or 'radio'. Those are meaningless generalities. Unfortunately there is no specialist media paper at CAM certificate stage.

5 The budget

A budget may be set, or one may be calculated to cover a proposed programme. Either way, it will require a careful estimate of the workload (time), materials and expenses. This is where the experience of the public relations practitioner will be important. From experience, it will be known how much time it will take to carry out various tasks, and the PRO will be precise in seeking estimates and capable of judging the merits of competitive quotations. The PRO has to be a skilled buyer of many services such as design, printing, photography, artwork, exhibition stands or materials, videos and so on.

6   *Assessment of results*

At the onset, it will be necessary to decide how the results can or will be assessed. There may be a continuous assessment, as with the evaluation of media coverage, or it may be some kind of test at given intervals or at the end of the campaign. Some results can be recorded, observed or experienced, and are apparent. Others, like change of opinion, awareness or attitude, may require an independent marketing research survey. Research may repeat that used in the first place to establish the current image or the extent and nature of hostility, prejudice, apathy and ignorance. Continuous research conducted or subscribed to already for marketing purposes such as omnibus surveys, consumer panels or dealer audits may provide evidence of public relations results.

Assessments will be related to the set objectives, and when these are realistic and practical the vagueness of intangible public relations will be absent.

A useful checklist

In his book *How To Manage Public Relations*,[5] Norman Stone offers the following:

'If you want to . . . develop a real PR programme, here are the 10 key questions. Simple to ask, they are not always simple to answer.

1   To *whom* are you talking?
2   *What* do you want them to do?
3   *Why* do you want them to do it?
4   *What* are you going to say to them?
5   *Where* are you going to reach them?
6   *When* are you going to reach them?
7   *Which* techniques will you use?
8   *How much* are you going to spend?
9   *What if* there is an unforeseen problem?
10   *How* did you do?

Strategic dilemma of consultancies

A subject which aroused some discussion in the trade press in 1992 was the fact that 'clients want outside PR consultants more for their arms and legs than their heads'. This leader comment in *PR Week*[6] was provoked by research conducted by Countrywide Communications which studied the public relations activity in 43 of the top 150 companies and 83 similar companies. Only 29 per cent regarded strategic counselling as an important consultancy service. Similar findings resulted from a survey in 1990 by Smythe Dorward Lambert, while a *PR Week* survey in July 1992 had 'highlighted the rise of the senior in-house communicator with access to the highest levels of management'.

These reports are of some significance in managing public relations programmes. Who is most or least capable of strategic management, the in-house PRO or the outside consultant? These revelations may be a surprise to *PR Week* which has been slow to discover the in-house public relations department, but it merely emphasises two things which were ever thus. The bulk of public relations work is conducted by in-house units. The consultancy either provides a media relations service for small clients, or specialist services for big ones, but except with some of the larger and superior-staffed consultancies they are rarely permitted to conduct complete campaigns. This is inevitable because public relations needs to be an integrated function within an organization, servicing every department, and working at boardroom level.

References

1 Jefkins, Frank, *Effective PR Planning*, 2nd edn, Frank Jefkins School of Public Relations, 1985 (O.P.)
2 Jefkins, Frank, *Effective Press Relations and House Journal Editing*, 3rd edn, Frank Jefkins School of Public Relations, 1985
3 Ross, Robert D., *The Management of Public Relations*, John Wiley & Son, New York, 1977
4 Jefkins, Frank, *Planned Press and Public Relations*, 3rd edn, Blackie, Glasgow, 1993
5 Stone, Norman, *How to Manage Public Relations*, McGraw-Hill, Maidenhead, 1991
6 *PR Week*, Leader, 8 October 1992

5

Appreciation of the situation

'Appreciation of the situation, is a military expression. The story is told of the late Field Marshal Montgomery, during the Second World War, calling for such a report, but when he was given a sheaf of papers full of information about the military situation he retorted 'put it on a postcard'. Admirable though this may have been, in public relations we are more likely to be greedy enough to welcome the sheaf of papers.

Although this is sometimes attempted, an objective public relations programme cannot be planned seriously without detailed knowledge of the situation, for public relations is not only a problem-solving business but needs to be the eyes and ears as well as the voice of an organization. It needs to have its own intelligence service, and it thrives on feedback. If we recall the IPR definition, public relations is concerned with *mutual understanding*, and that requires an inflow as well as an outflow of information.

Assumptions are not good enough, and they could be misleading. We need to be very cautious of management's convictions about external knowledge or opinions. Management may be entertaining illusions. A public relations campaign cannot be based on hunches. A public relations practitioner needs to be a pessimist but not a cynic, although an optimist when clear-cut plans are agreed.

The image

The word *image* is one of the curses of public relations, and is liable to mean different things to different people. 'Mirror image' is frequently used by journalists to mean the perceived image, whereas the opposite interpretation will be found below. We shall refer to different kinds of image, but the image in the broadest sense is the impression people have as a result of their knowledge and experience. This means that everybody tends to have a personal image of the same subject. Ideally in public relations we would like everyone to have a uniformly correct impression. However, some people are not satisfied with that: they want to obscure any faults and create a favourable image and sometimes they want to do the impossible and polish a bad one. The image can be only what it is, warts and all. However there may be occasions when a poor or false image exists simply because people are either uninformed or misinformed. Now let us consider the different kinds of image.

The *mirror image* is how management thinks outsiders see the organization. From the confines of the chief executive's office or the board room, it is assumed that outsiders know or believe this or that. The PRO or the consultant may be told what image is held by outsiders. This may be based on top management's pride or self-confidence, or on a situation that once existed. It is probably based on naive complacency. But in public relations nothing can be taken for granted. The alert practitioner has to be sceptical about any information supplied by an inside source. Always.

He has to discover the *current image* which is the one actually held by outsiders, and this may well conflict with the illusionary internal mirror image. It is a consensus of people's notions based on what they may or may not know, or on their good or bad experiences. But different images may exist among different publics. The community, staff, distributors, consumers, stockbrokers, academics and politicians may each have their own special images. A total public relations campaign may have to be planned after 'analysing trends, predicting their consequences' − to quote from the Mexican Statement − in relation to all the different current images of the various publics. For example, the image of a motorcar could be very different if one is a sales agent for the car, an owner, a motoring correspondent, a motor insurance assessor, a service mechanic or an investment analyst. The relevance of the current image, and its disparity with the mirror image, will have great bearing on how a public relations programme should be planned.

But if it is a new and unknown organization, product or service it will be necessary to project a *wish image* so that a true mental picture is created in the minds of our publics. Here, we have to be careful not to project a biased or overenthusiastic picture. It must not be confused with a *product image* which concentrates on distinctive characteristics or selling points. Of course, some products like Guinness stout, a Rolls-Royce motorcar, or the Concorde airliner do have justifiably distinctive images. There is no mistaking such products.

We may also have to consider the *multiple image* and its implications.

The multiple image can be a great handicap, and it occurs when representatives of the organization each create a personal image of the organization so that there are as many images as there are people. This occurs because the only, or the chief, image is created by, say, personal contact between the customer and the salesman. The image will depend on whether that representative is smart or untidy, punctual or late, obliging or unhelpful and so on. The answer to that dilemma is sales training to develop uniformly good behaviour. It is also the reason why chain stores, banks, supermarkets and building societies are given identical-looking premises, and a corporate image identity scheme is introduced so that through the use of a logo, house colour, vehicle livery, uniforms or dress and other standard physical appearances, a common image is created. This is done extremely well by airlines which establish an identical image wherever and however they operate on the ground or in the air. The physical *corporate identity* scheme contributes to the mental *corporate image* and removes any possibility of a confusing multiple image. It is the basic and one of the oldest forms of public relations.

It may also be necessary to accept that, because of the complexity of the subject, the most that can be achieved is the *optimum image*. With this kind of image the aim is to try to establish a reasonable but accurate impression of the organization, product or service, a layman's view perhaps of something very technical or complicated.

Finally, there is the *corporate image*, mentioned above, which is the way the organization itself is perceived by outsiders. This should not be confused with the physical corporate identity although that will influence the corporate image. Many things contribute to the corporate image such as the way the organization is seen to behave (e.g. its good or bad industrial relations and its social responsibility in respect of the environment), or how its management is seen to behave publicly, the performance of its products or services, or the performances of its quoted share price. The *current image* and the *corporate image* may be identical. The *product image* may be enhanced or harmed by the nature of the corporate image. When introducing a new product or service, it may enjoy the halo effect of a respected corporate image.

Some companies indulge in what is called 'image advertising', a kind of institutional advertising, with advertisements in journals such as *The Economist* and *Fortune*. Its value is somewhat dubious except perhaps when an Arab bank or a Japanese or Korean industrialist is trying to establish itself in world markets.

Methods of appreciating the situation

1 Marketing research

When it is necessary to understand the state of awareness, opinion or attitude, a marketing research survey should be carried out, using the *opinion poll* technique whereby a sample representing the public or publics concerned is asked questions calling for Yes, No, Don't know answers. The results can be represented graphically, and if subsequent polls are conducted to measure improvement or shift, the trend can again be shown graphically to record the results of the public relations programme. (See Figure 5.1.)

The sample may be a *quota sample* when quotas of people of the chosen sex, age and social grade groups are found by interviewers, or a *random sample* may be used in which actual names and addresses are taken from a list at regular intervals, and these identified respondents are interviewed. The random sample, providing a cross section of the chosen universe or population, is the more accurate method. But it is usually about three times the size of a quota sample, and at least three attempts are usually made to contact each named respondent before a replacement is used. Consequently, the random sample is more costly than a quota sample. The interviewer is responsible for finding the right people to fit the quota sample, whereas with the random sample the actual respondents are given. There is actually nothing random about a random sample.

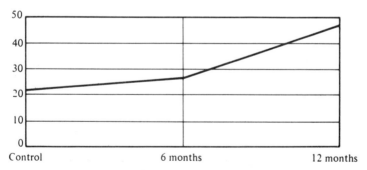

Figure·5.1 *Graph recording results of three opinion polls conducted at six-monthly intervals showing a shift from the original position of 22 per cent to 28 per cent and finally 47 per cent. If the aim was to reach, say, an awareness percentage of 40 per cent, the PR programme would have been very successful, but if the target has been 50 per cent there would have been a shortfall in expectations. (Source: Jefkins, Public Relations[1])*

However, the quota sample may be adequate when certain types of people (e.g. owners of sports cars, or young wives with small children) have to be interviewed, and the cross section provided by a random sample is unnecessary. But cost may be a deciding factor, and it will be noticed when reading the results of political polls that both quota and random samples are used by different research units, with possible effect upon the accuracy of their findings. The random sample involves probably three times as many respondents as a quota sample, and does not suffer from interviewer bias in finding people to interview.

Another form of research is the *image study* which seeks to make comparisons between the sponsor and rival organizations. This can be conducted by pre-arranged telephone interviews with an appropriate sample, say, of buyers or specifiers of an industrial product. They will be asked their opinions of the different organizations over a range of issues. The results of the study can be presented in the form of a graph such as Figure 5.2 which is also reproduced from the author's book *Public Relations*. This is actually based on an image study for a chemical company which was supplying an additive used in the paint, paper-making and other industries. It revealed to the client an unsuspected 'old-fashioned' current image which was very different from that held inside the company since its product greatly improved the quality of manufactured products. This type of industrial research can be inexpensive, using a small sample of buyers, interviews being by pre-arranged telephone call.

Understanding marketing research, the different methods available, their strengths and weaknesses, and the kinds of service offered by different research firms, is another management responsibility of either the PRO or the consultant. Significantly, the subject features strongly in the CAM and the LCCI examinations. Advice may have to be given

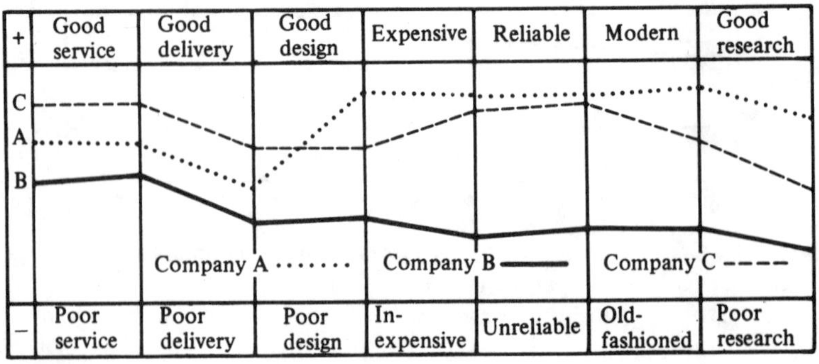

Figure 5.2   *Image study (Source: Jefkins,* Public Relations*)*

to employers or clients on the use of independent research, why it should be conducted, what it is likely to produce, what it costs and why it is a good investment before planning a public relations programme.

When it has been decided to carry out a study, the PRO or the consultant must be capable of working with a research unit. The choice of the sampling frame (who shall be interviewed and perhaps where), and the structure of the questionnaire (the information required and the questions to be asked) must be discussed. This is vital because the findings will depend on who was asked what questions. When reading a research report, it is necessary to study the nature of the sample and the content of the questions to understand why the answers were given. To take a typical example, a number of political polls may give conflicting reports, but the reason for this is likely to be found by studying the sample and the questionnaire used in each case. Generally, they will be found to vary considerably.

There was considerable criticism of the polls conducted prior to the 1992 General Election. But was it fair? Did the media misinterpret the findings, perhaps deliberately? Afterall, the percentage lead given to the Labour Party was far too small for a Labour victory let alone a hung Parliament, although it was also clear that the Conservatives would lose many seats.

It is therefore a public relations management responsibility to supervise the research, even at the point when the research report is being written because the researchers may interpret the results differently from the practitioner. An instance can be taken from a survey conducted into client–advertising agency relations. Client respondents, when interviewed, complained about the unpunctuality of account executives. The importance of this was discounted by the researchers yet, as we have seen in Chapter 2, punctuality is regarded seriously by clients, especially out-of-town ones.

An inexpensive form of research is the piggy-backing of questions onto an *omnibus* survey which a research firm mails to a recruited panel of respondents. Thus, advantage can be taken of using an existing research set-up. Again, surveys may be jointly sponsored by clients seeking the same information, so that costs can be shared. Knowing the market, a research firm could bring together compatible co-sponsors.

2 Desk research

Existing information should not be overlooked, whether internal or external. Internal departments may hold valuable information in the form of sales figures and salespeople's reports, while other studies may have been carried out such as those of the marketing department or the research and development department. Published reports and ones to which the company may subscribe, or those of the Central Statistical Office and trade associations, may provide indicators of the situation under review. The company's own annual report and accounts is bound to have information on policy, prospects and the company's performance. Valuable statistics will be found in the various yearly handbooks published by NTC Publications on behalf of the Advertising Association, e.g. the *Marketing Pocket Book*.[2]

3   Complaints

Useful feedback may exist in the extent or nature of complaints, both from the trade and consumers. It will pay to discuss this subject with those within the organization who receive complaints, such as the customer services department or the sales office. A survey of distributors might be useful, and a sample of retailers might be sent a postal questionnaire. This could be worded carefully so that praise as well as complaints would be elucidated. Another method is to tour a number of distributors in the company of a sales representative, and to interview members of the trade.

4   Financial situation

It may not be sufficient to read the City pages, financial journals and the daily share prices to appreciate the financial situation, and better to meet institutional share buyers (e.g. managers of pension funds and unit trusts), stockbrokers and particularly investment analysts who produce reports on companies as investment prospects.

5   Media attitudes

Feedback in the form of press cuttings received regularly from clipping agencies, or scripts received from firms which monitor broadcasts, can be very revealing. What are the media saying, or are they saying nothing? What is the quality of coverage? Do they get it right, are they critical or sympathetic? What sort of press are rivals receiving?

Media attitudes may also concern direct press relations. Are editors unhappy about the quality of press material they have received from the company? Do they feel fobbed off and unable to interview top people? Unintentionally (or because of the poor practice of a less efficient predecessor) the company or a former consultancy may have prejudiced editors and broadcasters.

One such investigation by a consultancy showed that editors had been writing to the client's advertising manager for information and, since he had filed their letters in the waste bin, these editors had received no information and so had omitted the company's products from important features and supplements.

On another occasion a group of trade journals boycotted a company because its consultancy had employed one of their journalists as an account executive and subsequently fired her!

The situation regarding media relations may therefore be critical to the success of a future press relations campaign within the proposed programme. Bad situations may have to be resolved very quickly. Editors and journalists tend to change jobs fairly frequently, and old contacts may have been lost. New staff may be unfamiliar with your organization, products or services.

6 Employee–management relations

An impartial, confidential and independent survey can be useful here, and this is usually included in communication audits, often revealing that management is unaware of employee attitudes. Bad industrial relations leading to strikes have resulted from 'grapevine' information and unfortunate misunderstandings rather than from genuine grievances. While it is not the place of the PRO to get involved in trade union negotiations, it is nevertheless true that public relations can provide a safety valve if there is a good flow of information upwards, downwards and sideways. A study may reveal the need for better internal communications, whether in the form of more open management, or improved communication techniques such as a more independent and participatory house journal.

In those organizations where staff have contact with customers, these individuals can perform an important public relations role if they are well informed. They can be the best image-makers!

7 Community relations

How is the organization regarded by the people who live and work in the vicinity of the company premises? Again, this is sometimes taken for granted or, worse still, ignored. People play various roles in the community. The policeman is a husband, parent, ratepayer and maybe member of a local club or society. Most people play many roles and according to these roles they could have a variety of attitudes for all kinds of reasons. For example, a company which ran an express bus service had very bad relations with pedestrians, parents, schoolteachers, the clergy and the police following a series of accidents in which children were injured or killed.

Community relations can therefore be very delicate and controversial, and a wide-ranging survey could produce some unexpected revelations. A company may be able to operate far more efficiently if it takes the trouble to find out how it can be a good neighbour. It may even help with staff recruitment. But if you fail to find out you will not know, and bad relations could be perpetuated out of ignorance if not indifference. The next time the company seeks planning permission from the Council it might be surprised by incomprehensible objections, simply because it was improperly understood or there was hostility towards it.

A current example is the hostility sometimes aroused when supermarket chains seek local planning permission to build huge new stores. The applications usually include offers of improved amenities which councils are loathe to dismiss, yet in some places local residents and tradesmen mount bitter protest activities. The two main contestants are Sainsbury's and Tesco and it is a curious fact that Sainsbury's tend to stir up less hostility than Tesco. Obviously, community relations need to be studied carefully when seeking new locations.

The Mexican Statement takes a step forward beyond 'analysing trends' and says 'predicting their consequences, counselling organization leaders, and implementing planned programmes of action'. This implies that the results of appreciating the situation must be interpreted. What will happen if wrong things are not put right or if corrective action is not taken? This is where the PRO or the consultant adopts the advisory role, and offers a plan in the form of recommendations to solve the communication problems which research has discovered. Thus the practitioner is responsible for taking the initiative, which is very different from doing what he or she has been told to do because management thinks it knows what it wants. A patient does not tell the doctor what medicines or treatment he wants: the doctor diagnoses the problem and tells the patient or prescribes what treatment is needed.

References

1 Jefkins, Frank, *Public Relations*, 4th edn, Pitman, London, 1992
2 *Marketing Pocket Book*, NTC Publications, Henley-on-Thames, annually

6

Determining objectives

Importance of defining objectives

The review of the situation, the directives of management and the needs of departments will combine to provide objectives. The public relations manager or consultant cannot plan without objectives and without objectives results cannot be assessed. This is tangible public relations. So what do we want to achieve? Have we the means of coping with all these objectives? The process of deciding priorities and applying constraints has begun. The plan may be for six months or one, two or three years. Some objectives will be short-term, others will require continuous endeavour. Together they will form the jigsaw of the complete scheme, time, money and resources permitting.

In Chapter 4 we quoted the Countrywide report. It seems incomprehensible that a consultancy can handle isolated assignments without having any say in the objectives. How can one even write a news release unless one understands the strategic purpose in getting it published? Without such knowledge the wrong story could be sent to the wrong media.

Let us consider some lists of strategies to achieve public relations objectives for various organizations.

A manufacturing company

1 Organize a community relations programme to promote understanding of the company among local community leaders who would act as innovators and spread their knowledge of the company.
2 Organize a programme of dealer activities to improve trade understanding of the company.
3 Develop international public relations in those overseas markets

where the company aims to set up agents or licensing agreements for manufacture, familiarizing these markets with the company and its products.

4   Improve the flow of corporate and financial news to city editors and the financial press, in readiness for a share or rights issue.

5   Make a video of a sporting event which the company has agreed to sponsor, and distribute this to organizations which arrange shows in order to perpetuate the public relations value of the sponsorship.

6   Increase reader participation in the employee newspaper in order to improve management–employee relations.

7   Develop more in-depth understanding of the company by relevant journalists by organizing a series of individual visits for them.

A local authority

1   Organize a programme of talks and slide or video presentations to schools and youth organizations to combat vandalism of parks, recreation grounds and public buildings.

2   Cooperate with local history society to organize a town history exhibition, organizing visits by school parties and seeking coverage by press, radio and television.

3   Edit and distribute a civic newspaper in order to make council tax payers better aware of the authority's services on their behalf.

4   Organize a team of councillors and officials to act as spokespeople about local affairs on local radio.

5   By acting as PRO to, say, a music or amateur dramatic festival, use this event as a vehicle for increased media coverage for the town and, for the first time, seek to gain television coverage of the finalists' concert or production at the end of the event.

6   Organize both local and national coverage of the opening of the town's new leisure centre which has won an international architectural award.

A charity

1   Increase public awareness of the charity's independence and that it is supported by voluntary contributions.

2   Make known the continuous story of the charity's work in developing countries.

3   Seek a sponsor for and make a video about the charity's work for people in disaster situations.

4 Organize a series of magazine interviews for the director following his return from an overseas fact-finding mission, in order to make known the charity's relief appeal.
5 Obtain maximum coverage of the air-freighting of relief supplies when these take place.
6 Seek industrial donors of advertising space in the press and on poster sites.

A trade association

1 Make better known the association's code of practice.
2 Revamp the association's newsletter for members, and issue it monthly instead of quarterly.
3 Obtain maximum media coverage of the association's campaigns to amend a law which is detrimental to members' interests.
4 Write, publish, publicize and distribute a pamphlet on this legal question.
5 Organize seminars for members.
6 Participate in the annual trade exhibition at the National Exhibition Centre or other venue.

In each case the list of possible objectives could be much longer, and the above are given merely as examples. The final choice of objectives will depend on the budget and how they fit into the available manhours. Time has to be allowed for general day-to-day affairs and administration, and the possibility of unpredictable calls on the PRO's time.

Here is how the European Economic Commission defined the objectives of its information policy in 1960:

> The immediate objective of the information policy of the Community is to make known the activities of the institutions of the Community to the public and to stimulate a public interest and comprehension. But there is more. The final objective is a political community in Europe in which citizens can live with greater security and prosperity and in this way better develop their personalities. To realise this objective it will be necessary to develop a new European public opinion which will replace the same autonomous, democratic function as national public opinion inside the frontiers of different countries.

It is perhaps a good example of how difficult it is to create understanding, for more than 20 years later it is evident that there is still little understanding of the European Community. The debate rages far above the heads of an uncomprehending public.

The process of listing objectives

The above examples are the priorities on which public relations programmes may be based, but how are they arrived at in addition to
research of one kind or another to appreciate the situation? Remember,
choice of these priorities, and the planning of the campaign, needs to
take place perhaps three months before the campaign starts.

If lines of communication have been established within the organization, the PRO will have little difficulty in arriving at a list of
potential objectives. The consultant will be able to do likewise if he or she
is able to talk to departmental heads, but may have to rely on the client
doing this. Let us take a hypothetical case and see how objectives can
be collated as a result of discussions with various departmental heads
plus the chief executive officer.

1 Personnel Manager

(a) Recruitment drive. Need to make the organization understood at
    sources of recruits, e.g. universities, technical colleges via careers
    advisers.
(b) Redundancy problem. Need to explain company policy, internally
    and externally.
(c) Relocation plans. Need to explain advantages of existing staff
    moving with company.
(d) Share issue. Need to advise employees about investing in the
    company. When there is a new share issue employees may be
    offered shares at a special price.
(e) Indoctrination of new recruits. Need to produce indoctrination
    material such as booklet, slides or video.
(f) New appointments. Will there be new senior appointments which
    need to be made known?

2 Production Manager

(a) Works safety. Need to explain safety-at-work procedures.
(b) New production equipment, techniques. Need to tell trade, market,
    of advantages or improvements.
(c) New quality control methods, in answer to complaint. Possibility
    of news material.
(d) New factory, and need to arrange official opening.

3 Company Secretary

(a) New share issue, rights issue or debenture. Need to keep the money market aware of the company's corporate and financial affairs, and ensure proper awareness prior to issue of prospectus, bearing in mind Stock Exchange rules on publicity.

(b) Acquisitions and mergers. Need to announce these if and when they occur.

(c) Takeover risks. If the company is endangered by possible predators, need to strengthen shareholder/investor relations. Has the share price fallen, or is it too low? Can it be raised or stabilized if money market is better informed about the merits of the company? Remember, share prices rise because people are buying them, and fall because people are selling them.

(d) Change of name. Is the company about to adopt a new name, which will require publicizing?

(e) Legislation. If the company is likely to be affected by new legislation, does this need public relations action?

4 Export Manager

(a) New overseas sales territories. Is public relations required, either through home agencies such as the Department of Trade and Industry, or through overseas or international media?

(b) New overseas subsidiaries, licensing arrangements, agents. Need for overseas public relations.

(c) Overseas orders, contracts. What is anticipated, and how can public relations be used to make them known?

(d) Overseas competition – can public relations help?

(e) Role of external magazine, documentary video. Are there production or distribution responsibilities for the public relations department?

(f) Overseas exhibitions. Need for public relations to support participation, both through British Overseas Trade Board and in the countries where exhibitions are being held.

(g) Overseas visits. Do company personnel travelling abroad on trade missions or personal visits require public relations support?

5 Sales Manager

(a) New sales organization, appointments. Need for trade press releases.

(b)   Sales conference(s). Need to contribute presentation on public relations.
(c)   Incentive schemes, sales contests. Need for public relations support, e.g. in house journal.
(d)   Trade deals. Need to make known in trade press.
(e)   Dealer relations. Efforts needed to educate trade about products, e.g. works visits.

6   Advertising Manager

(a)   Advertising schedule. Need to know where and when advertising will be placed, and possibilities for supply of supporting editorial stories. Also need to tell trade press about forthcoming campaigns.
(b)   Sales promotion material. Need to issue pictures and stories to press. Possibility of special public relations for special promotions such as prize contests.
(c)   Advertising/marketing trade press. Need for feature articles about new campaigns.
(d)   Advertising agency. Need to cooperate with them. Do advertisements satisfy corporate identity requirements? Do advertisements enhance goodwill?

7   Research and Development Manager

(a)   What new products/prototypes are under test? Do test reports need to be published or announced?
(b)   Research techniques. Need to make known company's research resources? Feature articles to be written?
(c)   Independent testing. Is a product under test in an independent laboratory, and should the results be made known?
(d)   New materials, components, ingredients, recipes? Need to make known such new uses or additives.
(e)   Can research results aid appreciation of the situation?

8   Marketing Manager

(a)   Marketing plans for existing or new products. Need to provide supporting public relations, including market education.
(b)   New packaging? Need to make known in trade press. Feature articles in marketing press. How does it respond to avoiding pollution problems?
(c)   New prices? Need to announce them to trade and consumer media.

(d) Test marketing. Need to stimulate a public relations programme in the miniature market.
(e) The after-market. Need to make known new after-sales services.
(f) Sponsorships. Need to organize public relations activities and support of various kinds.

9 Chief Executive Officer

(a) Company plans and policy. Need to know forward planning, especially in order to be well-armed with knowledge and information if media make enquiries.
(b) How does CEO view the importance of objectives gleaned from discussions with departmental heads?
(c) CEO's personal plans and activities. Need to organize public relations where appropriate. For instance, CEO may have other activities which can reflect well on the company, e.g. participation in a conference, trade association or voluntary body.

With the exception of the Chief Executive Officer, who may be visited last in order to consolidate ideas, select priorities and share confidences, the first eight are not in any order of merit and each may be visited as and when convenient appointments can be made. Another method is to assemble everyone at a discussion meeting when objectives can be tabled and priorities can be agreed. If neither of these methods is practical, perhaps because people are in different locations, the questionnaire method can be used and from the returns the PRO can assess what should go into his planned programme. From the items set out from 1 to 9 it will be obvious that not every issue requires regular and continuous public relations, but can be fitted into the overall programme. Some may be combined under single headings such as 'trade press' or 'financial public relations', and time and resources can be allocated to them according to their weight.

The lists in 1 to 9 are not exhaustive, and are set out merely as a thought-provoking exercise. Quite different people and considerations may apply to particular organizations, and here we have concentrated on a large manufacturer. There are some aspects such as staff training, a new corporate identity, crises management and Parliamentary liaison which have not been mentioned, but could involve very important public relations objectives for certain organizations. There could also be matters of a corporate nature such as social responsibility which should be discussed with the CEO.

It may be argued that the nine lists are not as precise objectives as the 34 possible objectives given by the author elsewhere,[1] and that they are a mixture of aims, goals and objectives. Norman Stone[2], makes the following observations at the beginning of his chapter on setting objectives:

> You would be well advised not to concern yourself overmuch with the distinction between objectives and aims . . . The question is, do they matter? . . . What are we to make, then, of the word 'objective'? It is a slightly more elaborate form of the word 'object' which expresses the idea of 'point to be aimed at'. Therefore an objective expresses the idea of both 'aim' and 'goal' . . . In practical terms, PR objectives are to do with specifying what changes need to be made in your relationships with your publics, to further the solution of business problems and the exploitation of business opportunities.

The strategy is beginning to emerge, and it is not unlike account planning in an advertising agency, except that the planner is more likely to be based in-house.

References

1   Jefkins, Frank, *Planned Press and Public Relations*, 3rd edn, Blackie, Glasgow, 1993
2   Stone, Norman, *How to Manage Public Relations*, McGraw-Hill, Maidenhead, 1991

7

Defining publics

Publics, *not* target audiences

'Publics' is part of the jargon of public relations, an invented word not to be found in the orthodox dictionary. It helps to show that public relations is rarely concerned with the 'general public' as dictionaries often suggest.

Publics is a very meaningful expression and one peculiar to public relations. This special word also helps us to strike yet another contrast with advertising, which has its own distinct jargon.

Advertising campaigns are usually directed at a *target audience* consisting of the largest number of potential buyers, or at a *market segment* of particular buyers. This selectivity is implied by the definition of advertising used by the Institute of Practitioners in Advertising, the professional body of advertising agencies:

Advertising presents the most persuasive possible selling message to the right prospects for the product or service at the lowest possible cost.

The right *prospects* can be defined precisely for an advertising campaign. For example, research may show that the prospects for an inexpensive battery-operated kitchen clock might be C2 housewives aged twenty-four to thirty-four or sales of a small, economical family car may be aimed at that segment of the motorcar market which is concentrated on family urban driving.

Such an identification of the sales market will be taken into account when planning a public relations programme, but it is much smaller and less diffused than the various publics with whom an organization has contact.

The identification of public relations publics is fundamental to the planning of a programme, for unless the publics are defined it is impossible to select media which will convey our messages to them.

Moreover, it may be necessary to list all possible publics in order to decide priorities because constraints of the budget, manpower and other resources have to be applied. But how can we choose priorities or media unless we first of all write down *all* the publics we would like to communicate with in an ideal world free of constraints? The problem will vary from one organization to another. Some will have such a diversity of minority group publics that it would be costly to try to reach them; others will have majority group publics which can be reached simultaneously through the mass media, especially if there is considerable role playing by the same people.

To explain role playing, a man may be a city office worker, a husband, a parent, a motorist, a golfer, a gardener and an amateur photographer who enjoys motoring holidays abroad. These are his roles. Such a person may read a lower middle class newspaper, listen to his car radio and watch television and is easily reached by the mass market media. Now, supposing an organization such as a bank, building society, travel agent, rose grower, camera dealer or car ferry operator wanted to reach some of the publics represented by this man's different roles it could do so very easily because such players of several roles enjoy the same popular media. But this would not be so if people with more specialized interests had to be reached, e.g. those who drove performance cars, played in golf championships, grew orchids, or made home movies on video cassettes.

Let us look at the example of a bank and its publics, the role playing of its potential customers and the ease of reaching them through the existing mass media. The bank's commercial objective may be to lend money to people who require finance for the purchase of houses, house improvements and extensions, motorcars, photographic equipment or holidays abroad. The public relations objective may be to educate relevant publics about the bank's services. The role playing aspect is important because it will show that many of the bank's prospects or publics are in fact the same people playing out different roles at different times. They can be reached simultaneously through the same media with the same public relations effort.

Nevertheless, this can be an oversimplification and concern only those publics containing large groups of people not unlike the advertising target audience. Most organizations will have numerous publics, as we shall see.

Understanding the nature of publics helps the public relations manager or consultant to determine the feasibility of reaching them economically within the budget. For example, because of their specialized minority interest it may be necessary to create private media in order to reach them – media such as slides, audio cassettes, video tapes, house journals, educational literature, private exhibitions or seminars.

Basic publics

The basic publics that apply to most commercial organizations may be generalized as follows:

1 The community.
2 Potential employees.
3 Employees.
4 Suppliers of services and materials.
5 The money market.
6 Distributors.
7 Consumers and users.
8 Opinion leaders.

Now we can see how much more varied are public relations publics than the target audiences or market segments of advertising. We are also spreading through the entire organization, taking in the production and financial functions of a business in addition to marketing. This immediately positions the public relations manager in relation to top management and the board of directors, and indicates that it is unrealistic to place him within the marketing function. Further, it shows how limiting it is to combine advertising and public relations within the one job specification. More and more we see that advertising and public relations are worlds apart, although it does follow that in those companies that do little advertising – such as industrial companies – advertising may well come within the responsibilities of the PRO.

According to the nature of the business, the eight basic publics may be subdivided or extended, so let us now review each of these publics in greater detail.

1 *The community*

The community consists of the organization's neighbours who may live or work close to the factory, office, store, airport, seaport, power station, research laboratory or whatever may be the organization's premises. Some complex organizations will have a number of premises of different kinds, or have different effects on different people and will have relations with various communities. An example of this is an airport where some members of the community will suffer from aircraft noise, others from road congestion, while still others will enjoy job opportunities.

Sensible companies are careful to develop and sustain a 'good neighbour' policy. After all, the community may contain potential customers, employees, actual customers and employees (and their families), and many people who can be friends or enemies.

The activities of the company may affect the community. Noise, dirt, fumes, smells — even the very presence of the organization — may provoke antagonism. People object to all sorts of premises. They could be potentially dangerous chemical works, waste disposal plants, or superstores however attractively designed and landscaped. Deliberate efforts may be made to overcome these problems and to make the organization acceptable. Tall chimneys, garden frontages, tastefully obscured buildings, waste disposal or conversion plants and noise abatement all contribute to good relations. But so also will more obvious public relations activities such as 'open days', participation in local events and the regular supply of company news to the local press. Nuclear power plants actually invite visitors.

Some manufacturers who make goods which are sold outside the community sometimes forget they are part of the community, and their works attain an almost 'Dracula's Castle' image. The author once visited the country house headquarters of a well-known company, and was surprised to find that local people had nicknamed it 'The Rattery' because it had a research laboratory. Firms like Cadburys and W. D. & H. O. Wills have, of course, been very much part of the community while others, like Bata, are sometimes accused of going too far with the creation of company towns.

Community relations can be matters of delicacy and diplomacy but, as with so much public relations activity, they represent thoughtfulness. Unlike the aggressiveness of advertising, public relations is about human understanding. The department store will try not to offend the job applicants it does not employ — they could be customers; provision of a car park will be a convenience appreciated by customers; good carriers (like those of Marks & Spencer) protect clothes on their journey home from the shop — and back to the shop if they have to be changed, but if form-filling formalities make the return or exchange of goods an embarrassment good relations will be sacrificed.

Some organizations take great pride in their community relations, supporting local theatres, musical festivals, flower shows, sports events and plainly being seen to be a responsible member and patron of the local society. In fact, some are great benefactors and down through history they have paid for churches, schools, hospitals, libraries, art galleries, parks and other important parts of the infrastructure. But one does not need to be part of the community fabric; brand new industries, perhaps located on a somewhat isolated trading estate which invites anonymity, still need to develop community relations.

2 Potential employees

Some future employees may live in the vicinity of the workplace – relatives or friends of present staff, local schoolchildren and students, employees in other local firms – but this will depend on the kind of employment.

Those who criticize the increase in immigration to Britain in post-war years forget that Britain had labour shortages in the 1950s and employers in the transportation and catering trades recruited staff from the West Indies. Similarly, hotels import staff from all over the world, just as early British railway builders imported Irish navvies, the Americans imported Chinese, and British colonists in Africa imported Indians for their railway construction and elsewhere for sugar production. It still goes on with Irishmen working on the Channel Tunnel, and Frenchmen building Mercedes-Benz cars in Germany. Migrant and immigrant labour is usually attracted by money, opportunity and better living conditions, and employers have great public relations responsibilities in today's race relations situation. The sons and daughters of immigrants and refugees are British-born citizens.

Recruitment may be from schools, colleges and universities where it is important that information about career opportunities is supplied to careers masters, advisers and appointments officers. This may be augmented by video, displays for careers evenings, visits to plants, and student weekends at training centres such as those organized by banks. Here we see public relations techniques being allied to the efforts of the personnel and training departments.

Other employers and industries may be sources of recruitment. Redundant workers may be attracted and trained in new jobs. The motorcar industry has recruited workers from coalmining and agriculture, and public relations itself has drawn staff from many spheres – not only from journalism. Where skilled staff are scarce they will have to be won from competitors. Vacancy advertisements alone will not always succeed: applicants of the right type will emerge more readily if they are aware of the merits of the employer seeking recruits. Public relations is about reputation: is the job advertiser a reputable employer, is the industry one with worthwhile prospects? Young people may be deterred by prejudices towards certain industries, as we have seen with engineering and chemicals, and public relations is about correcting false ideas.

3 Employees

Management—employee relations are considered to be one of the growth areas of public relations. In Britain — as compared with north European countries — lack of worker participation on the one hand and old-fashioned craft unions on the other tend to maintain a 'man and master' class division which does not encourage ideal industrial relations. Nevertheless, more open management, the training of shop stewards in new technologies, the encouragement of communications from the bottom up, the use of 'speak up' schemes, explanations of annual reports and accounts by means of house journals and video tapes, and so on are improving internal communications and relations.

A very different situation has emerged in the new Japanese-owned factories with their single unions and no-strike agreements. Gone are the days of trade union belligerence which handicapped much of British industry.

The employee public may have many subdivisions, and it is seldom satisfactory to rely on a single staff newspaper to cover the whole workforce. Some typical subdivisions may be:

- Management and executives, branch managers.
- Section leaders and foremen.
- Office workers.
- Factory workers.
- Field sales force.
- Transport workers.
- Overseas staff.
- Casual labour.

An airline is a good example of an employer with a great mixture of staff on the ground, in the air, at the home base and at overseas locations. On the other hand, a departmental store will have its staff concentrated within one building. It also depends on whether a large organization is structured vertically or horizontally. This kind of integrated structure results from amalgamations and mergers, a vertical company being an empire of complementary interests covering re-sources, supplies, manufacturing and distribution while a horizontal one is a combination of similar interests. Unilever is typical of the first; British Airways of the latter. Then there are conglomerates — holding companies like BTR which own companies of unrelated interests operating independently, and there are also consortiums of companies which may cooperate in a major venture as has been seen with construction projects in the Arab oil states.

These complicated structures may have considerable industrial communications problems. An obvious place to begin is at the recruitment and training stage to which public relations can contribute valuable induction material such as literature, slide presentations, and video cassettes, the effort being sustained by house journals and other regular forms of communication.

If there is a complete mixture of technologies and jobs, as with vertical amalgamations and conglomerates, each unit may have to be treated separately yet given a certain unity.

This is an area in which the International Association of Business Communicators is developing internal communcations beyond the traditional staff newspaper. Although based in San Francisco, the IABC has a British chapter.

4 Suppliers and services

These two external groups may include:

Suppliers
- Sources of raw materials.
- Sources of components.
- Suppliers of print and packaging.
- Suppliers of fuel.
- Suppliers of transportation.
- Suppliers of finished goods if it is a marketing organization, retailer, caterer, etc.

Services
- Professional – advertising, public relations, legal, accountancy etc.
- Public services – health, water, refuse, police, fire brigade.
- Educational – day-release training, industrial training board.
- Advisory bodies, research stations, trade associations.

Other suppliers and services will come to mind for particular organizations. Communications with these publics may be achieved through the external house journal, works visits, seminars, videos and other public relations media, but special efforts may be necessary in some cases. For instance, an organization conducting a dangerous trade would be wise to keep doctors, hospitals, ambulance and fire brigades and the police aware of special hazards.

The maintenance of good relations with suppliers and services is one that can be overlooked, yet it is an example of the thoroughness which is necessary when a PRO is planning a comprehensive annual programme and is listing objectives, publics and media. Remembering to put such people on the mailing list of the house journal, inviting them to social occasions, seminars and works visits, sending them copies of the annual report and accounts may be very useful indeed. But by listing such people among the publics new communication tasks and difficulties may be highlighted. How does one communicate effectively with the Chief Constable, the hospital surgeon, the water company and even one's advertising agent and public relations consultant? These are all part of the total communications of an organization.

5 The money market

Public companies, and private companies 'going public' and being quoted on the Stock Exchange, depend on the money market being well informed about their history, performance and prospects. This will affect the take-up of new share issues and the maintenance of share prices, and the latter may be necessary to avoid a takeover. The money market begins with one's local bank manager, and extends through building societies and insurance companies to shareholders and investors and those who advise them. At the top end of the money market are investment analysts, stockbrokers, merchant banks and institutional buyers of large blocks of shares such as insurance companies, unit trusts and pension funds.

Financial and corporate public relations has become a very important part of the overall public relations programme, with many specialist financial public relations consultancies. In fact, the City and Financial Public Relations Group of the IPR is one of its most active and successful sections, having more than one hundred members. The 'Big Bang' in the City, and the deregulation of share dealing, has imposed new demands on financial public relations such as the Stock Exchange ban on embargoed news releases to avoid insider-trader scandals.

6 Distributors

This is a very broad group and different organizations will obviously have different channels of distribution and use distributors best suited to their trade. Thus this very long list may include brokers, factors, wholesalers, cash and carry warehouses, rack-jobbers, supermarkets and chain stores, co-ops, neighbourhood shops, own shops, appointed dealers, clubs, hotels and holiday centres, direct response traders, direct salesmen, tally men (credit traders), exporters and overseas importers. To explain one or two of the less familiar terms, a factor is a wholesaler who takes over the collection of accounts while a rack-jobber is a wholesaler who specializes in stocking up supermarkets with non-perishable items such as toiletries and proprietary medicines. Direct response marketing through off-the-page press advertisements, TV, direct mail and catalogues has become a very sophisticated form of mail order.

Dealer relations is an aspect of public relations and marketing support which no manufacturer or supplier can afford to neglect, yet such neglect has been the cause of a number of product failures. Dealers are unlikely to sell a new product in which they have no confidence, no matter how beguiling the trade terms or massive the launch advertising. They have their own customer relations to consider. Pre-selling or market education must not be overlooked, especially with consumer durables and hi-tech goods.

Manufacturers of FMCGs, the small unit goods commonly found in supermarkets, have a major distribution problem in maintaining customer demand and combating the tendency for supermarket chains like Sainsbury's and Tesco to delist national brands in favour of own brands. These stores now stock 50 per cent of popular lines under their own labels.

7 Consumers and users

Consumers may be described as the final customers, users who make use of the product whether it be a component for a product or an ingredient used by a hotel chef. Users, industrial and commercial, come under the heading of 'business-to-business', but it is more sensible to refer to buyers of, say, garden insecticides or fertilizers as users rather than consumers.

Some products (and services) are never known to the final consumer, and the public relations operation is allied to the 'back-selling' operation of encouraging a manufacturer to adopt or continue to use a product. The public relations effort will be aimed at the designer, formulator or specifier. But although an architect may be the essential specifier he could be influenced by the wishes of a client who may have a preference for brick, tile, timber, metal or glass. The 'Brick is Beautiful' campaign reached various customers and users.

Final customers are not necessarily those addressed by advertising. They could be young people who will be eventual customers; or junior customers such as those for whom the Abbey National Building Society issues its twice-yearly journal. There can also be numerous minority groups, uneconomical from an advertising point of view, but approachable by public relations. Moreover, the consumer public can be broken down into numerous demographic subdivisions of sex, age, marital status, geographical location and so on which makes it possible for them to be reached by more specialized or local media.

Another comparison with advertising is that an advertising campaign may use different mass media from those used for public relations purposes. For example the advertising may be in the *Radio Times* and *TV Times*, but the press stories may be in local weekly newspapers, national daily newspapers, special interest or women's magazines in which there is no advertising, so directing the public relations information at certain sections of the consumer public. In fact, the *Radio Times* and *TV Times* would not print any public relations material.

Again, the public relations effort may be aimed at educating new, potential customers, or at breaking down the prejudices of people not normally regarded as being within the target audience for advertising. The motorcycle market is rather like this. The same applies to things as diverse as new forms of investment to new tourist locations.

8 Opinion leaders or formers

These can be any people who, whether well or ill informed, may express opinions and influence people because of their apparent authority. They may well be ignorant, hostile or prejudiced but certainly not apathetic. Or they could be knowledgeable, well disposed or at least tolerant. Their attitudes can be dangerous or helpful, according to the extent of their knowledge and understanding. Opinion leaders may be grouped like this:

- Parents, teachers, academics, doctors, clergymen.
- Central and local government politicians, political party politicians, trade union leaders.
- Civil servants and local government officers, officials of quangos.
- Commentators, presenters.
- Journalists and authors, radio and TV personalities.
- Authorities on specialized subjects, who may write, lecture or broadcast.
- Advisory services and information bureaux.
- Officials of societies, institutions, trade associations and professional bodies.

In this list an attempt has been made to group together certain kinds of opinion leaders. For some organizations there may be other individuals who may be regarded as relevant opinion leaders – for example, leaders of ethnic groups, the police or officers of the armed forces as might particularly be the case in some countries.

Here is a particularly good example of the role of public relations in effecting change. Some typical topics are the Channel Tunnel, the European Community, Sunday Trading and the environment, all of which abound in opinion leaders who express contrary views.

These influential people can be very important in a public relations programme. They may have to be dealt with on a face-to-face basis, through the medium of the spoken word, at private meetings or over lunch. Or groups of them may be invited on a visit, tour or to a reception.

There is not only debate about who is an opinion leader, but also about the source of their opinions, and this has a bearing on the purpose of media communication. In 1948 the Americans Lazarsfeld, Berelson and Gaudel[1] produced their concept of the flow of influence. They theorized that there was a two-step flow of communications, claiming that ideas often flow *from* radio and print to the opinion leaders and from them to the less active sections of the population. The implication of this in public relations terms is that, since opinion leaders are often dispersed among the population, and it is difficult to identify and isolate them, the best way to influence *them* is by informing the media which reach them.

There was an example of this when public relations was maligned in *The Independent*[2] in a remarkable article which described certain public relations consultants who were currently in the news as 'monsters', giving the impression that public relations practitioners in general behaved unethically. Next week the well-read Letters section of the paper carried a powerful protest from Pamela Taylor,[3] President of the Institute of Public Relations, stating 'Very few of the 5000 members of the Institute of Public Relations would recognize the fantasy figures described by Bryan Appleyard . . . Certainly the daily lives − and even the worst nightmares − of our 5000 members do not contain the sort of "quick fixes" that he described.' Thus mischievous opinions expressed by reckless journalists can be scotched at the fountain head.

Deliberately, we have looked at opinion leaders (or formers) as all kinds of people who influence others. This is a broader approach than that of regarding opinion leaders as people whose opinions should be respected, trusted or imitated. This is because in public relations we often have to deal with those whose opinions are ill-informed, biased and even dangerous.

The media

Some writers include the media as a public, but the media are really a means of reaching our publics. Media personalities such as columnists and broadcasters are best referred to as opinion leaders. Some of these personalities may combine the roles of journalist, author, public speaker, radio and TV broadcaster. They contribute to the media. Consequently we do not include media among our publics.

Examples of publics

The following are examples of possible publics for three organizations. These lists are not exhaustive, but they suggest how the PRO or consultant may project lists for his organization or individual clients.

1   Publics for an insurance company

- Employees – various grades.
- Potential employees, including students on business studies courses.
- Careers masters at schools, colleges, universities.
- Existing policy holders.
- Potential policy holders for the particular classes of insurance.
- Insurance brokers.
- Trade association, professional body, e.g. British Insurance Association, Chartered Insurance Institute.
- Members of Parliament.
- Economists and financial writers.
- Financial institutions, stockbrokers, investment analysts.
- Bank managers.

2   Publics for a holiday tour operator

- Employees – various grades including couriers.
- Potential employees, including students on tourism courses.
- Career masters at schools, colleges, universities.
- Previous customers.
- Applicants for holiday brochures, e.g. in response to advertising.
- Travel agents.
- Trade associations, e.g. Association of British Travel Agents.
- Motoring organizations, e.g. Automobile Association, Royal Automobile Club.
- Travel writers, and broadcasters on holiday programmes.
- Holiday clubs, women's organizations.
- Hoteliers associated with packaged tours, especially their PROs.

3 *Publics for a gardening product*

- Employees – various grades.
- Potential employees.
- Existing customers.
- Gardening societies, e.g. National Rose Society, Royal Horticultural Society.
- Trade associations, e.g. Horticulture Trades Association.
- Local horticultural societies, gardening clubs, e.g. in companies.
- Public park officials, keepers.
- Gardening writers, radio and TV broadcasters.
- Women's organizations.

The listed publics may vary according to the kind of insurance, holiday tours or gardening products but the above lists suggest the variety of publics which may apply. For example, the insurance company may sell mainly through brokers, the holiday tour operator may run tours to exotic places, and the horticultural company might be interested mainly in lawn care.

Having defined the publics relevant to our objectives we can now consider what media are available to reach them, or what special media may have to be created to reach special publics.

References

1 Lazarsfeld, Berelson and Gaudel, *The People's Choice*, New York, Columbia University Press, 1948
2 Appleyard, Brian, 'John Major ate our monsters', *The Independent*, 11 February 1993
3 Taylor, Pamela 'No place for "monsters" among PR professionals' (Letters), *The Independent*, 15 February 1993. Also reported in *Public Relations*, IPR. London, March 1993

8

Selecting public relations media

Media – a major area of study

A thorough understanding of communication media is one of the most
important assets a PRO can possess, and it goes a long way beyond
the gin and tonic caricature of a public relations practitioner who
excels at entertaining journalists. The media scene is a constantly
changing one with new media such as cable and satellite television
offering new opportunities, while the impact of new high technology
printing and international satellite transmission is rapidly changing
the press world. It is not limited to mass communications, and
so-called mass communication studies are only of partial value to the
PRO. For this reason, it is unfortunate that mass communications
courses are confused with public relations training.

Many public relations media are by no means addressed to the mass
public, the 'admass' as it is dubbed somewhat cynically. Effective
public relations may rely on addressing messages to small groups, or
face-to-face communication with individuals, or on the use of video
tapes and the small screen watched by small audiences. Thus we have
micro- as well as macro-media. The media may have to be specially
created, and may include audio and video cassettes, slides, notice
boards, internal and external house journals, private exhibitions, seminars and conferences, educational literature, books and sponsorships.

In developing countries, media may have to be mobile, and innovators
and folk media (oramedia) ranging from puppet shows to village gong
men, may be required. Throughout the developing or industrializing
world, media may have to be chosen which contend with problems of
distance, rural communities, illiteracy, multiplicity of languages and
dialects, and multi-ethnic and multi-religious societies. This subject
has been discussed very thoroughly in *Communication in Industrialising
Countries*[1] which the author has written in collaboration with the late
Dr Frank Ugboajah of the University of Lagos.

Media will be discussed more analytically in Part Three, but here let us consider the task of selecting the media mix. Unlike advertising, we do not have to buy space or airtime (except for a corporate advertising campaign), but the mistake should not be made of thinking that no cost is involved. Media are the vehicles of communication and the public relations cost lies in the time spent in working with them and the materials, postage and so on incurred in distributing releases.

Colour separation charges and advertorial rackets

Two contentious forms of cost have occurred in recent years but they have been opposed by the various publishing, journalist and public relations organizations. The first concerned colour photographs and the other advertorials.

For a time a number of magazines tried to charge public relations suppliers for the reproduction of colour pictures, charging colour separation fees. This was wrong for two reasons: the only reason for printing a colour picture should be because it is of sufficient reader interest to merit publication. To charge meant that only those willing to pay would get their pictures printed. It was a very bad practice which reflected on the reputation of the journal. No payment should ever be made for the publication of public relations material.

The second racket, which seemed to be a joint conspiracy between unprofessional consultants and inexperienced journalists, was the sale of editorial space to promote a product, the feature appearing to be independent editorial. In Britain at least, responsible editors do not sell space to public relations consultants and nor do responsible consultants buy editorial space, although this has proved to be an idealistic view.

Incidentally, a true advertorial is a merchandising scheme by a publisher who offers, as a reader service, a special price offer. A number of reputable women's magazines have helped to launch new cosmetics in this way, but the maker of the cosmetic bought no space.

'Reader advertisements', written in journalistic style and set to resemble editorial copy, must be distinguished by the words 'Advertisement' or 'Advertiser's Announcement' (which tends to nullify the editorial effect) in compliance with the *British Code of Advertising Practice*.[2]

The rules so far as journalists are concerned are set out in the *Chartered Institute of Journalists Code of Conduct*,[3] from which the following passages are quoted:

Section 3 paragraph (h)
Every member is required to subscribe to the code constraint in this schedule which stipulates that the following acts are discreditable to a journalist thereby carrying the penalties prescribed by Bye-law 26.

The writing or altering of editorial copy at the request of an advertiser or news feature pictures at the request of an advertiser or in exchange for advertising or any other consideration, or offering to do so, except for use in clearly marked advertising pages or supplements.

The implications of the above ruling are that any member who violates any fundamental rule of the Institute is 'liable to be excluded from membership or from office, or to be suspended from membership for any period not exceeding two years by a resolution of the Council. . .' .

The Code requires that:

(a) If payment is asked for or made for a picture it is mandatory that the picture is headed on a page marked advertising or advertising feature or advertisement.
(b) If it does not carry such a banner it is breaking the CIJ's Code of Conduct and the Member will face disciplinary proceedings.
(c) If a public relations executive pays colour separation charges he or she is in effect aiding and abetting a journalist to break the Code of Conduct.

The CIJ is opposed to colour separation charges because:

(a) They compromise the integrity of the journalist.
(b) They blur the distinction between editorial and advertising.
(c) They will lead to lower editorial standards.
(d) They deceive the reader into believing that a picture appearing on an editorial page is there because of news and/or feature alone.

The rulings are followed by guidelines of which the following is a particularly relevant example:

If on explaining the relevant paragraph of the Code of Conduct the editor insists on payment then he or she should be told that their name and the name of their publications will be reported to the CIJ for follow-up action. At this stage the IPR and/or the PRCA must write to the editor confirming that the matter will be reported to the Chartered Institute of Journalists.

The advertorial racket is also the subject of codes from the Periodical Publishers Association. But it was disturbing to read Torin Douglas's article in *Marketing Week*[4] which discussed the two-page advertorial on Norwich Union's Healthcare which appeared in *Good Housekeeping*, breaking all the rules, and revealed that 9 per cent of National Magazine's ad revenue came from advertorials.

According to a special feature on the subject in *PR Week*,[5] advertorials in *Best* and *Prima* cost over £17,000 and many of the leading women's magazines were selling advertorials at from £5000 to £13,000 a page. A well-known public relations consultant was quoted as saying, 'But to be successful an advertorial must look like editorial'. Sheer hypocrisy from a member of the IPR, which has a code of professional conduct.

Marketing Week[6] reported on 22 January 1993 that the Periodical Publishers Association had banned the word 'advertorial'. The PPA guidelines stressed that such features should be distinguished by the words 'advertisement', 'advertising' or 'promotion'. Deputy chief executive Peter Dear was quoted as saying, 'We want people to stop using the word advertorial because it is not generally understood by readers. People must be left in no doubt that what they are reading is an advertisement.'

Among the culprits were women's magazines which printed 'advertorial' sideways in the margin, where it was easily missed. But the racket was perpetuated in 1993 with publishers advertising their services to produce advertorials, and *PR Week* even ran a special report!

Some media and some public relations techniques occupy a lot of time: researching articles, photographic sessions, working with television producers, editing house journals, cooperating with video producers, or organizing press receptions, seminars, film shows and private exhibitions are all very time consuming. A story may appear in the press, and it may be only a paragraph, but considerable time was spent in its preparation and distribution. The question is: how much time have we got and how can it be divided up most economically and managed most effectively? This time does cost money, and there is a cost to press relations quite different from the purchase of advertisement space.

The choice of media will be derived from our decision regarding publics. Which media will best convey our message to our chosen publics? If no commercial or official media exists, what private media should we create?

Need to be specific

A weakness with some public relations students and even more senior practitioners is to generalize about the media instead of referring to specific media. Even the expression 'tabloid' is a generality, no longer describing the 'gutter press' but rather most newspapers, since broadsheets are rare. We do not send stories to 'the nationals', and ITV (with the exception of Channel 4) is not 'national TV'. Within newspapers, magazines, TV and radio stations there are pages, sections, features, columns and programmes all controlled by individuals. Media need to be analysed to know to whom or where to send material or make contact.

Britain is rich in media, and throughout the country there are nearly 100 regional dailies (mostly evenings), a few Sundays, thousands of local weeklies (paid-for and free) plus various categories of local magazines. Scotland, Wales and Northern Ireland can be regarded as having their own national press.

It is therefore important that the public relations practitioner should be as familiar as possible with this wealth of media and know how to incorporate it in his or her media mix.

Allied to this knowledge of titles, contents and locations (with the aid of directories such as *Advertisers Annual*[7] and *Benn's Media Directory*[8]) is the need to know how and when they are produced. Publications have deadlines which may be hours, days, weeks or months ahead of publication date. For instance, some magazines work three to six months ahead. Television programmes are often shot six months before they are aired. Modern newspapers, printed around the country by strategically located contract printers, print news no later than that seen on *News At Ten*.

Media provide a fascinating study, and he or she who knows the media best will win the greatest coverage.

The media revolution

The media demand continued and detailed study, and yet this is a subject about which many public relations students – and practitioners – are woefully ignorant. This has to be repeated and emphasized at the close of this chapter because in the past few years there has been a media revolution.

No longer is a reasonably acceptable news release subbed by hand. Instead, provided it has a proper intro (which few possess!) it is keyed onto the computer screen. We now have paperless newsrooms.

A totally different quality black and white photograph is needed now by newspapers which have abandoned coarse screen letterpress halftone reproduction in favour of fine screen web-offset-litho or flexographic printing.

We have seen the arrival of new newspapers, creating panic in Fleet Street, court disaster and stand to fight again under new owners and editors. *Today* failed to win a million circulation, and had to be sold, having first tried to compete with the *Sun* and the *Mirror* and then increasing its cover price to join the *Mail* and *Express*. Still even the half million mark evaded the new owners, until a workaholic editor sought a niche between the *Sun/Mirror* and the *Mail/Express* and changed *Today's* fortunes.

Television has changed for more reasons than the 1990 Broadcasting Act. Cash strapped, the news services have been unable to cover stories and have welcomed the video news release kits (see Chapter 22) which enable them to create the impression that it is all their own work. The auctioning of TV licenses has brought its disappointments as was seen in 1992 with the debacles at Granada TV and Good Morning TV.

Meanwhile radio has taken new directions with the national commercial stations, Classic FM and Virgin, while the future of the BBC is fiercely debated prior to the renewal of its licence.

We have seen many magazines fold, and watched the sliding circulation figures of the once all-powerful women's weeklies, and the growth and popularity of weekend magazines reflecting the styles of their newspaper sponsors, the quality of the rejuvenated listings magazines, and the invasion of English versions of foreign magazines.

Free newspapers (and magazines) continue to flourish, often with full colour pictures, while advertisers welcome the mass coverage of urban dwellers.

It is vital, therefore, that the public relations student or practitioner should be familiar with ever-changing means of communicating with mass publics.

References

1 Jefkins, Frank and Ugboajah, Frank, *Communication in Industrialising Countries*, Macmillan, 1987
2 *British Code of Advertising Practice*, Part 8, Clause 11, Committee of Advertising Practice, London 1988
3 *Chartered Institute of Journalists' Code of Conduct*, 1992
4 Douglas, Torin, 'Can You Trust These Pages?', *Marketing Week*, 16 October 1992

5   Dark, Stephen, 'Hiring an editorial lookalike', *PR Week*, 20 August 1992
6   *Marketing Week*, report, 'PPA bans use of the word "advertorial"', 22 January 1993
7   *Advertiser's Annual*, Reed Information Services, Windsor Court, East Grinstead, annually
8   *Benn's Media Directory*, Benn Business Information Services, Tonbridge, annually

9

Budgeting

Costing and controlling costs

Budgeting is not only a means of finding out costs and controlling them: it also identifies work to be done so that the D-Day timetable and the critical path analysis aids to planning and control, as explained in Chapter 4, can be drawn up in parallel. A budget is similar to the shopping list which a housewife prepares before going shopping, reminding her of what she has to buy which in turn is controlled by the amount of money in her purse or her credit limit.

The three principal public relations costs are time, materials and expenses. Until the volume of available time is agreed we cannot budget the materials or expenses which can be associated with the employment of that time. Thus time is the key to public relations budgeting, and all else follows. Some so-called budgets fail to recognize the reality of this simple truth.

Time

Time represents manhours, which can be looked at in two ways: the amount of time it will take to carry out a particular task (such as editing a house journal, handling a news release, or organizing an event), *or* the amount of time that is represented by a PRO's salary or a consultant's fee. The value of the time will be the hourly or daily rate.

To find out the PRO's hourly rate his annual salary has to be divided by the total hours of his working days — that is, the total after statutory holidays, weekends and annual holidays have been deducted. The same has to be calculated for the members of his staff. We now have a *time bank* which can be allocated to the tasks in the programme. If this fails to agree with the estimated manhours for the programme it will be necessary to do one of three things: make cuts in the proposed campaign, engage extra staff or augment the in-house staff with free-lance or consultancy services.

A more complicated calculation is required to arrive at the consultant's hourly rate because this rate has to recover the costs of running the business and produce a profit. The consultant's hourly rate will take into consideration salaries and all overheads such as light, heat, air-conditioning, rent, rates and so on, plus the percentage desired for profit. There are variations in the method, some consultancies basing the hourly rate on the salaries of the account executive and his or her secretary only, others working out hourly rates (salary plus oncost) for every member of the consultancy staff so that their work is both estimated and charged out according to its usage. A rough rule-of-thumb method is to treble the salaries of the account executive and his or her secretary.

In the case of an account executive, if the fee is £20,000 and the hourly rate is £50, the total number of hours available is 400, or about one day's work a week. It is important that the client should understand this for he or she may well imagine that a certain fee is worth more service that it really is. But the client can expect only what he or she pays for, and if the consultant exceeds the paid-for workload this is done at his or her own loss unless a supplementary fee is agreed. Correct calculations and expectations are therefore critical on both sides.

It is essential to calculate time and its allocation, otherwise it is impossible to plan what is to be done. In the case of salaries it is a matter of how best the time of the in-house PRO can be spent, and in the case of the consultancy fee it is a matter of how much work can the client expect for the money.

Materials

Materials consist of all goods which have to be purchased on the client's or company's behalf. Stationery, postage, photographs, print, slides, video, cassettes, exhibits and displays come under this heading. The consultant has to be careful to recover all such costs, otherwise they will come out of profits. Unless there are very expensive items such as house journals or documentary films, material costs will make up only a small proportion of the total budget.

The mistake is sometimes made of concentrating the budget on materials, with a round sum shown for fees and salaries. This is putting the cart before the horse. Normally materials are supplied at cost, perhaps paid for direct by the client, but if they are heavy costs, a handling charge may be agreed.

This type of budget is illustrated in Norman Stone's book *How to Manage Public Relations*[1] in which he either allows nothing for time, or refers to 'salaries' but no time bank, but does in one instance refer to 'outside consultancy (500 hours)'. Moreover, he refers to public relations expenditure as a percentage of advertising budget, which is an extraordinary way of looking at such expenditure which could be related to many things apart from advertising or even marketing in general. He also mentions a mark-up of 17.65 per cent on bought-in services or materials. Although time is referred to under his task-based marketing, it is not taken as an essential basis for the calculation of fees or what a salary represents in time. Moreover, his somewhat confused chapter on budgeting muddles up many advertising or extraneous expenditures such as direct mail, exhibition space, in-company training and so on which have nothing to do with public relations.

Perhaps this is why some consultancies call themselves 'agencies' because they are more like advertising agencies, with income based on percentages, than consultancies where the bulk of the income is derived from selling time and expertise. It is also true that some small con-sultancies, and especially ones overseas, do not charge proper fees (either because they lack expertise which justifies a certain price or their clients do not understand the fee systems) with the result that they charge small fees (which are little more than retainers) and earn their principal income from 17.65 per cent on costs. What this often means is that instead of selling their own counselling advice and services they are buying in other people's expertise. This may be justified in the case of, say, video production, but it should not be necessary to spend a lot of money on materials. Otherwise it is like a doctor making the sale of pills his primary source of income.

Some purists would say that a consultant should earn no commission, being a professional adviser and not an agent, and that major bills for materials (e.g. a catering bill for a press reception) should be sent direct to the client for payment. This has been the author's experience as a consultant.

However, if there is a mark-up it should be agreed with the client in the original contract. A mark-up is different from commission and is an *extra* cost. When a client uses an advertising agency under the commission system, the agency buys space or airtime at a discount. This discount may be 15 per cent, but the agency may require 17.65 per cent and will charge the client the difference of 2.65 per cent. However, mark-ups or on-costs are handling charges added to the full undiscounted price of, say, print or video production, or anything else which is 'farmed out' to an outside supplier. Thus a consultancy has no commission income but may have *mark-up* income. If the consultant is doing a labour-intensive job for a client, expenditure on materials and income derived from percentages should be minimal.

These minimal costs could cover such things as the printing of news release headings, photography, stationery, postage and so on which would provide little mark-up income compared with the major cost of time represented by the fee.

Expenses

These are the costs of fares, taxis, hotel expenses and hospitality, and will also include catering, transportation and other costs for press events. Again, this should not be a large item in the budget in spite of myths about public relations entertainment.

Three examples of budgets

In this section three kinds of budget will be demonstrated with dummy figures. The first is the kind which the consultant should include in a proposition to a client. The second is a budget for a press reception. The third is an estimate of the cost of running a public relations department.

1 Public relations consultancy budget

This calls for a little preliminary explanation. It differs from an advertising appropriation because no free services are covered by commission on media purchases. All time has to be paid for, including talking to the client. You will notice that progress meetings – regular monthly meetings – are chargeable, whether held on the client's or the consultant's premises. The calculations should be interpreted as the number of items multiplied by the number of hours multiplied by the hourly rate, which in reality might be 1×10 hours $\times$ £50 per hour equals £500. However, since from the reader's point of view the hourly rate may be different and he may not be thinking in sterling, dummy noughts are used.

12 progress meetings	$12 \times 00\,\text{hrs} \times £00 =$	0000.00
Public relations coverage of exhibition	$1 \times 00\,\text{hrs} \times £00 =$	0000.00
25 news releases	$25 \times 00\,\text{hrs} \times £00 =$	0000.00
Organizing 3 seminars	$3 \times 00\,\text{hrs} \times £00 =$	0000.00
Press visit to factory	$1 \times 00\,\text{hrs} \times £00 =$	0000.00

3 photographic sessions	3 × 00 hrs × £00 =	0000.00
Editing, designing, quarterly house journal	4 × 00 hrs × £00 =	0000.00
General information services	00 hrs × £00 =	0000.00
Contingency 10%	00 hrs × £00 =	000.00
		00,000.00

Estimated material costs	News releases	000.00
	Photography	0000.00
	Printing house journal	00,000.00
	Postage, stationery	000.00
	Press cuttings	000.00
Expenses	Travelling expenses	000.00
	Transportation	000.00
	Seminars	0000.00
Contingency 10%		000.00
	Total	00,000.00

Budget for a press reception

This is a very useful standard budget because press receptions are common public relations exercises. But it is very easy to forget things, make mistakes and miscalculate. A press reception may seem such a familiar event that the PRO may be tempted to be careless. Too much may be left to others, especially the caterers, and unexpectedly high bills may have to be faced. The practitioner must beware of management, who sometimes introduce their own last-minute and sometimes over generous ideas, and of company staff who are apt to stay behind after the guests have gone and so run up an unnecessary bar bill. It is sensible to control such expenditures by giving the barman a stop figure, and closing the bar by serving coffee.

Normally, journalists are not there 'for the beer', but want a good story. Hangers-on are usually freelance writers, and every PRO knows the saying 'first to arrive, last to leave'. It is also possible to control the volume of drinks consumed by guests. Never have a waiter walking round with a tray of drinks unless this is the easiest way of serving a large party. If the event is merely one of those old-fashioned cocktail parties where people stand around, and eventually someone makes a speech, the drinks will flow because there is nothing better to do. But if there is an organized programme, and for most of the time journalists are seated, listening or watching, the only time for drinking is on being received and following the business.

In recent years there have been changes in drinking habits. Journalists tend to prefer coffee on arrival, and tomato juice and dry white wine have tended to replace spirits. Nevertheless, one has always to be prepared to meet all tastes and one should allow for the occasional brandy addict.

The following *is* a budget of materials for a specific occasion. The time involved in preparation (spread over weeks) and running the event could make a total of at least three days, that is 21 hours, although the press reception itself occupies only two hours.

	£
Printed invitation cards, reply cards, white envelopes	00.00
Postage on invitations	00.00
Telephone: checking names on invitation list, following up non-replies	00.00
Hire of room	00.00
Hire of projector or VCR, TV set	00.00
Projectionist's fee	00.00
Hire of microphones	00.00
Average 3 drinks at £0.00 per head	000.00
00 buffets at £00.00 per head	000.00
00 coffees at £0.00 per head	00.00
Gratuities	00.00
Press kit wallets	00.00
News releases, copies of speech	00.00
Display panels for photographs	00.00
Photography and prints	000.00
Captions	00.00
Order forms for photographs	00.00
Visitors' book	0.00
Samples/souvenirs for guests	000.00
Lapel badges	00.00
Artwork for tent cards, displays, notices	00.00
Taxi fares transporting materials, staff	00.00
Special effects: costume hire, decorations, musicians, lighting, etc.	000.00
Incidentals	00.00
Contingency fund	000.00
Total	£0000.00

Budget for a public relations department

In-house public relations departments will vary in size and duties according to the type of organization so the budget given here is aimed to show a comprehensive range of activities and it can be adapted up or down as required.

It covers everything included in the consultancy budget except profit.

Overheads are identified instead of being calculated in the hourly rate. The variety of activities is likely to be greater than that of a consultancy budget because we are now dealing with full-time staff − not a share of a consultancy team − and the work will entail internal as well as external public relations responsibilities. It is assumed that the in-house department is self-sufficient and no consultancy services are used.

	£
Salaries: Public relations manager, assistants, secretaries	00,000.00
Overheads: Rent, rates, lighting, heating, air-conditioning, cleaning, share of telephone switchboard, etc.	00,000.00
Depreciation: Furniture and equipment	00,000.00
Insurances: Car, all risks on equipment, travel, pensions, health	00,000.00
Press events: Materials, catering, hire/rental charges	00,000.00
Visual aids: Preparation, production, distribution and maintenance videos, slides, audio-cassettes	00,000.00
News releases: Preparation and distribution	00,000.00
Press cutting service, television, radio monitoring services	00,000.00
Feature articles: Preparation and publication	00,000.00
Information service: Staff and equipping	00,000.00
House journals: Editing and production	00,000.00
Educational literature: Creation, printing and production	00,000.00
Sponsorship: Awards and coverage, hospitality	00,000.00
Seminars: Materials, catering, hire/rental charges	00,000.00
Photography: Shooting, prints	00,000.00
Vehicles: Car, van	00,000.00
Equipment: Camera, VCR, TV set or monitor, tape recorder, word processor, PC, software, copier	00,000.00
Stationery: Letterheadings, news release headings, photo caption headings, envelopes, etc.	00,000.00
Telephone, Fax	00,000.00
Postage	00,000.00
Travelling expenses: car expenses, taxis, rail/air fares, hotels, hospitality	00,000.00
Contingency: say 10%	00,000.00
Total	£000,000.00

It will be seen that several of the figures are totals and require detailed individual budgets, an example of which has already been demonstrated in the budget for a press reception.

Budgets can be produced in conjunction with D-Day charts or a critical path analysis chart. The one depends on the other.

Management is used to dealing in this businesslike way, and the proper planning of programmes, forecasting of results and budgeting of costs is the sort of accountable professionalism which will enhance the PRO in management's estimation. It will greatly diminish management's often false idea that public relations is something which happens on a day-to-day basis, perhaps subject to the whims of management, so that it could be regarded as intangible and dispensable. Of all things in an organization, public relations should be indispensable.

In some organizations, especially in less sophisticated countries, management sometimes does not know what to do with public relations. Thrust upon public relations are all sorts of irrelevant tasks such as servicing other departments by arranging travel requirements, 'protocol' (which in developing countries means the arrangements for social occasions), and even personnel management which is another job altogether. Budgets bring out the real responsibilities of public relations.

From experience, the public relations practitioner will know roughly what most things cost (in time or money or both) so that even in a meeting or during an interview he or she should be able to produce a tentative budget at short notice. This can always be confirmed afterwards with a more accurate calculation based on real figures.

Budgeting is therefore a primary management function of public relations for it implies time as well as money management. Both the PRO and the public relations consultant need to be capable of being good estimators who not only know how to go about obtaining and compiling figures but are cost-conscious and are aware of all the items that need to be costed. It is an attitude of mind and an ability that should figure strongly in the practitioner's job specification.

Cost-effective public relations means being greedy with money and time, and the practitioner has to be accountable for both.

These are very much considerations for doing things, but some additional costs should be considered overall. These could include professional fees (PRCA, IPR), and training including the maintenance of a library and sponsorship for courses and examinations. The library should not only be for staff training purposes, but should include the many excellent trade directories as shown in the Appendices.

Reference

1   Stone, Norman, *How To Manage Public Relations*, McGraw-Hill, Maidenhead, 1991

10

Assessing results

Three methods

There are three main ways of evaluating the results of public relations programmes:

1 By observation and experience.
2 By feedback and its assessment.
3 By research.

Observation and experience

Some objectives will be seen to be achieved. This is clearly the easiest and most inexpensive form of assessment. The following are some typical examples:

- The public relations manager may wish to stem a trend in staff instability, particularly if money is spent on training staff only to lose them to rival employers. The public relations programme may aim to inform employees better about company policies, performance and prospects. If this succeeds, the reduction in resignations will be a measure of the programme's success.
- The need may be to employ the right calibre of staff. Has a campaign to educate prospective recruits produced the desired result?
- The company may have had a poor reputation locally, resulting in a bad local press, public criticism, letters of complaint and poor response to vacancy advertisements. Has this situation been turned round as a result of a public relations programme to achieve a more deserved image? Is the company now respected locally?
- As a result of good communications with the financial media, has a new share or rights issue been successful, or has the stock market

price been improved? Has a takeover bid been averted?

- Are distributors better disposed towards the company, stocking lines, permitting displays, receiving salesmen more favourably, as a result of a trade relations campaign? Are distributors better able to inform customers about the company's products?
- Have industrial relations improved as a result of more candid or more personal management–employee communications?
- Are the media better informed, more accurate, less hostile, more sympathetic or more interested as a result of a media relations programme?

The above are seven possibilities. It may be disappointing to note that we have not mentioned sales and profits. This is because public relations is not only, perhaps not at all, concerned with the marketing and advertising aspects of business. This helps to emphasize that public relations does not belong to the advertising budget, nor is it a below-the-line activity. There *are* other aspects of business (e.g. to do with production and finance), and if public relations did not pay attention to these there would be no marketing or advertising.

Of course, too much should not be claimed for public relations and in making such assessments it is always sensible to consider whether other factors have influenced the result. Economic, political and other market forces may affect the situation. It would be silly to claim that public relations had been totally responsible for improved trade relations if one's principal rival had declined in popularity!

Feedback and its assessment

Since public relations is a two-way process, and the PRO provides the eyes, ears and voice of the organization, part of the public relations task is to initiate and receive a constant inflow of information. This may arrive in many forms, both internally and externally. It may take the form of complaints, ideas, suggestions, reports and recommendations, or it may consist of press cuttings, monitored broadcast materials, books containing comments on the organization, Parliamentary reports, independent research survey reports and so forth. Some of this may have been inspired by the practitioner, but much of it will be outside his or her direct control. Some of it may be provoked for good or ill by other people in the organization.

One of the practitioner's jobs will be to examine such feedback, and perhaps comment on it and report to those whom it concerns within the organization. He or she may have to act on it by correcting false reports or making sure that people such as journalists and broadcasters are better informed next time they deal with the subject. It is often poor policy to 'keep a low profile', which can be worse than making 'no comment'. Negative public relations is sometimes advocated when organizations are in trouble, but there is the adage that 'the best form of defence is attack', and this can be true of unfortunate public relations situations. Sometimes a bad situation can be turned into a good one as has been seen by the commendable way in which a crisis has been handled.

Among this feedback will be the material for which the practitioner has been directly responsible, e.g. press cuttings and the monitored scripts of broadcasts with which he or she has been involved.

Not entirely dead, though it should be even if it still favoured by those Americans who have a dollar measure for everything, is the evaluation of media coverage by its advertisement rate-card value. It is a nonsensical yardstick for the logical reason that editorial space and programme time is priceless, at least in most countries where editors and producers cannot be bribed or like Nigerian TV, where payment is expected for broadcasting public relations stories! Equating column centimetres or airtime with advertisement rates is also false because an advertising campaign would not have used similar publications or airtime, or have been booked for the same positions, dates or quantities. There is no sensible comparison between the two.

So, when someone says 'that two-page article would have cost so much if we had bought the space', or 'that hour's programme on networked ITV about our sponsored golf tournament would have cost *x* million pounds if we had bought airtime', they have not made a realistic comparison. For one thing, had they bought the space, and if they could have bought all that airtime, they could have said what they liked as favourably as they liked, provided it was ethical and legal. But they have no control over what is said or not said by editors, journalists, producers and commentators. Even now, with limited sponsorship of commercial radio and TV in Britain, the advertising content is comparatively trivial.

There are, however, five genuine and better ways of evaluating media coverage, for example:

1   One can note which papers or programmes have covered the story. What is the *quality* of the coverage? This can be important. Were they influential media? Half an inch in a multi-million circulation women's weekly magazine could be much more valuable than a page in a small circulation business monthly. A story in the *Sun* could be more valuable than one in the *Financial Times*, and vice versa according to the type of story. The *volume* of coverage could

be immaterial. Coming nearer home, a story in *PR Week* (with its penetration of the public relations world) could be much more useful than one in, say *Campaign*. Thus, it is valid to evaluate *where* a story has appeared. This can be represented on a value scale like this:

Publication	Rating	Story 1	Story 2	Story 3
Daily Blower	4	×		×
Daily Sizzle	2		×	
Sunday Scandal	2		×	×
Sunday Bore	4	×		
Weekly Gloom	4	×		
Weekly Hope	2		×	×
Score		12	6	8

The ratings would obviously be different for different organizations. The quality of the coverage can also be measured by the *tone* of the reporting. What did they say, and how did they say it? There can also be a recognizable difference or improvement in tone between past and present coverage.

2   One can also evaluate the **potential readership** or **audience** by multiplying each appearance of the story by the published circulation or readership figure of each journal or, in the case of broadcasting, by the published audience figures. Thus one could say that if a story appeared in journals with estimated readerships of 500,000, 750,000, 1 million and 4 million, 6¼ million people had the *opportunity* of seeing or reading the story. This is called an **OTS rating**. Or a television programme may have a recorded audience figure of, say, 15 million.

3   Picture usage can also be counted, and this may be a good indication of which publications should be sent pictures and which not, or whether it is better to *offer* pictures, perhaps submitting miniatures from which editors can choose and request pictures. Again, this exercise might suggest the wisdom of reproducing pictures on the news release with the offer to supply prints if required. Money is often wasted on sending expensive photographs to journals which are never likely to use them.

4   *Voice* is another form of volume measurement. What share of voice was achieved? How many publications, radio or TV stations covered the story irrespective of column centimetres or airtime?

5   *Response* may be yet another kind of evaluation if the media coverage produces enquiries.

Research

Marketing research techniques can be used when the objective of the programme is to effect a change or improvement in awareness, attitude or image. A base percentage of awareness or attitude is necessary, and this would have been obtained initially when the appreciation of the situation study or the image study was undertaken before planning the programme. There are two ways of going about this. A piece of primary research may be set up independently, or − very economically as described in Chapter 5 − questions may be inserted in the questionnaire of an already set up omnibus survey with its already recruited panel of respondents.

As Roger Haywood says in *All About Public Relations*,[1] 'Over the coming years, we shall see more serious attention paid to research. Public relations programmes that are research-based are demonstrably more effective − and while research may involve some cost, through focusing the public relations efforts, it can improve cost effectiveness.'

Suppose, in the case of an attitude study or opinion poll, it had been found that only 5 per cent of respondents had heard of the organization, or knew what it did, or liked what it did, and the objective of the programme was to increase this figure to 20 per cent. A post-programme survey would reveal the degree to which this had been achieved. Similarly, with an image study, the effectiveness of the programme in achieving a more accurate image would be revealed by a later survey to measure what changes had been brought about. These methods were described in Chapter 5 as means of appreciating the situation.

Thus, tangible quantitative results could be recorded because this type of research measures changes in trends over time, and this can be represented in the form of graphs, bar charts or pie charts. A typical graph was demonstrated in Chapter 5.

It is also possible to apply research techniques to news releases before they are despatched and after they have been published. James B. Strenski[2] says:

> Pretesting and post-testing specific communications campaigns of a random audience sample can be as helpful in public relations program planning as it is in advertising campaign planning. Pretesting is particularly effective in avoiding needless, poor impressions. Post-testing can help avoid repeating mistakes.

The problem, however, is how to induce management to accept the results of a pre-test when they have probably rewritten and 'approved' what they are adamant shall be issued! On the other hand, submission to pre-testing could be a way to discouraging management from ruining professionally written releases.

The lesson has to be learned by management that public relations can only be done 'on the cheap' if it is to be unaccountable. It seems a waste of money to commission public relations without knowing what it is expected to achieve, and not caring whether it achieves anything. Yet it is not uncommon for companies to spend an insufficient sum on unspecific public relations activity and then complain that it has not done anything. In such a case management is to blame for the waste of money and the ineffectiveness, not public relations. That 'sufficient amount' should be sufficient to cover the essential research, and should be enough to cover a programme capable of achieving the results which it is hoped the final research will show have been achieved.

The message, of course, if that if you want tangible results it is essential to have tangible objectives. If an architect designs a building he expects the finished structure to represent his plans. Similarly, public relations programmes should set out to achieve definite results: at the end of the programme the results should be capable of evaluation. It may not be a pounds and pence, or sales volume, evaluation because public relations has more diversified and less commercial objectives. But it may be an evaluation which helps the pounds and pence people to operate profitably.

For instance, millions of pounds have been spent on products which have flopped – from the Edsel car to New Smoking Mixture and the Sinclair electric tricycle. But they had no public relations (in the form of market education) to create a favourable marketing situation. In all three cases only the marketing and its promotional support could be evaluated in cash terms: the public relations would have been measured in growth of knowledge and acceptance which would have guided the advisability of marketing the product at all. Again, in each case, the public relations result would have been a measure of the risk rather than the actual profit of loss. In public relations we are talking about different things.

To take another analogy, for commercial purposes public relations can be more like the intelligence work and the artillery bombardment before the attack.

From this it follows that public relations is most likely to succeed when management understands what public relations can do, and when management knows what it wants it to do. When the PRO or consultant is properly briefed he or she can plan to operate effectively. Unsuccessful (and intangible) programmes result from practitioners being obliged to put forward proposals which are not aimed at satisfying management expectations. Worse still, they may be no more than pragmatic, 'playing it by ear' fumblings to support some other activity such as a marketing strategy or an advertising campaign to which, willy-nilly, public relations has been attached like a mascot.

In the long-term, the successful use of public relations can be seen in a company's overall performance. Few companies have applied public relations techniques more thoroughly than Rentokil, whose shares have been split three times since the company went public just over two decades ago, its profits soaring year after year. Its 30 year public relations programme is a major case study in the author's *Planned Press and Public Relations.*[3]

Year after year Rentokil figures high among the favourite companies in the survey commissioned by *The Economist*[4] with the assistance of Loughborough University Business School. Rentokil ranked third (after Glaxo and Unilever) in the Top 20 table, came top in the Business Services sector, top for quality of management, second for quality of marketing, third for capacity to innovate, fifth for use of corporate assets, and sixth for quality of products. Assessments were by their peers, namely 1900 of Britain's businessmen and financial analysts.

The Macro Model

So far we have discussed evaluation of the effects or results of a public relations programme in relation to objectives. This has been based on observation, experience or scientific research. This presupposes that the campaign was conducted efficiently, but in the event of a poor result the efficiency of the campaign could be subjected to a post-mortem. Of course, the campaign was as recommended and approved, but we have only to look at the quality and distribution of the average news release to see that operationally a good many programmes are conducted with little skill or experience. Where does evaluation stand now?

The Australian public relations consultant and author Jim Macnamara, chairman of the MACRO Communication Group, has evolved a different approach to public relations evaluation which he aptly calls the Macro Model of Public Relations Evaluation (Figure 10.1). This was described in the IPRA journal, *International Public Relations.*[5] This model is presented as a pyramid with *inputs* at the base, then sets out various physical *outputs*, and peaks with *results*. To quote: 'Each activity which forms a step in the communication is very specifically identified so that evaluation can be considered for that activity.'

Thus, evaluation is an on-going procedure, a form of continuous quality control using a cluster of technologies. There is no assumption

STAGES	ACTIVITIES	METHODOLOGIES
	Objective achieved or problem solved	• Observation (in some cases) • Quantitative research
RESULTS	Number who behave in a desired manner	• Sales statistics, enrolments, etc. • Quantitative research
	Number who change attitudes	• Qualitative research (cognition acceptance)
	Number who learn message content (e.g. increased knowledge, awareness, understanding)	• Qualitative research
	Number who consider messages	• Readership, listenership or viewership statistics • Attendance at events • Inquiry or response rates (e.g. coupons, calls)
	Number who receive messages	• Circulation figures • Audience analysis
OUTPUTS	Number of messages supporting objectives	• Analysis of media coverage (break down positive, negative and neutral – e.g. media content analysis)
	Number of messages placed in the media	• Media monitoring (clippings and broadcast media tapes)
	Number of messages sent	• Distribution statistics
	Quality of message presentation (e.g. newsletter or brochure design, newsworthiness of story)	• Expert review • Audience surveys • Feedback • Awards

INPUTS	Appropriateness of message content	• Readability tests • Review
		  (e.g. Gunning • Pre-testing
		  Flesch, SST) (e.g. focus groups)

	Appropriateness of the medium	• Case studies • Pre-testing
	Adequacy of background information, intelligence, research	• Review • Benchmark • Existing research research data

Figure 10.1 Evaluation of a public relations programme – the macro model. (*Source*: International Public Relations Review, 1992, 15(4), 28)

of efficiency but a critical analysis of every contribution to the programme. While this is not unlike what has been said above about the evaluation of media coverage, it calls for earlier evaluation of the actual message and choice of media.

Obviously, it is better to cure the patient than wait for the patient to die and then carry out an inquest. The Macro Model is ideal in intent, provided the practitioner is capable of being self-critical. It does call for a thoroughly trained, experienced professional. Judging by the uselessness of the 80% of news releases which editors discard, by the pointlessness of some public relations functions, by the amateurishness of so many house journals, and by the banality of a good many videos, the number of practitioners capable of knowing whether their inputs were good or bad is minimal. Independent opinions would therefore be desirable − if anyone would accept them!

References

1 Haywood, Roger, *All About Public Relations*, 2nd edn, McGraw-Hill, Maidenhead, 1990
2 Strenski, James B., *IPRA Review*, Longman, September 1980
3 Jefkins, Frank, *Planned Press and Public Relations*, 3rd edn, Blackie, Glasgow, 1993
4 *The Economist*, 'Britain's most admired companies', 17 October 1992
5 Macnamara, Jim R., Evaluation of Public Relations: The Achilles Heel of Public Relations, *International Public Relations*, IPRA, Washington, DC, vol. 15, no. 4, 1992

PART TWO

Media Relations

11

Role of the press officer

Press officer or media relations manager?

The PRO or consultancy account executive may have to be his or her own press officer, but in a large organization the public relations department will have one or more specialist press or information officers. Some organizations will have only a press officer, and not a full-time PRO. Much depends on the extent of the press work. The name 'press officer' is rather old-fashioned since this person has to deal with radio and TV as well. Some organizations, such as local authorities, have already adopted the more apt title, media officer or media relations manager.

When a company has only a press officer he or she may suffer a very lowly status, but on the other hand there have been some very famous press officers like the late Freddie Gillman of BOAC who could spontaneously dictate a news release over the telephone to the news agencies. He became President of the Institute of Public Relations.

The press officer may or may not be an ex-journalist, but he or she does need to be able to write a news release which resembles a newspaper report. Very few news releases received by editors measure up to that elementary criterion, but more on this theme in the next chapter. It is also necessary to understand how the media operate, and how to work with journalists. In this respect it may help if the press officer is an ex-journalist. However, if it is any consolation to non-journalist press officers, the author was never a journalist. In fact, he began his career in advertising, and was for eight years a copywriter, which is virtually the opposite of being a press officer!

Two responsibilities of the press officer

The press officer has two primary responsibilities — first to initiate media coverage, and second to supply information on demand by the media. To do this a two-way relationship has to be created so that the press officer is welcomed, accepted and respected, and the media come to him or her and find them helpful, sympathetic and efficient. It is the press officer's responsibility to supply communication media with material which will help them to produce publications and programmes of interest and value to readers, listeners or viewers. In so doing he or she will achieve maximum coverage and so satisfy employer or client. This is very different from issuing stories which management wants to have published irrespective of whether they are publishable. Let us return to the two responsibilities of the press officer.

To initiate media coverage

This is really a marketing proposition if we take the late David Malbert's definition that *marketing is producing and selling at a profit, goods that satisfy customers*. That can be adapted in a press relations sense to mean writing and publishing news stories that satisfy editors and readers and profit us by being published.

To initiate media coverage the press officer must first have a good story and then know where it can be published. Any story is not sent to every possible publication in the vague hope that it may get published. Rather, the fewest necessary publishable stories are sent to only those publications most likely to print them. This means that the newsworthiness of a story has to be evaluated, and also the most appropriate media have to be selected.

First, good lines of communication are required in order to encourage a flow of news from people in the organization. This is not easy because other people may not recognize the newsworthiness of their work, or they may think that things which are of great interest to them are of equal interest to others. But if these lines of communication are well established, the press officer has access to people who do have news-worthy information. Thus the press officer cannot work in isolation but has to know what is going on and where news can be found.

Looking in the other direction, the press officer has to study and know the media which are appropriate to the organization so that opportunities can be spotted for media coverage. The publications, journalists, features, columns or programme personnel on which efforts should be concentrated will thus be known to the press officer.

This will also entail understanding production requirements so that the supply of public relations material can be timed to arrive when it can be used. This may mean that there is no point in irritating an editor by sending him a good story which is hours, days, weeks or months too late. That publisher should have been omitted from the mailing list. This is another exercise in marketing! The press officer will not profit from failing to satisfy the customer.

To supply information on demand by the media

The press officer should make it known that he or she is the source of information about the organization, products or services, and this can be done in the following ways:

1   When newly appointed (either in-house or consultancy) appropriate editors and journalists should be notified that he or she is available as a source of information on the subject. In some cases it can be suggested that when articles are being written about the subject he or she − or a technical expert − will be willing to check them for accuracy.
2   An entry can be placed in the News Contact Directory in *UK Press Gazette*.[1]
3   An entry can be placed in the *Hollis Press and Public Relations Annual*[2] which will also give editors direct online database service.
4   If working for a consultancy it is common for a consultancy to operate named information bureaux for their clients which, again, are usually listed in the publications mentioned above. Thus, the Summer Orange Office, Le Bureau du Cognac Courvoisier, the British Bacon Bureau, the British Sausage Bureau, and the Pasta Information Office are operated by consultants.

Organizations which are constantly in the news will receive numerous press enquiries, usually by telephone. The press officer should make sure that he or she has a good library of up-to-date information and photographs so there can be a quick, accurate and reliable response. If the answer to an enquiry is not known, he or she should promise to find out and phone back without delay. Servicing the media is a major part of the job, and one which can create good or bad relations with journalists. If the press officer is obliging, this can produce future enquiries, and there are times when only that organization is approached and reported because the service is respected and sought. It is interesting to notice in the press and on radio and TV that when a certain subject is in the news it is usually the same organizations whose spokespeople are quoted. Obviously, a good rapport has been achieved between the media and these sources of information: very nice if the media do your job for you.

The press officer is also subject to certain advantages and disadvantages.

Advantages enjoyed

1 The press officer possesses or has access to information of interest and value to readers which is unknown to journalists.
2 He or she has the time to check the facts before supplying them to the media. The result of this is that the information can be trusted. This is important because the media work at great speed and, with so little time to check information, errors often appear in the editorial columns. When Ray Milland the film actor died, three national newspapers reported his age as being 51, 79 and 81! So public relations material can often be more accurate than the average press report. This is not always appreciated by readers, but newspapers rely on agency reports which they have no means of checking.
3 If he or she is a member of the IPR the press officer has a duty to be accurate for the Code of Professional Conduct requires that false or misleading information is not disseminated. This clause means that not only should he or she refrain from issuing deliberately false information but it should not inadvertently be issued. If the press officer is known to be a member of the IPR this should encourage the media to respect his or her integrity.
4 He or she is often in a position to help journalists to interview important people in the organization, and may be able to encourage or advise an organizational leader to give an interview when this person might otherwise be reluctant to do so.

Disadvantages encountered

1 The press officer may be the victim of demands from seniors to issue stories which are either lacking in news value, or poor in quality and presentation. In some organizations, a number of people have to approve a story before it is released, often resulting in an unpublishable version which may also have missed the deadlines. Editors will blame the press officer for poor stories which bear his or her name.
2 The press officer may not have the status to assert his or her professional authority.

3 The media may distrust him or her as a biased communicator.
4 The press officer may be regarded as a buffer between the media and management.

Keeping abreast of developments

Finally, the press officer has to understand the changes which are taking place in the media, and to adapt techniques accordingly. The increase in the use of new newspaper printing processes such as web-offset-litho and flexography, the use of direct input and computerization, and the greater use of colour photography, plus shorter lead times between editing and printing, all mean that he or she must be alert to the new demands of high technology.

Already in the USA camera-ready copy news releases are being supplied to the press by wire services. Online direct transmission of public relations stories to editorial computer terminals is arriving. In Britain, Two-Ten Communications has been supplying instant news via the PA Computer for some years. The day of the paper news release distributed by post, or even by hand, may well become archaic. These developments will mean that there will be no place for the typical unpublishable news release: in future news releases will have to resemble what is printed in the news columns. This could have a devastating effect on management approved releases! It could make demands on public relations professionalism such as we have never seen before, and it will be a very good thing. However, one reason why the paper news release may survive for some time is that not all publishers own their printers, and computerization may not be universally applied.

But one should be wary of the use of faxed news releases as these could be resented by editors who do not want their fax machines to be usurped by senders of unsolicited releases of no or very little editorial value. Faxed stories should either be acceptable because of their genuine urgency − e.g. a crisis or product recall story − or because the information has been requested or promised.

Trade unions

Mrs Thatcher did not destroy the trade unions during her period of government; they remain an important aspect of industrial relations, even though their membership numbers have been depleted by automation, robotics, slimmed down companies, the recession and unemployment. Several million British workers still belong to unions, and they are involved in communications regarding many topics.

The economic effects, and those of legislation requiring, say, secret ballots, have resulted in unions adopting more sophisticated communication techniques. Some unions have appointed press officers for the first time. Better use of opportunities to appear on television have been adopted, often arranged by wide-awake press officers. Sometimes the union cases are presented more efficiently than management's. Internally, many unions have forsaken their dull house journals in favour of ones resembling popular newspapers.

Within industry, senior officials and shop stewards are often engaged in management—employee communications, such as explaining new policies and techniques to their members. There are also (as with Japanese companies operating in Britain) single union companies with strike-free agreements. Trade unions are thus involved in more of a dialogue and less of a confrontation with employers.

Legislation has obliged unions to adopt communication methods, such as computerized membership lists in order to conduct democratic leadership elections, or to ballot members regarding industrial action. Such efficient membership lists did not exist in the past.

In time of recession the unions have been essential in the management of sensitive issues such as closures, amalgamations and redundancies, where strike action may be resorted to. They are also to be consulted concerning relocations to new sites.

There may be circumstances when a well-informed company press officer needs to inform industrial correspondents of the media as quickly, candidly and factually as the union press officer.

References

1 *UK Press Gazette*, weekly, London
2 *Hollis Press and Public Relations Annual*, Sunbury-on-Thames

12

Writing news releases

In Britain it is common to speak of editors filling their large plastic dustbins with 70–80 per cent of the releases they receive. In the USA the percentage is higher according to *IABC News*,[1] which carried the following report:

> **Editors toss 9 of 10 releases**
> Nine out of ten news releases sent to US daily newspapers from business, industry and organizations never see print, according to a recent study by journalist Professor Bill Baxter at the University of Oklahoma.
>
> Managing editors surveyed at 123 daily newspapers reported using only 9.2 per cent of all news releases received from public relations sources.
>
> Chief reason for rejection was lack of local or regional tie-in. Other reasons for non-use was too much advertising puffery, releases were too long and cumbersome, and, in many cases, they arrived too late to be useful.
>
> 'Too many PR people don't know the difference between news and advertising,' said one editor. 'It looks like the copy was written to impress bosses and not necessarily for print.'
>
> 'PR people should target their material more selectively and try to write more for individual papers,' said another respondent.

The third paragraph here describes some of the most common faults. Regrettably, this is true on a world scale. As long ago as 1906 the American public relations consultant Ivy Ledbetter Lee established the criteria that public relations material should be *of interest and value* to the reader, but sadly the public relations world has often ignored these principles the world over.

There is a wilful, obstinate belief by too many people in the public relations world that nothing has to be learned about writing news releases. This is intensified by the fact that managing directors, marketing and advertising managers, advertising agents and other press relations amateurs think that not only can *they* write (or re-write) news releases, but that they have the right to be published. The result is not only the adversarial situation between the media and public relations, but a senseless waste of time and money.

Writing news releases is easy

There is nothing difficult about writing news releases, except that it is different from any other kind of writing. The easiest way to learn how to write a news release is to read the news columns of a newspaper. There is one common style which anyone can copy. In fact, if this style is copied a story could be publishable as it stands. But to judge by the average news release its writer has never read a newspaper in his or her life.

To prove this point the reader is invited to pick up any newspaper and analyse its news columns — *not* its feature articles — and see whether they come to at least two perhaps surprising conclusions. Later in this chapter the way to write a publishable news release will be discussed in detail.

What is news?

William Randolph Hearst, one-time American newspaper tycoon, once defined news as being *what someone, somewhere doesn't want you to print — all the rest is advertising*. The press of the world seems to have adopted that advice wholeheartedly in its attitude to public relations material.

Journalists take a coy attitude to naming names. When the news is bad it is 'good news' and names will be named, but when the news is good this is regarded as advertising. The make of car involved in an accident is always named, for example. Journalists make little distinction between business or other public relations news and advertising. This, of course, is not helped by news release writers who do not understand the difference either!

On one occasion the author attempted to discuss this problem with the editor of the *Daily Mirror* in which a picture story had appeared without naming the company involved. The editor replied with a long sarcastic letter asking why they should not have named the makers of every item in the picture down to the boots worn by the man who was carrying out some special work on Buckingham Palace. Well, they did mention Buckingham Palace. Being a left-wing newspaper it was surprising that the *Daily Mirror* did not describe the Palace as being 'the home of a well-known monarch'. As the late Hannen Swaffer, one-time columnist on the *People* Sunday newspaper, said 'Freedom of the press in Britain is freedom to print such of the proprietor's prejudices as the advertisers don't object to'.

So, news depends a lot on the bias of the editor or of the particular publication, yet if the news release writer is to be successful he or she needs to supply original information of interest and value to the readers of the journals to which it is sent. News does not necessarily have to be 'new' if it has not previously been made known, but it must not be stale news in the sense that it is obviously dated. News may be defined as information the reader has not read before.

One also has to be careful about stating that something happened 'recently' for how recent is recent? This depends on how often a publication is published. A monthly magazine may print a story about an event which happened after the previous issue was published, but a daily will not print a story about something which happened the day before yesterday, unless it came from a remote destination from which news travels slowly. A weekly local newspaper printed on Thursday and sold on Friday is usually unable to report Thursday night's events, and will not hold such news for the following week's issue. Even so, if the item is sufficiently important, special efforts may be made as when Prince Charles opened a new police station in Croydon on a Thursday. Pictures did appear in the next day's issue of the weekly *Croydon Advertiser*, but this was a very rare exception which called for some very tight production scheduling.

Credibility

A quality which distinguishes public relations news material as being publishable in the eyes of editors is its credibility. We may have said some harsh things about journalists, but the right perspective is necessary. They are not white knights bringing their great reading public the unvarnished truth. They are making a living or a profit by giving people what they want to read. In Britain, what most people want to read will be found in the *Sun* and the *News of the World*, in Germany in *Bild*, in Nigeria in *The Punch*, and it was ever thus since the crowds cheered in the Coliseum and probably long before. The majority of people do not want to read newspapers like *The Times*. The news release writer needs to understand that on the whole few people want to read what he or she writes unless ....

Exactly. How does one compete with the murder and violence, the sex and corruption, and the other norms which make up the average person's reading taste? How do commercial firms succeed in getting into the dramatic columns of the *Sun* and the *Daily Mirror*? Or in any other publication? We have already said that releases must be of *interest* and *value* to the reader, but they must also be *credible*. Unless people are likely to believe in the story it will not get published.

Nowadays, people are sceptical about advertising, and they will be sceptical of any story which smacks of either advertising or one-sidedness. If an editor suspects that a story is a cover-up or an attempt to put the best side on things, he may well expose this effort to hoodwink the media and the public. Unfortunately, there are many releases which are blatant attempts to pretend things are what they are not. Whatever the biases of the various media or journalists, a news release must be impartial and factual if it is to be credible.

To be acceptable a news release has to be like a piece of plain wood which others can cut, shape, polish, paint or use as they wish. The cutting, shaping, polishing, painting or special use must not be pre-empted by the sender. Bare facts, without comment or self-praise, have credibility. Many rejected releases are simply unbelievable. On the other hand, the ideal is to supply a news release which is publishable as it stands because the journalist would have written it the same way given the same facts.

Local government PROs have a running battle with the media. The media believe that town hall news is little more than propaganda, while the elected representatives and local government officers believe that they are either misrepresented or inadequately covered by the media. In some cases, local authorities publish their own civic newspapers in order to get a fair and adequate press.

Language and vocabulary

It does not matter what sort of story it is — whether it is destined for the *Sun* or the *Financial Times*, *Heating and Ventilating Review* or *The Lancet* — short words, short sentences and short paragraphs are preferable. If there are unavoidable long technical words, fair enough.

Short words mean that more can be said in the space. Short words will not be broken in narrow columns. Short sentences, provided the effect is not too abrupt, and short paragraphs with their indentations, help to speed the flow of reading and the ease of understanding. Tortuous language and two-page paragraphs may have suited the leisured matrons who read Henry James, but Ernest Hemingway changed all that.

Some examples of short words which are preferable to long ones are the following:

live	*for*	reside	try	*for*	endeavour
death	*for*	mortality	climb	*for*	ascend
food	*for*	sustenance	poor	*for*	impecunious
job	*for*	employment	tiny	*for*	infinitesimal

This is not to say that to avoid the monotony of repeated use a different and perhaps longer word should not be used, but the news release does have a space problem. Longer words are better for articles and books which benefit from a rich vocabulary, a more literary style, and more reading time. Short words, sentences and paragraphs not only help the story to fit space that is scarce, but result in less sub-editing, less rewriting and less opportunity for editorial staff to get things wrong. It is very hard to alter a sentence which is so tight and precise that there is no better way of writing it.

Space *is* limited. A newspaper may have forty-eight pages, but a particular news release may be appropriate to only one section, page or even column. However good it is, it has to compete with other stories to be included. That is why, as we shall see, the opening paragraph is all important. It may be all that the editor can spare space to print.

The late Dr Rudolf Flesch, in his admirable work *The Art of Readable Writing*,[2] set the following criteria: 'Use short words − 150 syllables per 100 words; short sentences − no more than nineteen words per sentence. Human interest should be at the rate of 6 per cent names, personal pronouns or words referring to people or having masculine or feminine gender.'

Clichés should be avoided and to add 'at all costs' or 'like the plague' would be use of a cliché. News releases seem to have their own clichés, of which 'unique' is the worst since few things are unique, and 'exhaustive research', 'ultra-modern', 'this point in time', 'facilitates', and 'breakthrough' are common examples. Probably the most hackneyed expression used by all kinds of communicators is 'a wide range', for which there are many substitutes such as 'a wide variety', 'a large range', 'a large variety' or 'a wide choice'.

Apt words should be selected. Repetition of words should be controlled. The news release writer should use *Roget's Thesaurus* or *The Synonym Finder* to increase and sharpen the vocabulary.

Americans are given to long words, and to words which are peculiarly American. One suspects the German influence on American English! American scholars have tried to stop American newspapers using words such as 'parenting', 'medication' and 'orientation'. To these might be added 'escalation' and 'harassment'. Then there are those double emphatic bits of nonsense such as 'completely destroyed', 'true facts', 'most unique', 'really unique', 'utterly false', and 'totally untrue'.

We also need to beware of generalizations, which may be acceptable in more emotive and less explicit advertisement copy. We should explain why a product is 'economical in use', 'handy', 'easy to make', 'compact', 'lightweight', 'money-saving', 'generous' or 'convenient'. The facts, the details, must be stated in such a way that the attributes are implied.

Similarly, vague expressions such as the longest, tallest, shortest, biggest, smallest, or cheapest should be implied by facts, not used as puffs or left open to challenge. One also has to be very careful about stating that anything is 'first' — are you sure about this claim? Editors dislike receiving contradictions and having to print disclaimers. They may add the derogatory words 'claimed to be . . .' .

Expressions such as 'renowned', 'brand leader', 'world famous', 'leading' and 'foremost' are puffs which should not be used.

Writing the release

Journalists tend to follow the news story rule of the Five Ws: who, what, when, where and why. That is, *who* is the story about, *what* happened, *when* did it happen, *where* did it happen, *why* did it happen, and sometimes adding a sixth, *what* were the consequences?

A news release differs from this slightly if only that it is seldom a personal story. For *who* it is best to substitute the subject. But the subject may not be the *who*, and the organization or the product will replace the individual. Moreover, the subject is more likely to be what the organization has done or the product so that *what* displaces the journalist's *who*. We shall return to this again because the subject of the story is so important.

Importance of the opening paragraph

The above quotations all emphasize the importance of the subject and the opening paragraph, the two features which can make or mar the success of a news release. This is not understood by those who write the majority of rejected releases.

Nothing has given the profession a worse name than the bad news release — not all the gin and junkets for which public relations is supposedly infamous.

Nothing is done so badly by so many practitioners. Ask any editor anywhere in the world.

Yet it is perfectly easy to write a publishable news release. It is also perfectly easy not to write, or not to issue, an unpublishable one. Remarkable though this may be, some PROs do not expect their work to be published. They expect someone in an editorial office to rewrite it for them. Why should they? To prove the point, the author has published hundreds of news releases, mostly exactly as he wrote them. Sometimes, of course, they have been adapted to meet the particular style of a publication but in essence the message was identical.

Some releases are not addressed to the reader, but to the editor. They begin with flowery expressions such as 'We are pleased to announce', while others are written like letters with salutations. Pronouns should be avoided: the editor is not going to use 'we' or 'you'.

I can only repeat that the easiest way to learn how to write news releases is to read newspapers. This is not to be pedantic; if newspaper reports are studied it will be seen that the advice given in this chapter is sound. If other people think differently, and want to destroy professionally written releases, they should be shown actual reports in the press.

It will be found that in every story in every paper two things characterize press reports. First, the *subject* is stated in the first few words. Second, the gist of the story is given in the *opening paragraph*. There are no teasers, no clever introductions. The whole story is 'blown' or given away right at the beginning. The rest of the report substantiates the story. It is as simple as that. In fact, if one read the opening paragraph of each report one would have a complete digest of the newspaper's news.

Yet it is rare to find the subject of a news release in the first three paragraphs, perhaps not even on the first page. The mistake is often made of starting with the company name which is rarely the subject of the story. Four things are likely to result from writing a release professionally:

1 An editor can see at a glance what the story is about for, as the news editor of the *Financial Times* once told the author, an editor has 'one second flat' to judge each release in his daily pile.
2 If there is little space, *at least* the opening paragraph may get printed. If it is a good summary you are home and dry.
3 If a longer story is printed it will be capable of being cut *from the bottom up* as can occur when a story is printed at length in an early edition when news may be scarce – and then cut in each succeeding edition until perhaps only the first paragraph remains in the final

edition. This can happen in evening newspapers, the first edition appearing early in the day, and the final edition appearing when people are going home from work.

4   If the story is written as the editor would have written it there is no point in him changing it. Editors are busy people. On some publications (e.g. trade magazines) they have no assistants to rewrite stories and may well print the ones that provide them with the least work. Why should they burrow through three pages of terrible prose to find the thirty or forty words they have space to print? A news release has to compete with hundreds of other releases, but the professionally written releases, *the rarities*, really have no competitors. Moreover, with direct input, and with sub-editors subbing on VDUs, releases need to be ready for keying.

It may not always be appreciated that editors are receiving material from many sources, of which public relations may be regarded as the least important and often a nuisance. Stories will be coming in from staff reporters, special correspondents, 'stringers' in the regions, and numerous news agencies.

The subject

A major fault with too many releases is that they start with the name of the organization, which is seldom the subject. Unfortunately, to the sender, the organization is often all-important. Some stories begin with a long-winded presentation of the name, e.g. 'The Universal Engineering Company Limited, a member of the International Engineering Group, . . .' . Who cares – apart from the managing director and the company secretary? Of those twelve words only *Universal Engineering* are publishable in an opening sentence. Most journalists will make these the *last* two words of the sentence. Thus, an acceptable sentence might be: 'A new electronically controlled crane for the construction industry is now available from Universal Engineering of Luton.'

What is the subject? It could be different for different classes and categories of journal. It pays to write special versions of stories, not send the same story to every editor, and this will call for careful decisions about the appropriate subject for the opening paragraph. To take the example of the crane, subjects could range from its electronic interest to the fact that it was British, from its local manufacture to its use on an important construction job.

From many of these remarks it will be apparent by now that while it is not difficult to write a good release, the skilled writer will, in the words of Lord Geddes, 'squeeze the orange until the pips squeak'. Maximizing press coverage means marketing a story so that the fullest possible coverage is won. We shall return to this when discussing mailing lists.

Seven-point news release model

The discussion so far leads logically to the adoption of the seven-point model which the author created[3] to provide (a) a checklist when researching story material, (b) a plot for the release, and (c) a means of checking that nothing vital has been omitted.

The SOLAADS seven-point model

1 **Subject** — what is the story about?
2 **Organization** — what is the name of the organization?
3 **Location** — what is the location of the organization?
4 **Advantages** — what is new, special, beneficial about the product or service?
5 **Applications** — how or by whom can the product or service be used or enjoyed?
6 **Details** — what are the specifications or details of colours, prices, sizes and so on.
7 **Source** — if this is different from location, e.g. an airline will fly from an airport but the office may be in the city centre.

This is not a plan for seven paragraphs. The subject, organization and location will fall into the first paragraph together with highlights of the story. Thus we have an opening paragraph which summarizes the entire story and can stand alone if necessary. The story is substantiated by paragraphs which concentrate on certain types of information. Finally, it is a good idea to close with words such as: 'The Rondo lawn-mower is made and marketed by the XYZ Company Ltd, Richmond Road, Ilkley, Yorkshire.'

Different kinds of release

So far we have concentrated on the publishable release since the most typical release is the one we want to get printed. There are, however, other types of release, not all of which are intended for immediate publication. The six kinds of news release are:

1 *The publishable*, as already described.
2 *The background story* which is not intended for immediate publication, but is issued as background information so that journalists are kept well informed and have the facts on file when they are writing about the subject. This kind of release can be especially useful for a long-term project such as a civil engineering job or the development of a new source of energy. Organizations which are constantly in the news such as utilities, oil companies, airlines and new technology developers will issue regular background stories. Some firms consider it helpful to distinguish between news for immediate publication and background material by having separate release headings printed with the distinctive words NEWS FROM . . . and INFORMATION FROM . . . followed by the company name and perhaps its logo.
3 *The technical story with summary.* Ideally, a release should be confined to one sheet of paper, but some subjects warrant longer and very technical accounts. In such cases it is helpful to the editor if the main story is preceded by a brief summary. To identify the summary it can have wider margins or be boxed.
4 *The summary of a report, speech or document.* The objective here is to bring out the important or new features of something lengthy which is being sent to the media. Journalists may not have time to read the whole speech, document or volume, and even if they did they may not know how to make comparisons or evaluations. The accompanying release can pull out the newsworthy and most relevant stories.

   This may guide the journalist to read for him or herself what is most interesting; it may provoke questions; it may attract the journalist's interest when otherwise the material would have been ignored; and some busy journalists may take your word for it and print the summary.

   In the case of an advance copy of a speech, the opening paragraph technique already discussed is applicable. The summary might begin: 'The smoking of cannabis in public cinemas is opposed by the Conservative Party, Lord Wrigglebury told the Mapleton Conservative Party on Monday, January 10.' Once again we are home and dry with an opening paragraph which is a self-sufficient message. But the statement may well occur on page 10 of the speech, whereas the summary can put it in the first paragraph of a report.
5 *The extended picture caption.* When the picture is the real news item, a longer-than-usual explanatory caption can replace the news release. There are three ways of doing this. The caption may be attached to

the back of the print with Sellotape; a double perforated caption can be attached to the print, so that one copy can be used for editorial purposes and the other left to identify the picture; or the caption can be repeated on release paper, and this can accompany the captioned photograph.

6 *The brief announcement.* There is sometimes a mistaken idea that the submission of a press story is an opportunity to tell the editor as much as possible. Some releases read like confessions. On some occasions − if the sender has studied the media − they should not exceed one sentence or possibly a paragraph. This brevity will make them publishable and unalterable. One example is the change of address: some publications run a change of address column in which the essential facts are stated and no more.

Another example is the 'new appointment' story. Most publications say no more than that Mr X has left one company to join another, the job he is taking up, and maybe his age, or it may be a promotion within the same organization. Usually, many such items are published in the same 'New Appointments' feature. There may or may not be a portrait or portraits. Only a very few newspapers, e.g. *The Times* and the *Financial Times*, regularly print appointment stories; trade, technical and professional journals print very brief accounts, e.g. the cryptic items in *Campaign*, although somewhat longer stories may appear in some journals. Only the local newspaper will perhaps print a short biography if the person is sufficiently important or interesting. Yet, day after day, editors of countless newspapers receive three-page life stories, complete with large salon portraits, about hundreds of people who have been appointed or promoted.

This is a favourite area of public relations activity. Hours of research and interviewing can be spent to produce an approved biography, and money can be spent on special photography when in fact no more than a sentence or paragraph, and probably no picture, is required. Moreover, the expectations of the person involved can be built up out of all proportion to the coverage which is easily assessable at the start. A couple of lines here and there is all that can be expected. It is a case of studying the media and of marketing the story.

Example of an actual release

Here is an example of a release written by the author and issued by the Croydon Chamber of Commerce. With different headline and minor changes it was printed in four newspapers and one magazine. It is repeated from the first edition of this book because it is such a practical demonstration of what has been said in this chapter. It is purely factual, makes no comment and uses no advertising language. The headline is merely a working title because editors write their own headlines to suit their style, be different from others who may carry the same story and to fit the space. Also reproduced are three of the actual reports as printed. The word 'art' is added in one, while another has been shortened. Substantially, the message as written has been reproduced.

Public Relations Seminar

Press and Public Relations is the theme of a one-day course to be run by the Croydon Chamber of Commerce & Industry at Commerce House, Scarbrook Road on Monday December 9. The lecturer will be Frank Jefkins.

The course will cover planning PR programmes, PR departments and consultancies, mass and private media, photography, organizing PR events, and how to write, present and publish news releases and articles.

The course has already been run twice this year for the Birmingham Chamber of Commerce and Industry, and a return visit is planned for 1986.

Frank Jefkins of Ballards Way set up his mobile School of Public Relations in 1968 and has run courses in the UK and 22 overseas countries. He has 14 books in print. He is a Fellow of the Institute of Public Relations, serves on their Council and Board of Management and is Chairman of the IPR International Committee.

The course fee is £70 plus VAT (10% discount to Members) and details are available from Miss P. Culling, Croydon Chamber of Commerce & Industry, Commerce House, 21 Scarbrook Road, Croydon CR9 6HY, Telephone: 01–680 2165.

Chamber to run course

Press and public relations is the theme of a one-day course to be run by Croydon Chamber of Commerce and Industry at Commerce House, Scarbrook Road, on Monday, December 9.

The lecturer will be Frank Jefkins.

The course will cover planning PR programmes, PR departments and consultancies, mass and private media, photography, organizing PR events, and how to write, present and publish news releases and articles.

The course has already been run twice this year for Birmingham Chamber of Commerce and Industry, and a return visit is planned for 1986.

Frank Jefkins of Ballards Way set up his mobile school of public relations in 1968 and has run courses in the UK and in 22 overseas countries. He has 14 books in print.

The course fee is £70 plus VAT (ten per cent discount to members). Details are available from Miss P Culling, Croydon Chamber of Commerce and Industry, Commerce House, 21 Scarbrook Road, Croydon, CR9 6HY, Telephone: 01−680 2165.

Source: *The Advertiser*, Friday November 29, 1985

PR course

Press and Public relations is the theme of the one day course to be run by the Croydon Chamber of Commerce & Industry on Monday December 9.

The course will cover planning PR programmes, PR departments and consultancies and include how to write, present and publish news releases and articles.

The course fee is £70 plus VAT and details are available from Miss P. Culling, CCCI, Commerce House, 21, Scarbrook Road, Croydon, telephone 680 2165.

Source: *The News*, December 5, 1985

Day's course on art of public relations

The art of Press and public relations is the theme of a one-day course to be run by Croydon Chamber of Commerce and Industry at Commerce House, Scarbrook Road, on Monday, December 9.

The course will cover planning public relations programmes, public relations departments and consultancies, mass and private media, photography, organizing public relations events, and how to write, present and publish news releases and articles.

The lecturer will be Frank Jefkins, of Ballards Way, Croydon, who set up a School of Public Relations in 1968 and has run courses in Britain and 22 overseas countries.

Mr Jefkins, the author of 14 books, serves on the council of the Institute of Public Relations and board of management and is chairman of the institute's international committee.

The fee for the course is £70 plus VAT. Details are available from the Chamber of Commerce on 680 2165.

Source: *Croydon Post*, Wednesday, November 27, 1985

Mailing lists

The finest news release is useless if it is sent to the wrong media, or if it is sent to the right media at the wrong time. This is another area of criticism: too many public relations practitioners are either careless or ignorant about media. It is necessary to know your media − what they print, who their readers are, how they are printed, how often they are published, when they are printed and their latest date for copy. This means for each story a new mailing list has to be compiled, otherwise editors will be annoyed because they have been sent stories which are irrelevant or ill-timed.

The public relations practitioner can become professional at mailing list compilation if he uses the many resources available to him. *Benn's Media Directory* and *PR Planner* provide much of what he needs to know, while news release mailing organizations such as PIMS and Two-Ten Communications provide information and services which are updated regularly.

An experienced PRO, who has a thorough understanding of the media relevant to the story, should be able to dictate a mailing list.

One of the biggest faults with mailings is that too many releases are sent to too many publications. The rate of success should be considered. If one release is sent to one editor because only one editor is likely to print it, and he does, that is a success rate of 100 per cent. But if 100 releases are mailed and the story appears only once, that is a success rate of 1 per cent and a failure rate of 99 per cent! The point is that standard mailing lists, to which new titles are constantly added and defunct ones are never removed, are unprofessional. Each story requires its own carefully selected list so that the hit rate is maximized.

In compiling mailing lists it is necessary to restrict titles to those publications which:

1 *Are likely to print the story.* If publications are studied it will be found that some newspapers or magazines regularly, irregularly or never carry your type of story or any kind of public relations story. What is the editor of *Exchange and Mart* supposed to do with a news release? Therefore it is a waste of time and money sending releases where they are unwanted and unwelcome − yet it is not unusual for releases to be sent to 'all nationals' or 'all women's magazines' or all 'local weeklies'. Editors expect PROs to know what kinds of story they print. The *PR Planner* and *Editors* are useful guides to editorial requirements.

2 *Have time to print the story.* It is pointless sending a release to a publication which has been made up or printed already. Mailings, have to be timed correctly, and sometimes staggered. What is the lead time between editing and printing? In the case of a daily it could be hours, but a weekly will need the story four to seven days in advance and a monthly two to three weeks or even two to three months.

These two factors are vital, and with such understanding of editorial and publishing requirements it will be sensible to *eliminate* from the list those titles which are useless if immediate publication is desired. Some stories may be timeless, but few publications will carry forward a dated story.

The addresses of the above mentioned services and publications will be found in the Appendices.

News agencies

Several kinds of news agencies exist. The Press Association supplies the UK press with home news, and newspapers subscribe to this service. News releases sent to the PA should not exceed 100 words. Reuters supply and distribute international news. Two-Ten Communications (formerly Universal News Services) supply public relations news stories for their subscribers using the computerized services of their parent company, the PA. These are 'wire' services. There are also news agencies which specialize in the reporting of news and the supplying of features to the press. Reuters receive news from overseas, and transmit news overseas, using satellite services.

References

1   *IABC News*, San Francisco, September 1986
2   Flesch, Rudolf, *The Art of Readable Writing*, Harper Bros, New York, 1949
3   Jefkins, Frank, *Planned Press and Public Relations*, 3rd edn, Blackie, Glasgow, 1993

13

Writing feature articles

Exclusive signed feature articles

An article is not a long news release, but an entirely different literary form with its own special characteristics, uses and values. Here, we are concerned with the article written exclusively for one publication. It cannot be reproduced elsewhere without permission. One can, of course, rewrite the article, presenting the same basic information differently and with fresh examples to suit other journals but each paraphrased article will be an exclusive. When the same article is supplied to more than one publication this is called a syndicated article (syndication will be discussed separately). Sometimes permission may be obtained from an editor to publish an article elsewhere, such as in a foreign journal.

Whereas a news release is given broadcast distribution, could be printed at any time, may not be printed at all, and could be cut or rewritten, the article will be written for a particular issue of one journal and, if well produced, is unlikely to be seriously edited.

An article occupies a substantial area of space and is usually indexed. It can have permanent value in at least three ways: magazines especially are often retained in binders or libraries; articles are often kept as part of the literature on the subject; reprints can be made for future use as direct mail shots, enclosures with correspondence, or as give-away material in showrooms or on exhibition stands. An article can have a long working life, and the initial cost may be well recouped.

It can be authoritative, especially if the author is an authority on the subject, and it can be very informative and well-illustrated. Colour pictures may be possible, when they are seldom likely to be printed with news releases.

But an article will be more costly to produce than a news release because time has to be spent on obtaining permission to write about the subject if others are involved, negotiating publication with editors, researching the material (which may involve a journey), writing the article and checking the draft with those who have supplied information. This cost — it may be three day's work in all — has to be set against the cost-effectiveness of its long-term influence, and not against the achievement of only one press cutting.

When producing the budget the public relations manager or consultant should be careful to calculate this time element if feature articles are to be included in the year's programme. How many articles are to be produced, and what demand for articles should be anticipated?

Note that articles may be initiated by offering them to editors, or by suggesting them at press receptions, or editors may invite articles. There are also other ways of getting public relations articles published, as we shall see.

Two first considerations

First of all there must be an *idea, theme or subject*, not just a bare description of something. It could be how someone used a bank loan to make a fortune, how a new invention overcame a problem, why a new holiday resort is different from any other, how a dangerous task was made safe or how a new bridge has changed traffic patterns. It is this *idea* which is going to convince an editor that the article should be written and published. The chances are the practitioner is the only person who knows the idea *exists*.

Second, it must be possible to have *access* to the information which usually means getting permission from owners, contractors, customers or whoever may be involved. Several organizations and individuals may have to be approached. It must not be assumed that everyone will agree with the article being written, and only those with full responsibility for giving approval must be approached. It is both courteous and helpful to make initial approaches through the PROs of the various organizations, who can then assist the writer.

Negotiating with editors

Once the idea and the permissions are settled, the next step is to negotiate with the editor of the selected publication. The article should not be written speculatively and sent to an editor because (*a*) we do not know whether he or she will print it (*b*) we do not know what he or she wants, and (*c*) we do not know how many words he or she wants. The article must be written as instructed by the editor. By 'instructed' is meant whether the tone is light-hearted or serious, human interest or not, highly technical or non-technical, and so on. Even a serious subject can be lightened with anecdotes. One editor said to the author, 'you want to write about *rats* in *my* journal?' and he got an article full of amusing anecdotes which surprised him.

Moreover, there is also the question of *who* will write the article, for public relations articles can be written by the following people:

1 *The editor or a staff writer*. Large circulation publications may not accept articles from outsiders, and will prefer to be provided with the idea and with facilities for visits and interviews. They have their own staff writers. The initiator of the idea will then make the necessary arrangements, probably accompanying the staff writer and perhaps arranging for photography. This has advantages and disadvantages. The article will have the independent authority of the by-lined staff writer, but control may be lost over *what* is written and *how* the article is written. It can look better and less biased if the publisher has produced the article himself, but the piece can be inaccurate or biased by the writer's point of view.

2 *A contributor*. The article could be written by a contributor as when a professional writer supplies a regular feature to a journal. A lot of gardening writers do this. The PRO may be able to provide an idea and facilities to such a contributor.

3 *The PRO*. In this case the article could be written by the in-house PRO or by a consultant; or a freelance writer could be engaged; or a personality within the organization could be the author. A fourth possibility is that the PRO, consultant or a freelance writer could 'ghost write' the article for a VIP such as the managing director. This is rather like the biographies of famous people being written for them by professional 'ghost writers'.

There are therefore many ways in which public relations articles can be produced, and if they are fully exploited much valuable media coverage can be obtained, often of a volume, quality and authority far more significant than is possible with news releases. But it does take time, and has to be worked at professionally.

How to propose a public relations article

There is a false notion that in order to get a public relations article published it is necessary to take an editor out to lunch. This is not so if you have a practical proposition. The PRO has the advantage that the editor has neither the idea nor access to it until the proposal is put to him. Assuming that the PRO is responsible for producing the article the proposition can be presented on the telephone or in a letter. The author has published hundreds of articles in this way. He has not been known to the editor, and he has not known the editor, nor has he ever met the editor, a situation which can happen if, over a period of years, the PRO is dealing with scores of subjects. For one company he produced fifty articles a year for five years, using the technique set out below.

The *proposition* should present the idea, state that permission has been obtained to cover the subject and conduct the necessary research, and say that if the editor likes the idea will he please state:

1 The number of words required.
2 Any special treatment required, such as human interest, technical, non-technical.
3 If illustrations are required, what kind and what number, and whether black and white or colour.
4 The date of the issue in which the article will appear.
5 The copy date or deadline for delivery of the article.

If the article is accepted the PRO is commissioned to write it, and it must be supplied on the agreed date. There will be no fee for the article, and in any case it would be unethical for the PRO to be paid twice, once by employer or client and again by the publisher. It is wise to promise the editor that commercial references will be kept to a minimum, but the editor will probably safeguard him- or herself by agreeing to publish 'subject to sight of the copy'. It is up to the writer to supply a publishable article. This means that, as with a news release, the information must be factual and contain no puffery. It has to be a legitimate feature article which merits publication, and not be an advertisement.

How to write feature articles

Bad articles result from having too little to write about. A well-researched, readable article results from having to select from a wealth of information. If one is selective there will be no vague waffle, and every word will count.

The following model is a useful plot and discipline.

Seven-point model for feature articles

1   Opening paragraph.
2   The problem or previous situation.
3   The search for a solution or improvement.
4   The solution or improvement.
5   The results achieved.
6   Closing paragraph.
7   Check draft with sources of information.

This model is useful for writing a case-study article which enhances the current situation or experience by contrasting it with an inferior situation or experience in the past. For example, a journey once took days or weeks by ship, but now takes only a matter of hours by plane. Or production was inefficient and costly by hand or with old-fashioned machinery but is now faultless and economic by robotics. This *before* and *after* treatment gives a dramatic quality to an article. Points 2, 3, 4 and 5 become the ones requiring research. Then the article needs an opening paragraph to capture the reader's interest and attention, and a final paragraph to bring about a satisfying close to the account.

The topping and tailing of the article can be done after the heart of the article has been composed, and ideas for these paragraphs may spring from the central material. One should not 'write one's way in', and – unlike the news release – with an article the opening paragraph should *not* 'give the game away', but should lead the reader into the body of the article by means of an irresistible statement, question or perhaps an intriguing quotation.

The draft should then be submitted to *all* those who gave information or have the authority to approve its publication. This can be both a courtesy and an insurance. One owes it to all concerned, including the editor, that the facts are correct. It may be wise to draw attention to statements, figures and spellings which should be checked. And since a publication date is involved, there must be a deadline for the return of the approved or amended draft. If there is any risk of delay – readers of the draft will be busy people and they could be absent on business or holidays – it is a sensible precaution to state quite emphatically that the draft will be assumed to be correct unless returned by a certain date. This date should be early enough for the writer to supply the editor with a clean and correct final version. Even then, it pays to telephone if the draft has not been returned.

This checking with sources cannot be stressed enough. It is very easy, during an interview, for people to make statements 'off the top of their head' which are actually wrong. Such errors, which could be embarrassing all round, need to be detected before publication.

Other types of article

The seven-point model outline above is very useful when the previous situation was different and this can be used to enhance the present situation which has been brought about by the subject of the article. The contrast will imply the success of the replacement, improvement or whatever the topic may be. However, there are obviously occasions when this format does not apply.

If one is discussing new roses for the garden, recipes for Christmas fare, or the attractions of a holiday resort there will be more of a general flow of information. Another style might be to base the article on an interview with questions and answers. Yet another style, sometimes favoured by magazines when they serialize a non-fiction book, is to start with the current situation, and then flash back to the origins of the story, afterwards proceeding chronologically.

Another kind of article could be a paper presented at a conference by a company speaker, which could be edited to form an article with the speaker as named author. Such an article could interest the editor of a trade, technical or professional magazine, and should be negotiated in advance of the event.

Research

When producing an article it is necessary to research thoroughly and to collect as much information as possible. If visits or interviews are necessary, they will be of short duration — two or three hours at the most — and the scene may never be revisited. During that short visit everything must be collected, and it pays to come away with a hoard of information such as business cards, annual reports, house journals, catalogues and sales literature, photographs, photocopies of press cuttings and so on as well as one's notes taken during interviews. It will sound inefficient if one has to ring up for information not obtained during the visit, while the value of having so much background information is that the writer can be correct with names, spellings and other details.

Moreover, he or she will have such a wealth of material that they are obliged to be selective, and this will have the effect of forcing them to write concisely in order to cover most things. The result will be a tightly written piece packed with facts which will enjoy pace and be readable. The poor article is one that is padded out with generalities and long-winded parentheses because the writer had too little to write about. It is important to remember this advice if one writes only the occasional article. Fluency comes with practice.

Syndicated articles

Feature articles need not be exclusive, but can be *syndicated* − that is, supplied to and published in more than one publication − provided care is taken to see that they do not appear in rival journals. Articles should not be sent out in broadcast fashion like news releases. Unsolicited articles may be rejected, and control will be lost of offering them elsewhere.

The most practical procedure is to send a synopsis of the article to a selection of publications which do not have competing circulations (e.g. evening newspapers or free newspapers published at least fifty miles apart), and then, upon acceptance, to supply the article together with any requested illustrations.

Overseas distribution of articles is undertaken by EIBIS International Ltd, with translations as required, and with their long association with foreign editors they achieve excellent international coverage.

Syndicated articles are popular in the holiday and travel industry, often written by well-known travel writers, and they are usually aimed at the holiday features which appear in the regional press in January and February. The syndicated article usually succeeds best with products and services which are of interest to a large number of readers.

The services of Two-Ten Communications can be used for syndicated articles. Two-Ten will write the article, and supply the subject with a weekly basket of topics to 730 weekly newspapers, providing a computerized version of the complete article on request.

Writing style

This chapter began by emphasizing that an article is not a long news release. While it should follow the same rules of presentation as the news release and as set out in the next chapter, it is written quite differently. A principal difference is that the story is not 'blown' in the first paragraph which is essential to the writing of a news release. This reiterates what was said when describing the seven-point model earlier in this chapter, but it applies to any kind of article.

The writing style is also different for a feature article. Whereas the news release should be a disciplined factual account which can often be confined to a single sheet of paper, the author of an article can use a more imaginative style and a richer vocabulary, although he or she should avoid exuberant language, and not write an advertisement. He or she still has to be factual, but the information can be presented more attractively. For instance, he or she could make observations, use reminiscences or quote from interviews with people or from other acknowledged published work.

There may be a temptation to make frequent references to the company or the product or brand name, but care must be taken not to plug names. Names can be used when no other word would be suitable. Even so, it is often best to make very discreet commercial references, restricting them to the by-line, photo captions, or perhaps just one sentence.

Presentation

The article should be typewritten in a straightforward fashion, and be free of the tricks of word processors such as use of different pitch, bold type, words in capital letters, bigger type or underlining. All but opening paragraphs should be indented, and there should not be line spacing between paragraphs. In other words, it should be a manuscript, styled like a book, newspaper or magazine, and not resemble a business letter. The editor will use whatever style, including any form of emphasis, that he or she wishes.

Authorship

One of the advantages of the article over a news release is that it can carry the author's name. If the author is an authority on the subject, or it is ghosted in the name of someone important, this can give the article authenticity. But it would be silly to use an obviously commercial person as author if that tended to make the article look like an advertisement. However, there is no reason why the PRO's name should not appear as author, but best if his or her job title is not used.

In some cases – as with the travel articles already mentioned – it may pay to employ a well-known author to write the article.

14

Presentation of press material

How releases and articles should look

While this chapter concentrates on the presentation of a news release which should be typed as 'copy for the printer', most of these printing rules apply to any manuscript work whether it be a news release, feature article, photo caption, copy for the house journal or a whole book.

One of the first things a public relations practitioner has to do is teach his or her staff how to present press material. Most typists type news releases, feature articles and even book manuscripts as if they were typing a business letter. This is wrong, but common, making much press material look unprofessional.

Presentation of releases

A news release is a manuscript which provides copy for printing. A lot of releases ignore this requirement, simply because the practitioner has failed to instruct staff accordingly. *This is a management responsibility.* A secretary is trained to type letters with block paragraphs, courteously to give the managing director a capital 'M' and 'D', and to insert full points between initials such as 'I.P.R.'. None of these things apply to a news release. Again, in advertisement copy the company name may be written in all-caps, e.g. FORD, and numbers may be written 5, 7 or 9, but again this would be wrong in a news release.

A lot of news releases, especially if produced on word processors, look like advertisements because of unnecessary emphasis. A release should be typed as plainly as possible.

From these remarks it is easy to appreciate that if a release is typed wrongly the editor has to correct all these faults before he or she can send the story to the printer or input it into their computer. It is another way in which the release is unprofessional and helps to irritate the editor. Consequently, it is important that typists are properly instructed. They have to unlearn a good deal of normal secretarial practice. The following are essential considerations.

The news release heading

Flamboyant, multicoloured headings are not necessary. The heading should merely distinguish it from a business letter-heading, identify the sender (e.g. by means of a logo) and give the source details (preferably at the foot of the sheet). *The maximum amount of space should be given to the story.* One colour is sufficient, and this may be the corporate identity house colour. Do not contain the text area in a border or print anything in the left and right margins.

Typing style

Use a standard typeface – not all-caps or a fancy, imitation handwriting or italic face. Do not use an extra large face because this can spread a story over an extra page or pages. To comply with editorial and type-setting requirements all copy for print must be in double-spaced typing, with good margins on either side, and only one side of the paper may be used. No one is ever going to look at the back of the sheet.

The headline

The headline should simply declare what the story is about, e.g. New Soup From Heinz. Do not try to be clever and invent, say, *S'nice Soupier Snail Soup.* Editors write their own headlines to suit the space, to fit the page design, to be different, or in line with their house style.

Paragraphing

Normal publishing style is as in this book, with paragraphs indented. Most publishers do not, however, indent the first paragraph, either of a chapter, column or section a tradition dating back to handwritten bibles when the first letter (or drop capital) was drawn decoratively and very large. This is called 'book style'.

Subheadings or cross-heads

Do not insert them in a release (unless they help to clarify a long piece) because the editor will use subheadings or cross-heads as he wishes. This may be a typographical device to give a black and grey artistic contrast to the page.

Capital letters

The press use a minimum of capital letters. Not even the *Financial Times* gives managing directors and chairmen or other official or job titles capital letters. Normally, no word should be written completely in capital letters, even if the *Financial Times* chooses to print company names in caps in new appointment stories. (It also prints the person's name in black face.) Only certain top people are given initial caps, e.g. President, Queen, Pope, Prime Minister, Defence Secretary, Chief Whip, whereas job titles are not. One should also be careful about nouns which seem to be important. Some technical writers tend to capitalize nouns indiscriminately. Capital initial letters should therefore be restricted to proper nouns such as the names of individuals and organizations, registered names and geographical places.

Full points or full stops

The press do not use full points in abbreviations and print BT, EC, KLM, IPR, IBM, USA and so on, but retain full points in *i.e.* and *e.g.* A full point does not follow *Mr, Mrs, Rev, mph* and so forth.

Quotation marks

These should be restricted to quoted speech, not used for product names, ship's names, titles or anything else. The editor will have his own style — quotation marks, italics, bold face, caps and so on — which the news release writer cannot anticipate and must therefore adopt a neutral style.

Underlining

Nothing should be underlined as this is an instruction to set in *italics*, an instruction which only the editor can give.

Signs

Do not use the % sign in a sentence. Spell out 'per cent' or 'percent'. Do not use the ampersand (&) in sentences, nor the abbreviation 'etc.'.

Figures

Except in dates, times, prices, street numbers, weights and measures and similar special uses of numbers, spell out from one to nine, then use figures until they become unwieldy thousands or millions, when it is clearly better to say ten thousand, or 10 million. Thus, one writes: 'Two men spent five hours from 8 am to 1 pm considering whether 10 m tonnes of rice could reach the millions of refugees by August 30.' Never start a sentence with a figure — spell it out.

Dates

Most secretaries date letters the opposite way round to editorial style. In the press the month is given first, and 'th', 'rd', 'st' and 'nd' are not used. The correct style is December 1, *not* 1st December, although some newer newspapers do print 1 December, as do most book publishers.

Readers may be confused by the different dating styles used by some newspapers, and the following guidelines issued by Reuters to their staff are interesting regarding date lines:[1]

'The general style is to use the city, day and month thus: *London, 29 June — Reuters announced today . . .'*

'The RAM style includes the year thus: *Washington, D.C., May 4, 1992 — Reuters America announced . . .'* . Either style is acceptable if used consistently.

Continuations

If there are succeeding sheets, make this clear at the foot of the first page and at the top of the second page and so on if there are more than two pages. Write 'more' in the bottom right-hand corner of page one, and repeat the title at the top of the next page. Succeeding pages should be numbered.

Concluding the release

There is no point in writing 'ends' at the close of the story as this is obvious if the story is followed by the name of the writer, his telephone number and the date. Use of 'ends' is a hangover from the days of metal typesetting when copy was sent down to the foundry on a number of small pieces of paper, the last piece stating 'ends'. This is irrelevant on a news release.

Embargoes

Embargoes are not popular with editors, and should never be used unless there is a very obvious and justified reason which the editor can appreciate. Time differentials between countries, Stock Exchange rules, or the fact that a speech will not be delivered for some time are self-evident justifications. Ideally, an embargo should be a privilege, the editor being given advance information. Press embargoes are widely misunderstood: they should not be used to satisfy the convenience of the practitioner. If a story is not embargoed, there is no point in stating 'for immediate release'.

The question of embargoes has become so controversial that the Professional Practices Committee of the IPR has drawn up special recommendations which are published in a Guidance Paper *The Use, Misuse and Abuse of Embargoes*.[2] In this publication an embargo is defined as 'an accepted convention that the information to which it applies shall not be published in any form including broadcast before a specified time and date'.

A problem can occur if a story is embargoed for use by the media later in the day, but a breakfast television presenter wants to use it. This may have to be refused, otherwise its prior use might kill press coverage. On the other hand, it may pay to remove the embargo because breakfast television usage may heighten press interest later in the day. A delicate decision may have to be made.

An embargo can have an embarrassing effect, as occurred in November 1992 when Westminster City Council issued an embargoed news release which announced that a £42 m street cleaning contract had been approved. When the leader of the opposition Labour group arrived at the meeting waving a copy of the release he asked if there was any point in holding the meeting to debate approval of the contract. The excuse was made that had the contract not been approved the embargoed release could have been changed! Embargoes should not be abused like this.

Reuters[1] advise their own staff: 'Embargoes are fraught with difficulties. They are often broken. They pose regulatory problems for a publicly-traded company since they could lead to insider dealing. We should not use them.'

House style exceptions

Newspapers and magazines do have their own characteristics, and may not therefore adopt identical styles. Some magazines have an unjustified or 'free' right-hand edge; some business magazines do not indent paragraphs; *The Guardian* sometimes indents opening paragraphs, the *Sunday Telegraph* uses full points between initials (e.g. B.A.O.R.); various newspapers open stories in different ways – with drop capitals, bold face type, or all caps for the first word or two. These are 'house styles' over which the news release writer has no control, and he or she should not attempt to copy these individual styles. It is best, therefore, to adopt a printing and publishing style which is acceptable to the majority of editors. They can then introduce their own special styles as they wish.

Editorial and advertising styles

The rules stated above concern editorial material, and contrast with the styles adopted in advertising. The copywriter can break both printing and grammatical rules if it will be effective. The copywriter's English may seem appalling as, for instance, when use is made of a one word sentence or paragraph. Capital letters, full points, underlining, figures and tricks with punctuation may all be used. The news release or feature article writer cannot use such devices. English has to be perfect, and the rules set out in this chapter should be observed.

The person who has to write both advertising and public relations material, or deal with them, has to remember in which world he or she is operating, advertising or public relations. This can be a problem for advertising and marketing people who may not appreciate the special requirements of editorial copy. Another dilemma occurs when management approves a draft, and the PRO is given a freshly typed approved version. It usually has to be retyped to remove the wrong forms introduced by a secretary unfamiliar with publishing requirements.

Generally speaking it is highly unlikely that anyone who normally writes advertisement copy, sales literature or direct mail shots will be able to make the mental somersault necessary to write publishable press materials.

References

1 *Reuter External Relations Guide*, Corporate Relations Group, London
2 *The Use, Misuse and Abuse of Embargoes*, IPR Guidance Paper, Institute of Public Relations, 1986

15

Organizing public relations functions and events

Need for hospitality to be genuine

Public relations has a bad name for wining and dining; gin and tonics, 'good sloshes', junkets and jollies. This has to be balanced against the normal custom of welcoming a guest with a cup of tea or coffee, a beer or a glass of sherry, a cola nut or a date according to the custom of the country. In some countries a shopkeeper would not begin to discuss business until he had served his customer with a cup of mint tea. Elsewhere, it may be Turkish coffee or saki, maybe palm wine. There is a difference between hospitality which is bribery and that which is courteous. If there are a few journals and journalists, a press party may be welcomed and expected, but if – as in Britain – journalists may have to choose between any six press receptions occurring simultaneously, they want the stories, not the drinks. But they may be grateful for something to eat or, on a cold morning, some hot soup on arrival.

In this chapter we shall consider six kinds of public relations function and event: (i) the press conference; (ii) the press reception; (iii) the facility visit; (iv) the open day; (v) the press lunch; (vi) the exhibition press visit.

1 The press conference

This may be a regular event or one called at short notice. Its purpose is to give information to the media and to receive and answer questions. It will be a comparatively simple and informal occasion and hospitality will be minimal, such as a 'thank you' drink at the close. It may be held in the boardroom or conference room, or at a hotel, and if called at short notice there will be no printed invitation cards. The term 'press conference' should not be confused with the more elaborate 'press reception', although some people mistakenly use them as inter-changeable terms.

Regular press conferences may be held by heads of government and ministers to keep the media informed on an on-going basis. Sometimes a minister will advise the media 'off the record' or from a 'non-attribu-table source'. Based on such official 'leaks', journalists will refer the story to 'a usually reliable source'. But most press conferences are held at short notice because something unexpected has happened and a press statement is necessary, or a newsworthy person will be inter-viewed, for example, on arrival at an airport.

2 The press reception

This is more planned and socialized than a press conference. The planning may begin some months in advance, and it will be as thoroughly organized as a wedding reception complete with venue, invitations, catering, speeches and presentations. It will be more than a mere cocktail party. It calls for a timetable and programme of activi-ties which may include an audio-visual presentation and a product demonstration, a bar and a buffet. It must have an adequate purpose — that is, a good story — to justify a good attendance by the right people. The wrong people could be juniors sent by editors who think the event unimportant, but a kind of freebie that goes with the job. Guests should be limited to media representatives, and not mis-used as a party for company friends or clients.

3 The facility visit

This may be a press trip to a site, a factory or new premises; it could be a flight on a new aircraft or a voyage on a new vessel; it might be an official opening; it could be a visit to a country, an exhibition or a new holiday attraction. One way or another it usually means taking a person or a group of people by some form of transport to the location of the visit. If people are travelling from a variety of places they may have to make their own way. At least a day is usually involved, but overnight stops may be necessary. A great deal of organization is required. Again, because of the sacrifice of time, the visit has to be worthwhile from a story point of view.

Journalists will not respond if they have to travel 500 miles to see a jam factory that is no different from the one in their home town. They will be delighted to go behind-the-scenes of something unusual or unfamiliar. Such visits should not depend on complicated arrangements which could be wrecked by the weather or industrial action. A new motorcar was once launched many miles from London, but the press failed to arrive because of an air traffic controllers' strike. Sometimes helicopters have been engaged, only to be abandoned because of weather conditions.

4   The open day

This is an opportunity for the press to make a visit and see what goes on, though there is probably nothing new to be seen. Such a visit could be to a factory, college, hospital, mine, town hall, airport, charity home – preferably somewhere to which the press do not normally have general access. There may or may not be a direct story. More, it is a goodwill effort to familiarize the media with the place and what happens there. This may provide background knowledge that may help when news stories are being handled. Planning is still necessary, and management and employees should be aware of the visit.

A fiasco once occurred at a factory with an unfortunate industrial relations record resulting in hostile local press stories. The works manager had told the gatekeeper to refuse entry to the press. An open day was organized by the firm's public relations consultants who were unaware of the works manager's instructions. The press never got in.

5   The press lunch

This can be a pleasant way for journalists to meet the personalities of an organization, get to know them informally, and so discuss topics of mutual interest. It can be helpful in creating understanding between management and journalists. There may or may not be formal speeches, nor may there be an immediate story. Individual journalists or groups of journalists may be given lunch.

A good example occurred when, for no apparent reason, the entire trade press was hostile to a certain well-known company. This situation was reversed after each editor was invited to lunch with the consultant and two members of the company's top management. The problem had arisen because an assistant editor of one of the journals had become a member of the consultancy staff but had left their employ after a difference of opinion with the client. Delicate situations can be resolved in a relaxed atmosphere.

6 The exhibition press visit

This can take two forms, an open invitation to journalists to visit the stand for personal demonstrations, and a press reception on the stand itself.

Planning considerations

Planning and executing a press event is an exercise in good management, whether by the in-house PRO or the consultant. Control is necessary at every stage of the planning, budgeting, purchasing, stage-managing and direction of the event, otherwise it would be a disappointing waste of time and money. A lot of other people's valuable time is involved on both sides.

The purpose

Is the event justified − is it worth the cost to the organization and the time of the guests? Or would a news release be sufficient? This is a very important decision. As a consultant, the author found that clients enjoyed press receptions, and sometimes had to be dissuaded from holding them!

The date and time of day

The chairman may think it convenient to hold a press reception at 6 pm on a Friday evening, journalists may prefer one at 11 am on a Tuesday morning, and the chairman's wishes will be irrelevant. The event must be held when it suits the press, otherwise there will be a poor turn-out, little coverage and a heavy bill for a wasted effort.

There are two rules for the choice of date and time, and neither of them is easy to obey satisfactorily:

1 Try to avoid *clashing* with some major event or another press function. To some extent one can check that it is not Wimbledon Week, the Chelsea Flower Show or the Derby. One can ring press friends and ask if they have heard of anything else on the same day. However, a problem is that the public relations practitioner may plan his reception three months in advance and someone less well organized will choose the same date only three weeks in advance. Time of day is important, and for most receptions in London it is best if the proceedings begin in mid-morning and

close with a buffet lunch — that is, from about 11.30 am to 1.30 pm.
2 Try to choose a day which satisfies copy date needs. Day of the
   week is important because the end of the week is poor for daily
   newspapers, and too late for some magazines. The week in the
   month is important for monthly magazines which may go to press
   before the middle of the month.

So, as a general rule, early in the day, early in the week and early in
the month will suit the physical requirements of most publishers.
However, many of the big-circulation women's magazines will need
the story three months in advance. That is why receptions for Christ-
mas gifts are held in July/August, ones for central heating in April/
May, and those for summer holidays (January editions) are held in
September/October. To publish stories coinciding with the March
Ideal Home Exhibition, the press reception needs to be held in
November.

Venue

Again, the convenience of the guests is a first consideration, rather
than the glamour of the place. In a city centre, like London, the venue
should be easily reached on foot or by taxi. Remember that journalists
may have more than one reception to attend. In provincial cities it may
be more important that there are good car-parking facilities if guests
are coming from surrounding towns. The venue should have good
conference facilities ranging from catering to AVs.

Allowance has to be made for the fact that in London the press are
not centralized in and around Fleet Street, but are scattered in all
directions.

Programme

A timed programme should be drawn up when the event is being
planned. If it is a facility visit, the timetable must include everything
from the assembly of the party at a railway station, coach pick-up
point or airport to their return. There may not be a great deal of actual
visit time if a factory stops work for lunch at 12 noon and closes for the
day at 4 pm. How is the party collected early enough to reach the
venue in time to make a tour or see demonstrations before and/or
after lunch? This may determine the form of transportation, perhaps
require the provision of breakfast. It may be necessary for the PRO or
consultant to go over the route and tour and time the various stages —
on foot, by car and so on — allowing, for example, for the time it takes

to get a certain number of people on and off coaches and from point to point during the day.

The maximum number of people to be accepted may be determined by the size of a coach, aircraft, demonstration theatre, luncheon room or by the number of people who can be taken round. With most visits there is usually some such factor which controls the size of the party.

Guest list and invitations

People are naturally flattered if their names are known and they are invited by name. This may mean taking the trouble to telephone round and check names (unless one is a subscriber to PIMS or Two-Ten Communications and has a regularly updated list of names). If the guest list is large enough, a printed invitation is better than a letter. The invitation should state exactly what the event is about, not vaguely invite people to a reception or visit. A timetable can be printed on the back of the card. To ensure prompt acceptances or refusals there should be some means of reply, not merely an RSVP note at the foot of the card. This can be a tear-off reply coupon or a separate reply card, which should bear not only the PRO's postal address but a printed square for the stamp so that it becomes a postcard, otherwise recipients will put it in an envelope.

Rehearsals

Events need to occur without hitches — 'like clockwork' — and while a timetable provides the basis for a well-organized event, and it pays to time each stage, it is also important to rehearse wherever possible. Speeches, demonstrations, film, video and slide presentations should be rehearsed.

Press material

Guests should be supplied with only the minimum of material necessary for their information so that they can print a story. A news release, copy of a speech, a photograph and, on a visit, an itinerary should be sufficient. The mistake should not be made of overloading guests with elaborate press packs filled with irrelevant items. Remember, the guests may be standing, eating, drinking, smoking or walking round the site or premises. They will not enjoy having to carry a weighty press kit. Guests should be informed, not impressed. If there is a lot of useful information it may be better to supply it on the point of leaving, putting it in a convenient wallet, or on the return journey. Many an unwelcome press kit has been dumped under a seat!

The media can be scathing when a press visit turns into a junket and the proceedings invite cynicism. This is demonstrated by Peter Knight's feature in the *Observer*[1] about an international press facility visit to Silicon Valley, California, which is reproduced below:

How they put the hype into technology
'Is it a washing machine?' asks the man from the *Telegraph*.

No, and it's not a fridge either. It's Hewlett-Packard's new $200,000 computer, which has taken three years and 'many hundreds of millions' to develop. Hewlett's future as a computer manufacturer depends on the success of this smooth grey box and its effect on around 100 European computer journalists who were flown out to an unusually hot California for three days to see the machine, meet a few selected Hewlett people and generally 'get the feel of HP'.

Reporters love to get the feel of new products, but not always those for which the PR people are paying. The object of the Hewlett hype, for instance, appeared much less exciting than the 'super boost-cool' fridge being advertised on NBC breakfast television. At least the fridge looked high-tech, with buttons to push and digital read-out in the middle of its 'finger-spot-resistant' double doors.

Hewlett's new computer is a fine example of minimalism, both inside and out. It has no name, just a number (930), and its innards are based on a little-used design called 'reduced-instruction-set-computing' (RISC), an acronym that, when placed in apposition to the company's future, should give headline-writers a lot of fun. On the outside it looks like, well, nothing − no whirring tapes, no flashing lights, no booth-control, no finger-spot-resistant doors, not even a go-faster stripe.

Such engineering purity, a hallmark of Hewlett, gives the public relations men a headache. Clever people who understand how computers work are fascinated by RISC technology. But computer journalists prefer other pursuits, such as travel and wine. The PR people know their guests and organize a day of trivial pursuits involving a little travel and much wine. The day is designed to relax the hard-working hacks before The Launch, which will be televised on Hewlett's own international channel and seen by hundreds of staff around the world.

But first, as a warm-up to The Launch, Richard C. Alberding, executive vice-president (marketing and international), takes 100-or-so of us to dinner at a Chinese restaurant.

Richard ('hi, call me Dick') Alberding is relaxed and suitably international after spending 11 years in Geneva. The Hewlett table is so relaxed that one of the PR men, after downing a bottle of the best Californian Chardonnay, shouts: 'Hey Dick, have we got a drug problem?'

Some computer workers in affluent Silicon Valley, many of whom have million-dollar mortgages, consume vast amounts of cocaine and other substances to improve their lives. Silicon and narcotics don't mix and employers are worried about falling productivity.

Dick is such a nice guy that he doesn't even think of stabbing the questioner with his chop-sticks. By now the only sound is bean sprouts being inexpertly crunched by journalists who think they are about to get a little colour from Dick − a real feel of Hewlett-Packard.

'Sure we've got a problem' says Dick from somewhere in the 40 watt gloom. 'We try to sort it out with counselling, but sometimes we've got to fire them. It's no worse than anywhere else.'

The next day brings The Launch − and the Big Mistake called Joel S. Burnbaum.

Joel is straight from a Woody Allen movie. He is also vice-president in charge of laboratories, knows far too much about computers and makes terrible jokes about philosophy. His 45-minute speech, 'Beyond RISC: HP Precision Architecture', is so boring that even the chairman and co-founder, David Packard, walks out halfway through. The rest of us want to follow, but we're hemmed in by Hewlett heavies and our own politeness.

Having proved beyond doubt that there is no such thing as a free launch, Burnbaum finally sits down and we rush from the press room which we expect to be filled with Hewlett-Packard touch-screen personal computers and various high-tech methods of delivering copy to our far-away editors. Instead we find rows of IBM typewriters, most of which are older than Eddy Shah.

On the final day we're promised a last chance to question Hewlett's top people, including Joel.

Dick arrives, so does his Hollywood-looking chief executive and Sharon Jacobs, the only woman executive we've seen.

Joel's name-tag is there but he doesn't show.

Peter Knight

Reference

1   Knight, Peter, article, New Directions page, *Observer*, 6 March 1986

16

Broadcast material and opportunities for public relations

There is a lot more to broadcasting than sending news releases to the station news room or to Independent Television News, Independent Radio News or the BBC news services. In fact, merely to put the broadcasting services on the mailing list is likely to be ineffectual if only because the story will probably arrive too late to be usable. Airtime on both radio and television is divided into numerous programmes, not unlike the pages and features of newspapers and magazines except that (apart from the London radio station LBC) news is a small part of the total broadcast material.

Although the theory of broadcasting is that it should combine information, education and entertainment, the tendency is for the entertainment to pre-dominate, even to some extent in the information and educational programmes. This is because, as with popular newspapers such as the *Daily Mirror* and the *Sun*, radio and television cater for the mass public which prefers to be entertained rather than informed or educated. That is a statement of fact, not cynicism. Since the advent of colour television, newscasters have dressed colourfully, and the news is presented entertainingly with amusing tail-piece stories and quips by the newscasters. The studios themselves are decorated impressively and feature in the news picture.

With British television audiences numbering millions, most public relations material for television has to be 'of interest and value' to a very large number of viewers. Much of company news which might suit certain sections of the press, special interest columns or features even in the popular press (e.g. City Page) will be irrelevant. So this is a medium which has to be looked at very carefully. It can be a valuable public relations medium if programmes, presenters, producers, scriptwriters and research assistants are diligently selected, and if approaches are timed correctly. For example, a businessman might appear on *Question Time*, a topic might have a place in *EastEnders* or *Coronation*

Street, an export order success story could suit a regional news bulletin, or a holiday subject might be welcomed by one of the holiday programmes on either BBC or ITV. The story has to be marketed! A word of warning: while radio may be only a matter of a studio or outside interview (live or taped), television can be very time-consuming, with many hours taken up for a few moments of screen time. One has to weigh up the advantages of programme relevance and audience size with the brevity of the broadcast.

Before getting involved in television one should consider whether one has the time to spare compared with the value of the coverage. Television can be a temptation and a disappointment. It is a visual medium which invites critical viewing if the subject or personality is not attractive on a small screen in private homes. Some well-known personalities have suffered adverse publicity because they have come over badly on television. The viewing public does tend to look at, rather than listen to, television, but with radio it is the attractiveness of the voice which matters.

It pays to study the programmes printed in the *Radio Times, TV Times* and other listing magazines (or similar programme magazines in other countries) to see which programmes are being broadcast, and to note the names of presenters, editors and producers. There is no cast-iron rule about this, but for different programmes one may have to deal with the producer, the editor, the presenter or the researcher. If in doubt, it is best to contact the producer in the first instance, setting out the proposition in a letter or a telephone conversation with postal confirmation.

Moreover, it has to be remembered that while programmes may be networked to a national or partially national audience, they originate (with the exception of Good Morning TV and Channel 4) from a regional ITV station. The BBC also has its smaller number of regional stations.

As the BARB chart in Figure 16.1 shows, British television audiences total several millions for each programme on a number of channels, to which must be added Good Morning and BBC breakfast television, UK Gold and BSkyB and other channels which can be reached by satellite dish or cable television. The British television audience has been fragmenting since the 1980s when 15–20 million viewers might watch a popular programme. The programmes in first position have required repeat audiences on a Sunday to gain 1980s audience figures.

This fragmenting of audiences has also been influenced by many forms of alternative television, such as playing recorded programmes by means of video cassette recorder (VCR) and blank tapes; playing hired or bought films on videotape; playing of home movies shot on

	BBC1	Millions	BBC2	Millions	ITV	Millions	C4	Millions
1	EastEnders (Thu/Sun)	18.89	Top Gear	6.17	Coronation Street (Wed/Sun)	20.10	Brookside (Wed/Sat)	5.84
2	Neighbours (Mon)	16.15	Blackadder Goes Forth	5.58	London's Burning	14.30	Animal Squad Undercover	5.31
3	Keeping Up Appearances	13.71	Have I Got News For You	5.56	The Bill (Thu)	14.21	The Cosby Show	4.37
4	Casualty	13.53	Bottom	4.87	Home and Away (Wed)	14.16	The Golden Girls	4.35
5	Crimewatch UK	12.01	Star Trek	4.58	This is Your Life	14.07	Rising Damp	3.98
6	Boxing: Bruno v Coetzer	11.43	Rising Son	3.30	Strike It Lucky	13.69	The Cruel Sea	3.90
7	Birds of a Feather	10.99	The Living Planet	3.22	Family Fortunes	13.57	Fifteen-to-One (Wed)	3.51
8	News and Sport (Sat)	10.43	Fresh Prince of Bel-Air	3.21	The Krypton Factor	13.49	Desmond's	3.44
9	Porridge	10.35	The Man in the Iron Mask	2.99	Gladiators	13.27	Cheers	3.06
10	2 Point 4 Children	10.15	Food and Drink Special	2.98	Die Hard	12.95	Nurses	3.03

Source: Broadcasters' Audience Research Board (BARB) for 12–18 October 1992. When more than one episode is broadcast in a week the highest figure is given. If a programme is repeated the audiences for the first and repeat broadcasts are added together.

Figure 16.1 *Example of a BARB Top Ten*

camcorders; computer games, using the TV set as a monitor; and now multi-media such as Commodore's CDTV and Philips interactive compact disk system CDi. These interactive CDs will be time-consuming, which means absorbing normal off-air screen time. In addition CDi players will also show Kodak Photo CD on TV sets. Kodak's target for its first year beginning September 1992 was 250,000 households with a potential market of 10 million households.

But as TV producer Malcolm Quigan was quoted as saying about multi-media, in *Televisual*,[1] 'It's bound to affect TV viewing. People have only so much free time.' That is true in spite of greater leisure time resulting from unemployment, early retirement and longevity. A general risk confronting traditional television is that with an ageing population the endless repeats from money-strapped BBC and ITV must make these programmes increasingly less attractive. The James Bond films, for instance, have been repeated so frequently that the prints must be getting threadbare.

Seven points to remember about television

1 Some programmes are live or are produced only a few days earlier. For example, Esther Rantzen's *That's Life* is a combination of pre-taped material and studio performance.
2 Other programmes, such as holiday series, have to be filmed months in advance, usually during the holiday season. You may be able to get your topic into next week's show, or next season's. The author had coverage in a regular weekly programme, but discussions began in January and fifteen minutes of a day's filming appeared a week after shooting in March.
3 Sometimes material may be shot for a magazine programme, and one may be kept on tenterhooks wondering in which week's programme it will be used. Even then one may be told 'it's going on tonight' only to find it is held over to a future programme.
4 Television can be not only time-consuming but exasperating. The editing method of breaking up interviews and inserting bits in conjunction with bits from other interviews can be disconcerting. Juxtapositioning can give an entirely different meaning from what was discussed in the separate interviews! This can be unfair because those concerned are unaware of the other interviews from which they are isolated until the programme actually appears.
5 However, if there is a valid reason for seeking television coverage, and if the story is 'of interest and value' to the mass television audience, the public relations practitioner needs to understand the

technical demands of the medium. While it is simple and quick to tape-record a radio interview, television requires planning time, the use of equipment, proper lighting, sometimes many people, and probably a budget allocation to undertake the job. This implies, therefore, that the 'idea' has to be 'sold' in practical terms, facilities must be provided, and a lot of cooperation will be required in providing scenes or venues, or people for interview. For instance, it is unlike inviting a group of journalists to a press reception or on a press visit. One has to devote all one's time to a single television crew, and do so on a day convenient and for however long it may take to set up, script, rehearse and shoot the story. The author did nothing else but cooperate for two weeks in the making of a 23-minute television programme, after having negotiated for a year to get the idea accepted. In this case, one of the requests made by the producer was for a farm where part of the action could be shot. That section of the programme occupied a day and lunch had to be provided for a 12-man television crew in the heart of the country. On the actual day it poured with rain, everything was shot in a barn, where a visiting caterer served a four-course lunch with an immaculate butler!

6 If photographs are supplied they must be in colour.
7 If videotapes are supplied, and they contain any material which is not the copyright of the owner, this must be declared as repro- duction fees may have to be paid. The TV company will demand details of copyright ownership.

The public relations practitioner has to be aware of the pitfalls and peculiarities of television production which may prove to be merely a device to amuse rather than inform audiences. Inspired controversy based on innocent interviews is a form of entertainment. The wise practitioner may, therefore, find it a matter of responsibility towards clients or employers to advise them against participation in a television programme. This may require considerable tact since some people may be anxious to 'get on the box', if only to impress their friends. Vanity can prove costly.

Opportunities for public relations coverage

News bulletins

There are three kinds of TV news bulletins. There are national ones, which report major national and international news, and regional ones, which follow the networked news. To these terrestrial services must be added the satellite news services of BSkyB, some of which is supplied by Visnews and could include video news releases.

Video news releases are dealt with in the chapter on video, but can be mentioned here as a means of gaining news coverage which ITN and independent regional news services may be unwilling to cover, mainly because of cost.

Magazine programmes

Being regular, they are open to suggestions for material that is both topical and of interest to the particular audience, e.g. women, farmers, gardeners, motorists, businesspeople.

Chat shows, discussion panels, interviews

Opportunities exist for participation by interesting personalities, especially if they or their subjects are topical.

Two things are essential for live interviews:the interviewee must be articulate and must know his or her subject to be capable of responding instantaneously, authoritatively and sincerely to any question.

Serials

It may be possible to introduce a public interest subject into a fictional programme if it can be made relevant to the characters or storyline. A number of topics like this appear in 'soaps' if they are relevant to the storyline.

Current affairs programmes

A programme such as *Panorama, Weekend World or World in Action* may require cooperation in covering a subject or may be interested in a proposed topic. But sometimes such programmes are seeking to reveal something detrimental to an organization, and the decision has to be made whether to be frank or to withhold information. The problem is that investigative programmes are more intent on dramatic entertainment than on a fair treatment of the subject. Often it is wise not to get involved in such programmes.

Series

These may be produced in advance, and may appear regularly at certain times of the year. We have already mentioned the holiday series shown during the early part of the year when people are planning their holidays. But there are other series, such as those on gardening, which are made at shorter notice.

Archival material

This consists of ready-made videotape which can be inserted into programmes to give background effects or information – for example, scenes at a seaport or airport.

Library shots

Action films are often shot in studios, and outside scenes are borrowed or hired from libraries. Famous landmarks and geographical scenes are typical examples. Many airlines make available shots of their aircraft taking off, in flight or landing.

Properties and product placement

Many products have to be used in television films and series. They can be supplied to property rooms, and so used on sets, or they may be supplied for use on location. It is noticeable that Ford cars are often used in both American and British detective series, and credited in the subtitles.

The supply of products for use in films, plays and television programmes is called 'placement' and there are firms which specialize in getting products placed. Another name for this is 'presence advertising' which really means making payment for using products as 'props'. Theatre programmes often credit firms which have contributed props such as clothes, furniture or cigarettes. American films do big business in charging fees for the use of props, and at one time this was commonplace with British films. For example, if a shop featured in a film, manufacturers were invited (at a fee) to supply products or display material to dress the scene. This is not permitted on British TV, but many firms (through their agents) endeavour to supply props. *Coronation Street* abounds in such props on the sets for the Rover's Return public house and the local shops.

This has produced what *Marketing Week*[2] in a feature on placement called 'a twilight industry'. It quoted a number of product placement agencies, and remarked that 'Some marketing sources claim, if priced correctly, product placement offers a greater opportunity in terms of value to broadcasters than TV sponsorship. One estimate is that it

could be worth £100 m a year towards production budgets.' Presumably
the writer meant if the placements saved the production company the
cost of buying props such as vehicles.

There is another way of looking at this − the client's way − which
was expressed in a quoted interview with Charles Jackson, MD of programme sponsorship consultancy Howard Jackson. He said, 'There is
opportunity for growth so long as the ITC Code is not abused −
payment for use of products is prohibited. But you must remember
that what we're talking about is providing props for production.'

He went on, rather dubiously, to suggest (as the writer of the article
developed it) that 'if a product received a total of 30 second's exposure
during a single episode of *Coronation Street*, this could be valued at a
proportion of the network airtime cost of a centre break 30-second ad
costing, on average £100,000. This could make the value of exposure
through product placement about £10,000.'

This is arrant nonsense, and raises the old fallacy of measuring
media coverage by rate-card prices. It makes no sense. The mere
appearance of a bottle of HP sauce on a domestic table is no advertisement. It merely looks like the sort of thing you would expect to
see there and it conveys no advertising message. More sight of a
product aids awareness, but can do nothing to describe the product's
attributes or make any attempt to sell as would occur in a commercial.
In *Coronation Street* it would look a very odd grocer's shop or supermarket if there were no familiar brands in sight on the shelves, a
strange sort of newsagents shop if it displayed no magazines and
newspapers. Product placement does after all make a scene look
authentic.

Prizes for give-away and contest shows

These are purchased by the programme makers and are unlikely to be
identified (to avoid advertising) but if a product is suitable as a prize
and benefits from easy recognition, it could be useful public relations
to propose it to the producer. Most prizes, such as motorcars, are
recognizable.

Stills

Colour slides can be useful for news stories, being televised to coincide
with the reading of an associated story, but here is a case where the
video news release kit is superior, having movement and appearing to
be a natural part of the programme.

Documentary videos

Some may be of sufficient interest to be shown in their entirety. Clips may be taken from videos for use in programmes, usually with acknowledgement, but once again the collection of video news release shots is more convenient in use in the documentary or public affairs programme.

Differences between radio and television

Before listing the opportunities for radio coverage it is necessary to analyse how radio differs from television:

1 Radio is not confined to indoor audiences. Thanks to the portable transistor receiver, car radios, rediffusion and loudspeakers in public places, radio is available to more people, in more places at more times than television.
2 Even though television is no longer limited to those who can afford to buy receivers or to the availability of electricity − thanks to battery sets and community viewing in many parts of the Third World, plus rental systems − the time people have free for viewing may be limited even though TV may be available for many hours of the day and night. Television also requires the attention of immobile viewers. None of these restrictions applies to radio.
3 While the breadth and freedom of listening has its advantages it has to be admitted that viewers are more attentive. Radio can be a form of companionship, a background sound. One can listen continuously to any kind of enjoyable music − whatever one's tasks − whereas few people would wish continuously to watch music programmes on television. Radio does broadcast a lot of music.
4 Radio is more instantaneous than television. While it is possible to interrupt a television programme with a newsflash, instant news can be typical of radio. A radio programme can be produced at short notice, simply by going on the air. Television programmes usually require advance preparation. A play cannot be read on television − parts have to be learned as on the stage.
5 In Britain, television regions are quite large, embracing perhaps three or four counties, whereas local radio covers smaller areas more intimately.

With these differences in mind, and remembering that radio does not have television's realism and entertainment value or vision, colour and movement, let us now consider how to use radio as a public relations medium.

Opportunities for public relations coverage on radio

News bulletins

There are national, regional and local radio stations so that news of area significance will interest different radio stations. For example, information about traffic conditions or public transport, which is of interest to people only within one area, can be and is broadcast on local radio. When supplying news releases for broadcasting they must be written so that they are capable of being read aloud. There is great competition for radio audiences and stations are eager to cover local stories of interest to their listeners.

Taped interviews

Interviews can be produced by one of two ways. The station may commission an interview, either at the studio or with a reporter outside the studio, or the taped interview can be produced by a public relations source and supplied to radio stations. The latter is done more often than listeners realize, which shows that the public relations material was broadcast on its merits. The illusion of a genuine studio interview is created by the announcer saying 'We now have in the studio Mr X who is going to talk to Miss X about . . .', and then the tape is played. Afterwards, the announcer will say 'That was Mr X talking to Miss X about . . .' . No commercial reference will occur in the interview, but the identity of the company or product is usually mentioned in the announcer's introduction and close. Sometimes the identity will be obvious if the interview is about, say, a public event, a new entertainment or a new book. Or it could be a trade organization or professional body giving advice with the message more important than the source, e.g. advice in late October and early November about how to handle fireworks safely.

Professional services

Two-Ten Communications offers a public relations broadcasting service and its headquarters in Old Street, London, contains a radio studio. They have (under its present and former name of UNS) supplied material to radio since 1973. They know the names and addresses of every radio journalist and programme maker likely to be interested in a news release.

They can arrange for interviews to be conducted directly with local radio stations in London and throughout the country. These studio links are arranged in advance with guaranteed time slots with those who want to take the interview. Whenever possible, the interviews are grouped together within a few hours. Broadcast quality lines are booked, linking the Two-Ten studio with each of the radio stations. The interviews are conducted independently by the radio station's presenters or reporters, so the client has to be fluent and be fully informed to answer questions. The advantage of this is that the client can make broadcasts which would be physically impossible for him or her to cover since he or she could not visit all the radio stations involved.

Three- to four-minute recorded interviews can also be made in Two-Ten studios. Copies can be mailed to a selection of, say, 25 stations most likely to be interested in playing the interview, including both ILR and BBC stations. Message cassettes are another Two-Ten service, these being of a more promotional nature for distribution to members of a sales force, as direct mail shots, or as give-aways at exhibitions.

Studio interviews, discussions, talks

Being an audio medium, programmes based on talk and the human voice are characteristic of radio. Interesting voices, conversationalists, commentators or subjects suitable for a talk or discussion are all ideal for radio.

Phone-in

Borrowed from the USA, the phone-in produces listener participation and offers opportunities to phone in a public relations message if it is an appropriate and genuine contribution to the programme.

Serials and series

There are possibilities for including public relations messages in radio serials, as has happened a number of times on *The Archers*, provided they are of interest and value to large numbers of listeners. In spite of television and local radio, *The Archers* has three million listeners. Voluntary organizations have made good use of radio serials in order to advise the public on matters of health and safety.

Attacks on television programmes

Newspapers and magazines as different as the *Sunday People, Private Eye, The Guardian, New Society,* and the *New International* have exposed a great many scandals and strange doings. Some call it the freedom of the press, others call it gutter journalism. It can be either enlightening or mischievous, and either way it helps to build circulations and make money.

But there is a world of difference between muck-raking in publications which are read by selective groups of readers, and an attack from a television programme which is seen by millions of people, often in family groups in the home. There is practically no audience selectivity except between one channel and another. In Britain there are habitual BBC or ITV viewers. We do not have the selectivity that exists in the USA where there are numerous television stations in many cities. An attack or exposure broadcast on television is therefore a more serious matter than one in the press which thousands of people may never read. An exposure on television is discussed afterwards by viewers with people who may or may not have seen the programme, and the topic is often taken up by the press and radio the next day. The message spreads like shock waves.

The victim rightly or wrongly is crucified. An apology or retraction is usually too late. Newspapers may be anxious to avoid libel actions and will publish handsome apologies. Television seems to thrive on threats of libel. Esther Rantzen's attacks on inefficient organizations have produced responses in keeping with the programme, and apologetic victims have retaliated with verses and songs. However, a victim may go to law, but it is a long process and by the time the case has been won it no longer matters. For example, the BBC paid substantial damages and costs in settlement of a High Court libel action brought by a laundry group against Esther Rantzen's *That's Life* show; the BBC also unreservedly withdrew its allegations that the laundry had failed to pay proper compensation for clothes which had been lost or damaged; but it took five years for that victim of a television attack legally to recover its good reputation.

References

1 *Televisual*, 'TV's other half', London, September 1992
2 *Marketing Week*, 'Famous for 15 seconds', London, 13 November 1992

17

Photographs and captions

Three public relations requirements

Editors frequently complain about the poor quality of public relations pictures. The reason why public relations pictures are sometimes bad is that the practitioner does not understand three things:

1 How to tell a story with pictures.
2 The sort of pictures editors want.
3 How to work with a photographer.

   Without this knowledge and ability it is inevitable that the practitioner will fail to make the best use of photography, and will disappoint editors. It is therefore a managerial responsibility to see that public relations staff are proficient in the use of photographs, and in the briefing of photographers. It does help if the practitioner can use a camera, and with modern SLR cameras such as the Canon, Minolta and Olympus it is not difficult to take good pictures. The secret is to know how to compose a picture. With this knowledge one can create with a camera just as one does on a typewriter – and *instruct* a photographer. Let us now consider the three points set out above.

Telling a story pictorially

A public relations picture should convey a message, not be a mere record. But it should not be a blatant advertising message, and product or company names – if shown at all – should be discreet.
   Human interest may improve a picture, provided it is relevant and helps to explain the subject. For example, a holiday picture is more realistic if people are shown enjoying themselves, but a typical family

might be better than a model in a bikini. A brick looks better if a bricklayer is laying it, a sewing machine is better demonstrated by a dressmaker using it. But a power mower looks ridiculous if it is being driven by a blonde in a bikini and high-heeled shoes. People in pictures should be *concentrating* on what they are doing, not decorating the picture or grinning at the camera. If the size of the subject is difficult to judge the message is made clearer if, say, a tiny object is held in the palm of a hand, or a human being is seen standing beside something very large. A lot of public relations pictures could be made interesting and publishable if people were used properly. They do not have to be professional models.

Action is another device for giving pictures interest and realism. An aircraft in the air looks more interesting than one on the ground, while a static object such as a building looks better if someone is walking up the steps, or passing through the entrance. Action can thus be real or induced.

Three-dimensional effects give a picture depth. It is more interesting to see three sides of a matchbox than just the side. This applies to many subjects. Do not face the subject head-on: stand to one side and take it at an angle, whether it be a portrait, a piece of machinery, a ship or a loaf of bread.

It is more dramatic to *allow a little to tell the whole story*. A section of a building can look more impressive than if one stands back to get the whole building in the picture. The cricketer at the wicket, with the wicket-keeper crouched behind him, makes a better picture than a bird's eye view of the match in progress. Close-ups and telescopic lenses help here.

Show the subject in use. If it is a lorry, give it a load, show the crane working, have the fork-lift truck lifting things. Have the bus driving along a well-known street, the weighing machine weighing a parcel, and the pop-singer clutching a mike.

What editors want

Editors want pictures that enhance the page and flatter their ability to please their readers. Most of the public relations pictures they receive do neither.

They also want pictures which reproduce well according to the printing process and paper they use. Most newspapers and magazines are nowadays printed by web-offset-litho which permits the use of fine dot halftone screens. Advantage of this can be taken in three ways:

1   The picture can have gradations of tone.
2   In-depth landscape pictures can be used.
3   Pictures can be printed very small yet retain detail.

The public relations practitioner may be tempted to use pictures from newspapers, agencies or private individuals but must remember that these people own the copyright. It may be necessary to pay them reproduction fees, or print acknowledgements, and these pictures cannot be distributed to illustrate the public relations story as if they belonged to the practitioner.

Care has to be taken to observe the requirements of the Copyright, Designs and Patents Act 1988 which made at least two important changes to the former copyright law. First, the photographer now owns the copyright of the prints as well as the negatives, unless the work is undertaken for an employer. When the public relations practitioner commissions photography he or she (or his or her organization) does not own the copyright unless there is a written assignment of the copyright. Second, there is the requirement concerning 'intellectual property' or moral rights which are enjoyed by the originator of a copyright item. This means that the author of an original work is entitled to be identified (as could occur in the production of a video), but also that a work must not be altered in a way which the author considers derogatory, and that could relate to retouching or amending a design (which could be photographic).

Captions should not be *written* on the back of the print, but should be duplicated on a piece of paper firmly attached to the print, Sellotaped rather than stuck. A strip of tape top and bottom will fix the caption securely. Do not use a small single piece of tape so that the caption dangles and is likely to get ripped off. Flapped captions are best reserved for pictures in photo libraries. Pictures should not be pasted on to news releases.

Photographers should be told not to put their rubber stamps on the backs of prints, but the sender's rubber stamp may be used as well as the caption.

The caption should provide the information from which the editor may create his own caption. The editor will not remove the caption and send it to the printer for setting. The caption will remain with the picture to explain the picture and identify the source. The picture is likely to be stored in the picture library. This should be remembered. News releases may be discarded, but pictures are usually retained and may be used at any time in the future.

Even when captions are fixed to pictures it is extraordinary how often the senders forget to include their name, address and telephone number. The most efficient captions are those which have printed headings.

Fixing captions takes time, which is why they are often omitted: the reason may be that too many pictures are sent out! This may be related to the indiscriminate sending out of news releases on excessively large mailing lists. One fault leads to another.

Ways of avoiding wasteful distribution of pictures

- Pictures should be sent only to those publications likely to print them.
- Editors can be telephoned and asked if they would like a picture – for example, before sending an appointment story to the *Financial Times* which prints numerous appointment stories, the majority without pictures – but if a public relations appointment story is sent to *Campaign*, *PR Week* or *UK Press Gazette* a picture will probably be printed, although *Campaign* often prefers to take its own pictures!
- Pictures can be reproduced on the news release, and editors invited to request prints.
- If there is a set of pictures, a sheet of miniatures can be supplied with the story so that editors may choose which picture or pictures they want sent to them.
- At the foot of a release one can state that pictures are available.
- Colour photographs should not be sent unless requested. Most press pictures are printed in black and white and need black and white prints.

If these methods are adopted a great deal of money can be saved and fewer pictures will be wasted. Editors are normally inundated with pictures they cannot use, generally because they are unprintable.

From these remarks it will be seen that it is not difficult to produce publishable pictures, nor to get them published. It costs no more to produce a good picture than a poor one. The careful distribution of pictures is a budgeting consideration, and an exercise in good management.

Does the editor want black and white or colour pictures? It is a mistake to suppose that since we usually take colour pictures as amateur photographers, a good picture must be in colour. Hardly any public relations pictures should be in colour, unless this has been agreed with the editor. The majority of pictures in newspapers are in black and white. However, newspapers are making increasing use of colour pictures. This is also true of local newspapers. An exception is television: if photographs are sent to support a news story they must be in colour.

Some magazines have attempted to make charges for colour separations, but this malpractice has been condemned, as explained in Chapter 13.

Editors want sharp, well-focused glossy (*not glazed*) prints. They should not be snapshot size, but they do not have to be large prints if the subject matter fills the picture and cutting or cropping is unnecessary. A half-plate print without borders has the advantage that it is unlikely to be damaged in the post. Even card-backed envelopes are liable to be bent if the postman puts a string or elastic band round the bundle of letters for a particular address. Words such as 'Do Not Bend' are often ignored. Large prints really need personal delivery.

Working with the photographer

It follows that working with the photographer means knowing what kind of pictures are required. The photographer is not an expert who knows best and must be left to do as he or she pleases, although this attitude is all too common among those who, in the end, supply editors with pictures they reject.

The photographer cannot produce pictures which convey the right message, suit the printing process and encourage publication *unless* the practitioner knows what is wanted and instructs the photographer properly. The photographer is not a mind-reader. If a building is to be designed the architect has to know whether it is to be a bungalow, a house or a block of flats and then will want to know what kind of bungalow, house or block of flats. Similarly, it is useless sending a photographer to take pictures unless he or she is thoroughly briefed. In fact, the practitioner should accompany the photographer, help to set up pictures, and even look in the viewfinder to see if the right picture has been composed. When a good relationship has been developed, the photographer will probably invite the practitioner to look in the viewfinder. But this partnership is impossible unless first of all the practitioner has decided what pictures are wanted.

Photo captions

One of the strangest faults with public relations pictures is that they are often sent out without captions. The caption on the back of a picture should not be confused with the caption which the editor prints under the picture. The two can be very different.

Photo captions are essential on any picture when it is sent out and to whomever it is sent. It does not have to be an editor. It could be someone requesting a picture. Unless there is a caption the recipient does not know:

1 What the picture is about.
2 Who sent it.
3 Who owns the copyright.

Thus, the caption should say what the picture cannot say for itself. If is it a picture of a ship it is no use merely putting the name of the ship on the caption. Who owns the ship? What is its tonnage? Where it is going?

What is the source of the picture – what is the sender's name, address and telephone number? Captions should also be *dated* because good pictures are often placed in a publisher's photo library, and the information on the caption may be out of date in the future. For example, prices may change and so may people's names as a result of marriage, promotion or honours.

Whose is the copyright? Is there a reproduction fee or is it free of copyright? The practitioner should never submit pictures for which his or her client or employer does not own the copyright. When receiving a picture from a public relations source editors will assume that it is the copyright of the sender and can be reproduced free of charge. But do not add the silly proviso 'copyright – not to be published without permission'. If that is the case, there is no point in distributing it. Further information on copyright has already been given in this chapter.

18

Working with the printer

Three aspects

Printing is a craft on its own, and one that is rapidly changing with the introduction of computerized technology. A modern print shop resembles a hospital compared with those where hot metal was in use. While the practitioner does not need to have expert knowledge of printing, it can increase his or her efficiency if he or she has a working knowledge of printing processes and techniques, and can work intelligently with printers. Moreover, as a manager he or she is a buyer. Quotations cannot be invited, compared, understood and accepted if the practitioner lacks some technical knowledge.

It is extremely helpful to possess a brilliant little book called *Printing Reproduction Pocket Pal.*[1] No better, simpler, more compact and inexpensive guide to printing has ever been published.

There are three aspects to working with a printer:

1 An understanding of the different processes so that the best process can be used for the job, and suitable material can be supplied for printing by that process.
2 An understanding of production time schedules so that a print job can be delivered by the desired date. This is another management requirement.
3 An understanding of proof reading and correction.

This chapter will concentrate on these three aspects. There is great rivalry between printing processes and each is continually competing with the others through the introduction of new machines, inks, papers and techniques. Many years ago most magazines were printed by letterpress, then photogravure took over for large-circulation magazines such as the women's press and the Sunday newspaper colour magazines, but in recent years many such magazines have been printed by web-offset-litho. Similarly, while silk-screen printing was confined to short runs of rather crude posters, the process has become sophisticated with photographic reproduction, long runs and specialities such as printing vandal-proof posters on vinyl. Bus side and other large posters can be printed by silk-screen (or simply screen) printing.

Printing processes

The five main printing processes are letterpress, lithography, photogravure, flexography and silk screen.

Letterpress (relief)

Printing is achieved by having all printing surfaces raised or in relief so that when ink is applied and the inked surface is impressed on paper the image is transferred to the paper. This is similar to the typewriter or date stamp. Letterpress machines may be *flat-bed* with the printing material lying flat on the bed of the machine, sheets of paper being fed in and pressed down on the printing surface by an impression cylinder. Faster printing is achieved by moulding a copy of the metal printing material to produce a curved plate or stereo which is wrapped round a cylinder. This becomes rotary printing, the method that was used for letterpress newspaper printing.

The 'printing material' referred to above consists of metal type, line blocks to reproduce line drawings and halftone blocks to reproduce artwork such as photographs. This metal printing material together with spacing material which is not 'type high' and so cannot accept ink, is assembled in the forme and locked up in a frame called a 'chase'.

However, one of the developments by which new technologies have been introduced into newspaper and other printing is that the photo-typesetting, paste-up artwork and finer half-tone screens used for offset-litho – methods which do not require metal type and blocks – can be applied to letterpress printing. The pasted-up page or pages can be photographed and a plate, not unlike a litho plate, can be made for wrapping round the cylinder of a letterpress machine. The effect is to achieve a quality of reproduction difficult to distinguish from litho printing.

Letterpress printing has many advantages by which it retains its popularity. There are machines of all sizes and varieties so that the process can be used for work as small as a business card or as fine as a four-colour art book. It can also be used to print on a great variety of papers from cheap newsprint to chrome art. With heat set presses, which have driers, four colour work can be produced as a continuous process.

However, letterpress has been largely replaced by web-offset-litho printing, a few jobbing printers still printing by letterpress.

Lithography (planographic)

Lithography – which is often referred to in familiar terms as 'offset' and 'web-offset' – differs from letterpress in that the printing surface is not raised but is flat on the surface of the plate (see Figure 18.1). Years ago printing was made from a limestone surface known as 'the stone'. (This is not to be confused with 'the stone' in letterpress printing which is the steel-topped table on which printing metal is assembled in the forme for locking up in the chase before being placed on the bed of the machine, or moulded to form a stereo.)

The principle of lithography is that water and grease will not mix, which is why the porous limestone was used originally. In those days

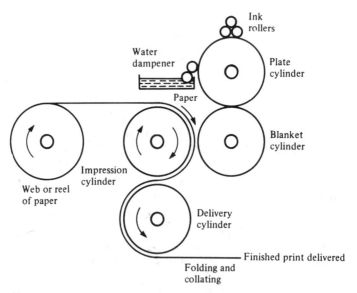

Figure 18.1 *Diagrammatic representation of the web-offset lithography process. The paper feeds from the web or reel. The plate prints onto the blanket which offsets the image onto the paper as it is fed through the impression cylinder. The delivery cylinder feeds the printed paper through to the folding, collating and delivery sections of the machine*

a litho artist would draw, say, a large poster in reverse on slabs of limestone, producing a separate stone for each colour. The drawn image would be greasy so that when ink was applied it stayed on the greasy printing image when water was next applied, washing away the unwanted ink from the non-printing areas. Although the process is today photographic, using metal or plastic plates, the same principle applies.

Offset means that the inked plate prints onto a rubber blanket which offsets onto the paper. On the rotary press there are three cylinders – the plate cylinder, the blanket cylinder and the impression cylinder – the paper passing between the blanket and impression cylinders to receive the image.

Web-offset means that a web or reel of continuous paper is used instead of single sheets of paper.

The advantages of offset-lithography are many. Machines are more compact than letterpress machines; inks have a lot of pigment and gloss so that rich colours are reproduced; the paper is not indented by metal printing surfaces (as with letterpress); the text is clearly produced because with photo-typesetting each character is of identical quality and there are no irregular or damaged letters; a good range of papers is now available whereas at one time hard surface cartridge paper was typical of the process; and fine halftone screens (about 100 to 120 screen) are used when letterpress might require much coarser screens (e.g. 65 screen for newsprint).

Lithography is used for the printing of inexpensive but beautiful picture books, and also for catalogues and sales literature such as holiday, horticulture, motorcar and fashion brochures.

Photogravure (intaglio)

There are two chief kinds of photogravure: the kind which economically produces large quantities of popular full-colour print on 'cheap' super-calendered paper, e.g. some women's magazines and commercial print such as labels and wrappings; and the second kind for the superb printing of reproductions of paintings plus the excellent printing of postage stamps.

Most gravure printing is by means of a recessed plate or 'sleeve' since it is cylindrical, the printing area being *below* the surface and consisting of minute cells etched to the depth required to contain the amount of ink necessary to print the gradation of tone. The surface of the sleeve is a square grid known as the 'resist'. Ink is applied and the surplus ink is scraped off the resist by a doctor blade. The paper passes through the machine and the ink is sucked out of the cells.

Being a volatile ink, the pigment stays on the paper and the solvent evaporates. A piece of photogravure print can be distinguished by the smell of the ink. The effect of the grid is to lay a fine square screen over the entire print area, and not just over halftone pictures as with the dot screens used in letterpress and lithography.

The quality of photogravure magazine printing (sometimes called rotogravure or colourgravure) tends to be poor, definition being lost by the velvety effect of reproduction, while the text is given a ragged effect by the resist.

However, as with the other processes, there have been revolutionary developments in photogravure. German print engineers have introduced the Klischograph hard dot cylinder which is not only a vast improvement upon the traditional photogravure sleeve with its comparatively crude reproduction but surpasses the fine definition of offset-lithography. Hard dot gravure still uses the cell system but instead of the cell being of varying depth it is of varying surface area. This is not unlike the halftone dot being of varying size, except that in Klischograph photogravure it is square, of varying size, and recessed.

Flexography

Originally used for printing on delicate materials such as foil, this special kind for letterpress printing has been adapted in the USA for newspaper printing and is used by the Daily Mail group. It uses photo polymer plates and bright Flexo inks, and print does not dirty the fingers.

Silk screen (stencil)

Probably the oldest printing process of all since the Chinese, centuries ago, stencil-printed through a mesh made of human hair, this is a remarkably versatile process. The principle is the stencil, a printing area being cut out to permit the passing of ink to the paper below. It is so simple that a home-made silk screen press can be made. In factories the process is used to print clock faces and instrument panels, and it can be used to print on curved surfaces such as soft-drink or beer bottles.

Its versatility lies in its ability to print on all sorts of materials such as paper, cloth, glass, plastic, foil, wood and so on. Readers will be familiar with ties, T-shirts, balloons, carrier bags, drip mats and other articles which have been printed in this fashion. It can be used for printing the price of goods posters seen on supermarket shop windows or pictorial posters seen on hoardings. But unlike the metal cut-out stencil used for marking crates, the silk-screen press has a mesh through which the ink is pressed. Presses can range from simple ones, hand operated with a squeegee roller, to electronically operated ones with photographic stencils capable of producing half-tone effects.

From these brief remarks it will be seen that printing is a fascinating subject, and a better understanding will be obtained by visiting printing works. However, most printers specialize in certain classes of work such as newspapers, books, commercial print, packaging, labels, picture postcards, calendars and so on, so that no one printing works will provide a complete picture of the craft.

For the same reason, when obtaining quotations for print it is necessary to pick the right printer for the job. Printers' estimates can vary astonishingly for the same job. This will be because they have different machines − faster or slower ones or ones printing from larger or smaller sheets and capable of printing larger or smaller quantities per hour. The price may also depend on how the job is set and made up. Human and machine time all have a bearing on price. It pays to talk to printers and ask them how the job will be produced, and to understand what they are talking about.

Production time schedules

The customer may want delivery by a certain date. The printer will say he can deliver by an agreed date provided a time schedule is followed. This is a discipline which must be obeyed, otherwise delays will result in rushed work, the need for overtime working and an increased price. A machine can set or print or bind only one job at a time, and production has to be planned to cope with the different stages of different jobs for different customers. A print schedule may look something like this.

Copy to printer	April 1
Proofs from printer	April 14
Corrected proofs to printer	April 21
Revised proofs from printer	April 28
Corrected revised proofs to printer	May 5
Delivery by printer	May 19

Obviously, there can be many variations on this example. It all depends on the job. 'Copy' means the layout, wording and pictures. If there is a lot of text, galley proofs may be supplied first (that is, long proofs without spacing and not made into pages), then page proofs will follow. If there is colour printing, machine proofs will be checked at the printers. If it is a lithographic job, photostat proofs will be supplied before the paste-up is photographed. There are various kinds of computerized photo-typesetting and proofs come in different forms. To avoid costly work, it is wise to heed the printer's instructions on making corrections, and to understand at which stage further corrections should not be made.

With modern typesetting it is so simple to make corrections that a proof may be submitted which is full of errors. It can be a frustrating experience to engage in the task of finding more errors than would have existed on a mechanically set proof, which had been read and corrected before submission. Printing has gone through a revolution from craftsmen printers who were artists in metal, to keyboard operators and paste-up artists whose attitude to print is as different as that of horse-carriage drivers and motorists to transport.

If copy is produced on a word processor, and the printer has computerized typesetting with online facilities, it is possible to transmit copy direct to the printer by telephone line without need for paper copy. Desktop publishing including copy and layout can be produced in this way, especially for house journals.

Correcting proofs

Two things should be remembered about correcting proofs. *First* it is too late at this stage to start rewriting copy. However, if serious amendments are vital, they should be made in such a way that the length of the column or page is not exceeded, otherwise subsequent columns and pages will have to be altered to take in the overflow of extra material. When deleting and replacing copy, the new copy should consist of the same number of characters, which includes punctuation marks and spaces between words. However, a feature of computerized typesetting is that whereas the old metal type was inelastic the modern keyboard operator can expand or condense type to fill more space or to accept more copy.

Second the corrections should be made clearly so that the printer can understand what is required. They should not be scribbled all over the proof, but confined to the margins and the proper correction signs used. Proof correction signs have been changed in recent years to conform with international needs, rather like traffic signs. The long-used *stet* (meaning 'let it stand' when something has been deleted in error) is now replaced by a tick in a circle. The current correction signs follow at the end of this chapter.

The following advice is helpful when correcting proofs.

- Author's corrections (i.e. changes introduced by the author or customer) should be made in black or blue. They may be chargeable!
- Corrections of printer's errors should be in red. (If the printer has read the proof he will make his own corrections in green.)
- Mentally divide the work with a vertical line down the middle, placing corrections on the left-hand half in the left-hand margin and those on the right-hand half in the right-hand margin.
- Read syllable by syllable slowly.
- Check the spelling of all names, especially those with alternative spellings such as Allan, Alan, Alain, and Allen, Francis and Frances, Sidney and Sydney, or Davis and Davies.
- Check figures, especially when there are noughts.
- Look up dates. It is easy to transfer dates from one year to another, or even look at the wrong year's calendar in a diary.
- Check prices. Have they changed? Is the currency correct?
- Check measurements − are there metric changes or requirements which have been overlooked?
- Watch out for transpositions of dates, such as 1918 for 1981.
- Check captions below illustrations. It is easy for a paste-up artist to paste captions wrongly, especially names of people. Such errors are very common in lithography.
- With litho proofs especially, look out for blank spaces where copy has run short. Can you fill it, perhaps by introducing a subheading? Also, in proofs based on computerized typesetting, watch out for long space gaps in lines, or wrongly broken words at the ends of lines. If an item is italicized, make sure that the typesetter has returned to roman where the italics should end.
- Watch out for words like 'of' and 'or' which are commonly mistyped in original copy, or misread by typesetters. Or 'i's' and 'e's' which can result in 'blind' instead of 'blend'. One of the most difficult things about proof reading is spotting an error which could make sense because it forms a normal word, as in the last example. Typesetters, using computer keyboards are apt not to worry about errors because they are so easy to correct, but the customer has to find them!
- Watch out for the typesetter's habit errors, or even the original typist's! There are some people who simply cannot spell certain words, e.g. 'seperate' for 'separate', 'liason' for 'liaison', 'personel' for 'personnel' and − although this has slipped into usage − 'all right' is better than 'alright'. There are also times when a peculiar, or even an American, spelling is correct for the job, e.g. 'disk' and not 'disc' in connection with computers or 'Travelers' with one 'l' for the American insurance company. Certain places names have

special spellings: Jakarta is nowadays not spelt Djakarta, and the country is Malaysia and not Malaya. Some countries have renamed capitals and major cities or given them new spellings, examples being Harare for Salisbury (Zimbabwe), and Beijing for Peking (China). One must not become confused between the different countries of the People's Republic of China (mainland China) and the Republic of China (Taiwan, formerly Formosa), the Democratic People's Republic of Korea (North Korea) and the Republic of Korea (South Korea). Both tend to use the name China or Korea as if the other did not exist. The Dutch prefer their country to be called The Netherlands rather than Holland which is a province.

● Finally, never be afraid to invite other people to check proofs, especially strangers to the copy who may well find errors which are overlooked by readers who are so familiar with the copy that they tend to read into it what they expect to find there.

New symbols for correcting proofs[2]

The symbols for correcting proofs used here are taken from a British Standard BS 5261: *Part 2 1976 Copy preparation and proof correction − Specification for typographic requirements, marks for copy preparation and proof correction, proofing procedure*. It was prepared by the British Standards Institution following discussions on an international standard of proof correction symbols to replace the former British Standard which used several English words or initial letters unacceptable internationally.

Extracts from the Standard are given below and all authors, printers, and publishers are recommended to adopt these correction symbols.

Instruction	Textual Mark	Marginal Mark
Correction is concluded	None	/
Leave unchanged	`------` under character to remain	(√)
Push down risen spacing material	Encircle blemish	⊥

Instruction	Textual Mark	Marginal Mark
Insert in text the matter indicated in the margin	$\wedge$	New matter followed by $\wedge$
Insert additional matter identified by a letter in a diamond	$\wedge$	$\wedge$ Followed by for example ⟨A⟩
Delete	/ through character(s) or ⊢————⊣ through word(s) to be deleted	⌀
Delete and close up	$\tilde{/}$ through character or ⊢═══⊣ through character e.g. charaꞔcter charaꞔcter	⌀
Substitute character or substitute part of one or more word(s)	/ through character or ⊢————⊣ through word(s)	New character or new word(s)
Wrong fount. Replace by character(s) of correct fount	Encircle character(s) to be changed	⊗
Change damaged character(s)	Encircle character(s) to be changed	✕
Set in or change to italic	———— under character(s) to be set or changed	⊔⊔

Instruction	Textual Mark	Marginal Mark
Set in or change to capital letters	▬▬▬▬ under character(s) to be set or changed	≡
Set in or change to small capital letters	▬▬▬ under character(s) to be set or changed	═
Set in or change to capital letters for initial letters and small capital letters for the rest of the words	≡ under initial letters and ▬▬▬▬ under rest of word(s)	≋
Set in or change to bold type	∿∿∿∿∿ under character(s) to be set or changed	∿
Change capital letters to lower case letters	Encircle character(s) to be changed	≢
Change italic to upright type	Encircle character(s) to be changed	Ⴑ
Invert type	Encircle character to be inverted	↻
Substitute or insert full stop or decimal point	/ through character or ⋀ where required	⊙
Substitute or insert semi-colon	/ through character or ⋀ where required	⁏
Substitute or insert comma	/ through character or ⋀ where required	＇

Instruction	Textual Mark	Marginal Mark
Start new paragraph		
Run on (no new paragraph)		
Centre	[enclosing matter to be centred]	[ ]
Indent		
Cancel indent		
Move matter specified distance to the right	enclosing matter to be moved to the right	
Take over character(s), word(s) or line to next line, column or page		
Take back character(s), word(s) or line to previous line, column or page		
Raise matter	over matter to be raised under matter to be raised	
Lower matter	over matter to be lowered under matter to be lowered	

Instruction	Textual Mark	Marginal Mark
Correct horizontal alignment	Single line above and below misaligned matter e.g. mi‿sa‿lign‿ed	‗‗‗
Close up. Delete space between characters or words	linking⌒⌣characters	⌒⌣
Insert space between characters	| between characters affected	Y
Insert space between words	between words affected Y	Y
Reduce space between characters	| between characters affected	⋔
Reduce space between words	between words affected ⋔	⋔
Make space appear equal between characters or words	between characters or words affected |	⋈

Reproduced by permission of the British Printing Industries Federation, from *Authors' Alterations Cost Money and Cause Delay* [2]

References

1 *Printing Reproduction Pocket Pal*, 14th edn, Creative Services Association, c/o R. Prior, D'Arcy Masius Benton & Bowles Ltd, 2 St James Square, London, SW1; International Paper Company, New York, 1989
2 *Authors' Alterations Cost Money and Cause Delay*, British Printing Industries Federation, 1979

PART THREE

The Media of Communication

19

The press

Still the most important mass medium

British public relations is remarkably lucky in having access to 12,000 publications according to *Benn's Media Directory*,[1] plus the novel facility of a national press. Few industrialized countries have the benefit of a centralized national press, but suffer a fragmented localized press at best linked by wire, facsimile and satellite transmission.

The reason for this is largely historical and geographical. London has been the British capital for 2000 years. Other countries have had various capitals, or they are either federations of former kingdoms and the old capitals remain as press centres (e.g. Italy), or there have been partitions and new capitals (e.g. Korea). It may also be a question of distance, as in Australia and the USA, which has resulted in city-based rather than nation-based newspapers. The exceptions in the USA are *USA Today* and the *Wall Street Journal*.

The press is the most versatile and resilient of all mass communications media. Sophisticated electronic media have not destroyed the press in industrial countries. As literacy grows in the developing world so the press develops to satisfy the demand for knowledge, news and entertainment. Kuala Lumpur had a direct-input computerized daily newspaper more than a year before Eddie Shah appeared in Fleet Street, News International became embroiled in the War of Wapping and *The Independent* arrived. In spite of a depressed economy, Nigeria has continued to see the launch of new press titles, including ones in languages other than English. In the Gulf countries the press has developed in recent years.

Radio, television and video cassettes cannot compete with the special merits of newspapers and magazines. What are these attributes? Why does the press continue to predominate?

Special merits and characteristics of the press

Depth of information

It can provide information in greater depth than transient broadcasting media. The extent of this will depend on the class of the newspaper, ranging from a brief account in a popular tabloid to more elaborate coverage in the business press or in magazines devoted to the subject.

Portability

It can be read anywhere, about the home or office, while travelling, sitting out-of-doors, over a meal, while waiting somewhere, at times and in places beyond the reach of electronic media where they may be inconvenient or unavailable. Newspapers and magazines are portable and can be carried almost anywhere, or they may be supplied at the reading point such as in a waiting room or reception area.

In fact, in developing countries educated members of a family may take newspapers to their villages and read them to illiterate relatives. A readership survey in Kenya has recorded the number of people who 'listen to newspapers'. On the other hand, people in other lands may, in spite of low income, be surprisingly literate and avid readers. In Hong Kong, for instance a hundred different Chinese-language newspapers are published daily, and great areas of the pavement are taken up by newspaper vendors who sell to Hong Kong's very mobile public.

Extended life

Publications often have an extended life because they are kept − binders are supplied by some magazines, or back numbers may be looked up in libraries − or because copies are passed on to other people. This is proved by the number of enquiries and orders which advertisers receive weeks, months and even years after publication. For some, this extended life is deliberate, as with *Radio Times* and *TV Times* which are published about four days in advance, are referred to daily, and so survive for at least ten days.

Some years ago, the regional evening newspaper was suffering from poor sales of both copies and advertisement space. The remedy was to extend the life of the normally quickly discarded copy by including features of home, entertainment and general interest. This encouraged the buyer, especially the male buyer, to take the newspaper home for the benefit of the family. This of course made the regional evening newspaper a good proposition for many advertisers who wished to reach domestic readerships. Eventually, it led to the home delivered free newspaper. All such newspapers are therefore valuable media for product publicity public relations stories.

Cuttings

Items may be cut out or photocopied and retained, either personally or by libraries which maintain files on many subjects, e.g. the Advertising Association and British Institute of Management libraries.

New types of newspapers and magazines

The change from letterpress to web-offset-litho printed newspapers, and from photogravure printed to web-offset-litho printed magazines, has been of special importance to the public relations practitioner. We now have newspapers such as *The Independent* and *The Independent on Sunday* which show an increase in intellectual readership, while the popular middle-class newspapers such as the *Daily Mail* and *Daily Express* and particularly the sensational tabloids such as the *Sun* and the *Daily Mirror* have all lost circulation.

With the new printing presses we have seen better typography and half-tone photographic reproduction, while colour pictures have become common in both national and regional newspapers. Generally, the quality of printing has improved, and we see this especially in the glossier, more colourful magazines printed by web-offset-litho, taking advantage of better quality paper, richer pigmented inks, finer half-tone screens and computerized photo-typesetting.

Yet another change has been in the inflationary spiral of cover prices, ironically at a time when there are hundreds of free local newspapers and magazines. With publishers enjoying production economies as web-offset printing, computerized typesetting and paper-less newsrooms have replaced the old over-manned presses, the metal typesetting and platemaking, and the newsrooms littered with type-writers and paper, the reader has had to pay more. Old newspaper reading habits have disappeared. There are fewer home-delivered newspapers. Many younger people never buy a newspaper. The habit of buying an evening paper on the way home has diminished. There is now only one London newspaper, and the *Evening News* which used to boast the highest evening newspaper sale in the world, vanished some years ago and resisted an attempted revival by the late Robert Maxwell. Meanwhile, magazine prices soar, often a pound or more instead of pence. Magazines like the *Radio Times* and *TV Times*, as a result of the removal of the monopolies on programme listings, and rivalry from the German *TV Quick* and the newspapers, have seen their circulations halved and their cover prices doubled.

The growth and popularity of the magazines supplied with weekend newspapers has seen the arrival of new titles and with their ready-made readerships they have been attractive to both advertisers and readers at the expense of the traditional big circulation consumer weeklies, especially women's magazines. No doubt cover prices have entered into this too.

The original 'colour supplements' printed by photogravure and issued with the *Sunday Times*, *Sunday Telegraph* and *Observer* have joined the offset-litho journals, and each Sunday newspaper has its characteristic magazine if not two. *The Independent* has its up-market Saturday magazine, for which the reader pays extra, while *The Independent on Sunday* has a tabloid business magazine and a large page colour magazine quite well printed on newsprint. There is therefore a rich variety of weekend journals, virtually a surfeit of reading material.

British magazines have also had to compete with an invasion of foreign magazines, from the USA, France and Germany, such as *Esquire*, *Elle*, *Bella*, *Best* and *Prima*. On the other hand, some British newspapers and magazines have acquired overseas circulations, *The Economist* selling more copies in the USA than in Britain, and the *Financial Times* being printed in Frankfurt, Roubaix, New York and Tokyo as well as in London.

A living medium

So, although newspapers used to be referred to as being ephemeral — tomorrow's fire-lighting or wrapping paper — there are circumstances in which they do have considerably long lives, and magazines may be retained indefinitely especially through secondary readerships in waiting rooms, hairdressing salons and reception areas, or through pass-on readership. The press is therefore very much a living medium, perhaps more so than has been suggested by advocates of electronic media who have tended to deride the press for its lack of participation and intimacy. By comparison with the 'cool' medium of films and television the Canadian academic Marshall McLuhan[2] called print and radio media non-participatory 'hot media'.

This does not deny that the electronic media have their special merits, but here let us go on and consider the demerits of the press as a public relations communication medium.

Special demerits of the press

Short life

While bearing in mind what was said above, it is nevertheless true that newspapers particularly can have short lives, and a morning paper may survive no more than a commuter's journey to work. Consequently, one has to be wary of the large circulation and readership figures claimed for them.

It is worth remembering at this stage that the circulation is the net average sales over a period, usually six months. That means that there can be days or weeks when sales are below or above the average. Readership is a very different thing. It is not a strictly counted and audited figure but an estimated figure of secondary readership based on an interviewed sample, and it takes into consideration that people other than the original purchaser may also read the publication. It is therefore important to interpret figures carefully. A business newspaper like the *Financial Times* could have a small circulation but, because of pass-round, reception room and library readership, it has a high readership figure.

Moreover, not every section of a paper is likely to be read by every reader: those who read the sports pages may never read the city pages and vice versa. In calculating 'opportunities to see' readership figures for press cuttings it may be necessary to estimate the *proportion* of a readership figure which will actually read the *part* of the publication from which the cutting was clipped. As an example of this, a reading and noting test showed that the most read feature in the *Financial Times* was not the financial news but the digest of general news on the front page. Similarly, we should not be deluded by the multi-million circulation and readerships claimed for popular tabloids: one such British paper has won a large circulation because it does not have too much to read in it, and its 'readers' are more interested in its pictures, cartoons and contests. So, the story in the *Sun* may have been hardly noticed, whereas the one in *The Times* could have been studied carefully, yet the former's sales are ten times those of the latter.

Bias

Most newspapers and magazines have their particular bias so that either they do not print certain stories or, if they do, they distort them. There is rarely objective reporting in the press, and it is often true that a good, factual news release from a professional public relations source is more impartial than the average newspaper report. *The Guardian*

and *Observer*, for instance, sometimes adopt an attitude of mock intel-
lectualism and parody public relations events or stories (as we have
already seen in the preface and in Chapter 15), whereas the *Financial
Times* welcomes and uses public relations material. In sending news
stories to the press it is wise to understand the peculiar traits of those
publications which insist on rewriting stories and getting them wrong.

Editorial bias has to be understood and accepted. It may derive from
political, religious, class, ethnic or simply proprietorial attitudes. The
occasion of the Conservative Government's decision in October 1992
to close 31 coalmines brought condemnation from every national newspaper, in an extreme and rare example of unanimity of opinion by the
British press. Bias can be observed by studying the way different
newspapers will treat the same story, and it has to be reckoned with
when sending releases to the press, or inviting journalists to press
receptions. Some papers may be best omitted from media and invitation
lists. It is not only public relations people who are responsible for the
adversarial situation.

Unreliability of reporting

Newspapers, especially, can be unreliable in their reporting, either
because of the speed with which they are produced or because journalists cannot be expected to know everything about anything, and they
cannot know for certain whether the stories they receive are either true
or accurate. Unfortunately, readers are apt to believe what they read in
the papers on the optimistic assumption that it would not be printed if
it was not true.

Some years ago, while I was writing the first edition of this book a
Russian defector returned from the USA to Russia. Some months later
reports appeared simultaneously in the British press that (a) he had
been shot and (b) he had just published a book on his American
experiences. No report made both claims. No London editor had apparently bothered to check the truth or otherwise of the two conflicting
stories, although one newspaper stated that the source of the execution
story had been an American newspaper. So much for the veracity of
the British press! There may be an adversarial attitude between journalists and PROs, and Polly Toynbee[3] writing in *The Guardian* may regard
PROs as 'disinformers', but PROs are entitled to be equally sceptical
about the press whose standards would seem to be considerably lower
than those required by the IPR *Code of Professional Conduct*.[4]

Behind this sort of controversy lies the illusion of the freedom of the
press, and the idea that the press is a democratic fourth estate, but as
will be observed if one watches the behaviour of our millionaire

newspaper proprietors, including the late unlamented Robert Maxwell, newspaper publishing is merely a business like (or perhaps unlike!) any other. Far from the public relations world attempting to manipulate the press it is often more nearly the case of the press exploiting public relations opportunities, even though they like to sneer at political initiatives as 'public relations exercises'.

However, to be realistic and to avoid being too contentious, the publishers are entitled to print what is most likely to sell papers, whether it be a law report in *The Times*, a knitting pattern in *Woman's Weekly*, or a nude in the *Sun*. In public relations terms, this means that stories are most likely to be printed if editors consider them, in the words of Ivy Ledbetter Lee, to be of *interest and value* to their particular readers. This will be coloured by the fact that in some cases readers dislike American multinationals and nuclear missiles or resent industrial disputes and protest marches. The PRO, in submitting press material, has to reconcile him- or herself to the facts of life about a commercially-owned press and the peculiarities of democracy in a free enterprise society which may not always work in his or her favour.

Location and distribution

Britain is unusual in having both a national and a regional or local press. This is because London, having been the capital for centuries, also became the country's press centre when good road and rail communications and a more urbanized population made it economic to produce national newspapers. The first popular national daily was Northcliffe's ha'penny *Daily Mail* of 1896. Overseas visitors are sometimes puzzled to find local weekly newspapers in Britain which have circulations as large as their national newspapers, and to be even more bewildered by the presence of free newspapers with circulations of maybe 100,000 copies weekly. There are about 850 free newspapers! The volume of the British press is phenomenal, and it is not therefore surprising that press relations forms such an important part of public relations.

If we take round figures, the circulations of the London-based British national dailies were roughly as follows in 1992:

Sun	3,500,000
Daily Mirror	2,800,000
Daily Express	1,500,000
Daily Mail	1,700,000
Daily Star	800,000

Daily Telegraph	1,000,000
The Guardian	400,000
The Independent	380,000
The Times	380,000
Financial Times	290,000
Today	500,000
Daily Sport	300,000

Circulation figures are issued every six months, and result from publishers returning audited figures for the number of copies printed, given away and actually sold to the Audit Bureau of Circulations which certifies the average net sale. *Readership* figures result from interviewing members of the public to discover which publications they read, and the demographic details (e.g. age, sex, occupation, etc.) of those readers. One is an arithmetic calculation, the other is the result of a national readership survey conducted by an independent research company on behalf of National Readership Surveys which replaced JICNARS in 1992.

NRS represents the publishers, advertising agencies and advertisers through their trade associations and is thus a tripartite body servicing all sides of the industry. While it operates primarily in the interests of advertising, the findings published in the National Readership Survey are valuable when evaluating media and public relations coverage. Thus, NRS is also independent compared to surveys which are occasionally conducted by individual publishers, or even the old Hulton Readership Survey of the 1950s which attempted to survey the press in general although sponsored by a publisher.

Readership figures are classified according to the social grades A, B, C1, C2, D and E which represent employment as distinct from socio-economic grades based on income. The latter are not used in Britain, but are still used in those developing countries where the majority of people are in the poorer groups and employment can be defined less distinctly. Although socioeconomic groups are still sometimes mentioned in Britain they were actually replaced by social grades more than 20 years ago.

Social grades

Social grades in Britain may be described briefly as follows:

A	**Upper middle class**	The head of the household is a successful business or professional	2.7%

		person, civil servant, or has considered private means	
B	**Middle class**	Quite senior people, not quite at the top	15.2%
C1	**Lower middle class**	Tradespeople, non-manual workers, 'white collar' workers	24.1%
C2	**Skilled working class**	Usually an appenticed worker, 'blue collar' workers	27.1%
D	**Semi-skilled and unskilled working class**		17.8%
E	**Those at lowest level of subsistence**	Pensioners, casual workers, those dependent on social security	13.1%

The British mass market thus consists of about three-quarters of the population, the readership of popular newspapers, and the audience for peak viewing television. It is very different from the 20 per cent literate elite in many developing countries, although in the case of India even that proportion is equal to the total population of Nigeria.

In a class-conscious country like Britain the national newspapers can be ranked against social grades, roughly as follows:

A	*The Times, Financial Times*
B	*Daily Telegraph, The Guardian, The Independent*
C1	*Daily Express, Daily Mail, Today*
C2, D, E	*Sun, Daily Mirror, Daily Star, Daily Sport*

Most popular papers are tabloids, only *The Times, Financial Times, Daily Telegraph, The Guardian* and *The Independent* retaining the old broad-sheet big-page format. Tabloids are no longer restricted to the 'gutter press'.

Kinds of publication

Daily morning newspapers

Daily morning newspapers are usually published six times a week — that is, except on Sunday in Christian countries (or Friday or Saturday where other religions predominate).

However, new technologies have brought about three changes.

1 Direct-input computerized editing and setting and web-offset-litho printing are calling for earlier copy times and dates.

2   Locally printed editions, using facsimile and satellite services, are leading to editions being printed simultaneously at strategically situated printers. In the USA, *USA Today* was the first American daily, being printed at fifty-three US locations and also in Europe and Asia.

3   Some newspapers have achieved international circulations by sending copy by satellite to printers in distant parts of the world, to mention only the *Financial Times*. The *International Herald Tribune* is printed simultaneously in Paris, London, Hong Kong, Singapore and other cities round the world.

4   Most London newspapers have moved to modern offset-litho printing works located in East London, or they print at strategically located contract printers outside London, e.g. Portsmouth. Newspapers may be edited in London and transmitted by facsimile to regional printers.

Regional or city daily morning newspapers

Outside Britain, it is common for morning newspapers to circulate within certain population areas, with perhaps a fringe circulation penetrating further afield. Like the *Washington Post*, the *Sydney Morning Herald* and *Il Messaggero di Roma*, their titles often take the city of origin.

But in Britain there are long-established regional mornings which compete with the nationals, although they tend to have a middle-class or business readership. Their circulations range from about 40,000 to 100,000. Three of the best-known are the *Western Morning News* (Plymouth), the *Liverpool Daily Post* and the *Yorkshire Post* (Leeds).

In addition to the English regional mornings, there are similar papers published in Scotland, Wales and Northern Ireland which really have their own national press, again in competition with the London nationals. There are the *Glasgow Herald* and the *Scotsman* in Scotland, the *Western Mail* in Wales, and the *Belfast Telegraph* in Northern Ireland.

Interesting variations occur in other countries. The popular German *Bild* (which is more sensational than the British *Sun*) has a huge multi-million circulation made up of local editions published in several German cities, and it is read by more than a quarter of the population. In the USA there are chains of newspapers which appear under separate city titles, but contain some standard material which is syndicated nationally to all newspapers.

In Nigeria there are newspapers based on regional cities like Enugu (*Daily Star*), Ibadan (*Daily Sketch*) and Jos (*Nigerian Standard*), but the

Lagos *Daily Times* seeks national distribution and achieves a circulation of some 400,000 (comparable to the small UK circulation of *The Times*). But in developing countries like Nigeria the majority of its 80 million people (50 per cent perhaps) are illiterate and very poor, and they are outside the mass market available to a newspaper in industrial, literate and much richer countries. Moreover, a Nigerian paper has the problem of reaching even literates scattered throughout a vast country where cities are often hundreds of miles apart (Maiduguri being 1000 miles, Kano 700 miles and Enugu 300 miles from Lagos). Even reasonable road transport can be disrupted by the weather. Yet the educated Nigerian is an avid reader, and newspapers and magazines sell readily.

Circulations of newspapers, or numbers of titles, may be restricted by other factors. Newsprint is a costly import and countries with balance of payments problems (Ghana and Zambia particularly) may have to limit the number of copies printed. In Nigeria, the competitive and popular *The Punch* — a sort of Nigerian *Sun* complete with page three pin-up — is restricted by lack of machinery, otherwise it would really challenge the *Daily Times* because it has often lived up to its name.

The situation is far simpler in the small island state of Singapore where the *Straits Times* can circulate to a largely literate English-speaking population (in spite of Chinese predominance), the paper containing a remarkable number of broadsheet pages and covering every possible interest. Neighbouring Indonesia, with an area as big as the USA but with its 160 million people of diverse ethnic groups scattered among hundreds of islands with three time scales, has nationally distributed newspapers. However, 80 per cent of their circulation is contained in the capital city of Jakarta. The largest circulation newspaper, *Kompass*, sells 500,000 copies daily.

A literate island community like that of Trinidad enjoys well-distributed newspapers like *The Guardian*, but because of Trinidad's interest in foreign places this country's papers are exceptional in their international news coverage.

A factor, apart from literacy, which characterizes Asian newspapers is that in addition to English-language newspapers there are ones printed in the languages of the Indian and Chinese communities or in the national Malay and Indonesian languages. There are also peculiarities that while English is the national language of Singapore, it is the second language in Malaysia, while in Indonesia (where English is widely spoken by the educated and business community) English-language newspapers (with much syndicated material from the Western press) are read mainly by local business people, expatriates and visitors from Britain, Canada, the USA and Australia. When a newspaper in a foreign country is printed in English one has to ask for whom is it published? In the Middle East there are likely to be foreigners from more than a hundred countries, and since they are unlikely to learn Arabic, English has become the common language with the exception of some Indian languages.

India presents a publishing enigma. It has famous English language newspapers such as the *Times of India*, published in Bombay with a daily circulation of 280,000. But the sub-continent has a population of 717 million, the official languages are Hindi and English, fourteen other languages are listed in the Constitution but newspapers are published in these sixteen and dozens of lesser languages. India has 835 daily newspapers!

Where newspapers are printed in a variety of languages (e.g. English and Swahili in Kenya, English and Greek in Cyprus) there are bound to be comparatively small circulations because the total newspaper circulation is dissipated by the different language versions. Thus, it is easier for British newspapers to have large circulations because only one language is common although some immigrant communities (e.g. Indian) do have their own language papers. An interesting move in the direction of non-European language newspapers is the existence of the Japanese daily *Asahi Shimbun* which has an international satellite edition published in London by the Mirror Group for circulation to the thousands of Japanese living in Britain and continental Europe.

Evening newspapers

This is a rather ambiguous description because so-called 'evening' newspapers often have early editions appearing in the morning, follow-up sports editions and lunchtime editions until the main city edition appears as people are going home from work. Publishers with new technology equipment may publish up to ten editions during the day. The London evening newspaper, *Evening Standard*, has a fringe circulation up to fifty miles from London, but within forty miles of the capital and in most of the large cities of England, Scotland, Wales and Northern Ireland there are regional evening newspapers. Some have extensive circulation areas, North Wales being served by papers from Liverpool and Manchester. While the number of regional titles has shrunk from the days when several cities including London had two if not three evenings, there are still 112 dailies published outside London, most of them evenings.

Evening newspapers have considerable circulations ranging from about 180,000 for the *Liverpool Echo* to 77,000 for the *Brighton Evening Argus* which is close enough to London to have to compete with the

Evening Standard. These newspapers cover many popular topics and can be valuable for public relations purposes. In Scotland, the *Evening Times* of Glasgow sells about 155,000 copies, in Wales the *South Wales Evening Post* of Swansea sells about 68,000 copies, while in Northern Ireland the *Belfast Telegraph* sells about 128,000 copies. While these figures are quite large, most evening newspapers show a falling circulation. This is partly due to the economic situation, and possibly some competition from television, including teletext, but it must also reflect the impact of free newspapers.

Sunday newspapers

The majority of British Sunday newspapers are national, but there are a few regional ones, and there are 'national' Sundays in Scotland and Northern Ireland. We have already discussed the weekend magazines.

A similar social grading breakdown can be made with Sunday newspapers except that the 'heavies' do not correspond with *The Times* and the *Financial Times*, and they have larger middle class circulations. The breakdown is as follows:

A, B	*Sunday Times, Observer, Sunday Telegraph, The Independent on Sunday*
C1	*Sunday Express, Mail on Sunday*
C2, D, E	*News of the World, Sunday People, Sunday Mirror, Sunday Sport*

The English regional newspapers are the Birmingham *Sunday Mercury*, the Newcastle-upon-Tyne *Sunday Sun*, and the Plymouth *Sunday Independent*. Scotland has its Glasgow *Sunday Mail*, and *Sunday Post*, while Northern Ireland has its *Sunday News* and *Sunday World* which also circulate in parts of the Irish Republic.

Local weekly newspapers

Britain's 2,127 weekly newspapers tend to fall into three groups (a) those published in the suburbs of cities like London, Glasgow and Manchester; (b) town weeklies; and (c) regional series or county newspapers.

In Britain most towns, and even suburbs of the largest cities, have their own weekly newspapers. In Greater London there are big circulation weeklies, and a number of groups like the *Croydon Advertiser* and *Kentish Times* with separate editions carrying the titles of nearby towns or boroughs. The *Croydon Advertiser* group (52,000) includes papers covering Croydon, Coulsdon and Purley, Banstead, Beckenham and Penge, Bromley, Caterham, Epsom and Ewell, Sutton and Wallington. Each 'Advertiser', with its separate title, publishes special pages of news, and some advertisements, which are of local interest, while the rest of the paper is standard to all editions. This is quite an editorial juggling feat, the more so when one considers that the papers are now printed by new technology methods (including colour) at Portsmouth which is eighty miles away from the Croydon office.

Weekly papers have been decreasing both in numbers of titles and in numbers of sales for some years. On the other hand, throughout the land most urban dwellers receive two, three or four home-delivered free newspapers. There are about 850 titles with a total weekly distribution of 26 million. During the early 1980s this figure increased five times. While these papers appear to rival traditional paid-for papers it is interesting that in many cases they are published by traditional publishers, some of whom had converted failing paid-for papers into profitable free newspapers. Others are owned by national newspaper groups. But some of the owners are a new breed of pioneering publishers who have installed new technology equipment and challenged restrictive trade unions, as Eddie Shah did long before he moved to national publishing with his *Today*.

Once given the rather derogatory name of 'free sheets', they have gained respectability with their own trade body, the Association of Free Newspapers, which produces a directory. Another form of recognition was the creation of Verified Free Distribution in 1981 as a subsidiary of the Audit Bureau of Circulations.

Magazines

These can be divided into many categories, and in industrialized countries there may be hundreds of titles. *Advertiser's Annual*[5] has 138 categories ranging from American Football to Yachting. In developing countries there may be few indigenous magazines, and many of those on sale will be imported (e.g. *Reader's Digest*, *Newsweek*), or published abroad and sold locally (e.g. *West Africa* and many Arab journals). The 'trade press' may be unknown, if only in that the majority of traders would be unable to read them.

The versatility, popularity and high circulations of magazines make them particularly valuable to the PRO in reaching his or her many publics.

Such is the variety of weekly and monthly magazines that it is possible to target almost any public with public relations material. Details of forthcoming features are listed in the monthly looseleaf *Advance*.[6]

This is one area of publishing which shows vigour and growth even though cover prices are expensive. Years ago publishers feared that television would harm the press, but it has created so many new interests that new magazines have found a good market among readers who want to know more, whether it be about sports, cooking, antiques, travel or any other topic introduced to them by television. Full publishing and advertising data will be found in *Advertiser's Annual*.[5]

Under the broad heading of Trade, Technical and Professional there are some 5500 British titles, while consumer and special interest magazines total around 2300 titles, according to *Benn's Media Directory*.[1] Let us look more closely at the various classes of magazine.

Consumer magazines

Covering popular subjects, many of these magazines have large circulations – hundreds of thousands, frequently more than a million. Sometimes called 'specialist' magazines, they cover every possible interest such as food, sports, hobbies, gardening, politics, religion, travel, fashion, motoring, house-buying and many other topics. They are called consumer magazines because they are bought by members of the general public and sold by newsagents. A visit to a High Street newsagent or to a bookstall at a large railway terminus will give a good idea of the range of interests catered for. Most are printed in colour, usually by web-offset-litho.

One of the most successful and interesting groups of consumer magazines, in which there are today many sub-groups, is that of the women's press. Some titles of very different character such as *The Lady* (1885) and *Woman's Weekly* (1911) go on for ever and with remarkably little change in their style of content. *Women's Weekly*, famous for its knitting patterns and romantic fiction, remains a great favourite. In recent years we have seen the arrival of new women's and home interest magazines appealing to different age and income groups.

A very specialized group of magazines which offers opportunities for public relations articles of interest to travellers and tourists are the in-flight magazines to be found in the passenger seat pockets of nearly every airline.

Mention has already been made of the 'listing' magazines covering TV, radio and satellite TV programmes. They include *Radio Times*, *TV Times*, *TV Quick* and *What's On TV*. They contain large editorial sections devoted to broadcast entertainment.

Trade, technical and professional magazines

Trade magazines although quite different, are sometimes wrongly lumped together under the general description of the 'trade press'. The trade press is addressed to the trade (distributors such as wholesalers, retailers, agents, brokers); technical journals are read by technicians such as electricians, builders, engineers and other craftsmen; professional magazines are published for professionals such as lawyers, doctors, architects, teachers and other qualified people. If the subject is very specialized, the national circulation will be small and the journals are sold internationally to make them viable, while many of the British and American journals are so authoritative that they are widely read abroad, especially in countries which have no such press of their own. Such journals often incorporate 'International' in their titles, e.g. *Coffee and Cocoa International*, *International Drinks Bulletin* and *Conferences, Exhibitions and Incentives International*. The British Medical Association earns considerable income from the international sale of its medical journals. Some examples of the three distinct classes of journal are:

Trade press: *The Grocer, Retail Fruit Trade Review*
Technical journals: *Food Manufacture, Electronics World + Wireless World*
Professional journals: *The Lancet, Architects' Journal*

These are all very useful publications for public relations purposes, but the size of circulation, coverage of the trade, industry or profession, and consequently their impact and influence, may depend on the method of distribution. This may also influence the type of material carried, that is, mostly news or mostly feature articles. Do readers *subscribe* to it, which could mean that the circulation is not large since it is dependent on payment? Is it *mailed to members* of an organization? If so, the circulation will depend on the size of the membership, but it would mean an official and regular distribution. Or does it have a *controlled circulation* – that is, mailed free of charge to a combination of selected readers and those who have requested copies? Most of the circulation of *PR Week* is of this order, and is substantial, whereas the circulation of *Public Relations* is limited to the membership of the IPR. Controlled circulation figures can be impressive, meaning good penetration of the subject area, more than 15,000 in the case of *PR Week* against 4500 in the case of *Public Relations*, but one is weekly and the other is monthly. Their content is very different, *PR Week* printing much gossip about the industry and recruitment advertising while *Public Relations* concentrates on news about the IPR and feature articles. The public relations practitioner needs to be aware of the very different content of journals with similar titles.

In selecting these journals for news release distribution, invitations to press events, or as possible journals with which to negotiate feature articles, all these factors need to be considered.

Directories, year books, annuals, diaries

In some of these annual publications entries are free, in others they are paid for, while in both cases charges are made for more prominent or more displayed entries. Absence from such publications, or inadequate information, can be very bad public relations, giving the impression that an organization is of too little consequence to be listed. It is therefore a managerial responsibility on the part of either the in-house PRO or the consultant to see that an organization is properly listed wherever possible. This may also include references in editorial features.

For example, the PRO or press officer of every British organization should be shown in the *Hollis Press and Public Relations Annual*[7] so that any editor can make contact whenever necessary, and so that PROs may contact one another. In the consultancy section it may be advisable to list clients, while overseas consultancies should be shown in the international section. The same applies to *Advertiser's Annual*.

The author has known cases where contracts (or invitations to tender) have been lost simply because a company or its products and services were not listed in directories which were consulted when offers were being invited. Certain yearbooks and diaries give advice to readers, and it will be in the public relations practitioner's interest to make sure that such published advice is correct, up-to-date or refers to the company's products or services if this is permissible.

A large part of a PRO's skill lies not so much in having personal contacts with editors and journalists – they may be too numerous for this to be physically possible – but in knowing the publications themselves. This may embrace their frequency, circulation area, readership profile or penetration of the subject area. How do they fit into public relations programmes, how well do they reach particular publics, and which ones should be chosen for, or omitted from, mailing lists for news release distribution, or invitations for press events? This intimate knowledge of media cannot be stressed enough.

A problem when compiling mailing lists is that the titles themselves may not define the nature of the journals or their readership, and unless this is known (and it can be found from the directories mentioned above) it is very easy to send stories to the wrong publications. This is not only a waste but it can irritate editors who will expect their journals to be better known by PROs.

Standard mailing lists are rarely satisfactory (unless the same publications are relevant every time), and it is best to compile tailor-made lists for each occasion. Far too many news releases are mailed indiscriminately, which is lazy, inefficient and unprofessional. It fails to take into consideration whether some releases are too late because the journal, e.g. a monthly, has already gone for printing.

How to know the press

1   Study newspapers and magazines at first hand as often as possible. They do change, fold or appear for the first time. Look at them in libraries. Browse through copies in newsagents' shops, or at railway or airport newstands. This is easy and can be a valuable and informative habit. The author has done this all his working life.
2   Read the profiles on publications in *Benn's Media Directory*. No PRO can afford to be without this annual.
3   Make use of the media lists supplied by PIMS or Two-Ten Communications, the editorial information contained in *PR Planner*, or the advance information in *Advance*. (Addresses will be found in the Appendices.)
4   Keep up-to-date with news of new publications and publishing plans as announced in *UK Press Gazette* published weekly and again listed in the Appendices.
5   Talk to editors and journalists, such as at press receptions, on the phone or whenever you meet, and ask them what they want and when they want it.

With such comprehensive insight, maximum coverage can be assured. Press relations has to be worked at, and it often calls for selectivity. It is wiser to send a story to one journal and get 100 per cent coverage, than to broadcast it hopefully to 100 journals, get only one cutting, and achieve only one per cent coverage! Far too many news releases are sent to far too many publications, simply because the PRO did not know the right ones to mail at the right time. The hit rate is more important than the number of releases distributed. Many up-to-date lists are published from which a minimal mailing list can be selected, e.g. *Editors*, PIMS and Two-Ten.

References

1   *Benn's Media Directory*, UK, Europe and overseas volumes, Benn Business Information Services Ltd, Tonbridge
2   McLuhan, Marshall, *The Medium Is The Message*, Penguin, London, 1967
3   Toynbee, Polly, *The Guardian*, 5 November 1984
4   *Code of Professional Conduct*, Institute of Public Relations, London, 1986
5   *Advertiser's Annual*, Reed Information Service, Windsor Court, East Grinstead
6   *Advance*, monthly, Themetric Ltd, Aylesbury
7   *Hollis Press and Public Relations Annual*, Hollis Directories, Sunbury on Thames

20

Broadcasting

How broadcasting media differ from the press

Broadcasting media are very different from the press, and television and radio have their special advantages and disadvantages. They do have one thing in common, which is that they are transient unless recorded on video or audio tape. Unlike printed messages, it is difficult to retain broadcast messages. They usually have to be absorbed at the exact time of transmission, and one cannot make later or repeated studies of the message. One has, therefore, to be satisfied with instant impact, and to remember that the message can be misunderstood or forgotten.

And yet these electronic media can be extremely valuable when the public relations manager or consultant is planning public relations programmes, if they are understood and used properly, especially as audiences may well exceed the readerships of newspapers or magazines. In Britain, a networked television programme may have an audience of up to 20 million viewers.

As a result of the Broadcasting Act 1990, the Independent Television Commission became responsible for commercial and cable television in 1990 and at the same time the Radio Authority became responsible for commercial radio. Previously, the Independent Broadcasting Authority had been responsible for both commercial radio and TV. New ITV franchises were awarded on the basis of auctions, while national commercial radio franchises were also awarded, the first being Classic FM which began broadcasting in September 1992.

Television

It is difficult to generalize about television because there are different systems in almost every country. In the USA there are many commercial television stations in each city, whereas in Britain there is the national BBC (non-commercial) and the fifteen regional commercial stations plus Channel 4 and Good Morning TV known as ITV (although the controlling authority is the Independent Television Commission). The BBC also has some regional programmes. The programmes of either BBC 1 and 2 or of the ITV companies may also be broadcast partly or wholly nationally or even at different times or on different days.

In Singapore there are programmes in English, Indian and Chinese, but in Indonesia they are entirely in the national languange. The expressions 'commercial' and 'sponsored' television have different meanings in some countries. By commercial television we mean in Britain that a company such as Central (Birmingham) or Granada (Manchester) will be responsible for the programmes, and will sell advertising time not exceeding six minutes in each hour and usually in two-minute slots. But in Nigeria there will be both brief commercials as in Britain, and whole programmes (mainly sports such as major and often international football or athletics) sponsored by an advertiser such as Coca-Cola, Cadbury's or Guinness with interpolated commercials.

Changes in sponsorship

However, major changes have occurred in Britain, both in regard to BBC and ITV programmes, and forms of sponsored programme now exist, although not quite in the form which created the original soap opera in the USA when an advertiser not only bought airtime but made the programme. The British compromise is that while programmes continue to be made by broadcasting companies or the BBC, they can be made in collaboration with a commercial sponsor. This sponsor is not allowed to influence the programme content, or to have its products included or mentioned in the programme, but for a fee it is entitled to credits in trailers, at the beginning and end of the programme and during breaks, the latter being called break bumpers. The programme may well be made before a sponsor is found.

The fee for such sponsorship starts at around £300,000 and depends on the frequency of the programme. For instance, there could be six episodes of a drama series but weather reports appear daily. Weather reports have been sponsored by Powergen and Legal and General Insurance. Sony sponsored the Rugby international matches. Kronenbourg lager sponsored a *Maigret* series, Croft Port sponsored the *Rumpole* series in 1991 and again in 1992, while Beamish stout financed an *Inspector Morse* series and repeats, and then a further series. Peugeot 106 supported the second series of *Prime Suspect*.

The time allotted to credits is very brief but creative firms such as Media Dimensions have exploited the opportunities very cleverly. A number of musical programmes have been made in association with the BBC, including the Young Musician of the Year competition sponsored on BBC TV by Lloyds Bank, who also sponsor fashion shows seen on BBC TV. Meanwhile, BSkyB has sponsored the Cricket World Cup and Premier League football.

Sponsorships on commercial radio are common, but are more localized because there are so many ILR stations. Sponsors are permitted a brief statement about what they make or do.

Both commercial radio and TV sponsorships are strictly controlled by the separate sponsorship codes of the Radio Authority and the Independent Television Commission. Primarily, this kind of sponsorship is a form of advertising, as distinct from the kind of sponsorship described in the special chapter on the subject in Part Four (Chapter 33). This latter type of sponsorship could be for advertising, marketing or public relations, but it seeks media coverage on its merits and this coverage will be at the discretion of the media. For instance, a company may sponsor a football strip, as Sharp do with Manchester United, and watchers of a match in which the team is playing, both at the ground and on TV, will be aware of Sharp's sponsorship. Similarly, when the results of various cricket and football matches are broadcast the sponsor's name will be given. So, too, with horseracing, whether it be the Whitbread Gold Cup or the Ever Ready Derby. But the games, races or results will be broadcast independently by the TV and radio stations and no payment will have been made for this airtime.

However, while the new kind of broadcasting sponsorships may be undertaken for advertising purposes, and they have proved to be very economical, they do nevertheless have a certain public relations content. This occurs in two ways. It can be very appropriate to associate a product with a characteristic programme, and it can also be a good thing to associate a product with a programme which is well liked so that the product shares in this goodwill. It is significant, for instance, that the three characters Rumpole, Maigret and Inspector Morse all enjoy a drink, and their sponsors are all drink firms. They are also, all three, distinguished and well-liked programmes. Matching the product to the character, the programme and the social grade of viewer is important and beneficial.

While the convention of a balance between entertainment, information and education may be the ideal, the tendency is for television to lean towards popular entertainment, especially if audiences are large and there is competition between stations, not forgetting competition between ITV and BBC. Sometimes there is competition between the stations of neighbouring countries.

Even the news programmes in Britain verge on entertainment with glamorous newscasters, quips between newscasters, and humorous news stories used as tail-pieces. Supposedly serious interviews have this entertainment appeal if the interviewer is provocative and can provoke argument. This has to be recognized by those who would like to introduce serious material into interviews, chat shows and so on. They are likely to be disappointed.

After all, television is watched as a form of relaxation, and has largely replaced the cinema and live theatre. London theatres are attended mostly by foreign visitors, most cinemas have closed, been converted into bingo halls, or have survived by being converted into smaller multiple cinemas.

In the Third World there has been a major change similar to the forests of aerials which appeared on Council estates following the introduction of commercial or independent television in Britain some 40 years ago. No longer is television an élitist medium in developing countries because not only has television become popular in urban areas but by means of community viewing in public halls it has been brought within reach of those who cannot afford sets. In some countries television is no longer limited to areas served by electricity because portable sets are available which are run off rechargeable 12-volt car batteries. Moreover, in Indonesia, for example, in spite of its size, programmes are transmitted throughout the country by means of a satellite and 96 stations.

Satellite TV

With the advent of satellite TV, many parts of the world now receive television programmes broadcast from stations hundreds of miles away. BSkyB has slowly built up a large audience in Britain. The Japanese in Europe receive their own satellite programme. The Gulf states enjoy satellite television, and mention has already been made of Indonesia. An interesting development in 1992 was the Hindi channel Star TV, broadcasting from Hong Kong. Not only does it compete with the Indian government's television stations, Doordarsham, claiming 8 million viewers with the prospect of reaching up to 30 million viewers in India, but Star TV's 'footprint' reaches from Turkey to Singapore. It could also be received by Pakistanis, whose Urdu language is similar to Hindi, and reach Indians and Pakistanis in the Middle East and South East Asia.

There is a partnership deal between Star TV and the BBC World

Television Service. The costs of Star TV are covered by Hutchvision which sells airtime to advertisers and broadcasts the service to Asia/ India by satellite.

This brings us to the BBC World Television Service (WSTV) and BBC TV Europe, modern counterparts of the BBC's long-established World Service Radio. While the latter continues to be broadcast from Bush House in the Aldwych, London, the international TV services operate from BBC Enterprises' building in White City, home of BBC TV. In 1992 this was a rapidly expanding BBC service, having launched in 1991 a 24-hour news and information service across Asia from Taiwan to Turkey, Siberia to Sumatra.

This followed the creation of a daily half-hour news bulletin to 2 million subscribers to BBC TV Europe. This grew into a half-hour bulletin every hour with 15 minutes of news from BBC correspondents world-wide plus business and weather information. This was extended to an African and a Canadian service with plans for Japanese and Australian services.

WSTV is often linked with other services, and via Canadian Broad-casting Company's cable service, Worldnews, it reaches 6 million cabled homes across Canada. The subscription service in Africa is broadcast in partnership with South Africa's M-Net Cable and Satellite. WSTV gives international coverage to programmes such as *Panorama*, the *Money Programme*, *First Tuesday* and *Whicker's World*. When such pro-grammes have public relations content those concerned may be interested and perhaps surprised if their message gets international coverage, or this may be a reason for seeking inclusion in such programmes.

The following extracts* describe an even more wide-ranging service:

> The pioneer of global television broadcasting has been the Middle East Broadcasting Centre (MBC) . . . From its headquarters in central London, MBC goes on air for more than 10 hours a day providing top quality news, sports, entertainment, health, science, religious and other programmes. The service is available to a potential audience of more than 100 million people, about half of the entire Arab population.
>
> MBC broadcasts on two satellites (Eutelsat 11 and Arabsat 1c), making it possible to receive it with simple and inexpensive equipment through-out the Arab region and Europe. Its daily service is also transmitted terres-trially in Bahrain, Kuwait and Morocco which means that anyone with an ordinary domestic television set is able to switch to MBC without any additional equipment.
>
> In other countries, receiving MBC was until recently only possible

---

* These extracts are reproduced with the permission of the editor of *Arab British Commerce*.

through a satellite dish (normally of about 75–120 centimetres in diameter), but the service has now become available also on cable. It is now estimated that about 400,000 homes in Europe are receiving MBC in this way and that about 200 hotels have subscribed to it. MBC viewers in Arab countries are estimated at 23 million.

MBC is subject to regulations issued by Britain's Independent Television Commission (ITC) . . . This ensures that there is a maximum time limit for individual advertisement breaks and that there is a clear separation between editorial and advertising material. Owned mainly by Saudi Arabian investors, MBC is the first Arabic network to use Western production styles with livelier programming than those in the Arab region which are mostly government-controlled and often dull and subjected to censorship . . . One interesting feature of MBC, however, is its ability to produce its own programmes through its production centres in Britain, Egypt, Saudi Arabia, Lebanon and Syria.[1]

Goggle television

At the time of writing the television equivalent of the Sony Walkman cassette player promises to fragment television audiences even more than the alternative forms of viewing which already exist. Goggle television or 'headgear television' are personal TV sets not unlike ski goggles. Having two miniature screens side by side, Goggle television is like watching a 3D picture with stereo sound under black-out conditions. Picture clarity and colour quality is achieved by means of a liquid crystal system which magnifies the picture. It uses a Microsharp system to create small pixels – the dots which make up a TV picture – and magnify them 10 times.

Goggle television, which can receive TV programmes, video cassettes and computer games, is the invention of Briton Willy Johnson and has been developed by a team from the physics department of Loughborough University. Its impact on television audience figures could be dramatic if different members of a household watched different programmes on their personal Goggle set instead of everyone watching the same programme on an ordinary TV screen.

Characteristics of television

1 Programmes are watched mostly in the home or other social settings, but may also be seen in schools and workplaces such as offices.
2 While not as captive as a cinema audience, the television audience has to view the programmes in a particular place, and remain seated. The viewer cannot be mobile like a radio listener. However, his assured attention can be unsociable and resentful of inter-

ruptions. In fact, television can have a time-consuming drug-like fascination, if only because the viewer watches in anticipation of something better turning up on the screen. It is sometimes criticized for its ability to destroy the reading habit in young people.

3 Perhaps its greatest merit is the blend of sound, movement and colour which creates realism. This applies to people, places and things.

4 But a special characteristic of television is that it is a *visual* medium. Viewers do tend to watch rather than listen to television. This means that people such as a company chairman or other representative of an organization should be visually interesting. This can be through the way they dress, but more especially how they look physically. Television tends to caricature people, highlighting their oddities. This can be critical and can demolish even famous people if they do not come over well. Very few politicians are successful on the small screen. The PRO should be careful not to rush the chief executive on to television, unless this person looks *interesting* and is sufficiently *articulate* to hold his or her own with an interviewer! Television familiarization courses can be attended, prospective interviewees being trained in interview techniques under studio conditions.

5 An important aspect of television has been its ability to introduce new interests to viewers who take them up actively and want to know more about them. This leads to a demand for information in more detailed and permanent form such as new magazines, new newspaper features and new books.

6 It is possible to record and play back programmes; to show one's own programmes with video cassettes, and to call up teletext information always provided that the viewer has the necessary equipment which at present is still costly. Millions of British television sets are equipped to receive teletext (ITV) and Ceefax (BBC) pages.

Disadvantages of television

1 Facilities — such as a factory or office background — are often requested and an organization can go to a lot of trouble without gaining any credit for it. If such premises are used it is best if they are recognizable by viewers.

2 Television can be very time-consuming, both in the negotiations and in the actual shooting. Many hours may be spent on rehearsal and shooting to produce a few minutes of scene time. However, that has to be weighed against the size of the audience.

3 If an organization is asked to provide someone for a programme

made up of several interviews, the edited version may be disconcerting when it is found that bits of interviews have been paired with bits from other interviews to produce a controversial juxtapositioning which was not apparent during the original shooting.

4   Television can be a wasteful medium − not only of the PRO's or the organization's time, but of audiences. While it is true that afternoon shows may be seen by housewives or children, and late shows may be seen by the more serious minded, and different audiences may watch BBC2 compared with ITV, nevertheless the audience is likely to be very large. Peak hour popular programmes may be seen by 10 to 30 million viewers. Is such an audience relevant to the public relations message? If it is about a mass consumer product, yes, but if the interest is more specialized, no. This also may govern acceptance of the subject by a producer, but not always. A television commentator may be happy to lampoon a multinational computer company even if few viewers are likely to buy a computer. Nevertheless, a vast audience may be admirable.

However, there may be times when it is wise to reject approaches from television producers who are concerned only with exploiting an organization or a personality for programme purposes. *One is not obliged to accept an invitation to be interviewed!* The negative and even damaging effects of television appearances have to be considered. Cliff Michelmore tells the story of the time he interviewed a famous personality who answered only *'Yes'* or *'No'*. Some of the people interviewed by David Frost have done themselves little credit, to mention only Richard Nixon and Rupert Murdoch. Few people have come over more disastrously than Henry Kissinger on the former *Parkinson* programme and that could also happen to a shy, hesitant or unattractive chief executive!

Additional reference to television as a public relations medium will be found in Chapter 16 on broadcasting material and facilities.

Radio

Perhaps the feature that makes radio different from all other mass media, and of special interest to the public relations practitioner, is that it can often be an instantaneous medium. Immediate announcements can be made on the radio. This immediacy has been valuable in ending a war (Morocco), calming the effects of a coup (Nigeria), and stopping a race riot (Singapore). In Britain, the state of the share market, traffic conditions and road diversions, the cancelling of trains, the arrival times of British Airways aircraft, sports results, requests for information by the police, and exchange rates for those going abroad are typical examples of instant news and information provided by radio. Local radio (both BBC and ILR) – especially the commercial radio station LBC (London Broadcasting Company) in the London area – have greatly increased this service, and much of it is derived from public relations sources or is a form of public relations.

The initials ILR stand for 'independent local radio', just as ITV means 'independent television', not the name of an organization.

Characteristics

1 In contrast to the visual nature of television, radio has the intimacy of the human voice, and therefore requires voices which please the ear. The history of radio is one of famous (or infamous) voices, to mention only Franklin Delano Roosevelt, Sir Winston Churchill, J. B. Priestley, Vera Lynn, John Arlott, Peter Sellers, Richard Dimbleby or, more recently, various announcers, presenters and disc jockeys such as Dicky Arbiter, Derek Jameson and Kenny Everett.

2 Not unlike the newspaper, radio can be portable thanks to the transistor. Many sets may exist in one household, or a portable set can be carried from room to room. Motorcars may be fitted with radios, they are often installed in public places, and there are still headphones for those who wish to listen without disturbing others in hospital beds. Radio can be listened to while doing many jobs in factories, on building sites, or while making deliveries.

3 The versatility described above also points to a variety of listeners who may tune in at different times of the day. There are the breakfast-time listeners who want to check the time, the commuters, the housewives about the house, the people at work, the business-people driving their cars, the home-coming motorists, and young people who often listen at night. The radio audience differs from the television audience with its peak hours during the middle evening. Consequently, the PRO can reach particular radio audiences if the material is properly timed for certain programmes.

4 Radio has long been an effective way of reaching people of different ethnic groups and languages in developing countries, including large numbers of people who cannot read, through either personal or public radios. It is easier and more practical to produce a radio programme in several languages, or to broadcast locally in the appropriate language, than to publish vernacular newspapers which people may or may not be able to read.

5 Radio provides companionship, whether it be by means of the human voice or music. But this can also mean that some people like to enjoy a friendly background noise without necessarily paying attention to what is being said. It has been found, for instance, that in landlocked states, where it is possible to listen to a choice of foreign stations broadcast from nearby countries, preference may be given to those which play popular music. In fact, in large countries like Zambia it has been found necessary to strengthen transmissions because people in distant parts of the country were finding it easier or possible only to receive programmes from foreign states.

6 Progressing from the above, it is also true that people listen in to overseas programmes put out by Britain, Germany, Voice of America and so forth, to obtain information and world news.

   The British World Service in English has programmes which discuss new British products and achievements, and this can be useful to PROs interested in export public relations. Many people in Singapore, for instance listen to the British World Service throughout the day. It broadcasts 18 news bulletins every 24 hours. The BBC External Services broadcast foreign-language programmes too: there is, for example, a large Russian audience for the Russian programme, although it was jammed during the Polish unrest. However, some people in Third World countries are critical of foreign broadcasts, regarding them as propaganda for foreign culture.

7 In Britain, the local radio stations of the BBC and ILR usually cover a smaller area than the regional television stations which makes them ideal for local information such as traffic and public transport announcements. Community radio may become an even more localized form of broadcasting.

   The British government's decision to open up commercial radio under the new Radio Authority, may offer public relations a new national radio opportunity.

Reference

1 *Arab British Commerce*, November 1992, London

21

Overseas media

How they differ from Western media

There are three ways of looking at public relations media in developing countries. First there is the dearth of Western-style mass media; secondly, there are the limitations of the existing mass media; and thirdly, there are the problems, special needs and special techniques of communicating with illiterate people and those, often remotely located, of different ethnic groups, languages, dialects, religions and lifestyles. These are problems which confront the PRO working in an industrializing country, or the PRO of an organization which exports to or operates in Third World countries. The main difference is that it is so easy to communicate in the North, but much more difficult in the South. Nevertheless, public relations does exist in these countries, and much of it concerns changing lifestyles.

Dearth of Western-style mass media

The number and circulation of newspapers, the number of television sets and number and kind of viewers, and the number of radio sets and listeners − in fact, the extent of what are sometimes called élitist media − will depend on the following factors:

1 *The extent of literacy*, which in turn will depend on the extent of primary education on the one hand and adult literacy education on the other.
2 *The sophistication of the economy and the number of people in the cash economy*. This will influence the size of the market, the justification for advertising, and the ability for media to be commercially viable. There are several ways of looking at this. A country may depend on

a particular crop or mineral — sugar, cocoa, copper or rubber — and if there is a slump in the world market the economy will suffer. A net exporter may become a net importer so that restrictions will be placed on imports as in the case of Nigeria; or a large number of people may be outside the cash economy either because they are subsistence farmers who sell little or no surplus produce and have no spending country. One can find nomads living in tents on the outskirts of town, and enjoying their television. A vast country like Indonesia has a widespread television service, using a satellite, and lack of electricity is overcome by the use of 12-volt battery sets.

3   While community viewing has popularized television, programmes are shown in the evening and since it is usually not the custom for women to go out at night audiences are limited to men. Young people are also likely to be excluded.

4   Programme material is usually poor. Video tape is expensive, studios have limited capacity and equipment, newsreading and acting experience are meagre, outside broadcasts are rare and foreign programmes may be too expensive or restricted by import controls. The poor quality of programmes also deters some people from watching television. However, the arrival of films on video tapes has put an end to the showing of very old American films.

5   The viability of television — which affects the quality of programmes — can be influenced by the lack of advertising revenue if the market economy is limited or depressed.

Radio

There is a common belief that radio is the answer to communications in developing countries because it can so easily penetrate distances, and one does not have to be able to read and write to listen to broadcasts. This has been found to be an oversimplification, and radio suffers its own limitation for the following reasons:

1   In large countries with large rural populations containing a variety of ethnic groups radio may represent a remote and distant centre, unrelated to local interests. Radio can therefore lack credibility, and there can be a great wastage of audience. This may not be realized by the broadcasting authority.

2   Nevertheless, all sorts of people may enjoy radio for its companionship and entertainment. In some countries in large land masses with neighbouring and nearby countries foreign radio programmes may be preferred if they provide the desired programmes such as popular music.

3 It is not always satisfactory to provide multi-language programmes for two reasons:
   (a) There may be too many languages.
   (b) If the programmes are broadcast from one station, only a short portion of the day can be devoted to each language with the result that speakers of other languages are deprived of broadcasts. Consequently, radio becomes a very limited medium.
4 Even more seriously, surveys have revealed that although large numbers of people are believed to possess receivers a surprising number of sets are not working. There are two reasons for this:
   (a) Developing countries suffer from being sold imported technical products which cannot be serviced or repaired, and they are often too expensive to be replaced.
   (b) Batteries are often expensive, and radios fall into disuse because people cannot afford to buy new batteries.
5 Electricity may not be available so that main electric receivers cannot be used.

These are problems which do not confront broadcasting in industrialized countries. Yet, in spite of all these difficulties radio can penetrate the large populations of developing countries. Box or rediffusion radio is cheap and popular and may be available in public places such as cafés. Radio can be listened to by illiterate people who are beyond the reach of newspapers. Thus, radio audiences are likely to be far greater than newspaper readerships. And radio has been shown to command authority in situations of emergency or national importance touching on the lives of the whole population – for example, in times of war, political upheavals or environmental disasters. In countries of vast distances, radio has also been successful for educational purposes, lessons being broadcast which can be listened to by individuals, listening groups or classes of students. This has proved to be very successful in Indonesia.

Other mass media

How else can one reach people on a broad scale in multi-ethnic, multi-language, multi-religious societies? One successful technique is through the use of pictures and diagrams which can inform without the need for words. Visual messages can be applied to give-away leaflets (useful in villages) or on posters where sites exist in or near towns. Posters can also be displayed on public transport which travels about the country. The poster method showing, say parents and two children, has spread the idea of planned parenthood in many parts of the world, especially in Asia. In a similar way, cartoon drawings can be used to explain many things to illiterate people. Even so, there are problems and the artist needs to beware of the literal meanings people may place on pictures. A simple matchstick figure may seem sufficient − but unless the mouth is curved to resemble a smile, it may be thought that the character disapproves!

Folk, traditional and other localized media

For centuries, people have communicated with one another, although in the past only scholars and scribes used written or drawn symbols. Many of these simple forms of communication are still practised. Even in Britain the town crier survives, and in villages in West Africa the *gong man* or court messenger still proclaims the news in the morning and evening, acting as the communication medium between the local ruler and his people. It may be necessary to have public relations messages conveyed in this way in order to give them credibility and to reach people who are outside the orbit of Western-style mass media. A detailed study of village and rural communication techniques − *oramedia* because it is mainly oral or conveyed by sound − was conducted internationally by the late Dr Frank Ugboajah of the Department of Mass Communication, University of Lagos. Much of this is contained in two books, *Communication in Industrialising Countries*[1] and *Mass Communication, Culture and Society in West Africa.*[2]

But to do this we must first convince the sender of the news − the king, emir, oba or headman. This is where the innovator theory comes into play: we have to gain the understanding, sympathy and acceptance of an innovator who will then influence others to adopt his advice. This method is not confined to unsophisticated societies. It has been used the world over: who would ever have flown the Atlantic if Blériot had not first flown the Channel? All new ideas need innovators who take them up so that others may follow. A typical example is the farm machine, the first user inviting neighbours to see a demonstration. In Third World countries the same psychology; the same follow-my-leader system, can apply when the use of modern mass media will fail. The techniques which McCormick used to sell labour-saving machinery to labour-starved prairie farmers in the USA in the 1860s is being used today to create a power farming agricultural revolution in Nigeria where urbanization has drained the little village farms of family labour.

Literacy is not only to do with reading and writing. There can be *visual* and *oral* literacy. So-called 'illiterate' people often possess visual literacy superior to that of Westerners, and have an 'eye-witness' skill which is quite uncanny. Similarly, in West Africa, for example, one finds 'illiterate' street-traders who act as postmen between villagers and their friends and relatives in town, carrying elaborate messages word perfect in their heads. These forms of communication should not be overlooked when communicating with people in developing countries.

Yet another important form of vocal communication is market gossip. In developing countries with small farms and surplus produce, or local craftsmen with wares to sell, the market provides a meeting place where news is shared. Consequently, market gossip is a medium for spreading information.

Open air events

Open air events are more common in warm climates and they appeal to the gregarious instinct of people who have little entertainment. It may be an exhibition or agricultural show, or a mobile demonstration or mobile cinema which tours villages where newspapers are unknown and radio sets may be rare or radio has little impact, while television is unknown. A crowd will gather to watch a film shown on a screen erected on the roof of a Land Rover. These may be called van cinemas, and the terms 'mobile' or 'static' may be used to distinguish between the visiting and the permanent city cinema (covered or drive-in). In some countries such as Malaysia, mobile video shows have replaced film shows.

But the audience figures and effectiveness of mobile cinema may be subject to doubt. Mobile audience figures have been researched in Kenya, based on an official or policeman estimating crowd numbers. The size of a crowd may not be very helpful if it includes hosts of children! There can be two other problems with mobile cinemas. First, they are infrequent, and even regular monthly tours allow a big memory or impact gap between one showing and another. This applies equally to advertising and information films. Second, the films may be too long to retain concentration, or too sophisticated and contain too many unfamiliar subjects to be comprehensible. An eight minute video is long enough, after which attention is likely to wander.

Thus they may defy the span of consciousness, the visual perception time and be outside the limits of experience. To be effective, a film shown to unsophisticated audiences should avoid the 'visual vocabulary block' by *repeating* the message; it should be short enough to hold the attention; and should avoid using scenes or objects which are *foreign* to limited local knowledge and experience. People in a land-locked country may have never seen the sea, while those in tropical countries will be unfamiliar with snow.

Very few Western-style documentaries are suitable for such audiences. The sight of a skyscraper to people used to mud huts may arouse howls of derision, disbelief or terror. MGM's lion has been known to empty a cinema in Africa. All this is little different from the fear of American tourists for British double-decker buses which they expect to fall over. It is perhaps hard to believe that Westerners are often more familiar with wild animals than natives of the countries from which these creatures originate. In Nigeria, the author found that a lion at Ibadan University zoo had been donated by Longleat, and when he visited Kano zoo his Nigerian companions were amazed at the huge size of *baby* elephants. Lusaka has a zoo in which Zambians often see for the first time the animals which roam in their great national parks. Such countries rarely have, as in Kenya, giraffes visible from the road and a ban on hoardings because they interfere with the view for the tourists! When Western firms make videos for showing to people in developing countries they should remember that the content needs to be credible to people with very different lifestyles and experiences. And it can be different in the sense that it is more intensely cultural, as in the East, and less materialistic than it is in the West. Different does not mean inferior.

Gregarious people living in simple surroundings often welcome entertainment when it comes to their village. The van may bring videos and song and dance teams may accompany it. There may be more local forms of communication such as the village theatre which can be used to dramatize a message, something which can be used for bringing new ideas to villagers. You can educate through entertainment.

Very effective when there are linguistic problems is the puppet show since messages can be mimed, and this is a medium which has been used for public relations purposes in Africa and Asia. In Malaysia and Indonesia, wire puppets and shadow puppets are used. In countries where 'public enlightenment' programmes are organized to improve farming, sanitation, hygiene, child welfare and so on, such methods can overcome the fact that millions of people are beyond the reach of so-called mass media. They are not to be dismissed for they buy goods, pay taxes, vote in elections and have rights to public services.

An intimate understanding of the media and communications problems and solutions in developing countries, especially in vast and heavily populated ones like Indonesia and Nigeria, is therefore vital to the public relations manager responsible for overseas public relations for an exporter or multi-national company.

References

1 Jefkins, Frank and Ugboajah, Frank, *Communication in Industrialising Countries*, Macmillan, London, 1987
2 Ugboajah, Frank (ed.), *Mass Communication, Culture and Society in West Africa*, Hanz Zell Publishers (imprint of K. G. Saur), Munich, 1985

22

Video and visual aids

The change from 16 mm film

Video has largely replaced film, and whereas the 16 mm film and the projector were once standard all over the world, the smaller book-sized videocassette has replaced the clumsy can of film, and the videocassette player (VCR) has replaced the cumbersome and noisy projector. This applies to the 'industrial' film; public cinema and TV films are still shot on 35 mm stock. TV commercials may be shot on film for the sake of quality and then transferred to video where post-production computer graphics and editing effects can be added.

Videos can be shown on TV sets or monitors or on large screens. In Europe the VHS format is common, but in other parts of the world, and where other TV systems operate, BETA may be the common format. It is possible to have a VCR which will accept every system, otherwise, say, a British video cannot be shown in North America or the Far East and vice versa.

Being compact, the videocassette is easy to store, carry or despatch, and if shown on a TV set it is ideal for a small audience, including showing in the home. The domestic VCR is popular for recording programmes, for playing home movies made on a camcorder, screening photographs, or playing hired, bought or borrowed films on video. Business offices are often equipped with VCRs. It is therefore a versatile form of communication with many advantages over film and few of its disadvantages. For industrial purposes the better quality U-Matic system may be used, from which VHS tapes may be copied.

Consequently, video is an important and specific field of created or private public relations media, and one which is distinct from commercial or mass media. Usually, such media are created to reach special, private, identified and sometimes small audiences. In public relations we are not only concerned with mass communications – in fact, sometimes not at all. The mistake is sometimes made of organizing courses in mass communications and confusing them with public relations. But it is often necessary to reach separate publics or groups of people – such as families regarding a re-location project – who cannot be addressed broadly and impersonally through the mass media. It is therefore very much a public relations responsibility to produce and use videos, or for the consultancy account executive to be able to advise clients on their applications.

Three basic rules

The three essential rules which applied to industrial films also apply to the modern video, especially in view of its greater versatility. They are (i) purpose and audience; (ii) production; and (iii) use and distribution. These three rules become more sophisticated with video compared to film, and as a result video has become one of the most versatile of all public relations media.

1   *The purpose*

Why is the video being made? Perhaps the reason is more definite with a video than it used to be with film. There used to be an almost casual attitude about making films, a 'let's make a film' approach, if only for the sake of vanity, whereas videos (possibly because they have so many practical applications) are made because they are needed to solve a communications problem. The question now is whether the video is the best medium for the purpose.

The *purpose* immediately involves the *audience*: to whom do we wish to show the video? Why do we need to show them one? Why is this likely to be more effective than some other medium? What can it do that other media cannot do? Such penetrating questions seldom preceded the making of a 16 mm documentary film. The answers will become apparent when we look at the numerous ways in which videos can be used, and the different kinds of video that can be made.

2   *Production*

The mode of production will follow on from purpose and audience. There are innumerable techniques not unlike films, e.g. a series of stills or slides; animation (cartoon); external locations; studio locations; live or dubbed sound; professional artistes or members of staff; and original or hired music. But to these basic techniques can be added specialities such as computer generated creative effects, which can be introduced at the post-production stage, that is after the shooting has been completed and computer graphics are applied. Examples of the wizardry of computer graphics are to be seen in both TV programmes and in TV commercials; some techniques, like morphing, when things or people are made to stretch or bend, have even been used in public relations films. Quantel, for example, have a whole range of paint (Paintbox) and digital systems.

One elementary aspect of production which can easily get out of hand is length. Far too many videos are too long, and either there should be fewer scenes or there should be sharper editing. When a video stretches to 30 minutes it is usually 10 minutes longer than viewer interest can be sustained. Some of the best public relations videos are shorter than 20 minutes. Unfortunately, there is a temptation to cram in too much, but this can destroy attention and interest, provoke boredom and obscure the message. This is very true of some of the tourist videos which are loaned to prospective holidaymakers.

Two important aspects of production should not be overlooked: the spoken commentary (with or without a visual commentator) and the musical accompaniment. If it heightens the interest and is not a distraction, the commentator may be a well-known personality such as a TV newsreader or an actor or actress. There is an excellent 20-minute video on the European Parliament with Peter Ustinov as a very appropriate commentator. Characteristic music, which fits the mood of the video and does not intrude, can make a big contribution. It is not necessary to compose special music, and all types of popular and classical music can be hired from music libraries.

3   Use and distribution

This links with purpose, and ability to use and to produce in large quantities for distribution makes video more versatile and flexible than film, as will be seen in the following sections. One could scarcely mail cans of film to lots of people, most of whom would not have projectors. If a film was supplied on loan, the time required for travel to and fro and showing could occupy a week and limit the number and use of prints. Now, videos can be offered free of charge and, if desired, retained by recipients. The hassle of keeping a library and repairing prints is avoided.

Different types and uses of video

Unlike films, which were often made for general use as and when the opportunity occurred, videos can be made for specific and sometimes short-term use such as an exhibition, conference, road-show or re-location. Let us break this down more explicitly.

Video house journal

Although this form of video may have enjoyed its hey-day, and corporate video (see later) is now taking over, the video house journal still has its value for some organizations, e.g. those with staff working in many locations at home or abroad, or where there are mergers and acquisitions and an inflow of new employers to a group. However, as has been proved, although the video house journal, resembling a TV news bulletin, has its human face-to-face advantages it has failed to replace the printed employee newspaper or magazine.

Documentary

This is the narrative type of video which tells the story of the organization, or some side of its work. A construction company might film a project, a brewer could animate the brewing process, or an airline might make a video about new aircraft. Such videos could have a variety of uses and could be shown to potential clients, at press receptions, on exhibition stands, in showrooms or to groups of visitors.

This is the kind of video which tempts sponsors to produce at too great a length, and sharper editing would improve them. Few subjects merit more than 20 minutes' screen time.

Recruitment

To recruit staff a video could be made which demonstrated the work conducted by, say, a bank, a retail store or an industry, and this could be offered to schools, shown at careers evenings and offered on free loan to youth organizations.

Safety

In hazardous industries, especially where it is imperative to wear protective clothing, a dramatic video can be made for showing to employees. It need not be purely instructional, but could demonstrate by example. To demonstrate the need to wear safety helmets a rock-climbing episode could be shot, showing how a climber without safety headgear is struck by a falling rock.

Induction

Videos can be especially useful as induction material for new recruits, explaining what the organization does and who is responsible for what. Because of likely changes in activities or personnel, the video could be made from stills or slides so that it may be updated inexpensively.

Relocation

Many videos have been made for this purpose, and they need not exceed 8–10 minutes in length. By showing the new premises and location, the shopping, entertainment, sports, educational and medical facilities, and concluding with a brief message from the managing director, members of staff can be attracted to move. Such videos can be taken home and played to the family, helping to overcome what is known as 'the trailing spouse' syndrome.

Annual reports and accounts

Here there can be two reasons for making a video, either to report to employees in locations at home and abroad, or to show to shareholders who cannot attend the annual general meeting and can be offered a copy. For employees the video could take the form of a celebrity interviewing the managing director who explains the figures. These are examples of the convenience of the short-life video, and of something which could not have been done with film.

Market education

These, too, can be quite short, and some amusing ones have been offered in press advertisements to explain investment schemes. The objective is to explain how a product or service works, and such videos can be screened in the home, in shop windows or in showrooms, on exhibition stands, or supplied on loan to clubs and societies.

Show reels

Also, a form of market education, show reels can be made by service companies such as advertising agencies to demonstrate their work to potential clients.

Corporate identity

When a corporate identity scheme has been created, including logo, typography, colour scheme, livery, dress and so on, its correct application can be demonstrated in a video which supplements the style book.

For visitors

Organizations which entertain groups of visitors may use videos to explain their activities, especially when these cannot be entirely viewed during a tour. This could apply where there are processes such as brewing or distilling.

In-house or outside production?

Whether to have in-house studios, equipment and staff or to use external production services depends on the number and frequency of programmes. Usually, in-house production units occur when, in addition to public relations videos, the emphasis is on training and sales support videos. Sometimes, in-house video units have developed as replacements for former film units.

The video news release (VNR)

This innovation has caught on slowly in the UK, but is becoming increasingly important as television companies, including the news services, are finding that their budgets limit their ability to cover outdoor events. The genuine professionally produced video news release kit can often secure coverage that would not otherwise occur. In the USA, VNRs have been common for several years, and in some areas, such as pharmaceuticals, there have been abuses of the 'free advertising' kind. Consequently, in late 1992, 'a special committee of the Public Relations Service Council (PRSC) . . . established the "Code of Good Practice for Video News Releases" to "affirm standards of accuracy and good practice in our industry"'.[1]

Video news releases are quite different from paper news releases. Before shooting anything negotiations are conducted with broadcasters to see whether they will take VNR material on a stated subject. The VNR itself is a kit of pictures which the broadcaster can combine to provide a visual report with his or her spoken newscast or commentary.

Another difference is that it may be supplied as a hard copy cassette or by satellite, and the latter can provide foreign coverage.

VNRs may be used in three ways: as live pictorial news material for news bulletins; as live pictorial material for documentary and public affairs programmes; and as archival or library picture material for future news or documentary programmes. An example of the latter is that even when the news story is a bad one of the VNR material can be up to date, e.g. robotics in a motorcar factory although the story is about lay-offs. From these remarks it will be seen that the supply of relevant VNR material is superior to supplying a documentary video. The video is ready-to-use footage. Television producers are less likely to use scenes from videocassettes.

According to a special feature on the subject in *PR Week*, 'Countrywide Communications in London set up a broadcasting unit towards the end of 1991' and it went on to quote Barry Leggetter, the consultancy's joint managing director, as saying 'With every major story we now assess the opportunity for a VNR. We don't consider VNRs to be a luxury – we know they work'.[2] Their clients include Gillette and the Co-op (and its environmental campaign on dolphin survival), the Drambuie round-Britain powerboat race, and the launch of Rolls-Royce's Bentley Brooklands.

The same feature described Abbey National's use of VNRs, quoting Paul Barker, head of public and media relations, who claimed 'We are getting a lot of requests for spokespeople to make comments on the effects of interest rate cuts. By providing VNRs we have considerably increased the amount of airtime Abbey National gets when there are stories on the housing market.' Abbey National works with VNR specialist Bulletin Television News Service on a retainer basis. Typical items in the Abbey National VNR kit are shots of types of houses, for sale boards, interviews on mortgages, and people using cash dispensers. The broadcaster can pick what he wants to use, but it is what the broadcaster might have shot himself if he had the money or the crew to do it.

The same feature in *PR Week* described the regular use of VNRs by Nissan on behalf of its Sunderland plant. Twice a year a general VNR about the plant is sent to every television newsroom in the UK, and special ones are issued when Nissan is involved in events such as the Motor Show. The company's European corporate office also uses VNRs.

How VNRs are produced and distributed

Production and distribution may be by separate companies or by one with combined resources. Visnews, for instance, with a history going back to cinema newsreels, and wholly owned by Reuters, has its Visnews Corporate Television division, and is the largest VNR distribution company. Founded in 1957, Visnews is now the world's largest supplier of television news pictures of all kinds to broadcasting stations. The network consists of 650 broadcasters and over 1000 affiliated stations in 84 countries. It also has 30 bureaux world-wide with main offices in London, New York and Tokyo. Visnews is the world's largest independent user of satellites, delivering daily feeds to the Middle East, the Americas, Japan, the Asia—Pacific region and Australasia. Moreover, their dedicated European satellite updates broadcasters with a constant supply of news, 13 hours a day.

Because of their reputation for distributing legitimate news material of high quality, Visnews is careful not to accept public relations material that is promotional, such as some VNRs which have offended news services in the USA. Provided, therefore, that company news VNRs are of equal quality to regular Visnews news coverage, they can be distributed world-wide, or wherever designated, using the Visnews satellite network.

Mention has already been made of Bulletin Television News Service, which has established a reputation for successful VNR projects. They make a careful assessment of what is viable and carry out every stage of the project, planning, research and production to broadcaster liaison, distribution, monitoring and reporting. Their clients include BMW, Hill and Knowlton, Abbey National, Grayling, BNFL, Help The Aged and Whitbread.

A large producer and distributor of VNRs is WTN Productions, which has experienced advisers and production teams throughout the world and so offers another international distribution service. Yet another VNR expert is Maxat, which is a wholly owned subsidiary of France Cables and Radio, part of France Telecom. Maxat acquired British Aerospace Communications and its Satellite Management International in 1992. Its clients include ICI, Porsche, Norwich Union and Digital Equipment.

Founded in the USA in 1986 by the Video Broadcasting Corporation, Medialink came to Britain in 1992, to provide VNR and other business television services. In the USA in 1991 they distributed 2000 VNRs to America's 700-strong television station network. Medialink negotiates use of VNRs by means of its newswire installations at television news desks.

One of the reasons for the development of VNRs, apart from the economics of UK television, is the international requirement of modern public relations. The ability to transmit public relations stories world-wide has been enhanced by the use of satellites, and also by the relaxation of broadcasting regulations in Europe.

Satellite media tours

Another facility offered by most of the companies offering VNR services is the media tour, whereby a celebrity, speaking from a centrally located station (e.g. in London) can give exclusive interviews by satellite to broadcasters in the UK, continental Europe or elsewhere in the world. These interviews can be used in live television programmes or kept for later transmission. Thus, a company spokesperson could address numerous audiences, or a personality such as an author could be interviewed. Prior arrangements would be made for the stations to receive the interview. The interview could be conducted at the sender's location, or by an interviewer at each television station.

Teleconferencing

This is another service offered by the business television companies whereby *ad hoc* point-to-point or point-to-multi-point video transmissions can be organized nationally or internationally for company meetings or press conferences, with great savings in travel time and costs by participants.

Business television

Business or corporate television is the modern counterpart of the video house journal. It differs, however, in being transmitted, usually by satellite, to viewers whose locations are equipped with special receivers, and it is generally a live broadcast rather than a pre-recorded one. It can be made in a studio, at the sponsor's premises or out-of-doors.

Once again, its origin is American with Merrill Lynch among its pioneers, but in recent years it has been taken up by a number of companies in Britain and continental Europe. These have included BMW, whose 165 UK dealers are equipped with a satellite dish to receive and decode weekly programmes, Norwich Union to communicate with 42 Life Society branches and hundreds of financial advisers and staff, Digital's contact with more than 4000 employees in 15 European countries (including use of five languages), and a Unipart programme broadcast to 4000 employees in 150 UK locations.

One of the most ambitious examples is that of The Body Shop, which Susan Nowak described in an article in *BAIE News*.[3] Every week a 20-minute video programme is transmitted to the 228 UK stores, and there is a monthly world service in a dozen languages to 24 countries from Iceland to the Gulf but not including the Americas which have their own video network. Anita Roddick appears in the video about every four to six weeks. The Body Shop programme (BSTV) is made by Jacaranda Productions.

In the article, John Bullivant, the director/producer, was quoted as saying 'There is more than sufficient material to warrant it going out every week because the Body Shop is involved in so many interests other than retailing.' The UK version costs about £5000 a week for material costs, editing, duplicating and distribution but not salaries. The international version costs £12,000 for a sub-contractor to translate and subtitle, which takes 10 days.

Business television uses a private satellite network. The original programme is converted into a signal which is relayed to a transmitting antenna, known as an uplink, which beams it up to a satellite. The satellite retransmits the programme back to earth. The signal is received by antennas known as downlinks and carried to the viewing screen. The signal may be scrambled at the upline and decoded at reception sites.

Audiovisuals and visual aids

In the preceding sections we have dealt with some of the latest developments in the world of video, but some of the older and less costly forms of visual aid remain as part of the public relations armoury of private or created media. They are not to be despised if used properly.

Slides are one of the oldest forms of visual aid, the 'magic lantern' preceding film. The simple slide presentation, using a carousel and remote control, is an excellent way of illustrating a talk. Kodak projectors are standard throughout the world, and there are additional facilities which have made slide presentations competitive with films. The slides themselves, apart from purely photographic ones, can be computer generated in colour with good lettering and diagrams or designs, and these make good bulletin points to summarize a talk. It is also possible to use projectors and slides which build up a succession of information on the screen, matching the sequence of information given by the speaker.

The continuous sound and slide presentation, with fade-in, fade-out or cross-fade, supported by vocal and musical effects on audio tape, give a film-like illusion even though the pictures are static. This can be a very inexpensive visual aid when the cost of making a videotape is not justified, as with a single presentation at a conference. For regular use the method has the advantage that slides can be replaced. It is necessary to have twin slide projectors, which may limit the presentation to locations which have the equipment unless it is conveyed there or hired for the occasion.

The multiple screen presentation, as used in a number of permanent exhibitions, can provide a dramatic presentation. By using banks of rear projection computerized slide projectors, the total screen can be filled by all machines projecting simultaneously, or it can be divided into 4, 8 or 16 pictures.

Flip-over charts, mounted on portable frames, can be prepared in advance, and the sheets turned back as required.

Cut-out charts, made of card, can be placed on a blackboard type of stand, and items can be slotted so that they may be disclosed by drawing the cut-out to one side.

Overhead projector (OHP) film. This is one of the simplest forms of visual presentation, but films should be professionally produced with clear wording, and the wording should be large enough to be read at a distance from the screen. Typewritten characters are seldom large enough and handwritten wording should be avoided. The mistake is sometimes made of using indistinct colours. The message should be as bold as possible, especially if the OHP is not used in darkness.

References

1 Code of Good Practice Created for Video News Releases, *Communications World*, November 1992, IABC, San Francisco
2 Purdom, Nick, 'TV exposure winning a wider audience', *PR Week*, 25 February 1993
3 Nowak, Susan 'Making everybody somebody', *BAIE News*, November 1992

23

Seminars, meetings and conferences

The organizing role

The organizing of seminars and conferences of short or long duration calls for the managerial skills of planning, budgeting, organizing and directing. Because the public relations practitioner is recognized as having these special skills, he or she may be invited to organize events other than solely public relations ones, for instance sales conferences, seminars associated with exhibitions, and maybe even the annual general meeting or shareholders' meetings in the event of a merger or takeover bid. Staff meetings, or ones to which the local community is invited when, perhaps, the company needs to face the public, may have to be organized.

These events may occupy a morning, afternoon or evening, one or more days or a weekend. Meticulous planning is important, and it really is true that a major public relations skill is the anticipation of disaster.

It is never too early to start planning. For instance, the author conducts an annual three-week international Summer School, and he starts organizing the next one just before the current one. It is a 13 months' task, beginning with deciding the date and booking the venue.

He learned to do this when for eight years one of his clients was an exhibition organizer for whom he provided press officer services for a number of exhibitions at Olympia. He observed that the organizers were busily planning the next year's event – and taking space bookings for it – in the course of the current show.

An essential factor for success is to establish a good relationship with those people at the venue who will be responsible for your arrangements. This could include a number of people such as the manager, banqueting manager, food and beverage manager, head waiter, receptionist, commissionaire, electrician, theatre manager, car-park attendant, gatekeeper and so on. They should be met and familiar-ized with the event, and it may be necessary to work with them from time to time in advance, and during the course of the event. A friendly liaison will help to avoid misunderstandings. Nothing should ever be taken for granted, never assume other people know what you want and mean. They need decisions, agreements, plans drawn on paper, numbers and maybe names. There are even occasions when the pro-prietors of the venue need car numbers, telephone numbers and even passports, or may have to give guests security badges or protective clothing. An event could be held at a venue where such requirements are necessary.

Conferences

A conference consists of a large audience and platform speakers and is less intimate than a seminar which may be attended by no more than 25 people, perhaps less, if there is to be participation.

A conference may last for a day or a number of days. It may be held mid-week or over a weekend. It may be residential or non-residential. Delegates may pay an attendance fee, or admission may be free of charge. Accommodation may be paid for by the sponsors or by the delegates who may be either enrolled or invited. There are clearly many variations on how the attendance will be achieved and how the costs are met.

These organizational details need to be thought out very carefully. The events may be so valuable to participants that they will be willing to contribute to the cost while another event may succeed only if people are invited on a non-payment basis. There is no reason why participants should not pay to attend, and there is always the danger that if the sponsor provides too much hospitality the event may provoke suspicion that it is only a publicity stunt. On one occasion a well-known pharmaceutical company paid all the expenses of doctors who were invited to a conference about new drugs, and the company was criticized afterwards for virtually bribing doctors to attend. Sometimes people will place more value and credence on something for which they have to pay, even if it is run for commercial purposes.

It may also be a question of whether delegates can afford to pay. A conference of local authority representatives could be poorly attended if the authorities were unwilling to pay for their staff to attend. Sponsor-ship may be possible as in the case of the CAM conference of examiners and lecturers which is sponsored by the Post Office at their manage-ment training college.

The important thing is to have a worthwhile programme with first-class speakers supported by good videos, slide presentations or other visual aids such as white-boards, flip-over charts and pads, and over-head projectors. The speakers should be experts (i.e. designers, technicians, scientists) rather than top executives, marketing or sales personnel. It may be a good idea to bring in outside speakers if they are familiar with the subject, either to give an authentic background or because they are users of the product or service. For example, a customer might present a case history.

Special considerations

1 *The date.* A day and time should be chosen which does not clash with another event of interest to prospective participants. It should be sufficiently far ahead to permit proper planning, and so that invitations may be sent out (or announcements may be published) in sufficient time for people to make arrangements to attend. The planning may need from three to six months, while the event should be announced four to six weeks in advance. The length of notice really depends on the time delegates need to get permission to attend and (as with international events) time to obtain visas and currency and make flight and hotel arrangements. For overseas visitors, up to six months' notice may be required.

2 *The venue.* A conference should be held at a venue which is (a) well-equipped for conferences, (b) attractive in itself or in an attractive location and, (c) easily accessible by road, rail, sea or air as the case may be, with good car parking facilities. Again, if foreign delegates are likely to attend allowance must be made for individual arrivals so that the venue must be easily reached.

3 *Recreational activities.* People cannot be expected to sit endlessly in a hall listening to speeches, and it is usually wise to include some recreation or entertainment. According to the type of audience, venue, time of year and so forth, this lighter side could involve a golf tournament, coach tour, boat trip, fashion show, theatre party, or some such social 'break' in the proceedings. It may be necessary to arrange activities for delegates' wives.

Planning a conference

When planning a timetable for a conference there are certain fixed times which dictate when sessions should be slotted in. These are the times for opening, coffee, lunch, tea and adjournment or closure. Thus, in a day's programme, there will be eight lecture sessions which can be subdivided into shorter lectures or in order to show videos or slide presentations. A day's timetable might work out like this:

First, we start with the skeleton plan of the day, and then we slot in the features of the programme in the time that is available.

9.30– 9.45	Delegates assemble	
10.00	First morning session	(Session 1)
11.00–11.30	Coffee	
11.30	?	(Session 2)
12.45–1.00	Cocktails	
1.00–2.00	Lunch	
2.00	First afternoon session	(Session 3)
3.00–3.30	Tea	
3.30	?	(Session 4)
4.30	Close	

The above outline shows that the periods 10.00–11.00, 11.30–12.45, 2.00–3.00 and 3.30–4.30 are available for speakers, videos, slides, demonstrations and discussion. The programme time is limited by the framework of standard items. Moreover, unless these items are controlled for time, the programme sessions will suffer. So, we arrive at the complete programme which may look like the following except that it will be filled out with the names of speakers and their subjects and the title of the video. Such a programme should be sent out with invitations, or at least in advance to those who have accepted. Guests should always know what they are attending.

9.30–9.45	Delegates assemble
9.45–10.00	Chairman's introduction
10.00–10.45	Speaker and subject
10.45–11.00	Questions and discussion
11.00–11.30	Coffee
11.30–12.00	Video
12.00–12.30	Speaker and subject
12.30–12.45	Questions and discussion
12.45–1.00	Cocktails
1.00–2.00	Lunch
2.00–2.45	Speaker and subject
2.45–3.00	Questions and discussion
3.00–3.30	Tea
3.30–3.45	Speaker with slide presentation
3.45–4.30	Questions and discussion
4.30	Close

Seminars

A seminar is a smaller gathering, and under this heading we can also include evening receptions. Generally, a seminar will be shorter than a conference and will be confined to an evening, half a day and at most a whole day. A large conference venue will not be required, and a medium-sized public room at a hotel or a lecture room at a professional institution will be adequate. Whereas in a conference with a large audience it will be more orderly to confine questions to question time, it is easier and often desirable during a seminar to permit people to participate at any time and for the speaker to encourage discussions rather than deliver a set speech.

Unhappily, the word 'seminar' is widely misused, but the general sense of the word is an informal gathering to discuss a topic with a speaker, and a chairperson may be unnecessary. In the academic sense a seminar consists of a group of students meeting with their tutor in a tutorial room to discuss a subject as distinct from a larger and more formal gathering in a lecture theatre to listen to a speaker. A lot of so-called seminars turn out to be conferences with an audience of a hundred people!

Evening receptions can be even more informal. A group of clients may be invited to listen to a talk and perhaps attend a video show on company premises or in a hotel room. The hospitality may range from sherry and biscuits to a private bar and light buffet. Bank managers adopt this modest but effective technique, as do motorcar distributors, and it lends itself to organizations with local branches or showrooms. The host and speaker is usually the local manager.

Business conferences

Organizing other than public relations seminars and conferences can again bring out the public relations manager's skills. This may also include the ability to produce print and audio visuals, and here creative, buying and planning skills including timing will be required. For a sales conference he or she may have to produce or have produced videos to demonstrate new products or selling propositions. If the company and the size of attendance is large enough to justify the cost, the video can be given extra dramatic or humorous impact by the casting of TV personalities such as John Cleese.

Annual general meetings also have their public relations elements quite apart from being events which have to be organized. Shareholder relations are important today, and they can play a big part in year-to-year affairs such as the election of directors as well as in traumatic matters such as takeover bids. Print will be required such as the annual general report (informative rather than prestigious) and maybe proxy cards for voting. Britoil sought the interest of their shareholders by enclosing with the report and accounts a poster-size map of the UK showing where North Sea and other oil fields were located. Not a bad idea to educate shareholders!

Other devices may be used to attract the interest of shareholders such as video presentations, and phone-ins to the meeting. Nowadays, the annual report and accounts matter to the staff, whether or not they own shares, and videos are frequently made and distributed quickly, often to locations all over the world. This is another responsibility of the public relations manager, a typical example being a video-taped interview between a TV personality and the chairman or managing director. One international company believes that all its staff world-wide will have seen the videos within seven days of the AGM. It can, of course, be made in advance, and may be featured at the AGM itself.

However, care should be taken not to irritate shareholders with weighty and elaborate annual reports and accounts which they regard as a waste of money. This has become such a problem − and such an expense − with nine million owners of shares in privatized companies such as BT and British Gas, that the option of a summary is offered.

Yet another problem is that a surfeit of junk mail has emerged as a result of shareholder lists being made public, and these ready-made mailing lists have been plundered by financial firms engaged in direct response marketing. Thoughtfully, some annual reports carry a warning about this practice and advise shareholders to ask the Mailing Preferences Scheme to delete their name from mailing lists.

24

House journals

A 150-year-old public relations medium

The house journal is one of the oldest forms of public relations, the Americans being pioneers of this medium with *The Lowell Offering* (1842), the *I.M. Singer & Co.'s Gazette* (1855) and the Travelers Insurance Companies' *Protector* (1865). This medium therefore supplies evidence that public relations is not such a new activity as is sometimes supposed. In Britain, Lever Brothers launched a house journal towards the end of the nineteenth century.

House journals have been given a variety of names, such as house organs, employee newspapers and company newspapers. They are private publications and are therefore discussed separately from the commercial press. Over the years they have tended to change from pulpits for management to more candid forms of management–employee relations. *Ford News* is a good example of a house journal which enjoys an independent editorship, and is not afraid to criticize management. While tabloid newspaper format is popular there is now a tendency for a number to adopt A4 size magazine format.

There are also two distinct kinds of house journals; *internals* for staff and *externals* for outside publics. The two are distinct and internals should not be expected to serve the dual purpose of serving, say, employees and customers.

House publications are not confined to the world of commerce and industry even if house journal editors have been given the curious title of 'industrial editors', and their professional association in Britain is called the British Association of Industrial Editors. In fact, private magazines and newspapers are published by almost every kind of organization whether it be in the public or private sector, commercial or non-commercial.

Types of house journals

There are basically five types of house journals.

1   *The sales bulletin* which is a regular communication, perhaps weekly, between a sales manager and sales representatives in the field.
2   *The newsletter*, which is a digest of news for busy readers, e.g. management, technicians. Mistakenly, *newsletter* is used very loosely to describe printed house journals in general.
3   *The magazine*, which contains feature articles and pictures and may be published at monthly or quarterly intervals. It is usually A4 size.
4   *The tabloid newspaper*, which resembles a popular newspaper and contains mostly news items, short articles and illustrations and may be published weekly, fortnightly, monthly or every two months.
5   *The wall newspaper* is a useful form of staff communication, where the staff are contained in one location such as a factory, department store or hospital. Wall newspapers are also used, in poster form, to communicate with British Rail and London Underground passengers, displays at London Underground stations being introduced some 40 years ago.

These are general descriptions. In very large organizations all five may exist, addressed to different types of reader. Tabloids are generally addressed to the majority of workers whereas the newsletter may be for executives and the magazine for more serious reading. Externals are likely to use a magazine format since they are more educational and informative, less full of news items, personal stories and gossip, but some follow the tabloid format.

House journals are popular throughout the world, and in developing countries they help to supplement a meagre commercial press. Indeed, some house journals − especially externals − may be seen on sale at bookstalls where there is a dearth of indigenous magazines.

Why publish a house journal?

This is not a silly question, but it may not always be asked and consequently the purpose of a company journal may not be clear. Such a publication should be one of the media used by the public relations manager in the effort to carry out a planned public relations programme which includes internal relations. In other words, the house journal should be a meaningful agent of public relations management. It is significant that although all kinds of innovations have been introduced into internal communications, the printed house journal has survived as the most effective medium.

But why is it published? It was once the means by which paternal management could preach to the staff, and there are still some journals which read like a galley master whipping his slaves at the oars. A house journal should be published because it is needed. Why should it be needed? Because management has things to tell the staff, or there is a need to create unity between staff who are scattered between different locations, or mergers and acquisitions are occurring and old and new staff need to know each other, or staff need to communicate with one another, or because a safety valve is needed so that staff can criticize or complain. When reasons such as these are considered, the house journal becomes an important instrument in the process of management–employee relations. In Britain it becomes a means of democratizing industry, and of escaping from the 'master and servant' syndrome.

A good example of a house journal with a purpose is *Barclays News* (Figure 24.1), edited by Kevin O'Neill of Barclays Bank and designed by Partners in Publishing. The 48-page A4 size two-monthly magazine is seen as the main vehicle for two-way communication in the Barclays

Figure 24.1 *Examples of* Barclays News

Group of companies world-wide. It circulates to all staff and pensioners — some 118,000 in all — in 40 countries.

By 1989 the magazine had fallen out of favour with both the staff and management. Staff felt that its content was either propaganda or the reiteration of circulars they had already seen. Management felt that the content in general was too flippant, inappropriate and in one case insulting.

A new editor, Kevin O'Neill, was appointed from outside the Group and given a commendably free hand to turn the magazine round. He was able to build and train a journalistic team, re-equip with basic desk-top facilities and select a consultancy to act as project managers beyond the copy stage.

The editorial philosophy is that while Barclays is the proprietor, if the Group is to achieve its two-way communications aim it should expect a 'warts and all' presentation of business operations and accept that readers may be critical in the well-used letters page. On one occasion a reader's letter resulted in the bank saving £65,000 a year on an outmoded practice. Although the philosophy has raised eyebrows at times, editorial independence has been maintained.

There are many signs of the readership regarding the magazine as their own. There is a constant demand from Group divisions for coverage: the submitted story rate is high; there are many cases of the magazine being used as an additional marketing aid; the letters column, sponsored by Jameson Whiskey, thrives and the response to reader competitions is well above average, reaching at times 7−8 per cent of circulation.

In 1992 *Barclays News* was named officially as the best staff magazine in Europe when the Federation of European Industrial Editors Association made it the first recipient of its Grand Prix de L'Europe.

Another successful international staff newspaper is *British Airways News*, a weekly tabloid with a print run of 55,000 which reaches 48,000 employers and others in 100 countries within 24 hours of publication. It forms part of an overall internal communication programme which includes *Newsbrief*, a daily teletext service which transmits news to 25,000 BA computer terminals world-wide, Forum meetings of the company's top 150 managers (who are responsible for cascade briefings), and Outlook, a six-monthly video programme. The campaign costs £445,000 which works out at £9 per employee per year.

For this British Airways won the Best Employee Communications Programme in the *PR Week* Awards 1992.[1]

In the following week's issue of *PR Week*,[2] Simon Dark wrote a feature on Communication Empowering Employees, quoting BA's *PR Week* Awards, and also quoting BA's corporate communication manager

Michael Blunt on the question of empowering staff with the information they need to do their job better, and be part of the decision-making process. Blunt was quoted as saying 'the programme aims to brief employees fully on company culture and make everyone realize they have a personal responsibility for customers wanting to come back'. The article went on to emphasize the need to make systematic evaluations to monitor staff attitudes.

An interesting aspect of 'empowering employees' is something revealed by the Two-Ten Barometer survey in 1992, which showed that 48 per cent of in-house practitioners and 43 per cent of consultants believed that, in spite of recession, there would be an increase in internal public relations activity.

This finding marries in very well with the question which heads this section – why publish a house journal? – because it reveals a new marketing approach to internal communications. Well, it seems to be new, but awareness of the necessity for good internal relations and understanding of what a company is doing and selling is the reason why Rentokil has been such a remarkable growth company over the past 40 years. But it is significant that at last the contribution that an informed staff can make to the success of a company is being realized, and it is recognized that the house journal is a major part of the armoury of two-way internal communication.

How should a journal be edited?

References to independent editing have occurred in the previous section. How independent can or should a house journal editor be? To some extent this depends on the status and authority of the editor. Is editing the house journal someone's part-time job, or is the editor a specialist professional?

In some organizations there is an editorial board or committee. In others the chief executive officer has to approve all material before it is printed. In others – possibly a minority? – the editor is completely independent, working on a typically professional 'publish or be fired' basis. The latter is the ideal. But that means employing a good editor who may, of course, be the public relations manager if the journal does not justify its own editorial set-up.

House journal techniques

There are special considerations concerning the publishing, editing, production and distribution of house journals which are best discussed under the following separate headings:

The readers

It is important that the sponsor and the editor of a house journal should be absolutely clear about who are to be the readers of the publication. Technicians will want to read about the technicalities of products; factory workers will enjoy reading about themselves and their companions; sales representatives will appreciate a journal which informs them about the company and helps them to sell. It is difficult for a journal to be all things to all people, hence the need for separate publications to cater for the different interests of different people. This is not always appreciated, and too many journals attempt to appeal to too wide a readership.

Frequency

For reasons of cost, it may be decided to publish a journal only so often, but there should not be too large a gap between issues otherwise the sense of regularity and continuity will be lost. Readers should look forward to the next issue, and it should appear on a regular day such as the first of the month. Frequency can also be determined on a cost basis by the number of pages and whether there is black and white or colour printing. There are obvious permutations such as twelve issues of an eight-page tabloid or six issues of a sixteen-page one. Frequency may also be determined by the need to publish news as soon as possible or the greater timelessness of feature articles. Another cost factor concerning frequency could be the number of copies required to reach all readers.

Title

Just as the naming of a company or the branding of a product is a form of communication which creates distinctiveness and character, so the title of a house journal establishes the image of the publication. If it is a newspaper it may be a good idea to incorporate a typical newspaper name like 'Times', 'News', 'Express' or 'Mail' into the title, while if it is a magazine a typical name such as 'Review' may be used; or a very distinctive title may be invented such as *The Black Dragon* if perhaps that is part of a trade mark. But one should avoid rather hackneyed titles such as *Link* or over-clever titles such as *Smoker's Smile*. Moreover, a title should be a permanent one, which makes it all the more important to decide on a good name.

Free issue or cover price

Some people argue that a company journal should be issued free of charge, others say a journal will be valued more highly if there is a cover price. It all depends on how important the journal is to the readers. Do they consider it is worth paying for? This will depend on how far the journal represents real upward and downward communication between management and employees and how valuable the contents are to readers. Some of the biggest circulation house journals are sold like commercial newspapers.

Distribution

There is no point in going to a lot of trouble to produce a fine journal, only to let it suffer from ineffective distribution. If an organization has many branches or locations, and bulk supplies are sent to each address, there should be a systematic distribution to individual readers. If employees are merely expected to pick up copies from a central point, even from an automatic newsvendor, they may not bother and copies will be wasted. Similarly, if copies are handed out at the work bench they may be discarded on the floor. Although this may be costly – in terms of wrappers, envelopes and postage, and the mailing list must be kept up to date – the best method is to post copies to home addresses. Employees can then read the journal at their leisure, and it may also interest their families.

Advertisements

The inclusion of advertisements can help to make a journal look more realistic and may be of value to readers. Three types of advertisement may be included: (a) those inserted by the organization about its own products or services or, perhaps, situations vacant; (b) outside commercial advertisements if the circulation makes the journal a good advertising medium; (c) readers' sales and wants advertisements. The latter can be a reader service which adds to reader interest, and – as with *Ford News* – they can be inserted free of charge as a further reader service.

Contributors

There should be a planned supply of editorial material, the editor planning future articles which he has agreed with contributors, while correspondents can be appointed who are responsible for collecting news and submitting regular reports. The editor should also organize the taking of photographs of newsworthy events. One of the advantages of web-offset printing is that generous use can be made of illustrations, costly half-tone blocks not being necessary as with letterpress printing. It may also be necessary to commission features from professional writers, while the PROs of other organizations may offer house journals free articles. Membership of BAIE provides access to such material.

Production

House journals call for a combination of writing, print design and print buying skills. A very amateur-looking journal can result if there is weakness in one of the these departments. Some editors are principally journalists, have little or no design or print knowledge, and rely on a printer to convert copy into a journal. The result can be disappointing. At the other extreme, there are sponsors who appreciate these deficiencies and appoint an expert house journal consultancy to produce a professional journal. Well-known specialists are Sam Weller & Associates, Paragon Communications and Partners in Publishing.

Some large public relations consultants such as Dewe Rogerson and Edelman Public Relations Worldwide have specially staffed and equipped desk-top publishing units which produce first class house journals.

There are various editing and production systems. Some journals may be fully produced in-house by DTP methods, finished pages going onto disk and being transmitted on line to the printer. With others, the reporting, commissioning and editing is handled in-house, and a consultancy is used for design and production. Some organizations may give everything to a consultancy, including collection and writing of editorial material. Much depends on the variables that are discussed in this chapter.

Desk-top editing does make large demands on both editorial skills and budget. Barry Duke of Citygate Publishing made some interesting comments in this regard in an article in *PR Week*.[3] He wrote:

> What all too often emerges from the in-house DTP operations is the technical equivalent of a genetic experiment gone horribly wrong.
>
> The appearance of such monsters is hardly surprising when you consider they are produced without recourse to any number of disciplines which have to unite the internal communications umbrella if one is to produce a successful staff newspaper or magazine.
>
> First, you need the expertise of someone capable of tailoring, then maintaining a credible internal communications strategy. Next comes the building of an editorial team: a designer who will create the right look for your newspaper or magazine; an editor who will, if necessary

have a good grounding in journalism in general and in staff communications in particular; and a project manager with knowledge of every aspect of production.

In short, you will need to set up your own professional in-house publishing department. Or place the whole job in the hands of a firm of professional communicators.

On the question of production quality, the mistake is sometimes made of using a paper which is either too highly finished or of too heavy a weight, and this looks incongruous in a web-offset printed tabloid newspaper. Credibility is vital: a house journal should look like a normal commercial journal, not be too prestigious or resemble sales literature. The editor of *Ford News* goes so far as to say it must be as good as the popular tabloids read daily by Ford employees, even though *Ford News* is published fortnightly. Again, care should be taken not to have a journal designed by a studio which is so design-conscious that legibility is sacrificed. House journals should seldom be entrusted to advertising agencies since they are usually unfamiliar with journalism and public relations. They are more likely to produce house journals that resemble sales literature.

Externals

Most of the above remarks also apply to externals except that the policy, readership and contents must concern readers outside the organization. Externals should not normally be aimed at a general external readership, like some of the lavish prestige journals of the past. An external should fit into the public relations programme as a private medium directed at a defined public for a precise purpose. There are some excellent technical externals, and the circulation list may include the relevant trade, technical and professional journals with the invitation to reproduce features free of charge. These chosen publics could be:

1 *The trade.* Distributors can be educated about a company and its products, with advice on business matters and how to display, demonstrate or sell the products.
2 *Users.* Specifiers, formulators, designers and others can be shown how to use products such as materials, components or ingredients.
3 *Professionals.* Products and services of interest to professionals can be described and explained, ranging from products they may recommend or use to services they may buy.
4 *Patrons.* The in-flight magazine is a good example, as are the journals

supplied to hotel guests. Added to these are the tourist journals provided by tourist information organizations which, again, may be found in hotels.

5   *Customer magazines*. These are journals issued to customers and clients, typical sponsors being hotels, insurance companies, motorcar manufacturers and retailers. Foyles bookshop has published *Foylibra* for more than 60 years. *Rapport* is published quarterly for Peugeot car owners and is sent to them free of charge for the first two years of ownership.

6   *Opinion leaders*. Some journals of a perhaps wider appeal are distributed to those who express opinions about the organization and need to be kept informed.

References

1   *PR Week*, Public Relations Awards 1992, 29 October 1992
2   Dark, Simon, 'Communications empowering employees', *PR Week*, 12 November 1992.
3   Duke, Barry, 'A word in their ears', *PR Week*, 5 October 1992

25

Exhibitions

Four aspects

Exhibition public relations can produce excellent rewards if the public relations manager exploits the possibilities. This begins when planning the year's public relations programme and being aware of the company's participation in exhibitions, or in travelling its own exhibitions. He or she will need to cooperate with the people inside the organization who are responsible for producing exhibitions and with those who are running the shows, especially the exhibition press officers. There are therefore numerous public relations opportunities to be exploited over many weeks or months.

Exhibitions (apart from some private or permanent ones) are not themselves a public relations medium, except on special occasions when a stand is used for public relations rather than selling purposes, such as a police exhibit. This point is stressed because sometimes public and trade exhibitions are classed as public relations by those who quite wrongly regard public relations as being, like exhibitions, a below-the-line advertising medium. This chapter is concerned only with the public relations aspects of exhibitions.

It is not sufficient just to arrive at the press office, on the day the show opens, with a pile of unwelcome and useless press kits. We shall return to the question of press kits in the section on Exhibition promoters' public relations.

In this chapter we shall consider *four aspects* of exhibitions: (a) participation in a public or trade exhibition for public relations purposes; (b) public relations support for a participant in a public or trade exhibition; (c) exhibition promoters' public relations; and (d) public relations exhibitions. Under public or trade exhibition we shall include trade fairs, but we shall not include the organization and running of commercial stands in public or trade exhibitions since they are advertising responsibilities.

Exhibitions take many forms. They may be indoor or outdoor. They can also be mobile using specially designed road vehicles such as trailers, caravans or buses; there are also exhibition trains and ships. They can be either portable or permanent. Once again, there is the public relations benefit of face-to-face communication with its opportunities for eliminating communication barriers. The public relations transfer process can be very effective through the medium of the exhibition.

Special characteristics

Attractiveness

Exhibitions appeal to the curiosity and have entertainment value. They are also gregarious so that there is audience participation. This blend of social and mental stimulation acts as a magnet and heightens the interest. Few media attract such effortless attention even if the actual walking round an exhibition can be an exhausting experience. Some shows like the *Daily Mail* Ideal Home Exhibition and the Motor Show have been held regularly for many years and attract millions of visitors.

Visibility

Unlike printed media and even more effective than film or television, an exhibit can be seen physically. It may also be touched, used, sampled or in some other way examined physically. But even if it is too large or inconvenient to include on the stand the subject can be represented by a model − preferably working − or by video tape. Static subjects like banks can be enlivened by interesting displays.

Personal confrontation

The ability for exhibitors and visitors to meet, talk, explain or complain is a big asset. Visitors can get first-hand information and resolve problems or misunderstandings: exhibitors can get reactions to new products or prototypes. The exhibitor can get close to the customer, something he or she cannot do when working through wholesalers, agents and retailers.

From these remarks it will be seen that exhibitions have a large public relations content even when they are primarily below-the-line advertising media. That is perhaps why there is unfortunate confusion as to whether the exhibition is an advertising or a public relations medium. The answer to that poser lies in the *purpose* of the exhibit: is it *to inform and educate* or is it *to persuade and sell*? The majority of stands or booths in public and trade exhibitions, including trade fairs, fall solidly into the advertising or second category. They are usually the responsibility of the sales or marketing manager.

It should be explained that a public exhibition is open to the public, but admission to a trade show is limited to those who are sent tickets or who are admitted on showing a business card. In the latter case, irrelevant visitors such as schoolchildren are excluded unless educational visits are arranged.

There are certain organizations such as government departments, public services, state enterprises, trade and professional bodies which may exhibit at public or trade shows as part of their public relations programme of communicating with their particular publics

Public relations support

The value of a commercial or advertising exhibit can be greatly enhanced if full advantage is taken of the many public relations opportunities created by exhibitions. Too often these opportunities are overlooked, or efforts are limited to placing news releases and photographs in the press room, which is rather a last-minute effort. It is usually a waste of time and money to place press kits in press rooms. Some examples of public relations support for a participant in an exhibition are:

1 Contact the *exhibition press officer* as soon as the contract for stand space is signed, and ask what help is required. Usually, he or she will be sending out advance information, and needs details from exhibitors (at least about the organization and what it does even if what is to be shown is undecided or secret). Some exhibitors fail to assist like this because they wish to be secretive, but there is no need to give away vital information. The publicity achieved by the exhibition press officer (sometimes overseas) will help to increase the number of visitors to shows, which is to every exhibitor's advantage. Big exhibitions have permanent all-year-round press office staff, but a small exhibition may employ a consultancy at short notice, say three months before the show. More details are given below under Exhibition promoters' public relations.

2 It may be that by finding out, at an early date, the identity of the official opener an approach can be made direct to him or her (even if it is a member of the Royal Family or a government minister) to

visit the stand during the official tour. This can be very important. The tour will last only a short time, and since an exhibition may consist of several hundred stands it is impossible for the official opener to stop at each one. Consequently, well in advance, the official opener will have an itinerary drawn up of stands to be visited. It will be necessary to make such an approach, usually through the VIP's secretary or PRO, weeks and maybe months in advance.

3 Newspapers and magazines may be publishing previews of the event. Often, they contact all exhibitors and seek information, and these invitations should not be ignored. Advertisement space does not have to be purchased unless this is thought to be valuable.

4 The exhibition press officer will usually call a press preview or, in the case of a big show, organize a press day. It is wise for exhibitors to have important company personalities available on the stand. The exhibitor may also invite journalists direct, or have a private press reception on the stand.

5 During the run of the exhibition there are often opportunities to secure media coverage, as when a large order can be announced, or the stand receives an important visitor. At some exhibitions there will be facilities for distributing such news (e.g. Two-Ten Communications).

6 If a new product with export potential is to be shown it will be useful to advise the Department of Trade and Industry well in advance as they may be interested in issuing overseas news stories, filming the exhibit or taping a radio interview through the Central Office of Information.

7 Newspapers, magazines and freelance journalists (who may be writing for overseas journals) may prepare reports on the show which will appear afterwards, and advantage may be taken of these opportunities to gain post-exhibition publicity.

8 The producers of relevant radio and television programmes may be invited to gain ideas for future programmes.

9 During the run of the exhibition a special press reception can be held on the stand, in a room at the exhibition hall or at a nearby hotel.

From these suggestions it is clear that an enterprising PRO can obtain a great deal of coverage from a purely advertising stand. But he or she must know about the company's participation in the exhibition as soon as the contract is signed, not be asked to supply news releases for the press room at the last minute. This also applies to consultants servicing clients who exhibit.

Exhibition promoters' public relations

There have been sufficient references in the preceding section to indicate that the PRO employed by the promoters or sponsors of the exhibition has a special type of public relations job to do. The efforts of the promoter are three-sided: he or she has to inform prospective exhibitors, then prospective visitors before and during the show, and finally achieve follow-up coverage. Moreover, much exhibition public relations is of a continuous nature, following on from one event to the next, the coverage for one helping its successor.

Large exhibition promoters have a permanent team of PROs who work on a number of shows. The Department of Trade and Industry Overseas Promotions Services Branch has a publicity unit which conducts public relations for annual all-British exhibitions and British participation in overseas trade fairs. Smaller shows may employ consultants, and sponsoring organizations such as trade associations employ their regular PRO to service their events. Dates and venues of overseas trade fairs, inward trade missions, outward trade missions, store promotions and EC supported events are given in the DTI's monthly *Promotions Guide*.[1]

The exhibition PRO may be involved in the following tasks:

1 The organization of public relations activities such as a press reception and issue of news releases to announce a forthcoming exhibition.
2 Issue of details to all publications which publish a diary of forthcoming exhibitions, e.g. *Exhibitions Bulletin*.
3 Cooperation with government agencies which circulate information abroad about exhibitions such as the Department of Trade and Industry.
4 Seek advance information from exhibitors.
5 Distribute advance information, including translated versions to the overseas press.
6 Negotiate, write and publish feature articles prior to the show.
7 Cooperate with arrangements for the official opening.
8 Organize a press preview or press day and media coverage of the official opening, and manage it on the day this including press, radio and TV.
9 Advise exhibitors of press preview or press day arrangements.
10 Invite news releases and captioned photographs for display in the press room.
11 Prepare the press room, displaying news releases on tables or in racks, and displaying photographs and captions on panels, the

photographs being numbered and stocks being kept in a filing cabinet.

Press kits are not required. Their destination is waste disposal when the show is over. Large sums of money are wasted on press kits packed with useless material such as the chairman's portrait, company histories, house journals, picture postcards, free gifts and sales literature.

Journalists rarely carry more than a briefcase when they visit press rooms. Sometimes they merely want a story to put in their pocket. They may even ask for press material to be sent to their office! It is unnecessary for exhibitors to use lavish press kits in order to 'sell' their stories. All journalists want is a good publishable story, ideally on one sheet of paper, and maybe a good half plate black and white photograph. The sensible exhibition press officer will not let press kits past his or her press room door. (The author was an exhibition press officer at Olympia for eight years and banned press kits.)

12   Obtain maximum coverage of the official opening in the press and on radio and television as this can produce important publicity at the beginning of the show and so attract visitors.

13   Maintain the press room throughout the run of the exhibition, assisting journalists with information, sometimes arranging to send material to their offices, and providing hospitality as required.

14   Invite exhibitors to inform the press room of any activities, such as visits by VIPs, which can be put on a noticeboard in the press room.

15   Some exhibitions publish a daily bulletin or house journal which the PRO will edit, have printed, and distribute.

16   Produce an end-of-exhibition report on exhibitors' comments.

17   Monitor and announce attendance figures, especially if it is a large public exhibition when, say, the millionth visitor will be celebrated. Supply statistics on attendance figures.

Different exhibitions will have their special needs and possibilities but the above is a typical list of duties. It is a very busy job and in some exhibition centres the press room can be small and placed in an obscure part of the building since most of the area is taken up by the exhibits. This work may go on all the year round from one annual event to the next.

Public relations plays an especially important part in the tasks of attracting exhibitors and then visitors. It is very difficult to use advertising effectively for a new event, and the period in which advertising is likely to have impact could be limited to three weeks including the run of the show. Thus an exhibition cannot enjoy the repetition which is vital in advertising, not even that of a play or film which may run for months.

Public relations exhibitions

Here we refer to the use of the exhibition as yet another private or created public relations medium, with or without a large audience. They may be portable or permanent. The various kinds are:

Portable exhibitions

These may be designed and constructed so that they can be taken apart and transported to a venue. They may be working models, or sets of panels or frames, forming mini-exhibitions which can be assembled at a conference, or in hotel rooms, public libraries, schools, theatre foyers, department stores, shop windows or other suitable situations. A number of building societies find that window displays on all sorts of unassociated topics attract attention to an otherwise uninteresting space, and these can be mini-exhibitions organized by enterprising PROs and toured from branch to branch.

Permanent exhibitions

These are usually on company premises, but for a number of years Monsanto enjoyed a permanent exhibition at Brussels Airport in the form of long stretches of Acrilan carpet which millions of passengers had to walk on when they arrived or departed. A permanent exhibition is ideal for an organization which receives groups of visitors. At its Lambeth headquarters the Pharmaceutical Society has a beautiful exhibition appropriate to its profession, serving as part of the décor of the building. Permanent exhibits can also be mounted at trade centres which governments set up in overseas markets (e.g. the American and Japanese centres in London, the British ones overseas), or in particular trade centres such as the Building Centres in London and provincial cities. On the shore beside the Thames Barrier there is an exhibition and video theatre on the subject of the Barrier, which aims to prevent London from being flooded.

Mobile exhibitions

Great ingenuity has been applied to the touring exhibition which can take a compact show from place to place by road, rail, sea and even air. The possibilities are endless, ranging from a simple caravan to a train which can stop in a bay at a local station or to a floating exhibition like the Japanese trade ships. There are also custom-built exhibition vehicles and converted double-decker buses, or simple Land Rovers that take combined video shows, demonstrations and song and dance teams to the villages in developing countries. Mobile exhibitions using road vehicles are set up in market squares, car parks, school playgrounds, hotel yards, or at agricultural shows, gymkhanas, sports events and so on.

Sponsorship of exhibitions

This special aspect of exhibitions — the use of an exhibition as a communication activity of an organization such as a trade association — is discussed in the exhibitions section of Chapter 33. Many exhibitions are sponsored by newspapers and trade magazines.

Reference

1 *Promotions Guide*, monthly, Department of Trade and Industry, Overseas Promotions Support Branch, London

26

Public relations literature

Analysis of public relations print

Print of various kinds, in addition to house journals, is another private public relations medium which serves the informative, instructional and educational role of public relations. It can be excluded from no public relations budget; the news release heading, the invitation card and the photo caption blank are necessities. The range of such print is great, and this chapter is confined to an analysis of twenty examples. Information about printing processes and how to work with the printer will be found in Chapter 18.

News release headings

The astonishing thing about British public relations is the array of gaudy news release headings which seem to represent an advertising agency's studio nightmare. Too many news release headings devote too much space to colourful displayed lettering which gets in the way of the story. In fact, the best headings − and the ones which editors prefer − are those which place the source details discreetly but clearly *at the foot of the sheet*. This then gives prominence to the headline and opening paragraph so that the editor is made aware immediately of the subject of the story. A news release should not look like a sales letter, unless the objective is to deliberately annoy editors.

Photo caption blanks

An excellent idea is to print photo caption blanks bearing, preferably at the foot, the name, address, telephone number and perhaps logotype of the sender.

Invitation cards

These are best printed for each occasion since each invitation card should state the programme, location and timetable of the event.

Video synopsis leaflets

Give-away leaflets presenting a brief summary and reminder of the content of the video and giving credits to producers, cameramen, scriptwriters, actors and commentators are valuable at showings of documentaries.

Calendars

While business calendars may be regarded as an advertising medium, they do create goodwill and may also be considered as public relations print. They can be informative about an organization. Stock calendars, supplied by firms like Evershed who specialize in producing calendars, may be overprinted, or special photography and printing may be undertaken to create individual calendars.

Posters and wall charts

Very popular with trade associations for products such as tea or coffee, public relations posters can be very detailed and instructive when the intention is to distribute them to schools. They can also be used to educate the public about safety precautions, or to provide information of public interest. Such posters are usually small bills or placards, the standard size being crown (15×20 in., 381×508 mm), double crown (30×20 in., 762×508 mm), or quad crown (30×40 in., 762×1016 mm). They may also take the form of wall newspapers as used by British Rail and the London Underground.

Educational leaflets, folders, booklets

Here we refer to informative literature which is different from sales literature. Subjects might concern lawn treatment, home decorating, care of clothes, or how to use a gas oven. Such literature helps the customer to gain benefits from the product, and should not plug the product in persuasive copywriting style.

Handy aids

Under this general heading may be included items which help the customer, such as calculators for quantities of wallpaper or metric conversion tables.

Instruction leaflets and manuals

Even if the PRO is not directly responsible for instruction and maintenance manuals he or she should advise on their production for they can so easily cause ill-will if they are not simple yet comprehensive. It may be that pictures and diagrams can say more than words. When producing for export markets it is more than ever important that translated instructions should be clear and accurate. Some manuals for Japanese products contain some very odd English.

Annual reports and accounts

Simplicity of presentation has become the hallmark of the modern balance sheet. With so many people interested in company performances − including the staff − the annual report and accounts has become an exercise in good communication. This subject is discussed more fully in Chapter 30.

Postage stamps and first-day covers

The postage stamp has become a public relations medium in many countries of the world, promoting public knowledge of road safety, 'grow more food' campaigns, industrial accident prevention and so forth. Germany has issued many such sets, and the British issued a set to coincide with the first elections to the European Parliament. First-day covers can be used to celebrate public relations events (e.g. IPR and IPRA conferences) or, when there is a new stamp issue, charities can issue appeals to prospective donors in first-day covers. Concorde has provided a whole philatelic theme with stamps depicting the aircraft and special covers flown by British Airways and Air France. There was a special commemorative set for the British Council.

Press kits

Although many press kits suffer from over-kill and are irrelevant, there are times when a useful wallet can be a convenient means of containing a number of loose items at a press event.

Picture postcards

Apart from advertising the subject, a picture postcard can be very useful and will promote goodwill, examples being those supplied by hotels, airlines and shipping lines.

Questionnaires

Confidence may be inspired when a hotel guest, airline passenger or customer is invited to complete a questionnaire which requests his or her praise, criticisms or suggestions.

Pocket and desk diaries

Lasting a year, diaries extend goodwill over a long period and even more so if annual refills are supplied.

Company histories

Provided these are not biased and pretentious, they can be important sources of information, especially if the organization has a good story to tell. The Americans are rather good at this, and Coca-Cola have an excellent full-colour volume. Centenary celebrations provide a good opportunity for such publications. The *Daily Telegraph* has produced a record of news stories as printed since the paper was first launched, making a very interesting historical record.

School project packs

Many industries and large companies receive requests from students who are undertaking projects, and very sensibly and generously some organizations have responded by producing informative school project packs.

School information material

Similarly, some organizations regularly supply schools with educational material (e.g. British Gas) in leaflet or pamphlet form.

Induction material

For any company which is frequently recruiting and training staff, good concise material about the organization, including charts of management structure, can be a public relations responsibility.

Reprints of feature articles

Ready-made pieces of print with a variety of uses as give-away material in showrooms and on exhibition stands are the reprints of public relations feature articles.

From the above it will be seen that public relations print can form an important part in a planned public relations programme, and perhaps absorb a substantial part of the budget. These needs and costs should be anticipated at the planning and budgeting stage, and are a serious part of the public relations manager's responsibilities. This calls for an understanding of the types of printing process best suited to a print job, knowledge of suitable printers, and how to go about requesting competitive quotations. When asking for quotations it is necessary to specify exactly the nature of the job, and it may be essential to check the printer's ability to meet a required delivery date. Ability to read proofs, and correct clearly by using the correction symbols given in Chapter 18, is most important. The advice on how to work with the printer in that chapter can be related to the literature described in this chapter.

When stocks are held of public relations literature it is necessary to maintain stock control so that the public relations department does not run out of stock, and − before re-ordering − to check whether it needs to be amended or up-dated.

Associated with public relations will be the use of the corporate identity scheme discussed in Chapter 29. This will involve correct use of logo, colour scheme and logotype. It could also be the public relations manager's responsibility to supervise all forms of company print to ensure that it conforms to the corporate identity, and also to avoid print design in which important information is illegible. Many business letterheadings have telephone numbers printed in small type and grey ink!

27

The psychology of communication

This chapter contains two sections: a reproduction of an address given by the author,[1] and a resumé of some of the points made by T. Mori[2] on the Japanese approach to marketing/corporate communications.

The psychology of public relations

The purpose of public relations is to create understanding through knowledge. That usually means that problems of communication have to be solved. People do not understand us and what we do because they have not received or comprehended information which would provide the necessary knowledge for understanding to be created.

All kinds of clever media may be used to convey our messages — the press, radio, television, video, exhibitions and the spoken word — but it all depends on how effectively the message is transmitted and received. Moreover, everyone is being bombarded with messages ranging from news to advertising, and our message may be buried in mountains of print and deluges of noise.

One rule emerges immediately: keep it short and simple. What could be more simple than the word STOP? This is far more effective than, say 'Do not move' or 'Stay where you are'. The secret of communication is to convey a message so that it is easily and clearly understood, like the sign which tells us to STOP!

Why is this sometimes so difficult? Because the recipient of the message does not have the same knowledge and experience of the subject as the communicator. This knowledge and experience develops with familiarity and repetition so that mental habit patterns are formed. Thus, we can communicate without words, as when a red light tells the motorist or the train driver to stop.

Communication is therefore part of the learning process, and public relations is about informing, educating, and creating understanding through better knowledge. It has to be done simply and repeatedly with regular news, frequent pictures, constant reminders, even by events such as sponsorships.

How do we communicate? There are five chief methods, which are:

1 By words, whether printed or spoken.
2 By sound, such as music or sound effects.
3 By movement, such as action in films, video, or TV or by gestures and body movement.
4 By the use of symbols such as corporate identity logos, badges and signs.
5 By the use of colours which have different effects or meanings.

In an educated, sophisticated society we may use all of these forms of communication. But in some societies these forms of communication may not exist, or they may have special significance. Remember, there are 125 less developed, underdeveloped and developing countries. Eastern Europe is becoming entwined with Western Europe but has different cultures, including religions. The USSR has become the CIS, with all sorts of new opportunities for communication with the world beyond Russia. In the changing world of Europe and Russia communications are concerned with conflicting sets of values.

The sheer size of populations and land areas also affects communications. There are 700 million people in India, 180 million in Indonesia and 80 million in Nigeria. The number of different races, tribes, languages or religions in such countries create barriers to simple communication and understanding. It is so easy to communicate and create understanding in Britain compared with countries outside Europe and North America, and that is why public relations is even more important and necessary than it is in countries where public relations is widely practised. People in Britain are sometimes surprised to learn that public relations exists at all in developing or industrializing countries, when in fact the need for public relations is far greater there than it is in Britain. For example, for many Western people the image of Africa is of one country, not a continent of 50 countries.

Nevertheless, there are millions of people around the world who never see printed words or pictures, and these cause cultural communication problems. Let us consider these together with the five methods of communication already defined.

Limits of experience

This is a constant problem because people with whom we wish to communicate will inevitably have less experience of the subject than we, who are closely associated with it, possess. For example, the sales assistant in the shop usually knows more about the goods he or she is selling than the customer who is enquiring about them. The same situation applies to journalists who have to write about countless topics and are experts in none. On one occasion I ran a press conference on a technical subject, and the journalists were addressed by the managing director. After his address he was asked questions which showed that those present had little understanding of what he had been saying. Later he complained to me about the ignorance and stupidity of the journalists and I had to explain to him that whereas he had lived with the subject for months they had been confronted by it for the first time.

This dilemma occurs all the time, the gap between the informed and the uninformed. To talk about the sea to people who live in a land-locked country in the middle of a continent, or about snow to people in a tropical country, is to talk about an unknown subject if they have never travelled abroad. During the Second World War, German soldiers, coming from an almost land-locked country, were surprised when invading Holland that they could not see England from the Dutch coast. Similarly it is difficult for people in Britain to imagine an earth-quake, a typhoon or a volcanic eruption. A few years ago parts of Britain were struck by a hurricane for about two hours one night; it destroyed thousands of trees and was a totally new experience for those affected by it.

Again, it is surprising sometimes to find that people living in African countries famous for wild animals have never seen them, except in a zoo. Once, on a visit to a snake farm I discovered my African companions had never before seen a snake. It is therefore very easy to assume that people have knowledge and understanding, but their experience may be very limited.

People tend to be very parochial, and their knowledge may be very localized. In London, those who live south of the River Thames are very often unfamiliar with north of the river and vice versa, regarding Londoners from the other side, as 'foreigners'. I once met a man only a few miles from London who had never been on a train. In public relations we have to recognize this major psychological factor, that we are all ignorant of a great many things.

For public relations – or advertising – to succeed it has to be credible. Two advertisements for Nigeria Airways help demonstrate how easy it is to communicate wrongly. One advertisement claimed 'Flies All Over Africa', which had an unfortunate double meaning. At one time the airline's symbol was an elephant because they flew jumbo jets, but people protested that elephants do not fly.

So, imagine this problem when trying to communicate unknown subjects. How do you explain powdered baby milk to people who have no means of measurement, no means of sterilization?

It is necessary, therefore, to appreciate the limited experience of people with whom we communicate, whoever they are and wherever they are. We may solve this riddle by using short words, short sentences and short paragraphs, or by using cartoons and diagrams which demonstrate step-by-step what has to be done. This is true whether people are educated and live in sophisticated societies or whether they are illiterate and live in primitive societies.

Problems of scale

These problems also stem from limits of experience. If people are unfamiliar with variations in size, other than perhaps the length of shadows, or the fact that a person moving into or from the distance changes size, they can be very literal about sizes. They expect them to be lifelike. Otherwise, credibility is lost.

An example of this was the supply of insecticide to destroy tsetse flies which were attacking cattle in the countryside of an African state. On the bags of insecticide was a picture of a giant tsetse fly. The farmers refused to use it because they had no insects that big, and consequently their cattle suffered. Similarly, villagers failed to use a pesticide against house flies because the insect illustrated on a poster was larger than those in their district.

Visual perception time

If a subject is new, different or complicated the information needs to be conveyed simply, slowly, in small doses and perhaps repeatedly. We have to consider how long it will take for a message to be comprehended. A number of subjects with which we may be very familiar today had their problems when first introduced. Holiday Inn sounded like a motel. Giro Bank meant what? And you might still be surprised to know what P&O, MG, Garuda, CAM or BMW stand for.

This problem particularly concerns messages that can be given quickly, such as in a film or video where the message is fleeting. Can it be simplified, can it be repeated, can it be re-presented in a different way, and can it be given over a short time? Whereas a feature film on television or in the cinema may run for an hour or much longer, the best length for a documentary or PR film or video is 20 minutes. For some subjects, it might be less. Videos made to describe new venues to staff when it is proposed to relocate, and it is hoped that staff will move with the company, seldom run to more than six or eight minutes. Similarly if films or videos are made for unsophisticated audiences, such as villagers in developing countries, it is usually best to keep them short and have repetitions of the message otherwise attention will wane and the message will be lost on the audience.

Span of consciousness

This is similar to visual perception time, but is more concerned with the extent to which people are willing to pay attention. A famous exponent of this was Dr Rudolph Flesch who said, 'People don't really like to read things they can just barely understand; they prefer reading matter they don't even feel any effort in reading.' In industrialized countries like Britain, Germany and the USA we see the difference between popular tabloid newspapers and the 'quality' broadsheet newspapers. Compare, for instance, the difference in literary style between the *Sun* and *The Times*. The give-away is that the *Sun* sells ten times as many copies as *The Times*.

Dr Flesch talks of six- to eight-word sentences in popular newspapers, but 30-word sentences in scientific papers. indicating the different intellectual spans of consciousness. This can also apply to sizes of vocabularies. The English language has a huge vocabulary because in addition to the original Anglo-Saxon we have borrowed words from the Latin, Greek and European languages. The American vocabulary is different from the British, especially in its adoption of many long German words. We shall return to the different meanings of words.

Understanding pictures

Here we are concerned with photographs, films and videos, and this is linked with the factors already discussed. Normally, when one looks at a picture it is rather like looking at a room or a scene, and we take in the whole as one piece. This action applies the *Gestalt* theory of seeing things as wholes rather than as sets of items.

However, if the viewer has little or no knowledge of the subject as a whole they will 'read' the picture according to the bits they recognize, and ignore the rest. Looking at a picture of the interior of an airliner a person who has never flown may well recognize the seats but little else. This may seem absurd but it is quite logical, in that we can recognize only the things we know. The rest becomes a meaningless clutter. A lot of information, whether it is in pictorial or any other form can be meaningless unless reduced to that which is meaningful. This should be remembered when taking photographs or shooting videos. Do not confuse the viewer. Keep it simple within the limits of the viewer's comprehension. You will notice in a good manual for a motorcar or a camera that each part will be explained separately and carefully with photographs, drawings or diagrams.

Another difficulty with pictures is that simple people who use few pictures can regard pictorial images quite literally. If they see a face or a head on a coin, or in print, they could assume that seeing is believing and that the person has been beheaded, or has been deprived of legs and arms.

Multi-language problems

How do we cope with a great variety of languages? You may say, let's have vernacular newspapers, or different language radio programmes. Up to a point that is possible and it happens, but it means that the newspapers are compelled to have small circulations and are uneconomic business propositions, while separate language broadcasts can mean that listeners are deprived of airtime when the programme is not in their language. In the Gulf states, where there may be more than one hundred nationalities in addition to the Arabs, one solution is to print newspapers in English for the foreigners with perhaps one in an Indian language. In some countries English may be a major second language, as in Hong Kong and Malaysia, or the predominant language, as in Singapore. English is a second language in Indonesia, where there are also many English-speaking people from Australia, Britain, Canada and the USA. English predominates in Nigeria, but there are also newspapers in Hausa and Yoruba. There are famous English language newspapers in India, but also others in Indian languages.

Multi-language countries present many communication problems. Even when English is spoken, the vocabulary may be limited. This can result in people jumping words they do not know and gaining the wrong meanings from what they are reading. For example, a question in a public relations examination asked 'Why do editors seldom want coloured photographs?' But candidates not knowing the word 'seldom' read and answered the question wrongly.

The vocabularies of native languages in some countries can be very limited. In Indonesia the local language, which is similar to Bahasa Malay, does not have plurals, so that they say 'man man' rather than 'men', and are trying to extend the vocabulary by borrowing foreign words.

Translations have to be meticulous, otherwise comic or misleading 'literal' translations occur. Dutch bulb growers are apt to write about tulips growing 6 inches 'low' when they mean 'high'. The French are very pedantic about their language and have difficulty in translating English jargon.

Different meanings of words

Some words have very different meanings in other countries. It is very difficult to promote the Irish Mist brand of whiskey in Germany where *mist* means dung! But even where people appear to speak much the same languages there can be surprising differences. There is, for example, English English and American English, and this can provoke great problems in, say, Singapore or Australia where the two languages may clash.

A billboard in American means a large poster, but in Britain it means a small poster board such as you see on the pavement outside a shop. We speak of the railway, Americans of the railroad, so our road show goes on the road but the American goes by rail. The British broadcast, and the American air, we eat sweets and they eat candy, we go shopping but they go marketing, we live in flats and they live in apartments. One of my books has been translated into American; a Canadian reviewed another one of my books and criticized the 'quaint' English.

So this is a problem for students taking exams in English but reading either British or American textbooks. Expressions like piggy-backing, billboard and sales promotion have completely different meanings. If you are taking a British exam do not read American textbooks.

There are other words which have different meanings in certain countries creating communication traps like these. Indians tend to call posters 'postals', although postal means sent by mail. In some Arab countries all lorries are called Mercedes because they were the first to be exported there. Nigerians tend to call a single cigarette a 'stick'. In the Caribbean, any drink may be referred to as 'tea', which confounded British market researchers who carried out a survey to guage the possible market for tea in Trinidad.

Colours

The language of colour varies round the world and is important in communications. Colours can have special national relevance. Britain tends to favour red, for example red Post Office vans and pillar boxes and scarlet Guards uniforms, while Scotland prefers blue, and Ireland green and orange. France tends to like pale blue and the Italians dark blue. The Australians like orange, as we see with Qantas airline and the shirts of Australian rugby players. Green is popular in Nigeria, and in most Muslim countries. The Chinese have quite a language of colour, with red representing prosperity and happiness, yellow meaning joy and wealth, but blue meaning sadness. When the Japanese tried to sell pale blue sewing machines to the Singapore Chinese they were a flop.

While red usually stands for danger, this was not understood when traffic signals were introduced for the first time in Gaborone, Botswana, in 1984, and they remained hooded until the authorities felt confident that motorists understood the meaning of red, amber and green.

There are differences in the acceptance of black and white. In the West black is the colour of mourning, but in some countries white is the colour of mourning. An African woman wearing black may appear to be a widow, but she may be protecting her colourful dress from the dust and dirt. Black is often associated with evil, white with purity. For the Malays, yellow is the royal colour while red signifies valour and might.

The language of colour is important in communications. The 'Made Simple' series of textbooks used to have red, yellow and black covers resembling the German flag, and it is interesting that they have been changed to blue and white. This could suggest that a German publisher had sold out to a French one, but it is actually a British publisher. Their use of colours is mystifying.

Imagine the red faces in Belfast when the Northern Ireland Office's Industrial Development Board sponsored a supplement in the German magazine Automobile Produkton only to find it decorated in orange, white and green the colours of the Irish Republic!

The colour of the labels on Gilbeys gin bottles was changed to meet demand as revealed by research. It was found that seven European, Far Eastern and South American markets preferred a red label to the traditional green one. Only the British preferred green. By adopting a red label sales were boosted world-wide.

Symbols

Certain shapes, creatures and people carry significant meanings, as will be seen in badges, trade marks and logos. Animals are particularly popular, the lion most of all. There are many products called Lion, and of course Singapore is the 'lion city'. Uncle Sam and John Bull are national symbols. Other countries adopt animals and birds (especially in the corporate identities of airlines), like the mouflon of Cyprus Airways, kite of Malaysia Airlines, and the garuda of the Indonesian airline. The label of Guinness beer pictures a bulldog in Malaysia but a black cat in Indonesia (the Indonesian waiter will know what you want if you ask for a 'black cat beer'). And yet while a black cat is lucky in Britain, it is regarded as unlucky in Nigeria. The crescent moon is commonly used in Islamic countries, appearing for instance on flags, and it is significant that while the cross of the Red Cross would not be acceptable, the similar organization is known as the Green Crescent.

Literacy

Finally, regarding developing countries, there is the question of literacy, which itself has different meanings in different countries. In the industrialized world people tend to be scornful of illiterates, meaning people who cannot read or write. But that is only one form of literacy. Other quite amazingly intelligent forms of literacy exist, such as visual and oral literacy, which so-called educated people in industrialized countries do not possess.

Very few people in, say, Britain can give a detailed visual description, as we see in police investigations. They do not remember what other people look like. It is not a case of all Chinese or all white people look alike: you can tell a Nigerian from a Ghanian by the way they walk! But it is amazing how people from developing countries carry mental pictures. I have arrived in an African hotel, and been asked by the boy on the newstand two years after my previous visit whether I want my *Guardian*. I did not recognize him.

But perhaps the most astonishing form of literacy − pure communication − is the kind one finds in Ghana. Sitting on the pavement in Accra will be a man selling mats, baskets and other village crafts. From time to time people will squat down beside him and converse at length. He is a postman or messenger who carries messages between village and town people, arranging marriages, land deals and all kinds of business matters entirely by means of memorized messages. That, I think is the most remarkable example of effective communications and of the psychology of public relations, which is based not only on information and understanding but on trust.

The Japanese approach to marketing/corporate communications

According to Takeshi Mori of the Brussels office of Dentsu, Japan's leading advertising and public relations agency, the Japanese are poor communicators. He quoted from a study of attitudes of European business editors to Japanese companies, and these findings offer a fascinating insight into the psychology of Japanese communications.

The report claimed that 89 per cent of those interviewed stated that Japanese companies were more difficult to communicate with than European companies or American firms in Europe. A UK business magazine said 'They are different. More wary. They are very good at what they are prepared to tell you, but that is limited.' In the opinion of a German high-tech magazine, 'One has to establish a common base of trust. Personal contacts are very important – more than with German companies – to keep a steady flow of information.' A Norwegian business magazine thought 'They are not very good communicators. This is due mainly to language barriers.'

Other comments were 'My impression is pretty negative. They appear very closed and defensive, particularly in South Wales. Very autocratic and inflexible' (UK financial magazine). A German trade magazine said 'Their management is more "closed shop", not as transparent as the German.' And a Belgian daily advised 'They have to be accepted and integrated, which means that they will have to modify their image as "invaders".' Finally, a German daily proposed 'In future the question will be: are Japanese firms able to adapt their communications systems to foreign markets, just like they were able to do with technology?'

With the Japanese establishing such a foothold in Britain and in continental Europe, they clearly have a public relations dilemma. Is it really a case of 'East is East and West is West and never the twain shall meet?' It is a subject which links with the psychology of public relations. Actually, it is not peculiar to Japanese relations with Europeans, and it not even a hangover from the Second World War. It is a question of national culture, and such clashes have been encountered by the Japanese in Asiatic and African countries. The Japanese have attitudes of mind which need to be understood by anyone having dealings with them.

So, Mr Mori posed the two questions: Why are the Japanese not good communicators; and Why have they been successful in the global market? The answers to these questions are given in diagrammatic form. Figure 27.1 gives a brief answer to the first question, Figure 27.2 to the second question, and Figure 27.3 elaborates on the differences in attitudes between the West and Japan.

In his presentation, Mr Mori went on to explain the difference

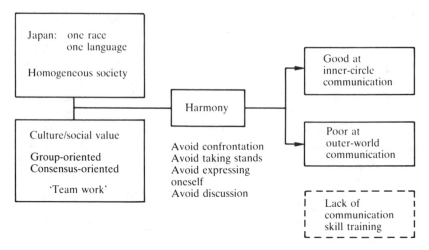

Figure 27.1   *Brief answer to question 1*

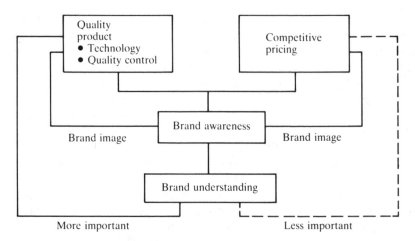

Figure 27.2   *Brief answer to question 2*

between Japanese and Western advertising. The Japanese place emphasis on familiarizing the name, and in creating a warm feeling towards the name. Thus − as may be seen all over the world − there are huge neon signs which simply say Sony, Fuji, Nikon or Canon. In Japan itself, television commercials say nothing about the product, but consist of an entertainer who is followed by a bold name display. One cannot imagine a Kellogg's commercial featuring a song by Tom Jones or a joke by Bruce Forsythe followed by the words Kellogg's Corn Flakes!

The West	Japan
• Emphasis on the individual	• Emphasis on the group
• Company's first priority is shareholders	• Company's first priority is employees
• Clear-cut description of functions	• No clear-cut description of functions
• Need for individual assertiveness	• Need for co-ordination
• Decision made by individuals	• Decision emerging collectively
• Confrontation/competition	• Harmony co-operation
• Strong need for contract	• Weak need for contract
• Short-term profits	• Long-term profits
• Specialist orientated	• Generalist orientated
• By-passing hierarchy is intolerable	• By-passing hierarchy is tolerated
• Stand up for an issue	• Uncomfortable in taking stance
• Management/employee wariness	• Management/employee trust
• The media needs careful handling	• The media is our ally
• Dealing with activism is way of life	• Little experience of hostile pressure groups and activists

Figure 27.3 *Differences in attitudes*

References

1   Jefkins, Frank, Keynote address, 13th International Summer School, Public Relations Management, London, 6 July 1992
2   Takeshi, Mori, Presentation, 13th International Summer School, Public Relations Management, London, 10 July 1992

PART FOUR

Special Areas of Public Relations

28

Public relations and marketing

The public relations − marketing relationship

Both the in-house public relations manager and the public relations consultant may encounter and have to resolve some strange problems concerning the relationship between public relations and marketing. The antipathy between the two has been provoked by misunderstandings about public relations on the marketing side, and antipathy towards promotion and selling by those in public relations who have so often been accused of producing free advertising. Moreover, public relations is concerned with many activities, even in industry and commerce, which have nothing to do with marketing. However, many public relations consultancies today are marketing orientated, and many marketing divisions of companies are making increasing use of these consultancy services.

From the in-house point of view much depends on the positioning of the public relations manager. Is he or she independent, reporting to the CEO and servicing the marketing department among others, which is the ideal and very proper positioning? Or does the PRO form part of the marketing team, which can be restrictive unless marketing management is enlightened about public relations?

There is no harm in public relations coming within the marketing department if the public relations manager enjoys independence as a specialist. This situation is common in the banking world.

Unfortunately, the marketing world has been brought up to regard public relations as little more than product publicity or even free advertising, placing it in the promotion box of the Four Ps (product, price, place and promotion). Marketing literature seldom mentions public relations, except in the narrow Four Ps context. Marketing lecturers do likewise, relying on their textbooks, and even confusing public relations with sales promotion, which is a very different activity, or they make the mistake of regarding it as a below-the-line activity. When dealing with the marketing environment, the public relations manager can, therefore, suffer from misunderstandings about his or her true role as a particular kind of communicator. The Chartered Institute of Marketing turns such a blind eye to public relations that holders of the CIM Diploma are awarded exemption from all except the public relations paper in the CAM Certificate. The unfortunate influence of Philip Kotler and his extraordinary definition of public relations was quoted in Chapter 1.

Public relations and the marketing mix

Marketing and public relations have so much in common — both are to do with human relations — that there is really great scope for the two to work together in pursuit of the company's success. The public relations manager can make practical contributions to the marketing strategy when it is understood on both sides that public relations can enter into almost every phase of the marketing mix. The marketing mix consists of all the elements that contribute to a successful marketing operation. Perhaps, because advertising is one of these elements it is thought that public relations is another, and possibly *optional*, single element. This is a common mistake, just as it is wrong to put public relations among below-the-line activities. It is not an isolated specialism, but is *inherent* in everything an organization does, and that includes marketing. Thus, in relation to marketing, the influence of public relations should be introduced as early as possible.

It could enter into product development, reflecting the feedback received from the media and various publics about products and services, ranging over complaints, suggestions and demands. The content of a packaged holiday could be changed because of unfortunate experiences in the past which had required assistance from the public relations department in dealing with complaints. Motoring correspondents may have criticized certain design defects of a motorcar. A woman's page editor — *as actually happened* — may have passed on the need for a product as expressed in readers' letters. All this feedback can assist product development, for public relations acts as the ears as well as the voice of an organization.

For practical purposes it is better to forget the Four Ps tidy box approach to marketing with its narrow groupings of product, place, price and promotion which invite exclusion of public relations, and adopt a chronological listing of marketing mix elements which is nearer to the real-life situation, such as the following:

1 Conception, innovation or modification of new product.
2 The place of the product in the product life cycle.
3 Marketing research.
4 Naming and branding.
5 Product image.
6 Market segment.
7 Pricing.
8 Product mix, rationalization and standardization.
9 Packaging.
10 Distribution.
11 Sales force.
12 Market education.
13 Corporate and financial public relations.
14 Industrial relations.
15 Test marketing.
16 Advertising.
17 Advertising research.
18 Sales promotion.
19 The after market; after-sales service, spares, guarantees, instructions.
20 Maintaining customer interest and loyalty.

These twenty elements are taken from an earlier book by the author, *Public Relations for Marketing Management*.[1]

From this list it will be seen that there are opportunities for public relations to service marketing throughout the preparation and conduct of a marketing programme. In this chapter we shall select a few of these elements for discussion.

The product life cycle (PLC)

Marketing strategy takes note of the position of a product in its life cycle. The traditional six-stage PLC shows a product passing through stages of development, introduction, growth, maturity, saturation and eventual decline. Different kinds of public relations activity will be required at these different stages, e.g. to educate the market, to coincide with advertising, to maintain sales, to describe additional uses or the use of accessories, and so on. Some products may be designed to have a certain life cycle. Fashion goods may live for a few months but a motorcar (with minor modifications) for ten years. This does not refer to the life expectancy of individual products but to the selling life of the total production. In the case of a motorcar a new model will be designed to replace the old model when sales fall below a given level.

Products like Guinness, Cadbury's milk chocolate or Coca-Cola may have an indefinite life cycle.

There are variations on the traditional life cycle which are also significant in public relations terms. There is the recycled PLC which applies to projects pulled out of decline by improvements or other changes such as additives, re-packaging or price-cutting. Then there is the leapfrog effect when one model is replaced by another, and the staircase effect when new product uses or new services are introduced. The classic example of the staircase effect PLC is nylon, but it can also be applied to shipping, insurance and banking which have diversified their services over the years. Changes in behaviour of the life cycle provide special opportunities for public relations activity, an example in the continuous story of nylon being the introduction of motorcycle wheels made of nylon.

Thus, here is a good example of how the public relations practitioner can work closely with marketing, for the public relations strategy will depend on the sort of PLC experienced by the product or service, and where it is now in the progress of the PLC.

The four types of PLC are shown in Figures 28.1–28.4.

Company names and product brand names

One of the most elementary yet foremost kinds of marketing communication is the name of the company, or the trade or brand name including other names attached to ranges of products. This can be confusing when the customer is asked to cope with three different names as used to be the case with Unigate's St Ivel Gold, which has been reduced to St Ivel Gold.

Many years ago it was natural to use the founder's name for the name of the company as in the case of Ford, Cadbury, Guinness and Fokker. As mergers have taken place, many such names have disappeared, like Morris, under a variety of corporate names culminating in Rover. Even then, the marques have continued as the names of makes of car, MG surviving after protests by former MG owners. Such names possess remarkable marketing magic.

In creating a new company name today it is necessary to consider all its communication aspects. Some new business names seem to be curiously anonymous, while others create a powerful corporate image. Choosing the right company name is an exercise in public relations, for the saying 'give a dog a bad name' is very true.

Some of the best names are simple initials, and while people may not know what the letters stand for they have a clear image of what

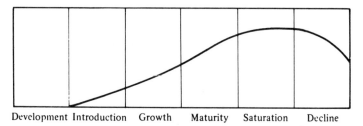

Development Introduction Growth Maturity Saturation Decline

Figure 28.1 *Traditional product life cycle*

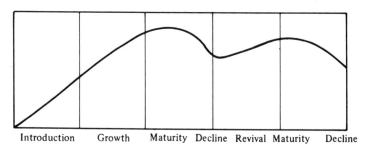

Introduction Growth Maturity Decline Revival Maturity Decline

Figure 28.2 *Recycled product life cycle*

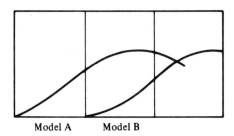

Model A Model B

Figure 28.3 *Leapfrog effect product life cycle*

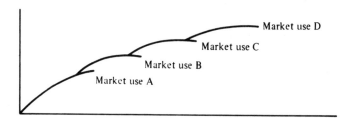

Market use D

Market use C

Market use B

Market use A

Figure 28.4 *Staircase effect product life cycle*

they mean in terms of products or services. Good examples are BBC, IBM, ICL, KLM and BMW. Three initials are often better than two, BA and even BT being weak whereas BOC was better than what could have been BO.

A simple device which helps names to be pronounced and remembered easily is the use of vowels (a, e, i, o, u), and the use of syllables which produce rhythm, although short words like Oxo and Omo are ideal if they are possible. But three-syllable names, with good use of vowels, like Rentokil, Texaco, Panama and Minolta are good examples. In spite of their strangeness in Europe or America, Japanese names have these qualities, e.g. Fuji, Honda, Sony and Kawasaki.

Another device, which converts long business names into excellent trading names, is the acronym, of which Fiat, Sabena, Toshiba, Daf, Caltex and Varig are good examples. Whether people know from what names or words they have been compiled is immaterial if the corporate image is clear.

In some cases a word with a definite meaning can be used because it satisfies the requirements of distinctiveness and memorability although it does not matter whether the meaning of the word is universally understood. Volvo is such an example. That 'volvo' is Latin for 'I roll' (*volvere*), and originated from a subsidiary which made ball bearings, is immaterial, but the two 'Vs' and the two 'Os' make it memorable.[2] Or the word may not have any special meaning yet by coincidence has a meaning in some countries. Elf came out of a computer, yet means a cheeky fairy in Britain, while Omo happens to be the name of an African river. Oxo was an accident, being a book-keeper's alternative for ditto.

Names can acquire affectionate variations like Marks and Sparks for Marks and Spencer, or succeed to a modern meaning like Rentokil which did not originally mean rent anything, the R being placed in front of 'entokil' for registration purposes, the 'ent' being taken from entomology.

Nowadays, many companies operate internationally, which requires that names are acceptable world-wide and do not have unfortunate, different or maybe offensive meanings in other languages or societies. Names like Coca-Cola and Elf, for example, have no problems, but the company at first called Malaysian Air Lines encountered problems because MAL suggested sickness to French-speaking people. The name was changed to Malaysian Airline System with the acceptable initials MAS although termed 'Malaysian Airlines' in 1987. In Hong Kong the original name for the underground railway was Mass Transit Railway, which began to earn a 'cattle truck' image; the system has now become known under its more pleasant initials of MTR.

Hundreds of names are often researched to arrive at the most popular or acceptable name, as occurred with St Ivel Gold, and more recently with the title of the newspaper *Today*, although in the latter case research produced nothing better than the original choice.

In deciding on a name the public relations manager can offer valuable advice, for he or she should be sufficiently broad-based regarding the company's affairs to see all the implications of a new name. For instance, when a name is changed this could affect the attitudes of recruits, employees, the trade, the stock market and the media. People may be suspicious of a new name or they may applaud it. Credibility, reputation and confidence are all involved. The test of a good name, whether company or brand, embraces the following:

Memorability

Is it easy to spell, say and so remember? 'The first name you think of' depends as much on how easy it is to remember, as on repetitive reminder advertising which keeps the name in front of people. One of the assets of sponsorship is having a name which is easily remembered and therefore benefits from being mentioned repeatedly. Sponsorship is often very much to do with name familiarization, but the cost and effort is wasted if the name is too difficult to remember. A name like Solpadeine is not easy to remember, let alone pronounce or spell.

Image

Does the name help to create an image of the kind of company or product it is? Do people instantly associate these vital characteristics with the name? Like 3-In-One Oil or All-Bran.

Some names may seem trite and yet they can be apt, like Whiskas cat food, Roll-on deodorant, Holiday Inn Hotel, Jetsave air travel, Evergreen lawn food, Winalot dog food or Every Ready battery.

Distinctiveness

Does it quickly identify and distinguish the company or product from all others? It could be an unusual made-up name such as Kodak, Pepsodent, Hovis, Sellotape, or Bisto.

Advertising advantages

Does it lend itself to advertising, whether in the form of a logotype or trade mark, or typographically in advertisements, on labels and packs and in sales literature? It is worth remembering that a short name can be displayed more boldly than a long one. This could be important on, say, a label on a small or narrow bottle. HP suits a sauce bottle very well.

From the above remarks it will be seen that naming and branding invites a public relations input since communication, corporate identity, corporate image, trade and customer relations and many other aspects of public relations are involved. This is when the knowledge, experience and advice of the practitioner can be valuable to top management or marketing management or both, especially at meetings where early discussions are being held on future developments. This is very different from calling in the public relations people to write a news release when everything else was decided months ago.

Packaging

Many considerations go into the packaging of a product, and services are also 'packaged' in the way they are presented to customers. An insurance proposition can be presented attractively, and that is a sort of packaging. The physical packaging of goods is a highly developed craft with specialist firms who will decide on materials and create shapes and designs and make use of numerous forms of packaging. The forms, in particular, can have public relations implications.

Do they please the distributor because of the way they store, stack, protect or display? Do they help the customer in ways beyond storing and protection? Are they easy to handle (and especially open!), and have they convenience factors? The latter can be extremely important so that choice of the most conveniently packed product will be a selling point above all else. The sachet, the aerosol, the dispenser and the blister pack are typical examples.

The sachet contains exactly the right amount to use, and it could be anything which has to be mixed with a quantity of water such as a soup, hair shampoo or garden insecticide. It removes the awkwardness and possible inaccuracy of using measuring devices such as lids or spoons which might not be available. It is also immediately disposable unlike a bottle or can whose contents have to be used up eventually, or perhaps wasted. So the sachet is satisfying, economical, gives the user confidence and creates a good relationship not only with the manufacturer but with the stockist. Good public relations all round.

The aerosol is a very costly container, but the customer willingly pays this extra cost because of the convenience of using a shaving cream, paint, insecticide or hair spray in this way. The aerosol therefore makes a very saleable, and a very satisfying pack.

Dispensers of various kinds are again very satisfying all round, examples being those for razor blades, artificial sweeteners, and some forms of confectionery.

The blister pack has made many friends because it has replaced many cumbersome liquid medicines, and often dangerous loose tablets in heavy bottles. Packed in foil, small tablets can be supplied in small, lightweight and very convenient packs.

Other convenient or safe packs are those with rip pulls, screw caps which require pressure, and pilfer proof packs.

The significant thing about the packages described above – and there are many others – is the *thoughtfulness* behind them. They answer the question *what will please the customer*? Of course, this is not wholly public relations but carries out the marketing concept of anticipating and providing what the customer wants, and doing so profitably. But surely this is where public relations and marketing thinking fuse so well? The pleased customer is unlikely to complain. The pleased customer regards the manufacturer well. Good relations emanate from satisfied customers, and we must not forget the distributor who has also created good customer relations by making the product available. He is seen as a wise and helpful stockist.

Long ago it was Beecham who claimed that his pills, which cost very little to make, were worth a 'guinea a box', but it was only because he put them in a box and made them marketable. Although packaging is more sophisticated today, thanks to plastic materials in many cases, it is the care with which goods are packed that not only makes them marketable but creates that public relations quality, goodwill.

Nevertheless, a new element has now entered into packaging and this is the avoidance of pollution. Some excellent devices are refillable detergent packs, the use of less packaging material, and the use of degradable materials. The 'green issue' now plays a big public relations role in packaging, and there are also EC directives to consider.

Packaging is not limited to manufacturers. Retailers can introduce their own packaging, as when they gift-wrap items whether they be boxes of chocolates or menswear, or supply convenient forms of carrier bag, put cakes in a box, or gently wrap bouquets of flowers. Gone are the days when fish and chips were wrapped in old newspapers. Customer service has not disappeared. It pays to please. The continental habit of gift wrapping purchases is being copied in Britain.

Distribution

This is an area where public relations really comes into its own because the practitioner can offer his or her special skills in developing good dealer relations which can strongly support the sales force, advertising and sales promotion aspects of the marketing mix and the marketing operation when it is in action. Some of the special public relations contributions may include:

External house journals

Published solely for the trade, they can be circulated to wholesalers, retailers, franchisers, agents, brokers and so on according to the kind of business and the kind of distributor used. The content should be of value to these special readers, and not merely publicity for the company although it is important to keep distributors aware of company news which will encourage understanding of the supplier. Features can be published which will help the distributor to sell the company's products or services, and this can range from educating distributors so that they are knowledgeable when dealing with customers or clients, to advising them on shop display or general business management including book-keeping and relevant new legislation. This is an example of how the external house journal can be made to work because it is aimed at a specific readership.

Inviting dealers to exhibition stands

It may be either a trade or a public show, but an exhibition is an opportunity to show distributors one's latest products, and to meet them face to face beyond the periodical sales representative's call. Again, goodwill can be engendered and this is something the public relations manager can propose and organize. It may be done by inserting a ticket in a trade magazine (or in the external house journal mentioned above), by sending a ticket direct, or by having tickets given out by travelling sales representatives. This can also be an opportunity for distributors to meet the management of their suppliers.

Dealer conferences

These may be initiated by the marketing department, but the public relations manager's experience in organizing events, knowing venues, and arranging visual aids will be valuable to the marketing manager. Here is a good example of how the two may work together. Dealer conferences can sometimes be organized at ITV stations to see previews of forthcoming commercials.

Training dealer staff

Again, the public relations manager's skills can be helpful, as with the production of slides and videos. These may be used on training courses, or for portable counter display units carried by sales representatives. Training can also be incorporated in the dealer magazine. Proficiency certificates can be awarded for display at the distributors' premises.

Works visits

These can also be a form of training since distributors are able to learn at first hand how products are made, and the quality control applied so that, again, they are knowledgeable when talking to customers. This not only includes factory visits but tours organized for other trades such as wine sellers or travel agents. The shop assistant can recommend the product because he or she has seen it made, and seen the quality control processes.

Trade press relations

In industrialized countries with a substantial range of trade publications, this is an area of public relations which will be fully exploited as part of the press relations work of the practitioner. It will include news stories about the company, its products and their packaging and advertising campaigns; feature articles; personality stories about new appointments; interviews; works visits for journalists; press receptions; and invitations to exhibition stands plus releases and pictures for exhibition press rooms. All this needs to be done in close cooperation with the marketing department so that the practitioner is kept constantly aware of public relations opportunities. Exhibition public relations is discussed in Chapter 25.

Dealer contests

These have proved popular in a number of trades, and a typical example is the window dressing or in-store display contest in which the shopkeeper submits a photograph of his or her display. Other contests may be based on sales figures, run on a regular or seasonal basis according to the nature of the trade. Contests can also be included in dealer magazines. They have the public relations effect of encouraging dealer participation, and they have the marketing effect of getting goods displayed and sold. The organization of contests, choice of prizes, and award ceremonies with media coverage in the trade and local press, all call for the skills of the practitioner.

Sales force relations

Here we have a mixture of management—employee relations and marketing communication. Field sales representatives often feel neglected and remote from the company's central headquarters. This lone-ranger attitude can be harmful to the maintenance of good staff relations, and can also be detrimental to dealer relations. The danger of a multiple image is always present when the only visible representation of the company is the visiting sales representative. Rightly or wrongly, the company will be judged by this person. Part of sales training should be the public relations role of presenting a uniform image of the company without destroying the individualism of the sales representative.

Some of the ways in which the practitioner can service the sales manager are:

1   Through the corporate identity scheme which will include business cards, vehicle liveries, letterheadings, price lists and other sales literature, which present the company physically. Whatever the distributor sees via the sales representatives should conform to the corporate identity scheme. This is discussed more fully in Chapter 29.

2   A special house journal, newsletter or bulletin can be produced solely for the sales force. Such a journal can concentrate on topics of interest to sales representatives, and which may not concern the staff in general. Field sales representatives are seldom interested in the domestic affairs of factory or office staff which usually appear in staff newspapers, and may pay little attention to these publications. It could promote sales contests.

3   Audio cassette news bulletins are even more convenient than printed bulletins, having the advantage that the sales representative can play them in his or her car, and they have more curiosity value than a piece of print that can be glanced at quickly.

4   Regional and national conferences are useful get-togethers and with his or her organizing ability, knowledge of venues, and access to videos and other visual aids, the public relations manager can again help the sales manager. It can also be useful for the public relations manager to meet and talk with sales representatives. There may be opportunities to glean public relations stories, especially in servicing companies where news of new contracts can be valuable. Moreover, these meetings give the practitioner the opportunity to develop internal lines of communication, and to explain to sales representatives what kind of material he or she is looking for.

5   Incentive schemes and sales contests have their public relations value in maintaining closer relations between HQ and the representatives in the field, and here again the practitioner may be able to assist with the organization of these schemes.

6   A mistake to avoid is the sending of news releases to sales representatives because they will not understand why they do not always appear or why, when they do, they may have been edited or shortened. But it is an excellent idea to send them *reproductions* of press cuttings and *reprints* of published feature articles. They are evidence of back-up, and they can be shown to customers. And if customers mention them, they will have been seen in advance by the sales representatives. This is one way of getting value out of press cuttings instead of just burying them in a guard book in the office. Press cuttings can be made to do a job of work.

7   It is important that sales representatives are familiar with the annual report and accounts − for their own sake and again because company results may be something their customers may have read about in their newspapers or trade press and want to discuss. The report and accounts can be explained in the house journal, or on an audio tape and a number of companies make special videos for their staff, the chairperson being interviewed by a TV presenter or professional interviewer. This video could be the occasion for a regional sales meeting.

8   Sales representatives also need to be kept informed of advertising plans, and this information will help them to convince retailers to stock up in readiness for the demand stimulated by the advertising. The supply of media schedules and pulls of press advertisements can be devised, even storyboards of the forthcoming TV commercials. Ideally, sales representatives should see TV commercials before their customers do. Previews can be arranged at regional sales conferences, or, with the cooperation of regional ITV companies, this can often be arranged at the local ITV station if the commercial is being shown in that region. Previews of commercials can be combined with a reception for distributors at the ITV station. Again, there is good staff relations public relations in this, the salesperson feeling that HQ is keeping him or her informed. It can also help with the representative's dealer relationships.

9   In some companies sales representatives are encouraged to give talks to local clubs and societies, address Rotary Club and Chamber of Commerce luncheon meetings, and also to organize evening receptions for customers. The public relations manager can assist by supplying speaker's notes, videos and slide presentations. This brings the sales representative (or perhaps a branch or area manager)

into public relations activity (which can include reports on such meetings in the local press). Again, the local speaker receives back-up from HQ, and is encouraged to feel part of the national effort. Local talks have been carried out very successfully in a number of companies, especially where training is given in public speaking.

Market education or pre-selling

This is a subject worthy of a book to itself, and yet it is an area of marketing which is too often neglected, too much reliance being placed on the power of advertising to sell to an uneducated market. It is like an army advancing with heavy artillery without knowing anything about the disposition of the enemy. Marketing education is based on the principle that people are more likely to respond to promotion when they understand what is being sold. To take the military analogy again, it is like carrying out a softening up bombardment before going into the attack.

A. C. Nielsen have claimed that even after test marketing, 50 per cent of new products fail. Many of them could have succeeded had the market been better aware of their purpose and qualities. In recent years we have seen the major disasters of the New Smoking Mixture non-tobacco substitute for ordinary cigarettes, and the Sinclair C5 electric 'car'.

How do you sell pest control services and products unless the market understands the nature of pests, how they breed and live, what hazards they present, and how they can be eradicated? Rentokil has become a successful international growth company, in spite of recession, because through its comprehensive public relations programmes using every technique and medium it has concentrated for more than 30 years on educating the market. It has spent remarkably little on advertising.

Media advertising will produce enquiries for glossy holiday brochures, but interest in foreign travel has been stimulated by newspaper and magazine articles, film shows, videos that can be seen on the home VCR, 'weeks' in shopping centres, holiday programmes on the BBC and ITV and publication of numerous photographs. The world has been brought to the very sitting room of the tourist public. It is no longer just fish and chips and bingo in Majorca. People travel to places they would never have thought of visiting only ten years ago – the USA, the Caribbean, Seychelles, Singapore and Hong Kong.

The computer industry has thrived on market education, and IBM was one of the first to realize that the customer – often the chief executive officer – had to be educated first before parting with thousands of pounds for both hardware and software. Market education has continued right down the line to desk-top and home computers. More recently, market education has been applied to camcorders, and Philips' CDi and DCC.

Many domestic goods from paint to gardening aids have benefited from marketing education, as have more expensive items such as central heating, insulation, modern kitchens and double glazing. People like to read and learn about such things, or see them demonstrated at private and public exhibitions, before spending their money.

An essential part of the marketing of many products and services – and that includes banking, insurance and investments – calls for a sustained marketing education programme leading up to, but sometimes coincidental with, the advertising campaign. We have seen large-scale examples of this with the privatization of public enterprises. In the cases of British Telecom, TSB, British Gas, and the electricity and water undertakings the market was educated not only about the forthcoming share offer, but about buying shares since one objective was to extend share-owning. One of the most interesting, controversial and competitive market education exercises has been that of Eurotunnel, making use of most public relations techniques – press, literature, TV programmes, video, exhibition centre and visits.

A fairly new way of educating the market has been the offering of free video cassettes so that prospective buyers can enjoy an educational show on their own television set. Others offer audio tapes. These are more positive and convincing devices than traditional media advertising which can be too persuasive when people are at the negative stages of hostility, prejudice, apathy or ignorance. Once again we see how the public relations transfer process can be applied, this time as an early effort in the marketing strategy.

The effect of market education or pre-selling, using any, or all, of the public relations techniques described in this book, is three-fold in respect of advertising.

1 It will help to make advertising more quickly acceptable and productive of response.
2 It could make less weighty advertising possible. In fact the cost of a preliminary public relations campaign is likely to be less than the saving of unnecessary advertising.
3 Whatever advertising is conducted, it is likely to be more economical.

Thus, the overall marketing budget could be reduced if more was spent on public relations.

A paper on market education is reproduced as Chapter 36, Pre-selling through market education.

Sales promotion – not to be confused with public relations

The mistake is sometimes made of expecting the public relations practitioner to organize sales promotion schemes. Some people think that the two are synonymous. Perhaps it is because they think the organizing talents of public relations can be used for sales promotion schemes, or the two are confused because both are thought of as below-the-line activities. Sales promotion consists of special promotional exercises, usually of short duration, to boost sales, and they are often used instead of traditional advertising. Mostly, they give the consumer extra benefits such as a wine glass with the purchase of so many gallons of petrol. Because so many goods are now available at competitive or discounted prices in the shops, the once popular premium offer has lost favour.

Most sales promotion schemes no longer require the saving up of tokens, or any mailing requirement, but provide benefits at the place of purchase. There are also High Street redemption schemes, cash vouchers being redeemable at other High Street shops, vouchers towards railway tickets, money-off offers, scratch card 'bingo' and other contests with instant prizes being given by the retailer.

Strictly speaking, sales promotion is neither advertising nor public relations, nor really is sales promotion a below-the-line activity. Sales promotion is generally accepted today as a form of marketing.

However, it can become very bad public relations for a company if, like Hoover's infamous free flights scheme for purchases of Hoover machines, it turns into a fiasco. Hoover thought it had included enough provisos in the rules to prevent too many take-ups of the offer.

Many of these schemes are organized by specialized sales promotion agencies, and it has become very big business. Alan Pascoe, a consultancy mentioned in Chapter 33 as one specializing in sponsorship, also handles sales promotion schemes. Sales promotion features are run regularly in the trade press, and there is a professional body, the Institute of Sales Promotion, which recommends rules for prize competitions, makes annual awards, and is associated with the Advertising Standards Authority through the Code of Sales Promotion Practice.

As will be appreciated from the above remarks, public relations and sales promotion are clearly two different things. However, there are distinct public relations implications in sales promotion, for if a scheme fails to please and provokes disappointment or complaints, this will be very bad public relations for the promoter. It has happened that inexperienced or over-zealous brand or product managers have organized schemes and failed to ensure that there was either a sufficient supply, or that supplies could be delivered sufficiently quickly, to meet the huge demand for the premium offer.

In recent years, the word 'free' has come under fire, especially in some continental countries such as Germany where free gift claims are banned as being misleading. They may be right, for nothing is ever free, and a so-called 'free gift' is only a manufacturer's alternative way of spending the promotional budget for which the consumer ultimately pays in the price. One of the worst sales promotion abuses, which invites poor public relations, is the so-called 'Free Draw' which is an illegal lottery. Attempts to pretend 'no purchase is necessary' may be hypocritical for is there any point in such a promotion unless it increases sales?

It is also possible that a sales scheme will provide the public relations practitioner with opportunities for press stories, ranging from trade press releases about the scheme to announcements of prizewinners of competitions, particularly in the prizewinners' local press.

Sales promotion schemes may be associated with the PLC described earlier in this chapter, being efforts to launch a product or maintain the product at its optimum level, and help avoid decline.

Added value

There is nothing new in adding value to a product to encourage sales, and it can take many forms, from gifts to after-sales service, but the recession years produced a spate of added value inducements. The buyer of a motorcar, for instance, is offered free petrol, free insurance, special credit terms and so on. Some retailers, such as Currys, offer 0% interest on credit terms. But the added value may be in some enrichment of the product, a larger chocolate bar, more fruit in the cake or petrol that reduces engine wear.

Giving the customer something extra, if it is only the helpfulness of well-trained sales assistants, obviously has strong public relations implications. In this analysis of the public relations that are inherent throughout the marketing mix this is a good point at which to refer to 'added value', since much of it ranges from sales promotion to the after-market. Its effect is that the consumer will give preference to the product (or the distributor) offering added value.

However, there is another side to this. Giving things away can have the anti-public relations effect of implying that the product is hard to sell. Even when motorcars were selling badly in the early 1990s there were some dealers who refused to condescend to 'deals' and sales promotion gifts, among them Alfa-Romeo, BMW and Mercedes.

The after-market

This is where many a marketing strategy has come unstuck, often through failure to understand the public relations implications after the product or service has been bought. How the company will handle the after-market needs to be built into the marketing strategy, for goodwill and future sales, including recommendations, are at stake. Some companies are foolishly indifferent to the after-market.

An infuriating situation so far as customers are concerned, and this is very true of the office machinery market, is the way some manufacturers regard products as obsolete after a very few years (perhaps simply because their inventory control system is based on economics rather than customer service). As a result, spare parts cease to be available. Quite cynically, they give products a life expectancy far shorter than that reasonably expected by the customer. Whereas a rugged old manual typewriter would last a lifetime, today's electronic typewriter, word processor, copier or personal computer is unlikely to survive more than four or five years. The complacency with which today's manufacturers view the in-built obsolescence of costly machines does not enhance the reputation of the office machinery industry.

In contrast, the motor industry − which used to expect people to change their car every two years − has been working in the opposite direction for the past decade. Cars are actually advertised with the promise that they will last longer, and some even major on the eventual second-hand value.

Care of the after-market − which means being jealous the company's reputation or corporate image − is the most effective public relations aspect of the entire marketing strategy. It breeds satisfaction, admiration, recommendation, and above all repeat purchase. It creates trust, confidence and reputation − the objectives of public relations. It can only be earned, not bought. All this is expressed in the simple abundant promise rather than the guarantee with the miserly clauses printed in small type in grey ink. It is expressed in the efficient after-sales and spare parts service, in the explicit, well-illustrated instruction manual, and in follow-ups to ensure that the product is cared for. Added to this may be public relations efforts to maintain interest (e.g. customer magazines, feature articles in the press), and to extend enjoyment of the product's benefits, either by continuing to educate the customer about additional uses, or by offering accessories or other means of extending the product's use.

What is the point of creating a fine product, packaging it well, educating the market, setting up good distribution and indulging in advertising if no thought is given to what happens next? All those people who have bought the product or service should be ambassadors, a reservoir of future customers who should remain permanently sold. This is where public relations and marketing can consolidate their efforts, but it may be the public relations person's initiative and far-sightedness which is called for.

Yet another feature of the after-market which can reflect credit or discredit on a company is the manner in which it treats the recall of a defective product. Sometimes the frankness and helpfulness with which a recall is handled can turn an apparently bad situation into one of respect and appreciation from customers whose interests or safety have been preserved. Again, the public relations implications are obvious. This particular aspect of the after-market will be discussed again in Chapter 32.

References

1 Jefkins, Frank, *Public Relations For Marketing Management*, 2nd edn, Macmillan, 1985 (O.P.)
2 Room, Adrian, *Dictionary of Trade Name Origins*, Routledge and Kegan Paul, London, 1982

29

The corporate image and the corporate identity

Some false ideas

The corporate image and the corporate identity are two different things, although the second may contribute to the first. Put very briefly, the first is mental and the second is physical — what one thinks about an organization and how one sees or identifies it.

A lot of nonsense is talked about creating, improving, polishing and projecting a corporate image (and it always has to be a *favourable* one), none of which is possible. Let's forget the managerial myths and pleasantries, some of which are perpetuated by advertising agents and journalists. In this chapter we shall deal with practical realities. It is very important that public relations practitioners should understand what they are about when dealing with the corporate image. They also need to explain to management what a corporate image actually is. Consultancies have even been known to be engaged to create or improve corporate images, which they cannot possibly do, and there is even one consultancy called Image Makers which is surely a contradiction in terms.

A corporate image can only be what it *is*. It is not something one can invent. *But*, and this is what it is really all about, members of the organization's publics may not know what it is, or they may have an incorrect idea of what it is. That, of course, can be put right.

It is also possible that one organization has a bad image in the minds of people, either because the organization is *misunderstood*, or because it *has* a deservedly bad one. The first can be righted by means of public relations techniques, but the second can be corrected only by the organization itself. The public relations manager or consultant may have to advise on how this should be done. It might, for instance, require staff training.

Corporate image defined

So what is a corporate image? It is the impression of an organization based on knowledge and experience. Since everyone's knowledge and experience of an organization will be personal and will differ from other people's, the corporate image will vary from one person to another. Here's a fine muddle, you may say, and so it often is. The public relations task is therefore to increase people's knowledge and experience — and we are back to *understanding* again — so that they have as clear and as correct an impression of the organization as is possible.

It may not necessarily be a favourable impression. For example, a Protestant and a Catholic, a Christian and a Moslem, a Russian and an American, will benefit from having a clear image of each other. It may not lead to love but it could lead to understanding and tolerance. In the world today there is great strife simply because of lack of understanding between such pairs of people. We have only to consider the muddle of ideas about the future of Europe to see how easily misunderstanding occurs.

This dilemma can be brought down to the level of commercial and other organizations and their publics, even between management and employees. The lack of clear corporate images in all sorts of social, religious, political, industrial and commercial situations is the cause of conflict and misunderstanding. We even have it in the absurd adversarial situation between the media and public relations in which neither side has a clear image of the other.

To bring all this back to the purpose of this book, it is important that all the publics of an organization — the community, staff, investors, distributors, customers and opinion leaders — have the most accurate possible corporate image.

It is perhaps another piece of nonsense to make this the separate responsibility of a special communication unit dubbed the public affairs department, because it is the most elementary public relations. It must be integrated in the whole public relations endeavour.

Simple and complex corporate images

Some corporate images can be simple and distinct. It is not difficult to establish a corporate image for a gas or electricity undertaking, a hotel group or an airline. It is less easy to establish a corporate image for a conglomerate or a multi-national which has a diversity of businesses. For instance, British Telecom has a developing corporate image because it not only supplies telephone services, but is developing or acquiring a variety of high technology services. Sometimes it is necessary to accept that other people can never have a comprehensive corporate image, and it is necessary to establish what may be termed an optimum image which is a digest of what they can be expected to reasonably accept.

A lot of corporate image public relations work has to do with unravelling confusion and misunderstanding. A few years ago Reckitt & Colman was badly misunderstood in the City because the company's overseas business was not understood, and a public relations consultancy was engaged to explain to City editors, financial institutions and investment analysts exactly what sort of international trade Reckitt & Colman were in.

Very often it is necessary to conduct an image study to find out what the current image is. This, as was explained in Chapter 4, is really a matter of defining negative and positive attitudes. It is not a case, as some managements think, of saying this is the kind of image we want people to have, and then proceeding to impose it on people. If it is the policy of the company to make cheap or expensive products, specialize in holidays in Europe or the Far East, supply gas or electricity it can only have the corresponding image. If it offers different products or services from its competitors, then the image will reflect that difference.

The image will go on developing in the minds of various publics, just as the character of a person develops on better acquaintance. The corporate image is the character of the organization, and the way the company is seen to behave will influence the impression people have of it. We can see this idea of character in the images of our national newspapers. It lies in their individuality so that we would not confuse even fairly similar newspapers such as the *Sun* and the *Daily Mirror*, and the *Guardian* and the *Independent*.

Different publics

We mentioned above 'various publics' and it is important to realize that some people will have a different impression or image of the company because of their particular association with it. An employee, a distributor, a consumer and a shareholder may view the company quite differently according to working conditions, trade discounts, quality of products and dividends. The idea of corporate image is sometimes too often oversimplified in terms of corporate and financial relations, as if it was only at this superior level that a corporate image mattered.

This is a theme which could occupy much thought by the public relations manager or consultant when planning a corporate image programme. To whom is the information being directed in order to make the organization properly understood, and what information should be directed in each case? We are beginning to refine the corporate image in some interesting ways. Not every kind of information is necessarily relevant to every public. To demonstrate this, here are some elements which could constitute a total corporate image.

1 The company is a publicly quoted company founded in 1880.
2 It has factories in the Midlands, Europe and Australia.
3 It makes building materials, but has diversified in recent years into aluminium windows and solar heating, and has taken advantage of new marketing opportunities.
4 It has an excellent industrial relations record and has a profit-sharing scheme.
5 The chairman plays an important part in trade association affairs, and is a spokesman for the industry. He is often seen on television.
6 The share price is steady but rising, dividends are conservative, and profits have been invested in new factory equipment and the development of the replacement window and solar heating business.

The overall corporate image may well please a shareholder or an investment analyst. It is a sound company with modest growth potential and unlikely to be the victim of a takeover. But not all these elements (which can be expanded in detail) interest the factory worker, the window salesman, the architect or the builder. In establishing the corporate image in their minds the information will need to be selective and relevant. Which of all the various publics will be interested in the employee's profit-sharing scheme or the factory in Australia? The builder putting in the windows could not care less, but he will be interested in the fact that the architect has specified materials from a firm which makes good products which will be delivered on time, are easy to use or instal and will enhance the building.

Thus the corporate image can be interpreted differently by different groups of people, and consequently it will need to be presented appropriately. This also tends to make the division between public affairs and public relations an irrelevancy, for all these applications of the corporate image to various publics come properly within the orbit of the public relations manager or consultant, and not only the public relations consultant who specializes in corporate and public relations.

In fact, most consultants of the City-based variety would probably be out of their depth if asked to handle non-financial corporate image presentations, and this might be best left to the in-house public relations manager.

The corporate identity

Whereas the corporate image may be relevant in different ways to different people, rather like the role playing of individuals who may be seen differently by various people, the corporate identity will be the same for all people who are aware of it. Obviously, a foreigner coming to Britain for the first time may not understand the relevance of the corporate identity of a British company, but many corporate identity schemes like those of Coca-Cola or Holiday Inn will be significant internationally.

Even so, some corporate images take on local interpretations. For instance, the Guinness corporate identity, as expressed by the typography, the dark stout with a white head (which is often pictured in advertising), the brown label with the harp insignia, are familiar in many countries. Not so for the Malaysian Chinese or the Indonesians where the labels carry a dog or a cat in addition to the harp. The Malaysian Chinese says Black Dog beer or simply Black Beer, and the Indonesians say Black Cat beer, not Guinness, which is unpronounceable.

Corporate identity has a historical background. Centuries ago a king would lead his army and identify himself by means of an emblem on his shield, such as the cross of St George or the cross of Lorraine. But since this was rather dangerous it became the fashion for all the king's knights to wear the same emblem, which was confusing to the enemy. Emblems became flags, and later troops wore uniforms.

When transportation began to develop, stagecoaches were decorated distinctively. Then steamships were given coloured funnels. Buses and trams had their colours, as did railways. The colourful buses of London disappeared in the 1930s as the General Omnibus Company and then London Transport amalgamated them in London red but deregulation has brought back the colourful buses. The oil companies have their road tanker liveries. But the most splendid liveries are those of the world's airlines which make the aprons of international airports look like artists' palettes. It is very costly to paint a fleet of aircraft, especially when, as occurred with British Airways, a new corporate identity is introduced, but the paint protects the metal from deterioration by the weather and de-icing. Livery is one of the most effective ways of establishing corporate identity.

However, designers have to be careful. The Holy Cross is one of the world's best known identification signs. Saudia, the Saudi Arabian airline, was dismayed to find that its original logo displayed an unmistakable white cross between the letters s and a of its name! (See Figure 29.1.)

Change of name

The need for a new corporate identity often occurs when either a number of organizations have been united by amalgamations, merger or acquisition, or when the nature of an organization's activities has changed and the old identity is misleading or inadequate. This can be very confusing when there are too many changes of name and identity, such as Rootes becoming Chrysler and then Talbot followed by Peugeot Talbot and now Peugeot.

When a change of name has a unifying effect the company gains new strength. An interesting example of this is Rentokil which is today accepted as the simple and memorable name of a very successful international pest control company. In 1980 it adopted a new look which was based on the lettering for the word 'Rentokil' and the use of Pantone 483 red and white as the house colours. This had developed from the renaming of the whole organization as Rentokil, and its subsequent placing on the stock market as a public company. Before this, in the 1960s, the original and holding company was called British Ratin (which was not particularly attractive) and over the years it had acquired a string of companies with even less attractive names such as Disinfestation, Fumigation Services, Woodworm and Dry Rot Control, Scientex, Rodine, Chelsea Chemicals, Insecta Laboratories and also the small retail product company, Rentokil. Wise management decided to dispense with all these names except Rentokil. In 1991 the identity was

Figure 29.1 *Old Saudia news release heading with cross effect between the s and a*

revised and in 1992 the Royal Warrant was incorporated in the logo. This more recent change is of considerable significance as the company has now been officially recognized as the supplier of environmental services to Her Majesty Queen Elizabeth II. This permits the Royal Warrant to be used by every Rentokil business (except office machine maintenance) on an international basis.

The effect of the adoption of the one name in 1980 was seen in the new company's first corporate identity scheme. Within a few months vans and lorries were on the roads bearing the Rentokil livery. This national fleet of vehicles suddenly made the company visible as a large organization. The vehicles had been there all the time, but in various guises and some had been plain green vans, discreet enough to park outside a West End hotel plagued with cockroaches. The new red and white Rentokil van, bearing the Royal coat of arms since the company had become a Royal Warrant-holder, like the horse in the White Horse whisky advertisement, could be taken anywhere. Thus, name changing and corporate identity went together with impressive impact which has no doubt been yet another example of how public relations has contributed to the company's success. Credit for this is largely due to the company's former chairman, Bob Westphal who, as joint managing director and a public relations natural, insisted on adopting the name Rentokil, of having hygienically white vehicles, and on applying for the Royal Warrant (Figure 29.2).

The logotype

The *logotype*, usually shortened to logo, is a special way of presenting the name of the company. Strictly speaking, symbols are special designs or shapes like the British Rail double arrows or the British Oxygen half chevrons, but name displays and symbols are often loosely called logos. Many logotypes are based on a signature or handwriting such as Boots, Cadbury's, Canon, Fokker, Ford, Coca-Cola and Kellogg's. Others use a distinctive typography like Dunlop, Guinness, Kodak and McVitie's. The logotype may be accompanied by a symbol or, like

Figure 29.2 *The new Rentokil logo incorporating the Royal Warrant*

a number of motorcar badges, name and symbol may be combined as with BMW, Fiat, Rover and VW, whereas the Mercedes-Benz symbol appears alone on the bonnet. The logotype for Goodyear has the two syllables divided by the symbolic figurehead, while Birds Eye is set on the white wings of a bird symbol. These designs are also usually registered trade marks, but sometimes the trade mark is an older symbol and the logotype has been designed later. Some symbols last for years, then disappear and return perhaps when an advertising agency decides on a revival.

Obscure symbols should be avoided since they may be distinctive but scarcely meaningful. The Dunlop arrowhead-shaped symbol is helped by carrying the letter 'D' and this is noticeable on the rubber matting of the moving walkways at airports. A clever design which is not readily comprehensible is a failure of communication. There are also some designs which tend to be repeated, such as swastika-shaped 'Ss' and arrow effects like British Rail's. One of the cleverest symbols is possibly Plessey's oscilloscope effect, while the wise-looking penguin of Penguin Books is very apt.

Trade characters

Corporate identity may be associated with a trade character, some of which seem to live on for ever like Johnnie Walker, Bisto's urchins, the Michelin rubber man and the White Horse whisky horse. Some emerge for special campaigns like Mr Cube of Tate & Lyle, while others like Mr Therm of gas advertising are dropped after a while. Usually, a sense of humour is attached to trade characters and they may typify the mood of society at a certain time. It is therefore remarkable that the Bisto Kids, who belonged to the depressed times between the two world wars, should have survived to modern times. They belonged to the era when the Save the Children Fund was set up for starving British children!

Slogans

Certain evocative advertising slogans – because they have been retained long after disuse – also belong to the devices of corporate identity. Although Guinness have not used the slogan *Guinness Is Good For You* in British advertising for many years, few people realize this, so characteristic is this slogan. In Nigeria the slogan does appear on the neck label of Guinness bottles.

Another type of slogan, the strapline or signature slogan, has become internationally adopted. The same strapline may be used, or a new one may be created for each advertising campaign. These appear at the end of an advertisement – and may also be used as a jingle in TV commercials – and they go beyond corporate identity and tend to sum up the corporate image in a few words.

Examples of straplines are *In touch with tomorrow* (Toshiba); *The serious alternative* (British Midland); *Don't leave home without it* (American Express); *Something special in the air* (American Airlines); *As sure as taking it there yourself* (United Parcel Service); *Corby Works* (Corby Industrial Development Centre); *Technology that works for life* (Samsung); *Designed to perform* (Braun); *A taste for life* (Remy Martin); *We believe in life before death* (Christian Aid); *Get through to someone* (BT); and *A certain flair* (Renault).

These examples may seem out of context when isolated like this, but their repetition in advertising does make the strapline yet another way of creating a corporate identity and contributing to the corporate image. Primarily, they are the creations of imaginative copywriters, and may form the copy platform for an advertising campaign. Nevertheless, if such a slogan is intended to be permanent the public relations manager or public relations consultant should be consulted at the visual and draft copy stage because of the obvious public relations implications. It would be silly if the slogan was out of key with the public relations message, especially in a corporate image campaign, and vice versa.

A slogan should not be thrust down people's throats, but should reflect the knowledge and experience of those to whom it is addressed. In other words, they should willingly accept the slogan as their opinion. This could be true of the satisfied passenger of an airline or patron of a hotel. A slogan must be credible, not just a gimmick.

Items involved in a corporate identity scheme

The creation and introduction of a corporate identity scheme is a costly and extensive business, yet it can be very necessary when one sees the messy collection of unrelated pieces of communication which some organizations accumulate because there has been no standardization and direction. When there is a corporate identity scheme, everyone responsible for ordering or buying advertising, print, paintwork, decorations, furnishings and so on is obliged to follow the instructions contained in a corporate identity kit. For instance, even the corridor lampshades in a Hilton hotel conform to the Hilton corporate identity scheme, as do the serviettes on most airlines, or the cheque books issued by banks. In a department store or supermarket there is no doubt whose shop one is in, for the corporate identity is explicit in many things visible such as the dress of staff, price tags and shelf labelling, in-store displays, store layout and carrier bags.

Here are some of the items which may be involved:

1 The livery (paintwork) of road vehicles, trains, ships, aircraft and other forms of transportation.
2 All stationery, including letterheadings, news release headings, invoices, order forms, receipts, compliment slips, business cards, tickets, etc.
3 Name displays on premises such as factories, offices, shops, warehouses, depots, garages, etc.
4 Exhibition stands, showrooms, mobile exhibitions.
5 Sales literature, price lists, catalogues, sales promotion material.
6 Labels, packaging and containers.
7 House journals.
8 Instruction leaflets, service manuals.
9 Uniforms, overalls, blouses, headgear, cap, pocket and lapel badges.
10 Point-of-sale display material.
11 Advertisements in all visible media.
12 Credits on video tapes and slide presentations.
13 Diaries and calendars.
14 Give-aways such as key-rings, pens and novelties.
15 Annual reports and accounts, share prospectuses and any special communications with shareholders such as proxy forms.
16 Cutlery, crockery, food packs, serviettes, menus.
17 Drip mats or coasters, table mats and table cloths.
18 Ash trays.
19 Company ties.
20 Cuff links.
21 In certain premises like hotels and restaurants, door-handles, lamp shades, and other fittings.

Not every item applies to every organization, but organizations which are much in the public eye, and operate very close to their customers such as stores, hotels, banks and airlines, will take up a long list of such items. It may not be necessary or even possible to scrap everything and start afresh, but the corporate identity scheme can be incorporated as new things are bought. Such a scheme has a consolidating repetitive effect which has a great psychological impact, and it can also enhance the morale and pride of those working in the organization.

Few companies have made such remarkable efforts to establish and maintain their corporate identity as Coca-Cola, even to the extent of legal battles with rival firms. It is significant that Coca-Cola have scored on a massive international scale by their consistency. The well-known script logo has scarcely changed since 1886 when it was penned by Frank M. Robinson, bookkeeper to the creator of Coca-Cola, Dr John T. Pemberton. True, the freehand copies of the script have been tidied up and the logo containing the trade mark script has changed shape from time to time. The company has issued a style guide worldwide and ruled that only faithful reproductions may be used. Corporate identity has also been associated with the pack; the bottle with the badge. This goes back to the company's early days when a pinched-sided bottle to confound imitators was designed which could be recognized even if held in the hand in the dark, and even if it were broken. However, today there are other packs.

Generic terms

It may be flattery when everyone refers to vacuum cleaners as 'hoovers' (except to Electrolux) or to thermos flasks, pyrex dishes and sellotape, but there is a loss of true identity which can be serious. A product may also be unfairly associated with inferior or rival brands, as when one orders a Coke and is served a Pepsi-Cola. Some of these names have slipped into the language. For example, the *Shorter Oxford English Dictionary* says: 'hoover v. to clean (a carpet, etc.) with a vacuum cleaner.[1] So much for decades of advertising and selling Hoover vacuum cleaners. The housewife goes to the electricity showroom, asks to see a 'hoover' and buys whichever make pleases her.

The press dislike capital initial letters, yet many companies insist on protecting their registered trade names, and state in or on news releases that names are registered. They include names such as Pop rivets, Tannoy, Burberrys, Thermos, Fibreglass and Vaseline to the extent of supporting a quarterly journalists' guide to registered names which has been published for many years in *UK Press Gazette*[2] about their correct usage. The guide gives a glossary of trade names. It also lists unregistered and so unprotected names, a sample of which include:

aspirin	mac(k)intosh
cornflakes	melamine
dynamite	mimeograph
escalator	petrol
hovercraft	polythene
lanolin	shredded wheat

Another responsibility of the public relations manager may be to see that trade names are registered, or are registrable. It may be necessary to avoid names which are place names or simply ordinary descriptive words, which cannot be registered. It depends how exclusive a name should be.

There follow three case studies supplied by SampsonTyrrell Limited as examples of their work for Castrol, ScottishPower and the Murray-field Debenture Issue.

Case Study 1: Castrol

Revised December 1992

Project: corporate and brand identity

Background: the client

Castrol is the world's largest specialist in the blending, distribution and marketing of lubricants and allied products. The company employs over 9000 people and is represented internationally by operating companies in over 36 countries and an agency network covering more than 100 others.

Now owned by Burmah Castrol, Castrol accounts for more than 48% of the parent company's trading profit. In 1989, Castrol's total turnover exceeded £1.25 billion, representing increased global market share, despite a background of static demand.

Castrol operates in principal markets in the following sectors: automotive, industrial, marine and fuels. Of these, automotive engine oils are the most important part of Castrol's business.

Castrol divides its markets into four geographical areas, namely: UK and Ireland, Continental Europe, Western hemisphere (the Americas) and Eastern hemisphere (Australia, Japan, South Africa, Far East). Of these, Continental Europe is the leader in both turnover and profit. Of the individual markets, the USA is the largest, followed by Germany and the UK.

Castrol's operational management is highly decentralised, in order to provide the freedom to tailor product specifications and marketing to the particular demands of the national market. For this reason, products and their positioning will often vary significantly from market to market. This variance is also apparent in the production and presentation of communications material.

The need for change

The case for undertaking a review was a strong one, particularly in the current market environment, where competitive pressure is increasing and strength of brands will be the deciding factor in continuing success. A review in 1990 was timely in preparation for the decade, particularly as several of Castrol's international competitors are investing in their images and identities.

Castrol's current visual identity was introduced during the 1960s. Since its introduction, the company has expanded both geographically and in products and has acquired a number of related companies and brands. The existing identity guidelines were last updated in 1982 and were incorporated in a manual for use worldwide.

How to change

Castrol wish to rationalise the use of their identity, and coordinate its varying applications across the group, and produce revised guidelines for distribution internationally to marketing managers and all design specifiers and suppliers.

Over the years, a number of issues have arisen which have accelerated the need for an identity review:

- **Use of the Castrol name**
  The Castrol name is used not only as a corporate name and endorsement of a variety of brands, but also as a brand name itself. It could be seen as a company, masterbrand, consumer brand, consumer range name, industrial brand and industrial range name. This is potentially confusing and a clear relationship structure and strategy between all these functions and identities needed to be established.
  (Key question of when to use the name and when to use the mark.)
- **Decentralised structure**
  Castrol is a broadly decentralised organisation and has focused its marketing and business strategies successfully at a national level. This has implications for the control and maintenance of consistent corporate and brand identities, with particular relevance for the future development of multi-national products and businesses. A substantial number of agencies and print suppliers across many markets adds to the difficulty of quality control and makes imperative the effective communication of visual identity guidelines.

- **National differences**
  As a major player in a fast moving and competitive market, Castrol is constantly developing and introducing products. Increasing product specialisation is in turn likely to lead to an increase in sub-branding and a need for more information to be projected, especially 'on-pack'.

The brief

The company's aims include greater geographic penetration; a more highly specialised sales force, and extra commitment to research and development. In order to achieve these goals, and taking the above areas of required change into consideration, Castrol appointed SampsonTyrrell to:

- Assess the performance and usage of Castrol's current visual identity system.
- Assess the effectiveness of the manual and methods for maintaining visual standards.
- Put forward recommendations for the future communication and maintenance of the Castrol identity system.

The process

SampsonTyrrell put forward recommendations to approach the brief in four phases:

- Research, including a comprehensive Communications and Visual Audit.
- Design system refinement.
- Production of revised guidelines (published January 1992).
- Subsequent implementation and communication programme (January 1992-December 1993).

Research

The first stage of the research programme was to establish an overview of the actual versus the ideal visual image visual for Castrol. This would act as a yardstick for any subsequent evaluation. This included:

(i) Desk research.
(ii) Investigation of existing research.
(iii) Briefings with key personnel.
(iv) Board presentations.
(v) Further research.
(vi) Point of sale and site visits.

   (vii)   Discussions with marketing personnel and suppliers.
 (viii)   Internal image research.
   (ix)   External research.
    (x)   Conclusions and recommendations.

Design system refinement

During this step of the design process, SampsonTyrrell developed solutions to any identity problems or opportunities which were defined in the research. This covered areas such as how the corporate identity should be applied throughout the company, different degrees of corporate endorsement across brands, the roles of brand identity as opposed to corporate identity, the relationship with the Burmah identity and how the identity works across different practical applications and in different environments.

Once agreed, the system was refined and developed, and consultants looked in greater depth at applying the revised system to the full range of manifestations.

Guidelines and manual

Four printed documents and a video have been produced to date:

Setting the Standards – a rigid set of identity guidelines breaking away from traditional 'corporate identity manual' style, to present a highly visual, innovative, internationally understandable reference point for chief executive officers, marketing managers and all people involved in the briefing and design of visual material for Castrol.

Framework for the Imagination – an on-going series of publications to supplement 'Setting the Standards', addressing specific topics such as Motorsports livery; retail signage and point of sale; acquisition and non-core branding policy. These offer advice and ideas to all marketing personnel, showing how the Castrol identity can be exploited in new and imaginative ways. 'Communicating the Castrol Brand' – the first 'Framework for the Imagination' publication, explains the importance of Castrol's premium pricing position. It demonstrates how this position can be protected by working creatively with the visual identity tools established in 'Setting the Standards'.

Celebrating the Castrol Brand – an employee brochure and video explains the importance of the Castrol brand, and why it is important to maintain visual consistency.

Brand Matters – a regular magazine dedicated to the communication of the Castrol brand. Each edition focuses on topical worldwide Castrol communication issues, providing help and guidance at a local level.

SampsonTyrrell team

Dave Allen, Josie Bowman, Fran Lane, Pip Llewellin, Rowan Bray, Lee Hoddy, Mark Wing, Ralph Ardill

Case Study 2: ScottishPower

In early 1990 the South of Scotland Electricity Board was a set of initials – SSEB. It produced, distributed and sold power and appliances to the industry and inhabitants of the area dominated by Glasgow and Edinburgh. By the end of 1991 it had become the most favoured of the new electricity companies among UK institutional investors, under its new name and style – ScottishPower. This evolution was planned and designed in close cooperation with SampsonTyrrell.

Background

Whereas the English power companies born out of privatisation are generators of electricity or distributors or marketers, ScottishPower is a vertically integrated supplier producing the original energy and marketing it to both the commercial and domestic sector.

The company is large, 59th largest in the UK, 135th in Europe, with a market capital of £2,066 million. It serves a population of 4.5 million, and has the capacity to produce 6700 MW of electricity a year, drawing power from a number of sources; coal, nuclear, oil, water and gas. Identity is important for several reasons:

1 In Scotland, it is the leading industrial company. Electricity has played a vital role in the development of the Scottish economy. The identity of the company is bound up with a sense of nationality.
2 In the newly privatised electricity industry, there is competition at all stages, from generation to retail supply. Competition in the large industrial sector is already very keen and this will shortly spread to commercial customers.
3 The proportion of electricity exported to other regions – England, Wales and soon Ireland – is increasing. This is likely to be a principal

source of growth. Capacity for 'interconnection', i.e. export, will soon be doubled.

4 Sales of the company's expertise in engineering and technology will also be an important source of income.

5 In all of these markets, non-cost factors, represented by the corporate identity in its fullest sense, are likely to prove decisive. A highly visible reputation for reliable, uninterrupted fault-free service may prove more valuable than low price to large users.

6 As a publicly quoted company, ScottishPower's identity will help the process of distinguishing the company from its competitors.

7 Internally, a complete change of attitude was necessary; from that of a state institution, with assured supply and protected markets, to a commercially and competitively oriented private company seeking to satisfy customer needs.

The change

The new company was to be different from the old and different from the competition, in spirit, structure, motivation and geography. New accountable divisions were set up, costs cut, new enterprises undertaken. The real change of identity needed an external focus, a visual and verbal change that proclaimed a new company – a brand.

This new brand had to represent: Scottish allegiances, power in its broadest sense, technology, stature, quality – seen as a balance between commercial enterprise and public duty and the multi-faceted nature of the business. It had to have meaning for three audiences – staff, customers and the financial community. In an industry at the core of progress, moreover, it had to be a focus for rapid change.

Timing

Name chosen	
Appointment of SampsonTyrrell	June 1989
Research and briefing	July 1989
Design work begins	July 1989
Designs agreed	November 1989
Launch of new identity	February 1990

The name

The name ScottishPower had been chosen for its breadth of meaning, including its patriotic undertones. It covers the huge range of company activities, both present and potential, and capitalises on Scotland's reputation for engineering excellence. It also differentiates from Scottish HydroElectric, and Scottish Nuclear, separated out at privatisation.

The identifier

The brief to the designers was to embody those aspects of 'power' which were appropriate, i.e. energy, potential, success, strength and security, in a Scottish context. It had to be made to work over a huge range of applications, from power stations to invoices to animated sequences on television.

Any of the traditional symbols of electricity, such as lightning flashes, were to be avoided − especially since the range of the company's activities was certain to expand. But the Scottish values − of engineering quality, care, innovation and community spirit − were, if possible, to be retained.

The chosen symbol combines these qualities: precisely arranged elements 'pulsate' from a central core, suggesting technology and dynamism. At the same time, the colours and the pattern suggest familiar Scottish themes; the tartan and the St Andrew's cross.

ScottishPower

The launch

The identity was launched in February 1990, to an audience of thousands in Glasgow. It was a major event in Scotland, featuring Scottish orchestras and stars. A video of the event was shot, and became part of a roadshow led by ScottishPower directors, which was circulated among those employees who had not been present.

The implementation

The new name and visual identity were then applied to the whole of the company's communications and interfaces; vehicle livery, shop fascias, stationery and literature, uniforms, power stations and advertising, including television. For television and video an animated version of the Power Mark − as it is known internally − was designed by SampsonTyrrell and implemented by Charles Barker Scotland and Electric Image. This sequence, ten seconds long in its full version, was adapted for corporate advertising and for retail appliance commercials.

The results

The latest research figures available show that ScottishPower is viewed favourably by investors and analysts, when compared both with its own sector and with industry generally. Interviews carried out among institutional investors by MORI in November and December 1991 gave the following results:

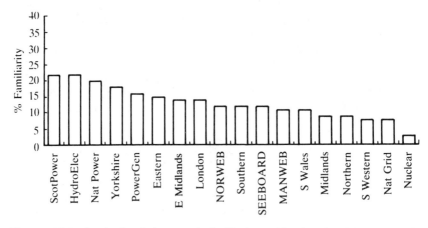

Figure 29.3 *Institutional investors' familiarity with the electricity companies, winter 1991. (Source: MORI)*

- ScottishPower is the second most familiar electricity company (after PowerGen).
- It is the most favourably viewed.
- It is seen as the one that stands out above the others for quality of management and potential for growth.
- In terms of overall familiarity, ScottishPower scores 69th among all companies in the UK, higher than such long-established names as Halifax, Thames Water, Citibank and Johnson & Johnson. Its favourability is even higher, at 43.

These research results are even more remarkable when the corporate advertising spends of the largest power companies are compared. For the year January to December 1991, the relevant figures are:

ScottishPower	£76,647
PowerGen	£324,590
NationalPower (incl sponsorship)	£4,082,028

In the months following privatisation, the company has pursued a successful policy of cost-cutting, restructuring and exports of power and services.

The contribution of the new identity

Clearly, a number of factors have contributed to the successful reputation of the new company, as well as the new identity:

1 Its successful position as a vertically integrated supplier.
2 Efficient management and a loyal workforce.
3 The effect of privatisation and the resultant newness of the company.
4 An established reputation for low-cost and reliable supply.

Other companies in the same sector, however, have had similar advantages, with the exception of vertical integration.

The new identity has, in our view, accomplished four things:

1 It has synthesised the favourable qualities of the new company into one name and readily recognisable mark − a brand.
2 It has made the company instantly recognisable to a very wide public, including export markets, investors and the financial community.
3 It has spearheaded a new spirit of entrepreneurism within the company.
4 It has made the necessary management measures such as cost-cutting and job-shedding easier, due to improved morale within the company.

Case Study 3: The Murrayfield Debenture Issue

Background

The Rugby World Cup turned rugby into a major spectator sport, popular as never before. This was a window of opportunity for the Scottish Rugby Union (the SRU). Murrayfield, where Scotland plays its international matches, needed huge investment in order to upgrade its facilities for the growing numbers of Scottish rugby supporters and meet the recommendations of the Taylor Report. In a bold initiative, the SRU decided to go ahead immediately, to raise the money via public subscription and begin development without delay.

The method they chose was to sell debentures − a right to buy specific seats at every event for at least the next fifty years.

Objectives

The objective was to raise £37 million in order to build a modern 65,000-seat all-covered stadium. Debentures ranged in price from £9900 to £1200 in the stands behind the goalposts. It was important to raise the bulk of the money quickly, while consumer interest was high.

The SRU were also keen to draw a balanced response – between Scottish and external applicants, and between private and corporate. In particular, they did not want the issue to be seen as an opportunity for big business to outbid the real rugby fans.

Two features widened the appeal of the scheme; an after-market in the debentures, enabling them to be sold like stocks and shares; and a loan scheme on advantageous terms from The Royal Bank of Scotland that spread the purchase for individuals.

Murrayfield draws spectators from a very large catchment area. It attracts strong loyalties and is rich in tradition, having been the scene of some notable victories over the 'auld enemy' since inauguration in 1925. In the championships it is used only twice a year; but the new stadium will become the venue for many other events in the future.

Means

A total budget of £500,000 was made available by the SRU to spend on a multi-media campaign. At the core of the campaign were, first, the visual identity and second, the mailing package containing the details of the issue. It was not possible to apply for a debenture by any other means.

Twenty-five thousand packs were sent out to rugby clubs, while an advertising campaign invited the general public to respond. Press was used over a three-month period in the UK and some overseas locations, such as Hong Kong. In Scotland this was reinforced by an outdoor poster campaign. The advertising generated 35,000 requests for the prospectus. The bought media was supported by a public relations campaign, including an exhibition, which was effective locally.

Results

The mailing pack achieved a conversion rate of 9.46 per cent – a high figure in any circumstances, but especially so where 41.66 per cent of the original recipients had not requested it, and where the *minimum* purchase was for £1200. The bulk of the funds was raised very quickly following the launch on 4 September 1991; by 25 November £22 million had been raised (60 per cent of overall target). At the end of March, 71.78 per cent of seats had been reserved – amounting to £24.5m. It was particularly gratifying that of this total, over £15 million has come from Scotland. A further £2 million has been received in the form of a grant from The Foundation for Sport and the Arts.

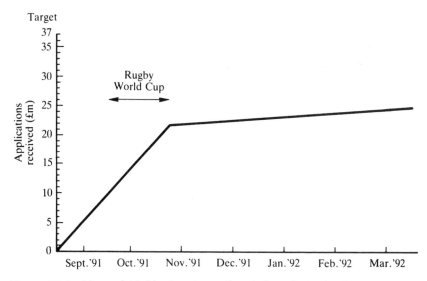

Figure 29.4 *Murrayfield debenture issue: the window of opportunity*

The role of design

Design had two key roles to play in this remarkably effective fund-raising scheme; one strategic, the other tactical.

Strategic

SampsonTyrrell created not only the 'brand identity' for the debenture issue, but also planned the integrated communications that would exploit it to the full.

The target audience were to be exposed to messages coming from a number of media simultaneously; press advertising, posters, news stories in the press and television coverage of the World Cup, and finally, the mailing. It was vital that each should be recognised immediately as relating to the same subject, from the same source. And all these messages had to be delivered, received and understood in a matter of months – before the heightened awareness of rugby brought about by the World Cup and the Five Nations competition that followed, faded from minds. The issue, therefore, was consciously branded with an easily reproducible and instantly recognisable identifier. This was prominent on every communication to do with Murrayfield and found its way on to many unpaid-for reports and news items in the media. Style, too, was carefully controlled, on everything from letterheads to application forms for the loan. Identity was tightly integrated.

Tactical

But in the final analysis, everything would stand or fall by the mailing package. The Offer Document and Prospectus had to be clear and carefully explained, and the application form easy to complete, to attract, reassure and stimulate action. It was a once-and-for-all sell of an expensive product and, moreover, one that was totally unfamiliar to its recipients.

What the mailing succeeded in doing was to build a vivid impression of the yet-to-be-built stadium, and show how each debenture holder might claim a seat there. It explained the novel concept of the debenture, made it simple and attractive, and relatively easy to attain.

The problem was a classic one of communication and persuasion to act, solved by design. SampsonTyrrell's work in coordinating the overall campaign, both visually and conceptually, and in producing the desired response when and where it mattered has played a significant part in the success of the Murrayfield Debenture Issue to date.

References

1   *Shorter Oxford English Dictionary*, 3rd edn, Oxford, Oxford University Press, 1985
2   *UK Press Gazette*, quarterly journalists' guide to registered names

30

Financial public relations

A specialist world of public relations

Some public relations managers and consultants may be active in financial public relations on a day-to-day basis because that is the nature of their or their client's business. Other in-house public relations managers may use financial public relations rarely, and the public relations consultants who handle financial public relations will be specialists. Among the first group are those engaged in public relations for banks, insurance companies, building societies, unit trusts and other financial institutions plus the Stock Exchange and various dealers in stocks and shares. The latter have become very active following deregulation. Both groups have to communicate with shareholders, institutional buyers, city editors and investment analysts.

Institutional buyers are those regular buyers of shares because they have an inflow of funds which need to be invested, for example insurance companies, pension funds and unit trusts. They have their own public relations but are also the targets of public relations from those whose shares they buy. The latter is known as investor relations.

City editors are not to be confused with the news editors of newspapers. The meaning of 'city editor' is different in some overseas countries. In Britain it means the editor of the business or financial section of a newspaper, and the more up-market the newspaper the more extensive the coverage of City news. These editors have their offices located in the City, rather than wherever the newspaper has its main editorial offices.

Investment analysts prepare reports on public limited companies which are listed on the Stock Exchange, and make recommendations regarding their investment prospects. The accuracy of their reports may depend on the information they receive from public relations sources.

Returning to the opening paragraph above, the majority of in-house PROs' normal responsibility for financial public relations may not extend beyond shareholder relations and preparations of the annual report and accounts, unless there is a share issue, rights issue or a takeover situation when a specialist financial public relations consultant is likely to be engaged. Nevertheless, they ought to understand how the money market works.

Shareholder relations are important and must not be neglected. Shareholders have voting rights and can attend company meetings or issue proxies with voting instructions. They have to be kept informed periodically, and not only sent interim and annual reports and accounts. Nowadays, shareholders may also be employees. Shareholders may be tempted to sell during a takeover bid, and their loyalty can be crucial. Some companies have a large number of shareholders other than institutions and speculative buyers who merely seek to take a profit by buying cheap and selling dear.

An important part of management—employee relations (whether or not employees are shareholders) consists of keeping staff aware of the company's financial performance. This can be done through explanations of the annual report and accounts in the printed house journal, or the video house journal. A number of companies produce videos in which a well-known TV personality interviews the CEO and the accounts are explained. Annual report videos are distributed throughout the organization for showing to employees.

Effects of deregulation

The effects of the Big Bang, on 27 October 1986, as deregulation of the London Stock Exchange has been popularly termed, were far reaching. Deregulation meant a move away from dealings on the floor of the Stock Exchange to the buying and selling of shares through other agencies. Shares may be bought and sold at High Street, doorstep and letterbox level, subject to control by a number of new regulatory bodies.

The ownership of shares has been greatly widened by the privatization of industries such as British Telecom and British Gas. Moreover, the availability of share registers has already made thousands of people subject to direct mailings from firms selling financial services. However, these huge potential mailing lists have been so abused by direct response marketers that some annual reports carry a warning and advise shareholders who do not wish to be pestered by irrelevant mailings to seek the help of the Mailing Preference Service in having their names excluded from mailing lists. The whole financial market has therefore been extended, and one new aspect of financial public relations is the protection of the corporate image and integrity of reputable sellers of shares.

Financial public relations has therefore become a very important part of a listed company's public relations activities. It may be separated from other public relations work and come within the scope of a public affairs manager, but this can be an artificial device, largely an invention of American corporations. Most British, as distinct from American companies, will make no distinction in jobs. We shall therefore speak of the public relations manager. However, on the consultancy side it is more likely that there will be a separate financial consultancy, or a large general consultancy will have a specialist financial division.

During the past twenty-five years or so we have seen the arrival and development of the City-based financial consultancy, so specialized that it is probably incapable of handling any other type of public relations. Its staff has been recruited mostly from financial journalists and graduates qualified in economics rather than arts. Firms such as Dewe Rogerson have built impressive reputations, handling accounts like the British Telecom flotation and takeover battles.

Why financial public relations is different

One of the ways in which financial public relations differs from other forms of public relations is that the 'product' is a very sensitive one. Share prices are mercurial as if one only has to blow one's nose to provoke a rise or fall, and that could make one either a target or a predator in a take-over struggle. Fortunes, careers and company ownerships are at stake. Public relations activities need to be diplomatic. Unlike ordinary public relations which may relish maximum media coverage, in financial public relations this could either stampede the market, produce criticisms of insider trading, or arouse the suspicions of City journalists and investment analysts. Frank, informative one-to-one relationships with influential individuals may be more productive than a flow of news releases to the business newspapers. The City is not nicknamed 'the village' for nothing and, as in an African village, market gossip is a public relations medium.

A few years ago some New York financial public relations consultants were upbraided for overdoing their media coverage so that share values were overvalued. There is a subtle difference between creating overconfidence which produces a bull market, and confidence in a company which stabilizes its shares at a realistic price.

The public relations manager or consultant has to beware of the computers and online instant information facilities, and the satellite-fed international dealings, which have now replaced frenetic trading and shouting matches on the trading floors of isolated stock exchanges and bourses. Traumatic situations can occur such as that in mid-1986 when an American computer matched futures with current stock prices and prophesied a fall which was actually so small it would have been ignored when it eventually occurred. But it caused a huge fall (which was also felt severely by the London share market) when otherwise the market would have remained high. Worse still was the world crash of October 1987.

Nowadays, when financial public relations has become such a big province of public relations, it is necessary to understand the changes occurring in the stock markets of the world. With the computer and the satellite now linking stock, futures and commodity exchanges worldwide, it is a fast-moving scene. All this is aided by the latest information being provided by the international publication through a network of overseas printers of journals like the *Financial Times, International Herald Tribune, Wall Street Journal* and *The Economist*.

Reuters supply real-time financial information regarding money and capital markets, equities and stock markets, and commodities, doing so on a world scale and at incredible speed, using computers, landlines and satellites. Reuters have 980 journalists world-wide, and production centres in Hong Kong, London and New York which cover different segments of the 24 hours. Anything affecting a share price will be on a Reuters subscriber's screen. In London, for instance, 34 journalists deal with the top 1000 companies. While the London Stock Exchange regulates dealings, and provides information on companies, Reuters seeks and transmits the same information.

London Stock Exchange

When the London Stock Exchange was deregulated in October 1986 it was preceded a year before by the Company News Service for the benefit of those disseminating information about listed companies. Since that time there have been changes and earlier London Stock Exchange publications have been replaced by new ones, notably by the *Regulatory News Service Procedural Guidelines*.[1] Major changes are that hard copy news releases are discouraged in favour of instantaneous electronic messages, that for security reasons fax releases are discouraged, and there is a very precise eight-line specification for 'header messages' at the top of a financial announcement. Some extracts are given below but anyone concerned with the dissemination of financial information should obtain a copy of this booklet from Company Liaison Officer, Company Announcements Office, The London Stock Exchange, Old Broad Street, London, EC2N IHP.

The Regulatory News Service (RNS)

The Company Announcements Office (CAO) of the London Stock Exchange is responsible for the Exchange's Regulatory News Service (RNS), a service for the receipt, validation and publication of regulated announcements provided by companies in compliance with the Continuing Obligations of Listing and the USM General Undertaking.

RNS is designed to ensure that regulated announcements, particularly those which might reasonably be expected to have a material effect on market activity and prices of securities, are validated and communicated promptly to the market through the RNS subscriber network.

The key features of RNS are:

- A computerized system to validate the authenticity of all regulated announcements.
- A telephone confirmation of release service, confirming publication of an announcement by RNS to the issuer (or authorized agent).
- The simultaneous publication of regulated announcements by computer-readable feed to all RNS subscribers.
- Each announcement consists of two elements: a headline, containing the company name and type of announcement, prepared by the Exchange; and the full text of the announcement as prepared by the company.

How RNS works

RNS has four stages:

1 Receipt of announcements by the CAO.
2 Validation of the source of the announcement.
3 Processing of the announcement.
4 Publication to RNS subscribers, through a computer-readable feed.

A secure delivery point is available, at all other times, at the main entrance to the Stock Exchange Tower.

Facsimile transmission

Facsimile transmission poses additional security risks and may cause operational difficulties if copy is handwritten. For this reason, facsimile is not a recommended method for delivery of announcements. Typed facsimile may be used when no other method of transmission is available.

Hard copy announcements

1 A 'header message' must precede all announcements. This will assist the Company Announcements Office in identifying the source of the announcement.
2 Submit original documents rather than copies.
3 Avoid coloured inks and coloured paper — red and blue are particularly difficult colours to scan. Black ink on white paper is the preferred combination.
4 A4 size paper should be used. A paper size of less than 6" × 6" (150 mm × 150 mm) or larger than 9" × 14" (228 mm × 350 mm) is not suitable for scanning.
5 There should be a margin of 2" (50 mm) from the top of page to the beginning of the text, at least ½" (12 mm) border at each side, and 1" (25 mm) clear at the bottom of the page.
6 Avoid 'skewing' the text by checking line alignment.
7 The misuse and thus confusion of characters should be avoided, e.g. zero and capital 'O' for zero; capital 'I' or small 'l' for the figure one (1).
8 Typestyles should be restricted to one of the 13 which are recommended by CAO. Examples can be supplied on request. Print wheels should be set at the pitch and point size recommended.
9 Do not use proportional spacing other than with typestyles model 2051 Madeleine, model 2052 Cubic, model 2053 Bold, model 2054 Title.
10 Avoid a change of typestyle or print font within the document.
11 The use of bold type, underlining and boxes around figures or text should be avoided.

Specification of RNS header message

Every announcement should carry a header message, as set out below. This speeds up validation and lessens the likelihood of missed deadlines due to inadequate instructions.

Line 1:   Listed or USM designated company name.
Line 2:   Name of the issuing agent (if different from line 1).
Line 3:   Announcement Validation Service (AVS) security number.
Line 4:   Date and time of release.   Note A
Line 5:   Request for telephone confirmation of release   Note B
            service.
Line 6:   Contact name and telephone number (for CAO   Note C
            purposes).

Line 7: Announcement not given to third parties.   Note D
Line 8: No unvalidated version to be issued.   Note E

Notes

A Clear indication of the required time of release should be given, e.g. 'Embargoed until 12 noon', or 'Please release at 9 am', or 'Do not release until receipt of a telephone call from A. Jones, Company Secretary'.

B Line 5 should state: 'Confirmation of release is required' or 'Confirmation of release is not required' as appropriate.

C Line 6 should carry the contact for CAO queries regarding announcement content, validation questions, or contact to confirm release. If companies wish to release a contact name and telephone number for market enquiries on the text of the announcement, these should be given at the end of the announcement text.

D This will indicate that RNS is the only channel of release.

E Specific instruction not to pass an unvalidated version to RNS subscribers. (This instruction may be overridden if Line 7 indicates that the announcement is being given to third parties.)

Note A refers to embargoes, which used to be discouraged by the Stock Exchange because of the danger of sensitive information appearing on hard copy announcements (paper news releases) and the opportunities this accorded inside traders. With electronic supply of information this danger is less likely. Note D refers to third parties, which could mean Reuters.

Commercial Company News Service (CCNS)[2]

The London Stock Exchange's CCNS is the leading supplier of UK company news and economic data, although closely rivalled by Reuters whose financial services have already been described, Reuters being international. CCNS provides comprehensive coverage and is relied upon daily by analysts, brokers, market-makers and investors.

All company announcements issued by listed and designated companies are received by the RNS described above and displayed in real time on CCNS. These announcements (releases) contain vital price-sensitive information comprising:

- Preliminary, interim and final financial results.
- Takeovers, mergers, acquisitions and disposals.
- Changes in directorate or substantial shareholdings.
- New share issues.
- Major contracts.

- Future board meetings.
- Temporary suspensions and restorations.

In addition to regulatory news, that is, financial news validated by the Company Announcements Office, CCNS covers economic and commercial information likely to affect the stock market or individual stocks. This includes non-regulatory announcements sent direct to the Exchange by listed and non-listed UK companies, public relations consultancies, brokers and advisers as well as companies listed on overseas exchanges. It also includes the latest major UK economic indicators such as the retail price index, UK trade figures, retail sales figures, the money supply, PSBR, bank lending, official reserves and changes to interest rates.

CCNS News goes out by TOPIC teletext system in six formats. The CCNS Full Text carries all regulatory company announcements in full. The CCNS Edited Text provides a digest of key points of all price-sensitive announcements. The Blue Chip 'Story in a headline' warns of an impending announcement of a price-sensitive announcement. CCNS Benefits offers information about shareholder benefits, such as dividend declarations, news of new issues and forthcoming board meetings and AGMs. CCNS Historical Database stores all CCNS Edited and Business announcements for up to an additional four business days.

Investor relations

With some 9 million British shareholders, largely as a result of privat-izations, a new kind of shareholder relations has become a cross between a public relations and a marketing exercise. One form of this is the external house journal addressed to shareholders, a typical example being the tabloid *British Airways Investor*.[3] The issue quoted in the References not only carried a summary interim statement and numerous news items about the airline's activities, but offered 20 per cent discounts on flights.

Trading with shareholders makes marketing sense when a company has thousands of potential customers. A BP shareholder can be encouraged to buy BP petrol, a Sainsbury's shareholder can be likewise urged to shop at the store in which shares are held.

Annual reports and accounts

The public relations manager is usually responsible for the writing, design, printing and at least some part of the distribution of the annual report and accounts. What considerations dictate the style of this important and necessary publication? Cost? Prestige? Information? What about the public relations *effect*, and the public relations *usage* of the annual report? Some of them look as if they are mostly windfalls for designers and printers. Not many are worth keeping.

Readership

Who will read the annual report – to which publics will it be addressed? Some reports appear to be aimed at pleasing the vanity of management, forgetting that these publications are *communication tools*.

Shareholders, both institutions and private investors; financial journalists; investment analysts; distributors; potential investors; employees; Members of Parliament; business studies lecturers and many others could be readers. The readership can also be spread to all kinds of people interested in the company such as visitors and inward foreign trade missions. Copies may be useful on exhibition stands, particularly at international trade fairs. Annual reports can act as ambassadors on many occasions. The question is, does it measure up to all these communication demands? Have all the opportunities for exploiting the annual report been analysed?

Does it, for instance, have a place in the media list for reaching the public selected in order to achieve the objectives of the public relations plan? Can a special public relations exercise be built around the annual report itself? Once we start thinking in this practical way the annual report takes on fresh significance, and is no longer a chore for non-public relations people like the company secretary who should be no more than a source of information. In a modern company, all this information should be on a computer anyway, accessible by the public relations manager.

However, privatization, with its millions of often quite small share-holders, has produced a public relations problem since these people, often with small holdings in many privatizations, are bewildered by weighty, sophisticated annual reports. They regard them as a waste of money. Wise companies invite shareholders to forgo the full report and accept a digest.

Design

Outlandish originality is not necessary. Some of the Arab reports, printed in gold and silver ink on expensive paper, only suggest that the company is filthy rich, which may offend more people than it impresses. An American one peppered with jokes was not appreciated.

Design should be distinctive, perhaps characteristic of the company, but the objective of the exercise is to get it read and understood and most people do not like reading figures and cannot read a balance sheet. Annual reports interest many more people than accountants. Having decided the first point about readers, the design, typography and general presentation should follow the need for simplicity, readability and legibility.

Usually, the text is too long and judicious editing should be applied, even to the chairman's report. Sometimes the type is too small, it is printed in a light colour on a tinted paper, the paragraphs are too long, and there are no sub-headings to break up the vast areas of copy. In other words, there is either design for design sake, or it has just been given to the typographer to set as typewritten.

All this means is that no attention has been given to the reader. Is the message easy to read and absorb? All this comes back to the writer, who should have command over how the words will look. The insertion of captioned figures, charts and pictures may help, and it is up to the writer to use them as devices to achieve clarity and comprehension. But some reports look as if a sheaf of typescript and a bunch of photographs were passed to a designer. How does a designer know what you want to *say* and to *whom*? Design can so easily get in the way of communication, so that a report looks pretty. Are all those colour photographs necessary?

One piece of information that is sometimes missing is the company's address!

When it comes to the presentation of the figures in the accounts, they may follow bookkeeping rules, but some producers of house journals have found unorthodox ways of setting out the results, such as by ranging information text against them.

Many companies insert advertisements with a summary of the report and accounts and the invitation to write in for the full report. Much can be learned by making a comparative study of as many reports as can be collected. Faults can be avoided and good ideas adapted. This can be important to the success of the annual report when its all-round purpose has been planned. It will help to avoid the biggest hazard of production and that is that designers tend to think in terms of shapes and how to balance or arrange them attractively, generally forgetting that these shapes actually represent words which various people are expected to read, not merely look at.

References

1 *Regulatory News Service Procedural Guidelines*, The London Stock Exchange, 1991
2 Commercial Company News Service, leaflet, London Stock Exchange
3 *British Airways Investor*, British Airways, Winter 1992

31

Internal public relations

Importance of management−employee relations

Internal communications have advanced a long may beyond the rather fuddy-duddy, management-sponsored house journal to well-organized systems of internal communication. There are three reasons for this.

1 A greater requirement for companies to inform their employees about policy and financial affairs including the annual report and accounts. In Chapter 24 on house journals, reference was made to 'empowering employees', and the value employers are placing on this and customer relations during a period of recession.
2 Increasing democratization of industry − however timidly − on the continental European pattern of worker directors, works councils and works committees, plus the effects of management buy-outs, the influence of profit-sharing schemes, and encouragement to take up equity ownership. A feature of privatization has been the allocation of shares to employees at advantageous prices.
3 The availability of new communications technology which makes it easier to organize and conduct internal communications. With these techniques everyone is brought much closer together, as was seen in Chapter 22. Among these new techniques are video, including video magazines, audio tapes, business TV, journals, desk-top publishing, teleconferencing, use of satellite, mobile telephones, electronic mail and computers.

All this reflects a much changed industrial climate as the old industrial age is replaced by the new technological age. The 'them and us' attitude diminishes as the power of the unions decreases, management learns to manage, workforces are slimmed down as computers and robotics take over, and electronic man emerges from the twilight of recession. Even this book echoes the theme since it stresses the role of the public relations manager, not the PRO who was often no more than an executive with no real managerial responsibility. The public relations manager envisaged in this book is not just a departmental manager, but part of the management team who is either responsible to the board or has a seat on the board. In large companies where public relations is recognized as a major activity, he or she is the public relations director or at least the public relations adviser to the board.

So with internal public relations. This may be the responsibility of the public relations manager, but in some large companies there is also an internal communications manager. This person's task may be limited to a particular location such as a factory, and each location in an organization may have its local communication manager just as each hotel in a hotel group will have its own PRO. He or she will be responsible for editing the house journal and any other form of communication, writing speeches for the CEO, conducting community relations, organizing incentive schemes, controlling noticeboards, and working closely with the personnel manager, the training officer and the industrial relations officer.

These latter links will range from providing induction material for new staff (such as videos and literature) to assisting labour relations by keeping employees well and quickly informed about management policy. Wise managements have come to realize that many of the unofficial lightning strikes were the result of rumours gleaned from the grapevine. They could have been avoided had they opened the door more often and allowed the public relations manager to tell people what was going on.

Internal public relations is therefore one of the keys to successful management, requiring open management and closing the gap between the two sides. The influence of so many Japanese companies in Britain has also contributed to the new climate of internal relations, although we have not quite reached the stage of having company songs. Nevertheless, the common canteen and the loss of the managers' dining room is a sign of the new spirit in industry.

There are even occasions when the grapevine is a good way of disseminating information, provided that information does not get distorted. But is 'cascading' information down from top to bottom of an organization such a good idea? Evan Ivey, quoted in a *PR Week* article,[1] disagreed. This senior consultant with Aspen Business Communication said: 'Cascade has a very bad name everywhere. Information starts at the top and arrives six weeks later, often patchily. Also, not every manager is capable of holding effective briefings.'

Internal communications audits

A number of companies today take the trouble to invite professional research units to conduct internal communication audits. It is often surprising how little management knows about its own company, and likewise how little employees know about the company in which they work. All this can be revealed by an independent survey with confidentiality guaranteed to all who are interviewed. This should not be confused with the investigations conducted by management consultants who are mainly concerned with the way a company is managed.

Some of these internal audits are of long standing, and Rank Hovis McDougall have conducted such studies every three years for the past 15 years. Cadbury—Schweppes also have such a scheme, and Burson—Marsteller have made a speciality of communication audits both internally and externally. The method is not unknown in the developing world, and it is a service performed by the Zimbabwe public relations consultancy, Spectrum. In Zimbabwe, political independence produced new relationships between management (usually white) and employees who were black, members of new trade unions, and protected by new labour laws.

In the PR Week[1] article already mentioned, Michael Blunt of British Airways was quoted as saying: 'We have just committed ourselves to doing census surveys of staff attitudes every 18 months.'

Internal public relations can be placed under the three headings of *upwards*, *sideways*, and *downwards* communication as detailed by the author elsewhere.[2] These three headings indicate that management-employee relations are no longer a matter of management preaching to the disconcerted, but of people talking to people, and of the public relations principle of mutual understanding being invoked. Moreover, it works both ways: employee—management relations as well as management—employee relations. To this can be added employee—employee (sideways) relations.

To take two examples, if a house journal has an independent editor, and readers can express opinions, this is enlightening to management, and if management can be interviewed for a video house magazine or for business TV this can be enlightening to employees. An entirely new, frank and relaxed relationship is created. Again, if there is a works council it may slow down the decision-making process, but it can result in some different and more enlightened decisions. This is a very sensible and practical way to run a company. It could have prevented Britain's twelve-month coal strike which only succeeded in discrediting both management and union, and the government as well. Most strikes, as the Industrial Society has often pointed out, are wholly unnecessary and principally the fault of management's failure to communicate. Unions may be perverse at times, but in well-managed companies such perversity is pointless. Strikes rarely occur in Germany or the Netherlands where there are worker directors or works councils. Sadly, it is Britain's resistance to such things which has made EC relations so strained.

Taking this broad look at internal public relations, let us reconsider the three divisions of upwards, sideways and downwards communications.

Upwards communication

How can employees communicate with management? Moreover, how can they be encouraged to do so, because it may not have occurred to them that they should or could? They may have thought that their only means of communication with management was through their trade union shop steward, and then only when they had something to complain about. But upward communication is not only, or even, about grievances. The facility to talk to one's leaders is the ability to belong, to join in, to contribute, to be more than a regimented drone. Money isn't everything. Job satisfaction is derived from enjoying one's work. While it is true that there are still factories in Britain which resemble the Charlie Chaplin film *Modern Times* and almost the Charles Dickens novel *Hard Times*, the modern factory or office does invite greater job satisfaction, and does bring management and employees closer together. This is so if only because numbers are fewer and machine-minders have been replaced by technocrats.

Some of the methods of upward communication are:

Readers' letters

When employee newspapers like *Ford News* print readers' letters, two things happen: (a) There is reader participation and (b) the publication contains one of the most popular features of the press. Thus, readers' letters not only provide the opportunity for people to have their say but they add reality and credibility to the journal. They are what people expect to find in a real newspaper or magazine. They give pleasure to hundreds, perhaps thousands, of readers who may never bother to write a letter themselves.

Speak-up and suggestion schemes

Again, the opportunity may not be exercised by everyone, but the fact that anyone may propose something creates a good feeling that one's ideas are valued. The means of doing this should be conveniently located, as when boxes are fitted to corridor walls.

Incentive schemes

These can work both ways, as upwards or downwards communication, and the suggestion scheme can be coupled with awards for ideas which are put into practice to the company's benefit. A downwards incentive scheme would be a reward for achieving a sales target or some such stimulant for special endeavour, while awards are often made for ideas that help productivity. An example is given in the item about *Barclays News* in Chapter 24.

House journal articles

Another way of communicating upwards can be the contribution of an 'own job' article, or an interview about one's job which could appear in printed or video magazine form. By this means members of staff may describe aspects of their work experience which could be quite unknown to management. Remember, business leaders including directors have seldom grown up in the company, and they are often remote from what actually goes on in the working lives of employees. This could be regarded as a management education exercise!

Correspondents for house journals

Such people may be scattered throughout the country and possibly abroad. They are like local stringers for a national newspaper, and are in a position to feed to the central editorial office a variety of ground roots information. From their listening posts they can help employees to express themselves through news of their activities.

Quality circles

This ingenious Japanese system can be a great aid to productivity, as when a group led by a supervisor attacks a problem with vigorous discussion which produces ideas on how to improve performance. While geared to greater efficiency, the quality circle does give employees responsibility for contributing to that efficiency instead of being, say, the puppets of time and motion studies.

Sideways communications

Sideways − or crossways − communication is appreciated in organizations where there are good relationships between members of staff and they are interested in each other's affairs. This may simply be because there is a friendly working environment, or because staff move about and have different assignments and friends and associates like to keep in touch with one another. A company with many branches, a hotel group, an airline or a shipping company belongs to this category.

This type of internal communication may be achieved through the house journal, controlled noticeboards and business meetings and social get-togethers. Another idea is to arrange staff visits between one location and another, or to take field or shop sales staff to the factory where the company's products are made. Here are a few special ways of achieving sideways communications.

Sales and wants advertisements

Usually inserted free-of-charge, but restricted to a certain length, a marketplace can be established in the employee newspaper. In journals such as *Ford News* they fill a couple of pages. Like readers' letters, classified ads are very popular. They not only add to the interest of the publication and give it a realistic appearance, but they encourage reader participation and create many staff contacts.

News about staff clubs

Reports in the house journal and announcements on a controlled noticeboard provide further links between staff when there are staff clubs and societies covering sport, hobbies and other interests. Controlled noticeboards means that wherever there are noticeboards they are of standard design, and only an authorized person is allowed to mount notices, usually in allotted spaces or on clips reserved for specified subjects. It is a good idea if this uniformity is maintained by the public relations department producing the notices from supplied information. Thus, the boards can be kept tidy and attractive and employees know where to find different kinds of information.

Staff news

Special columns in the house journal can be devoted to topics like 'On The Move', 'New Appointments', 'On Leave', 'Marriages, Births, Retirements' and so on so that employees can learn about people they know. Many journals are distributed to all retired staff, and this sort of personal news can maintain reader interest even among those who have left the company.

Downwards communication

A house journal should be neither a pulpit nor a platform for top management, but there are various ways in which they can keep the staff well informed about developments, prospects and finances. Well-informed staff are likely to work more satisfactorily, and if it is a service company, being well informed will enhance customer relations. Some of these methods are:

Annual reports and accounts

These can be explained graphically and in straightforward language in the printed house journal or visually in the video magazine. However, a method adopted very successfully by some companies is to produce a video in which the chairman is interviewed by a professional inter-viewer such as a TV presenter. Financial reports can interest a consider-able number of staff now that so many employees own shares in the company for which they work (or may consider buying some), or have unit trust shares and the company is included in the portfolio, or there is a profit-sharing scheme.

Company policy

There is nothing worse than for employees to learn about company plans at second hand, say, in the press or on TV, or as a rumour. It will pay to delay a public announcement until the staff have been told. This is where works councils are valuable. But there are times when the staff are the last to know, simply because management thinks it is none of their business. The public relations manager, who should be aware of all company plans, may have to use a form of communication more urgent than waiting for the next issue of the house journal. Today there are many methods of achieving immediate communication such as electronic mail. By this means a message can be transmitted by personal computer. Cascading information can be effective; it is quick and can exploit the advantages of face-to-face communication.

Top appointments

Equally, all new managerial appointments or changes should be given to the staff as soon as possible. The staff should always be familiar with the management structure. Reminders of this can appear in the house journal in the form of a 'family tree'. Meetings and visits can also be arranged, or tours of premises can be made to meet the staff. Top management personalities should not remain remote in boardroom eyries, or be merely names painted on car parking bays.

Advertising

Before campaigns break, employees should have an opportunity to see pulls of press advertisements − on the noticeboards, for instance − or ads can be reproduced in the house journal. If it is possible, commercials should be shown to the staff before they see them at home on their television sets. It depends on the size, nature and location of staff whether these advance showings are possible. By being given prior knowledge of advertising campaigns, employees can see what is being done to promote the prosperity of the company which is, after all, very much in their interests since their jobs depend on successful sales.

The above is just a sample of items which can be included in downward communication, but they give an impression of how management can be forthcoming and can generate interest, enthusiasm and above all understanding. All the time, we return to this basic purpose of public relations − *understanding*, and better still *mutual understanding*.

Empowerment

The article in *PR Week* quoted above[1] was entitled 'Empowering employees' and dealt, among other things, with the development techniques in British Airways, thus encouraging greater customer care. Empowerment has become one of those buzz words, rather like 'added value', introduced by Americans who have re-invented the wheel. Just as good retailers and manufacturers have been giving 'added value' for decades, so 'empowerment' is something most wide-awake managements have been pursuing for the past 40 years at least. However, it is a nice bit of jargon which suits a recession situation, where some managements have woken up to a communications gap between their staff and their customers.

An advertisement for Marriott Hotels[3] carried the following copy:

> There were no taxis and no chance of catching my plane until the Marriott receptionist took a personal interest in the matter. Without hesitation she made an executive decision. If she couldn't order a car in time to get me to the airport, she'd take me in her own. It was no stretch limo but thanks to her I made the flight. I believe, at Marriott, they call it Empowerment. It means that the staff see their roles as being more than just a duty. They're really sensitive to guests' needs and assume responsibility for attending to them. I needed to catch that plane and they ensured I did. It's been the same whenever I've stayed at a Marriott and the new UK hotels will be no different, I'm sure.

Quality and internal relations

Quality circles from Japan, productivity councils in Singapore, quality assurance in Britain, and just plain 'quality' in the USA are all expressions of a desire for perfection. Perhaps it is an antidote to recession. But what are the implications from the point of view of internal relations? Is 'quality' another excuse for management to exhort the workers to excel themselves?

> In its literature Marketing Quality Assurance Ltd of Egham says PE International plc has established Marketing Quality Assurance to provide assessment services to companies wishing to develop quality systems based on best practice for their Marketing, Sales and Customer Assurance activities. Among its objectives are 'staff and organizations responsive to the market place'. Among the nine reasons 'why MQA registration is vital to your organization' is 'Committed Staff. Staff who have a better understanding of their role and objectives are more motivative and effective.' The specification in brief says, 'Resources, Personnel, Training and organization structure − requirements call for well-trained, experienced staff who are responsive to the needs of the market place.[4]

All very cold-blooded 19th century stuff. Not a word about telling the staff what management is up to and so inspiring their confidence. No wonder Britain rejected the Social Charter at Maastricht!

John Fraser-Robinson has written an interesting book, *Total Quality Marketing*,[5] which is about what has to come next in sales, marketing and advertising. But you cannot sell, market or advertise something unless there are people to produce it. Robotics have not usurped manpower altogether. Yet here is a book which purports to explain total quality marketing and yet never mentions anyone in a company below management level.

The idiocy of this sort of situation was brought out by Dan Koger and Greg Brower in an article in the IABC magazine *Communication World*.[6]

The authors began with a definition rather different from the British concept of the subject. 'Total quality — the involvement of all employees in continuous improvement of an organization's products and services to customers — has been called a thought revolution in management'. This is more like it, and harks back to what has been said earlier about 'empowerment'. However, the authors have some blunt things to say about the lack of management communication, saying 'when employees don't trust managers to behave in keeping with their public messages, the best media campaign for quality is doomed to disappointment if not outright failure.' The article went on to quote Roger D'Aprix, who said 'The boss makes the weather.'

> D'Aprix's point is obvious. All the feel-good efforts in the world won't warm the company climate if management, especially senior management, doesn't visibly support the quality effort with appropriate new ways of running the organization.
>
> Does this mean traditional media should never be used to communicate quality?
>
> Of course not. They're too valuable.
>
> But in a total-quality environment, the true value of traditional communication media — videos, newsletters and such — comes primarily when they are used as part of a carefully planned and coordinated communication strategy to support an equally well-crafted total quality strategy.
>
> Only management can build the quality strategy.

TQM — magic or moonshine?

Is Total Quality Management (TQM) another fad, like work study, operational research, organizational development and other magic formulas which have gone before it? Very mixed views from business leaders were considered in an article by Alison Edie in *The Independent* business and city section.[7] She quoted the enthusiastic Eugene Anderson, chairman of Ferranti, who saw TQM as 'the main plank of the company's rehabilitation', having recovered 'from the brink of bankruptcy'. Even though Rank Xerox was the first winner of the European Quality Award, the article quoted Bernard Fournier managing director of Rank Xerox in Europe as saying rather cautiously, 'It is not a substitute for technology or research, as the Japanese have shown.' When asked what he was doing about TQM, Alan Sugar, chairman of Amstrad, asked whether it was a disinfectant.

The aim of TQM is to make customer satisfaction the top priority, and this begins with employee attitudes to customers. BT, for example, now deals with 'customers', even on its bills, whereas they used to be called 'subscribers'.

The idea of TQM originated with a pair of American academics, Edwards Deming and Joseph Duras, who failed to convince Americans about the merits of quality control and customer satisfaction and so took the idea to Japan. The Japanese were not impressed and passed TQM on to the Europeans where it was adopted by Rover and Rank Xerox for quality control and product quality, and then customer satisfaction. It has even been applied in the public relations profession. The problem with TQM has been trying to prove that it works.

Case Study: The Texaco Charity Challenge

Here is a case study which shows how a sponsorship can become a staff relations exercise and exploit the use of both videotape and satellite business television, as described in Chapter 22. The complete scheme is described in a booklet *Charity Challenge, The Story*,[8] produced by Texaco's Public Affairs and Advertising Department in London. The case study was reported in *BAIE News*[9] following a presentation by David Robinson, public affairs manager for Texaco Ltd.

Texaco, like most large companies, reserves a fund for charitable donations, but in this case the management decided to involve the staff in raising monies, which it would match, for the National Children's Home. The company's chairman, Glenn Tilton, challenged employees to raise £37,500 which the company would match pound for pound to a joint total of £75,000. In nine months that total was far exceeded.

This challenge was issued by the chairman in a dramatic fashion. On 29 November 1991 nearly 2000 Texaco employees celebrated the company's 75th anniversary in the UK. Whether located on an oil platform 120 miles off shore in the North Sea, more comfortably seated at the Grosvenor House Hotel in Park Lane, London, in a marquee in the grounds of Pembroke refinery in Wales, or watching in Aberdeen, Manchester, Swindon, Slough or Birmingham, employees simultaneously celebrated the event by satellite link. The transmission was produced by G. Force, a division of MetroVideo.

To quote from the booklet:

> The company has long had an active relationship with the communities in which it operates and the Charity Challenge was a

way of developing this relationship still further. Because it had employees in all parts of the country, Texaco was keen to be involved with a nationwide charity such as NCH. The choice of NCH was also consistent with the company's policy of providing support and encouragement to children and young people, as with its 'Children should be seen and not hurt' road safety campaign and many of its community affairs and sponsorship activities.

During the next nine months hundreds of employees became involved in more than 200 events. Examples were a competition offering a Renault Clio car as the prize for guessing the distance covered by the car on 7.5 litres of petrol, which raised £7514; proceeds from weekly meat raffles at a local pub, totalling £500; a piano playing marathon which produced £1002.60; a communal slim which raised £1592.65; and a gala trivia quiz night which achieved £443.35. The initial target of £75,000 was exceeded in March, and eventually by the end of October the total reached £301,774.

> It was decided that the money should be spent primarily in geographical areas close to where it was raised. The balance will be used to support NCH's national programme of activities.
> These are concerned with all aspects of child and family suffering. Whether it be physical or sexual abuse, mental or physical disabilities, homelessness, poverty or the damaging effects of family breakdown or emotional neglect. NCH can intervene offering help and long-term solutions.

The grand total of £301,774 was celebrated at the Houses of Parliament where Texaco's chairman, Glenn Tilton, made the presentation of a token cheque to NCH president Viscount Tonypandy, former Speaker of the House of Commons. Financial support was given to the Springfield Family Centre, London; the West Swindon Family Project; Stepping Stones Family Support Group, West Glamorgan; Llanelli Community Family Project; Family Link Scheme, Billingshurst; and Merkinch Family Resources Centre, Inverness.

Finally, Texaco recorded the whole story in both a 16-page full colour booklet and on a videotape that shows many of the 200 fund-raising events and also visits each of the NCH projects that received financial aid as a result of the Charity Challenge.

References

1 Dark, Stephen, 'Empowering employees', *PR Week*, 12 November 1992
2 Jefkins, Frank, *Public Relations for Your Business*, Mercury Books, London, 1990
3 American Express Europe, advertisement, Marriott Hotels, *Expression*, November/December 1992

4 *Executive Guidelines*, Marketing Quality Assurance Ltd, Egham, 1991
5 Fraser-Robinson, John, *Total Quality Marketing*, Kogan Page, London, 1991
6 *Communications World*, article, 'If Total Quality seems like a revolution, that's because it is', IABC, San Francisco, October 1992
7 Eadie, Alison, article, Business and City section, 'It may be total but it's not all', *The Independent*, 8 March 1993
8 *Charity Challenge, The Story*, Texaco Public Affairs and Advertising Department, London, 1992
9 Robinson, David (manager, public affairs, Texaco Ltd), Report on talk to BAIE members, *BAIE News*, October 1992

32

Crisis management

Public relations in disaster situations

What does one do when disaster strikes? There used to be an idea that one called in the PRO who, because of the devious nature of his or her business, could wave a magic wand or spread a smokescreen and pretend it had never happened. The PRO got a deservedly bad reputation with the media as a troubleshooter, and has often appeared as such in many a novel or film, rather like the lawyer that gangsters call their 'mouth'.

It was not always like that. The pioneer of public relations, Ivy Ledbetter Lee, was called in by the American anthracite coal industry, and the Pennsylvania Railroad, *in 1906*, to handle crisis public relations for them when they had pit disasters and railway accidents. He was not an expert in black magic. He demanded access to boardrooms to get the facts, and access by the press to the scenes of disaster. Lee achieved fair and accurate reporting instead of the exaggerations and inaccuracies based on rumour and hearsay which had been published on previous occasions.

Lee's proper public relations behaviour remains the example which should be followed today, except that he had to act when it was almost too late. In recent years we have seen some terrible events which have shown a lack of preparation or crisis management to mention only Bhopal, the Shuttle rocket disaster, Sellafield and Farley's. This is not to say that public relations people did not go into action afterwards, but management was often left floundering when trouble occurred.

Today, when we live in the midst of chemical, nuclear, electronic and also terrorist and activist hazards, it is necessary to accept that anything can happen, not merely take precautions about the most likely. The modern public relations manager has to reckon with the unlikely, and − like a fire station − be organized to go into action at the ring of a bell. This is being realistic, not idealistic, and it is a special area of public relations which calls for *management* skills in prevention, preparation and provision, not just ability to call a press conference.

Crisis public relations frequently occur in CAM examination papers and the prime weakness in answers is lack of a sense of urgency. There is talk about making videos when there would be scarcely time to get a news flash on television. There is talk of calling press conferences the next day when the news agencies have got to be phoned immediately.

A great problem today is the fantastic speed of communication, and the world may know of our disaster before we can decently think about what to do. We have WSTV and CNN providing world TV coverage of events, and Reuters capable of transmitting a story to editorial terminals world-wide in less than five seconds.

Let us discuss those three Ps − prevention, preparation and provision − and then consider some particular kinds of crisis situations.

Prevention

It is easy to be wise after the event and say if only we had done so and so this would not have happened. Too often, disasters occur through bad management. They happen all the time in everyday public relations life let alone in large-scale industrial circumstances. But today there is a risk of destroying large numbers of people, whole communities, even the planet. It is time to take stock and not leave it to voluntary guardians of our conscience like Ralph Nader, Greenpeace, Friends of the Earth or *Which?* magazine. The causes of disaster vary between the extremes of casual optimism and selfish greed. In some cases there is evidence of downright corruption. It is the public relations manager who should represent the conscience of an organization because he or she is more than just a spokesperson and is the guardian of its goodwill and reputation. Carol Friend,[1] president of the IPR in 1986, made this virtually her definition of public relations.

When advocating that public relations should be planned, an excuse is sometimes made that public relations often has to deal with the unpredictable. Crisis public relations means planning to deal with the unpredictable.

Prevention procedure should be based on trying to anticipate what could go wrong. This can be done by building two lists, one of the disasters or crises that are possible because of the nature of the organization, and one of more unlikely ones that might, perhaps in a million years, occur. *How often is this ever done?*

Let us compile two hypothetical lists to demonstrate the above, taking the familiar landmark of St Stephen's tower, Westminster, which houses the clock with the bell known as Big Ben. We usually refer loosely to the whole edifice as 'Big Ben'.

Possible crises

1   Could be struck by lightning.
2   Could be hit by aircraft.
3   Could be blown up by terrorists.
4   Could collapse on House of Commons.
5   Could collapse in River Thames.
6   Could be destroyed by wartime bombing or rocketry.
7   Clock could be stopped or time changed by fanatic.
8   Could be daubed, or have banners hung on it.
9   Bell could disintegrate.
10   Belfry could be invaded by thousands of starlings.

Impossible (?) crises

1   Could be stolen by false contractors removing it like previous London Bridge.
2   Could be occupied by demonstrators or other fanatics.
3   Could have time mechanism distorted by some electronic or laser device.
4   Could be privatized by, the government, and BBC etc. charged royalty for reproducing sound of Big Ben.
5   Destruction could be threatened by a terrorist organization if prisoner not released.
6   A kidnapper could hold a victim in the clock chamber.
7   Legislation could be passed to have the bell silenced.

How many of these possible or even unlikely crises have been considered by the custodians of Big Ben? One suspects less than half of the above, and then by whom − Ministry of Works, Metropolitan Police, Home Office? And do they have an emergency plan including public relations requirements? They were probably better organized when they discovered Guy Fawkes.

One of the ways in which such emergency lists can be compiled is by running a press cuttings check on disasters, and adding new kinds of hazard to one's list as and when they are spotted.

Preparation

Two things are necessary in order to be prepared for crises.

First, there should be a basic crisis committee comprising such people as the chief executive officer, personnel manager, works manager, safety officer and public relations manager, or whatever is the appropriate minimum committee according to the kind of organization. If there are several locations, each should have a representative on the committee so that it could go into action locally, nationally or at both levels. Or perhaps internationally.

Secondly, these people should have regular contact by meeting (which could include teleconferencing), computer terminal, telephone, fax or correspondence so that procedures can be reviewed and up-dated, including means of rapid communication in the event of a disaster. For instance, media requirements are constantly changing, including access to media by online computer facilities.

One of the objectives in this planned procedure is to make sure that all members of the crisis committee have access to, or are in receipt of, the same information, are agreed on what can be said to the media and are consistent on giving out the same information. This is necessary because release of information has to be controlled, not because the organization is afraid to be frank but because there may be restrictive commitments. For instance, if people are killed, next of kin must be informed first, and if there are any legal or insurance implications liability must not be admitted. The latter was a problem experienced by CPC, maker of popular foodstuffs, when mercury was discovered in a corn product ingredient for cattle foods produced in the Netherlands. Fortunately no one died of the meat affected by the mercury.

Provision

The media will demand every kind of information, although they have no *right* to anything. They are in business, and for them bad news is good news which helps to sell papers and attract audiences. The organization has its own responsibilities to itself, employees, distributors, shareholders and others. So a balance is necessary, coupled with the knowledge that any crisis invites criticism rightly or wrongly. The immediate conclusion is that the organization is to blame when something goes wrong, and it is unlikely to receive any sympathy. We are back to our negative situations of the public relations transfer process, especially hostility, prejudice and ignorance and it is the organization which may be accused of apathy.

It is therefore necessary to be organized regarding provision of information, and organized in order to provide it. A media statement should be written and agreed by the crisis committee as soon as possible. Ideally, the media should be assembled wherever this is feasible and given every reasonable facility. They should not be allowed to exploit the situation, and it may be necessary to be frank but blunt, and keep control of the situation. The public relations manager must be the ringmaster and not the performing pony.

This is difficult, but it all depends on how far the public relations manager's skill is able to satisfy and convince the media representatives. Once he or she slips into a defensive, apologetic and therefore weak position he or she is lost and the media will walk all over him or her. It is better for him or her to make frank, authoritative statements as far as he or she can go at the time, and promise additional facts as soon as they are available. Under no circumstances must the PRO (or others) adopt a 'no comment' attitude, and if a question cannot be answered he or she must explain why. The PRO must carry the media with them, and earn their respect, understanding and tolerance, however fiercely and irresponsibly he or she may be badgered. The 'name of the game' applies to both sides.

There may be an initial statement, followed by more detailed statements at press conferences or facility visits. If it is possible to lay on tours, these should be made with facilities available such as telephones, fax machines, computer terminals, transport and so on so that media representatives may despatch their stories, pictures or tapes.

When the problem has been resolved, the media should be re-invited and told what has been done and why there is no longer any problem, even if this is at some time in the future. The new situation may well be to the credit of the organization. But it depends on the nature of the catastrophe and sometimes it may be wise to leave well alone: it is surprising how short people's memories are! There is no point in reminding people of a disaster. On the other hand if an old bridge collapsed, and it has been replaced by a fine new one there is every reason for seeking recognition of this achievement.

Much may depend on the ability of the CEO to handle the media, for such a person will carry authority and avoid criticism of a cover-up. Two excellent examples were those of the Piper Alpha oil platform disaster in the North Sea when the chairman Dr Armand Hammer flew from Los Angeles to deal with the media and the British Airways Boeing 737 crash on the M1 motorway when the chief executive, Michael Bishop, took charge immediately.

What is the state of crisis management?

Experience has obliged some of the most endangered and hazardous industries to adopt excellent crisis procedures, as has been seen in Britain by the oil companies following North Sea oil rig and tanker calamities. But according to a report published by Western Union Corporation,[2] following a survey of 1500 American corporations, only 53 per cent had a plan which would enable them to communicate quickly and effectively in a crisis. These plans were mostly developed *after the event* of an earlier crisis. The report was prepared for Western Union by Burson-Masteller.

The types of crisis identified in this report are industrial accidents, environmental problems, investor relations, hostile takeovers, rumour suppression, strikes, proxy situations, product recall and government regulatory problems.

Western Union have themselves published a kit *When Every Second Counts – Crisis Communications Planning*,[3] and the following checklist is quoted:

Dos

- Gather all the facts, and disseminate from one central information centre.
- Speak with one voice, consistently, via designated and trained spokespeople.
- Select credible spokespeople, train them and make sure they are well informed.
- Be accessible to the media so they won't go to other sources for news.
- Report your own bad news. If the media has to dig it out, they may decide you are guilty of creating a crisis.
- Tell your story quickly, openly and honestly to allay suspicion and rumours.
- If you can't discuss something, explain why.
- Provide sufficient evidence of statements.
- Record events as the crisis evolves, including photographs and video tapes, so later you can present your side of the story.
- Update crisis communications plan periodically.

Don'ts

- Avoid 'no comment', as it leads to speculation.
- Don't debate the subject.

- Don't attempt to assess blame; rather, address and solve the problem at hand.
- Don't overreact and don't exaggerate the situation.
- Don't deviate from corporate policy or agreed-upon crisis procedures.
- Don't make 'off-the-record' statements; there is no such thing.

In addition, Western Union issues a folder *How to Develop a Crisis Communications Program*,[4] which sets out specific planning suggestions and operational details. A particularly interesting item concerns telephone accessibility within an organization in the event of any kind of crisis:

1 Tell lobby desk and telephone operators how to deal with visitors and callers in a crisis.
2 Assemble a crisis phone index to reach key people 24 hours a day:

- Corporate attorney
- Board members
- Officers and key management
- Corporate executives
- Crisis team leaders
- Travel agent
- Public relations and advertising people
- Twenty-four hour food service
- Office machine repair and maintenance crew
- Mailroom staff
- Telephone company
- Western Union
- Local and overnight messenger services
- Executive secretary
- Typing pool

Contamination of products

Activists, such as animal rights groups, have provoked a double-edged crisis situation. If confectionery, baby food or some other product is impregnated with dangerous substances, or there is even a hoax to this effect, both retailers and manufacturers are under attack. Recent examples of victims of such action are Mars and Heinz, and in November 1992 it was a theme in the TV series about the fictional lawyer Kinsey. There is usually a ransom demand, but the perpetrators may be satisfied with the publicity given to their cause.

The retailer − often a large supermarket chain − does not want to lose trade by appearing to stock the offending product, and will clear the shelves. The manufacturer will be expected to take back perhaps millions of pounds of stock. A double crisis has to be solved. The retailer will not restock unless the manufacturer can guarantee a safe product. This may mean repackaging, or introducing a new tamper-free pack. Then the consumer has to be convinced that the product is safe.

These can be costly crises, running into millions of pounds in losses. In most cases such crises have been resolved in a few days, and sales have been recovered in a few weeks or months, but it is a terrifying situation all round for manufacturer, retailer and consumer, especially in such cases as when bits of broken glass were found in jars of baby food.

Crisis by criticism

Laws, codes of practice and investigative journalism can all provoke crises of confidence. Many companies have received unfortunate media coverage as a result of prosecutions under the Trade Descriptions Act, Consumer Protection Act and various labelling laws − and there are more than 100 such laws. They have ranged from misleading descriptions in holiday brochures to inadequate labelling of food products.

Codes of practice such as the British Code of Advertising Practice (BCAP), those of the Independent Television Commission and the Radio Authority, plus those of the Institute of Public Relations and the Public Relations Consultants Association, can lead to adverse publicity if their recommendations are breached. In the case of the BCAP, a monthly case report is published and items are widely published in the press, as are complaints to the ITC even though TV commercials are vetted before they are screened.

Investigative journalism, especially on TV, can be very hurtful and over the years many famous firms have been pilloried, or dangerous products like inflammable clothes and furniture, dangerous children's cots and push-chairs, and dubious treatments and foods have been criticized, on programmes such as *That's Life*, *World in Action* and a number of consumer protection programmes.

Rightly or wrongly, all investigative TV programmes which appear weekly in Britain have tremendous impact. If it was any relief to British business, the producers tended to concentrate in late 1992 on programmes about the deficiencies of the government; as was seen at that time, crisis situations can apply to politicians and personalities as much as to organizations and products. Much, for instance, revolved around the Matrix Churchill machine tools for Iraq affair and the provision of British machinery to make munitions used against British troops in the Gulf conflict. Both ministers who had approved export documents and manufacturers were under fire. In the USA the Gulf War caused problems for the American office of an international consultancy which was criticized for accepting millions of dollars to persuade the American people to support a war to return the scarcely democratic rulers to Kuwait, which was not to be confused with removing Saddam Hussein.

Crises in public service industries and events organizing

One of the penalties of running a public service, whether publicly or privately owned, is that it supplies a multitude of customers who depend on it. The fact that one can boil a kettle of water at any time of the day means that gas, electricity or water undertakings are taken for granted and rarely thanked or praised. If the supply fails the undertaking is heavily criticized. When the Hong Kong Mass Transit Railway was launched a few years ago the biggest public relations worry was that a breakdown would bring the trains to a halt. The same applies to many services such as the railways, airways, Post Office or waste disposal services. These are consequently crises of great magnitude.

When organizing conferences which require delegates to travel to a distant location, both rail and road transport should be booked to be on the safe side! A good organizer should avoid crisis possibilities. Press events have been ruined in the past because of such crises as an air-traffic controllers' strike in one case, and bad weather preventing use of a helicopter in another.

Product recall

An ever-present crisis risk is that of product failure. It may not seem very good public relations to have to admit that a product is faulty, yet the best way to retrieve goodwill is to climb right down the greasy pole and admit the fault, and organize the speediest possible recall so that the defect can be remedied. It is no use being timid about this, and attempting to hide behind excuses or deal with the problem discreetly, because this will only worsen matters.

There was protracted argument over a small number of Volvo 340 Automatic cars whose drivers had accidents or frightening experiences because the car apparently developed a mind of its own and drove off unexpectedly. Volvo were puzzled and could find no fault. Were the drivers to blame? The complaints persisted. Finally, the cars were withdrawn so that a new safety device could be fitted. The following statement appeared in the news column of the press, in this case the *Daily Telegraph*.[5]

Volvo Recalls
Automatics
By Our Motoring Staff

Volvo is recalling 30,000 of its 340 Automatic cars to modify the selector mechanism and prevent the wrong gear from being used. There have been cases of cars moving off out of control when drivers thought the lever was in the 'Park' position.

A warning light and buzzer will alert the driver if the lever is wrongly positioned.

Thus, the company has actually been able to produce a more efficient car which it can turn to its advantage. The device was fitted to all models manufactured between 1978 and 1986, and cars were recalled gradually between 12 May and 1 September 1986. However, this new gadget had to be designed and manufactured, and then fitted, and the cost was a financial loss to the company.

The cost of some recalls has been phenomenal. The John West salmon recall cost £2 m, and when it is a serious one because a food product is dangerously tainted, or an electrical product is dangerously wired, there is not only loss of goodwill but loss of sales when products have to be stripped out of shops. Loss of goodwill extends to stockists as well as customers, can be demoralizing for staff and can bring about a fall in the share price. There can be a crisis of confidence all round.

The key to product recall is speed. It may be quicker to place advertisements in the press than to rely on news releases being printed, and posters or showcards may be advisable at the point-of-sale. A problem with some recalls is that the fault is in a certain batch made some time ago, and their present location is not always easy to trace. This happened when plastic handles fell off coffee pots made many years earlier by Corning[6] of America, but a redoubtable nationwide and mostly public relations endeavour failed to trace every coffee pot. Sometimes the fault is in the wiring of a recently bought appliance, which is easily rectified by taking it to the nearest stockist who has been instructed how to repair the fault.

Simple things can turn out to be dangerous, and a recall advertisement has to temper urgency with reassurance. The thing has happened and it is no use pretending it has not. And although the fault does the manufacturer no credit, what is done about it could show that it is a caring company. A faulty door on a refrigerator could create all sorts of problems and dangers for a family, but, the following extracts from a Hitachi[7] recall advertisement are commendable. The advertisement was illustrated with the rating label to be found inside the refrigerator, and there was a simple coupon which asked for both a home and a daytime telephone number.

WARNING
IMPORTANT SAFETY
NOTICE
HITACHI REFRIGERATOR
MODEL R11LC1

As a responsible manufacturer, Hitachi wish to advice that there is the possibility of the refrigerator door hinge assembly failing on a batch of larder refrigerators, model type R11LC1. Testing has shown that under certain conditions the door may come away from the hinges whilst being opened. The products concerned can be identified by the serial number which is located on the rating label inside the fridge at the top right hand side.

The serial numbers in question are between:

91010001 to 91529999 or 11500001 to 20299999

If your Hitachi Fridge has a serial number in this range or if you are in any doubt please telephone:

FREEPHONE 0800 525357

(Lines open 7 am−10 pm daily)

Quoting the model and full serial number. Alternatively please complete and return the coupon below. Arrangements will then be made for our service engineer to visit, inspect and modify your product free of charge.

In the meantime we strongly advise that you do not subject the door to any heavy or additional loads which may stress the door hinges. Please take extra care with young children.

No other Hitachi products are affected.

Thank you for your cooperation.

Reproduced here is a no-nonsense recall notice about a faulty plug on Tricity Bendix microwave ovens (Figure 32.1), and once again the manufacturer is to be commended on its effort to make amends. Such recalls can be difficult to conduct because while some customers can be contacted through guarantee cards and retailer's records, appliances are sold through a variety of outlets and customers may not necessarily buy for themselves.

So many organizations have become prey to disaster and crisis

RECALL NOTICE

TRICITY BENDIX MICROWAVE OVENS

This is an important safety announcement to owners of Tricity Bendix microwave ovens

Model <u>MT520</u>

Model <u>MV510</u>

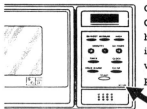

Our continuous Quality Control Programme has identified an isolated case of a wiring fault on the plug of the MT520 and MV510 microwave ovens sold in 1992.

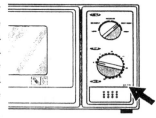

To check whether you own one of these ovens, you will find the model number located above the 'Door Open' button at the bottom right of the control panel on your microwave, as shown here.

If you own either of the models mentioned above, please **stop using the product immediately and remove the plug from the socket.**

Then telephone **0800 626090** (the call is free), and we will arrange for one of the Tricity Bendix Service team to visit you to carry out a free safety check.

We have already contacted some of our customers possibly affected by this notice, and we hope to contact the remainder through this advertisement. If you have recently acted on a letter from us on this matter, then ignore this notice.

We apologise for any inconvenience this may cause, and thank you for your co-operation in this matter.

This notice does not affect any other Tricity Bendix microwave oven or any other Tricity Bendix appliance.

**Tricity Bendix, 99 Oakley Road, Luton, Bedfordshire LU4 9QQ.
Tel: 0800 626090 (Freephone) Fax: 0582 588380**

Figure 32.1 *Example of a product recall notice*[8]

situations – often as a complete and devastating surprise to quote only the Bhopal tragedy – with serious anti public-relations implications, that this has become a major area of public relations. Moreover, it falls into the overall need to plan public relations strategy for the future.

The problem is how to detect and even accept the unthinkable and be prepared for its possible occurrence. Too many organizations do nothing because they sincerely believe crises are impossible. There is nothing new or remarkable about this: it was believed of the Titanic which proved not to be unsinkable although every previous ship had been. Other organizations are careless, as we have seen with airlines from whose aircraft bits have fallen off, even though it is well-known that this is not unusual. Refusal to recognize the fatigue-factor in much-flown workhorse aircraft has provoked bitter criticism of both plane-makers and airlines.

Following the terrible Amsterdam tragedy in 1992 Boeing and airlines flying 547s did not hesitate to publicize the fact that the bolts securing engines to wings were being tested and if necessary replaced.

The following account demonstrates the public relations role in the oil industry.

Bombay High blow-out

On Friday 30 July 1982, at 9.00 pm, a blow-out occurred in well SJ-5 that was being drilled from the jack-up rig Saga Vikas which the Oil and Natural Gas Commission (ONGC) was operating in the South Bombay High oil field. It was the first time such a disaster had occurred in India, and it created a picture of a volcano in mid-ocean.

A blow-out is a costly and spectacular hazard in oil exploration, but a known risk in the search for oil. It happens when the formation pressure so exceeds that of the drilling gear (and the chemical mud that is pumped in as the hole is drilled) that the formation fluid gushes out with an uncontrollable force.

On the fateful night of 30 July an uncontrollable flow of reservoir fluids – gas, muck, traces of oil and stones – was observed by men on the rig when well Number 5 was being drilled at a depth of 1660 metres. The rig was 78 nautical miles off Juhu coast in the Arabian Sea. The wind velocity was 13 knots and swell 15 feet high.

Immediately, the crew of 74 men were evacuated and ferried by helicopters to the Sagar Pragati, about 5 kilometres away. When the message reached the shore-base at Bombay, senior officials made helicopter flights at night to assess the situation and make plans for combating the blow-out. At the same time international help was sought to control the well.

The ONGC had a scoop situation with the sudden news which aroused a number of reactions. The media became restless for more news. The government was worried. The ONGC as an organization was stunned and depressed. Parliament, which was in session, awaited a statement from the Petroleum Minister. Ecologists were worried about pollution of the sea. A puzzled public wanted to know what had happened and why.

Next day an air force helicopter landed on the rig, and the emergency generators were switched off. The danger area was guarded by the air force, navy coastal guards and multi-purpose vessels for, in spite of efforts to prevent it, fire broke out on 2 August. It was put out in the afternoon of 5 August. The world-famous blow-out surgeon, Paul 'Red' Adair, was rushed to the rig and the killing and capping of the well was completed on 5 September. Even so, media attention lasted for 48 days.

The way the disaster was handled by the public relations department of ONGC, under the direction of M. L. Kaul, Additional Director (Public Relations), has become a celebrated case study which has since been reproduced as a full-colour pictorial report[9] with reproductions of press cuttings.

For three reasons, the blow-out attracted media and public interest. These were: the importance of petroleum in the national economy; the reputation of ONGC as India's number one public enterprise, which was now at risk; and the curiosity attached to an unprecedented disaster situation.

The Commission enjoys a responsible and participative management which coolly identified its priorities in the following order:

1 To contain the blow-out, fight fire, and mobilize resources, equipment and expertise internationally.
2 Maintain morale of the staff throughout the organization.
3 Ensure participation of the media in the effort to share information with the public and the opinion leaders so as to avert any blow-out of public opinion.

The media responded well and well-informed coverage resulted. Accurate news reached employees at their various workplaces. The policy of participative communication was sustained with the employees, the media and the public. The following communication strategy was evolved:

1 No room to be allowed for rumours.
2 Top ONGC management to become the spokespeople during the crisis.
3 Regular media briefings to be held in the evenings at the offshore headquarters in Bombay.
4 Press notes to be issued regularly and relayed to all the major centres of work.
5 Media to be given full facts and figures as well as any assistance in filing their reports.
6 Information level of the eagerly curious media personnel to be upgraded, particularly regarding technicalities involved in the blow-out.
7 Media to be taken to site for a fly-over as soon as helicopters become available.
8 Public Relations Office to remain in constant touch with radio room and collect eye-witness accounts of the happenings at the site from those reaching base.
9 Provide evidence, as far as possible, to substantiate statements made.
10 Monitoring of published media reports, particularly those not based on facts. Immediate clarifications to be given at the evening's media briefing.
11 Personal visits by top management to other installations in the area for direct communication of facts.
12 Blow-out and subsequent activities to be filmed for future reference, training and education.

A positive stance was achieved from the time of the original rescue story which demonstrated ONGC's responsibility for the safety of its employees. From then on ONGC had no need to be defensive or reactive.

On the night of the event the chief executive of ONGC, Colonel S. P. Wahi, made a report to the nation on the 10 o'clock TV news. In Parliament, the Minister of Petroleum made a full statement.

There were also some side-lights. The arrival of 'Red' Adair produced demands for extra media stories, and ONGC screened various films of blow-outs including *Hell Fighters* about 'Red' Adair.

Out of calamity came certain rewards, and perceptible gains were that:

1 ONGC added another dimension to its image.
2 Its own people developed a sense of pride and faith which gave it strength to rise to the occasion.

3   Capability to deal with the difficult situation made known ONGC's vitality and potential.
4   Blow-out received public acceptance as a normal hazard in oil exploration.
5   Experiment in participative communication proved successful. Media got involved in the entire operation from the start to the end, as they found each day a new day for 48 days.
6   Public relations came to be recognized as a key management function within the organization.

In the oil industry the *nature* of a possible crisis is predictable, but with a hotel, an airline or a manufacturer anything can happen, and it may be the result of external influences. In Europe and America, the oil industry has suffered many crises, sometimes with heavy fatalities. Nowadays, these companies have prepared emergency drills, including how to deal with the media.

References

1   Friend, Carol, interview, *PR Week*, 2 April 1986
2   *Crisis Communications in American Business*, prepared by Burson-Marsteller Research, New York for Western Union, Upper Saddle River, NJ, June 1984
3   *When Every Second Counts – Crisis Communication Planning*, Western Union, Upper Saddle River, NJ, 1984
4   *How to Develop a Crisis Communications Program*, Western Union, Upper Saddle River, NJ, 1985
5   'Volvo recalls automatics', *Daily Telegraph*, 26 April 1986
6   Jefkins, Frank, 'Corning case study', *Public Relations for Marketing Management*, 2nd edn, Macmillan, London 1984 (O.P.)
7   Hitachi advertisement, *The Independent*, 21 November 1992
8   Tricity Bendix advertisement, *The Independent*, 23 November 1992
9   *Communication in a Crisis Situation*, A public relations case study of the Bombay High blow-out, Oil & Natural Gas Commission, Dehra Dun, India

33

Sponsorship

Growth of sponsorship

In the past many arts and social services were sponsored by wealthy patrons. Composers, performers and artists depended on the patronage of the church, royalty, aristocracy and businessmen. The latter included people like Carnegie, Tate, Ford and Morris. Today, sponsorship has taken on a more commercial meaning, is applied to a variety of subjects and personalities, and is invested in for very specific business reasons. These reasons may be to do with marketing, advertising or public relations or be a blend of all three.

At the outset modern sponsorship should be regarded as a business investment for it is seldom a philanthropic gesture. Nor, for public relations purposes, is it to be mistaken for an image-building exercise, if only that images cannot be invented and different people perceive corporate images for particular reasons. Regrettably, a lot of nonsense is talked about images. When we have looked at the numerous reasons for undertaking a sponsorship it will be realized that to restrict it to image-building is to trivialize an important form of communication. This is a mistake often made by journalists.

As evidence of the growth of sponsorship, Coca-Cola spent $33m on the world-wide sponsorship right to be the official soft drink of the Barcelona Olympics, and a further $40m for the category exclusivity on US games broadcaster NBC; Carlsberg spend $1.8m a year supporting Britain's most famous football club, Liverpool; while according to Mintel, 75 per cent of British sponsorships favour sport to the tune of nearly £250m.

Does sponsorship pay? According to the Italian firm Montedison, its £100m yacht *Moro di Venezia* had the effect of increasing the company's share price[1] by 10 per cent when the yacht won the 1992 Americas Cup. Incidentally, it is interesting that SampsonTyrrell, whose corporate identity work is described in Chapter 29, also created the Venetian team logo for the 73 foot yacht which represented the company's latest technology and materials. This identity scheme and logo is featured in the author's *Public Relations*.[2]

More evidence of the phenomenal growth of sponsorship was the publication in 1993 of the 450 page *Hollis Sponsorship and Donations Yearbook*.[3] In its Foreword it quotes ABSA research showing a total investment in arts sponsorship of £65,459,894 in 1992, while sports sponsorship, according to Sportscan, grew by £1m in 1992 to an approximated £250m, confirming the Mintel figures quoted above.

Much of sponsorship is undertaken because it is capable of achieving media coverage, which is why subjects that gain regular media coverage such as football are the favourites. Why is media coverage sought? For many more substantial reasons than so-called 'image-building'! It can make names familiar, position them in particular markets, be more cost-effective than traditional advertising, or create goodwill.

Two kinds of sponsorship

There are two kinds of sponsorship, and until recently only the first kind was permitted in Britain. The first kind resembles the patronage already mentioned. The second kind, now allowed by the Independent Television Commission, the Radio Authority and to a lesser extent by the BBC, concerns the sponsorship of actual programmes, although limited to credits in the breaks. This chapter is mostly devoted to the traditional forms of sponsorship such as sponsored events and prizes, but closes with references to sponsored broadcast programmes.

The nature of sponsorship

Sponsorship may not be undertaken wholly for public relations pur-poses, but even when its primary objectives are marketing or advertising there can be an important public relations element. If we consider some of the marketing and advertising aspects first it will be easier to detail and define the public relations content.

Most of the larger sponsorships of sports are conducted because these popular events receive extensive TV coverage resulting in either repeated naming of the sponsor by all the media or by supporters. The Ever Ready Derby[4] is talked about for months in advance, and when the winning horse enters the winner's enclosure it is covered with a large saddle-cloth bearing the words *Ever Ready* which fills the TV screen. Similarly, other horse races, football and rugby championships, golf, tennis, snooker, bowls, darts and other sports events receive wide coverage by all the mass media. Sponsorship of the Football League over the years by Canon, *Today* newspaper and Barclays Bank has given them many months of media coverage, results being broadcast nightly and 92 teams being involved. Moreover, some aspects, such as football and Formula One motor racing, have international spin-offs. A Japanese company even sponsored a British golf tournament in order to get coverage on Japanese TV!

The tobacco industry is not permitted to advertise on radio or TV and is excluded from magazines with young readers. The cigarette companies have therefore taken up sponsorship, mainly in the arts and sports ranging from art shows to flying events and motor racing. The John Player Special and Marlboro racing cars are well known. Other sports such as golf, rugby and tennis have been supported by tobacco firms.

There is a large and influential anti-smoking lobby which objects to the tobacco firms either financing healthy pursuits, or subverting the ban on TV advertising by having their name-bearing racing cars and race circuit banners so that they are picked up repeatedly by TV cameras. The controversy hinges on whether it is good public relations for the tobacco companies (being manufacturers of allegedly harmful products) to promote sports and athletics, and to some people their activities may seem to be hypocritical. In fact, TV coverage of Grand Prix racing had to be abandoned in France because TV regulations forbade coverage of tobacco sponsorships.

Sponsorships do not have to be as costly or as extensive as those described above. They can be more modest, appealing perhaps to a smaller or more specialized audience, or they may be local ones such as supplying shoes, shirts or strip for local sports clubs.

An interesting development in recent years has been that some TV advertisers have recognized that there is a point when further purchase of airtime is not cost-effective, and that a given expenditure on sponsorship (with TV coverage) is more preferable. It can also be more economical than conventional advertising. At the end of their three-year sponsorship of the Football League Canon reckoned that to get one of their machines into most offices of Britain would have cost far more in advertising than the £3m sponsorship costs.

Threat of ambush marketing

Ambush marketing is an abuse of sponsorship which is often associated with major events such as the Olympic Games and various world cup events where an official paid-up sponsor has to compete with a pirate publicity seeker. The subject is featured in the *Hollis Sponsorship and Donations Yearbook*. It is defined by lawyers François de Zedtwitz and Nicholas Couchman who say 'Ambush or parastic marketing consists of the unauthorized association by companies of their business or brands with a sports event or competition through a wide range of marketing activities; unauthorized in the sense that the controller of the commercial rights in such events, usually the relevant governing body, has neither sanctioned nor licensed the association.'

It can be a grey area, as when arena or perimeter boards encircle a stadium where a sponsored event is being held, and the advertisers could be the sponsor's rivals. There can be more obvious examples when bodywear and souvenirs are hawked as being 'official'. The authors quoted above give the example of the Fuji airship, in its striking green and red colours, flying over the Seoul Olympic Games when Kodak had bought the official sponsorship rights. It is therefore unethical to exploit situations in this manner, but the offence has been committed by some famous firms.

Organization of sponsorship

There are two sides to sponsorship, those seeking funds and those who wish to engage in sponsorship. They may not necessarily be sympathetic to one another. A potential sponsor may wish to support something which traditionally has had no commercial connections and may consider them undesirable. In contrast, an organization or person in need of funds may make the mistake of imagining that businesses are wealthy and therefore likely to be willing benefactors, not realizing that commercial firms will ask what's in it for them. In between there are specialist agencies which match would-be sponsors with appropriate beneficiaries, and they plan and run the whole complex sponsorship programme. Among the best-known consultancies that specialize in sponsorship are Alan Pascoe Associates, Strategic Sponsorship, CSS International Holdings, DSM Sponsorship and Shandwick Sponsorship. The *Hollis Sponsorship and Donations Yearbook* lists more than 130 sponsorship consultancies.

Kinds of sponsorship

Subjects for sponsorship fall into certain broad categories of which sport predominates. These categories are sport, arts, books, exhibitions, feats and expeditions, educational and charity. The latter became more important when the 1986 Budget made charitable donations (including those in sales promotion schemes) more attractive to companies.

Sport

This form of sponsorship predominates all over the world, and also includes the special sports which are native to certain countries. Other sports are conducted internationally and may be supported by multi-nationals because of their coverage by world media. Grand Prix motor racing takes place at many circuits round the world, and is watched by television audiences everywhere. Sponsors will choose the sports which are most appropriate to their markets, whether it be the mass market, a particular market segment, or the women's or youth markets. Coca-Cola has concentrated on young people's interests such as swimming and athletics, while Cornhill chose test match cricket to reach the household insurance market.

However, motor sport attracts some unlikely sponsors. Benetton, infamous for some of its poster advertising, supports Formula One motor racing in its anxiety to make people aware of its jumpers and franchised retailers. When handicapped by a name which could mean anything, extraordinary efforts may be considered necessary to make people aware of it, let alone what it stands for.

Dating from the 1930s, one of the oldest and an almost unofficial form of sponsorship, is the bottle of Robinson's Barley Water underneath the umpire's chair at Wimbledon. The idea originated when a Colman's employee thought the tennis players needed refreshment and so he provided a complimentary bottle! The 'sponsorship' has been repeated for some 60 years.

Britain's biggest sports sponsorship began with the 1993–4 football season, with the FA Premier League which became the FA Carling Premier League with a four-year £12m sponsorship package from the parent company, Bass. The brewers already sponsored the Tennents Charity Shield, the Tennents Scottish Cup and the Stones Rugby League Championship.

Earlier, there had been reluctance to accept the Carling sponsorship because a number of clubs such as Liverpool, Manchester United, Tottenham Hotspur, Nottingham Forest and Blackburn Rovers had shirt sponsorship contracts.

The Carling sponsorship differs from that of Canon and later sup-porters of the Football League, with its 92 clubs. Carling will be funding the 15 elite clubs of the Premier League. Another difference is that BSkyB bought the rights to televise Premier League matches, limiting viewers to those with satellite or cable TV, but this is offset by the popularity of the BBC's *Match of the Day*. Each club receives about £136,363 per season.

An increasing number of minority sports have found sponsors, such as netball and Evian mineral water, who have been able to associate their product with a healthy pursuit. Football has won many sponsors, and a number of teams have their strip blazoned with their sponsor's name, as with Manchester United and Sharp.

In 1993 McDonald's announced a £2m-plus sponsorship of British athletics, which was a change from its usual support for children's and community activities. Initially a two-year deal, it covered the Young Athletics League which in the past had launched the careers of several athletic celebrities. The sponsorship was negotiated by Alan Pascoe Associates, and included title sponsorship of ITV and Channel 4 coverage of the Don Valley Stadium athletics meeting in Sheffield. This particular sponsorship had special values since it was a televised sport which interested men and women equally of all social and age groupings.

A large number of sports sponsorships are Japanese. The Japanese rely heavily on name displays and creating awareness of these names. There are possibly two reasons for this. In Japan, television commercials are entertainments which conclude with bold, simple name displays, unlike our type of commercial in which products are demonstrated. World-wide, Japanese firms favour bold lighted night signs which spell out company names like Sony or Fuji. Throughout the world, Japanese firms have indulged in sponsorship, sometimes to create goodwill towards a former enemy, and particularly in the West to familiarize markets with unfamiliar Japanese names. They include Canon, Citizen Watch, JVC, Mitsubishi, Nikon, Panasonic and Seiko.

According to RSL Sponsortest Weekly Tracking studies, the public awareness of who sponsors what is remarkably high, and people still remember sponsorships that occurred three or four years earlier if there was strong media exposure.

Tobacco companies have resorted to motor, golf, snooker and tennis sponsorships in order to gain TV coverage in spite of the ban on TV advertising for their products. This has aroused the hostility of both the anti-smoking lobby and politicians to the extent that both EC directives and national legislation will make such sponsorship less possible. Motor sport, with its international Grand Prix events held in different countries and enjoying world-wide TV coverage, has already led to France's banning the televising of events in which racing cars were sponsored by tobacco firms. Australia has decided to ban sport sponsorship by tobacco firms from 1995, which means a loss of £8m in backing money. A problem for the BBC is that cameras can inadvertently pick up perimeter boards promoting tobacco products at sports meetings.

Arts

Historically, with the patronage of the arts by wealthy people, this is where sponsorship began. Today, there are sponsored orchestras, concerts, operas, ballets, theatricals, recordings, art shows, theatres, museums, book awards, and many other cultural organizations and events. Many of them, such as symphony orchestras, would not survive but for commercial support. Arts Council or local authority grants are often inadequate or not made at all. Some politicians have quite cynically said that the arts should be supported by commercial patrons, rather than by the tax payer.

The problem with many arts is that they represent minority public interests. Why, it may be asked, should pop enthusiasts pay for symphony orchestras with 120 players? Shakespeare's plays may be part of the national heritage, but should the public pay for their performance? And if a commercial sponsor funds cultural subjects, what benefits is it likely to enjoy? It is an interesting question but nevertheless a number of arts survive simply because organizations as diverse as British Gas, Lloyds Bank and Royal Insurance are willing to be seen to finance them.

An example was the sponsorship by Royal Insurance of Royal Shakespeare Company performances at Stratford-upon-Avon, tickets being offered at only £6, limited to two tickets per person per day. These 'armchair proms' were advertised in journals such as the *Independent's* Saturday magazine with an application form for tickets. Even if one did not wish to buy tickets the gesture no doubt helped to enhance the reputation of Royal Insurance as a responsible company. Feeling nice towards Royal Insurance could influence one's choice of an insurer, and is rather more substantial than image-building. It does little to create an 'image' since the announcement of the sponsorship gave no hint whether the company offered life, fire, motor or any other kind of insurance.

Digital is a firm which saw sponsorship as a better way than advertising in order, as a newcomer to the UK, to communicate with its 8000 most important potential buyers, sponsoring dance events to which it invited 6000 of its buyers between 1986 and 1992.

The Prudential is also an arts sponsor, giving a £75,000 prize to the 1992 dance festival Dance Umbrella, and it has also sponsored Opera North and the Huddersfield Contemporary Music festival. The Prudential spent £260,000 on arts sponsorship in 1992, an increase on previous years in spite of the financial problems of the insurance industry.

This is an area of sponsorship which has seen remarkable growth since the 1980s, and the Association of Business Sponsorship of the

Arts reported an expenditure of £57m in 1990−1 compared with £30m in previous years.

In some Third World countries sponsorship is one of the few expressions of public relations by commercial companies, possibly because of the limitations of media and literacy. Years ago, in Trinidad, sponsorship proved to be socially valuable. There used to be rival gangs which would meet and fight in the streets. Each gang had a steel band. An oil company had the bright idea of sponsoring one of these bands, and other companies copied. Energies were transferred from gangland battles to steel band competitions, and so sponsorship became an excellent public relations medium. A steel band can have a large number of performers, like an orchestra, and hours can be taken up in practice sessions.

Books

In addition to the sponsorship of book awards, such as the Booker and the Whitbread, which may also be forms of arts or cultural sponsorship, there is also the sponsorship of publications. Many of these are sold through booksellers and can be legitimate and profitable ventures, like the series of Guinness publications of which the *Guinness Book of Records* is the most famous. There are also long-established sports and motoring annuals, guides, maps, DIY guides, gardening and cookery books, to which firms such as Rothman, Shell and Michelin have lent their names.

In addition, there is the specialized publication of authoritative books on technical subjects which are expensive to produce, are written by company experts and carry the imprint of a well-known publishing house. The sponsor contributes to the production costs, provides the author, and usually buys a quantity of copies for distribution to staff, friends or customers. The Rentokil Library of books on pest control is a good example of this.

Another form of sponsorship, which is common in the American academic world, is for a commercial company to sponsor the research and publication of a work by a university academic. Unfortunately, this sometimes leads to some large tomes which would not normally be commercially viable or even desirable. This practice is less prevalent in Britain.

Exhibitions

Many exhibitions, both trade and public, are sponsored by newspaper and magazine publishers, or by trade associations, professional bodies and voluntary societies. The *Daily Mail* Ideal Home Exhibition is an example of a public exhibition and it has been held for a great many years. Attendance at a trade exhibition may be encouraged by the issuing of free admission tickets in the sponsoring magazine which in turn helps to attract exhibitors to participate. A number of trade magazines sponsor exhibitions.

Feats and expeditions

Many feats, such as mountain climbs, exploratory ventures, one-man voyages round the world, journeys to the North Pole, and other endurance tests have to be financed, and this is done by a single sponsor, by a number of companies which contribute either funds or equipment and supplies, or by a publisher or TV company.

In supporting these remarkable endeavours the sponsor needs to be clear about its likely rewards. Is it purely a question of philanthropy or are media coverage and other credits expected? Sometimes the sponsor's name will be publicly associated (as when a boat has the sponsor's name on the hull or sail), but it is possible for sponsored contributions to be virtually anonymous. Sponsors of such subjects need to be aware of the scope or limitations of their support. On one occasion a bank was criticized for financing an expedition, but when there was world acclaim for its success the bank was congratulated on its foresight. Smiths Industries once gained considerable publicity by providing Tensing with a watch for his conquest of Everest, but a brewer complained that he got no credit for supplying a round-the-world solo yatchsman with a keg of beer.

Educational

Bursaries, scholarships, awards, fellowships and university chairs may be sponsored by commercial interests. This may contribute to the advancement of the industry, provide the sponsor with high-calibre recruits, and often be a long-lasting form of support. There are many colleges or college buildings which bear the name of the sponsor in perpetuity.

Charity

The 1986 Budget made charitable donations more attractive to companies, as stated in *Sponsorship News*.[5]

Up until now, charitable advertising – with a few exceptions – has tended to be more associated with patronage than with the modern meaning of sponsorship: a two-way commercial agreement of equal benefit to both.

Charity sponsorships can take many forms, ranging from the Texaco example in Chapter 31, which involved employees, to those which are sales promotion schemes whereby tokens from products have value as contributions which the manufacturer promises to make to a charity. Some charities, such as Marie Curie Cancer Care, are actually seeking funds from commercial sponsors in addition to their regular sources of income like legacies and direct mail appeals for donations. One major supporter of charities is Tesco, which receives some 1000 letters a week begging for funds. One of Tesco's chosen charities is Birthright, which finances research for the benefit of women and babies. Birthright reciprocated by producing a healthy eating advisory leaflet which was distributed through Tesco's chain of supermarkets, which have 9 million customers a week.

Another example of charity sponsorship was that by Lyons Tetley brand World of Coffee on behalf of Cancer Relief Macmillan Fund. Coffee mornings for more than 300,000 people were held across Britain, providing sampling opportunities and media coverage, and raising £250,000 for CRMF in four hours from the world's biggest coffee morning.

Some of the leading charities depend very much on funding by corporate bodies, and the National Trust is a good example. It may be thought that membership fees from more than 2 million members, entrance fees to 200 houses and parks, plus catalogue and shop sales would provide income enough. The National Trust also has to maintain those properties, including their restoration, and it also protects 600,000 acres of land. Consequently, it needs sponsors and according to the Trust's annual report[6] for 1992, it has 23 corporate sponsors, while 19 others have financed special projects, gifts in kind have been received from 11 companies, and monies were received from 70 trusts. Among all these contributions was £40,000 from Ford of Britain to finance the Trust's well-known Handbook for Members and Visitors which every member receives, £50,000 from Northumbrian Water Ltd for coastal management in Northumbria and Yorkshire, and £20,000 from Fisons plc to finance the Information for Visitors with Disabilities booklet.

Reasons for sponsorship

As will have been demonstrated by some of the given examples, sponsors have very definite reasons for spending money on sponsorship. It was rarely for a simplistic reason such as creating an image, more often because it actually did something such as being more effective or more economical than conventional advertising. The modern businessperson is not a philanthropist.

So, clear objectives should be established before indulging in sponsorship. We may be talking hundreds of thousands, even millions, of pounds. Why should a sponsorship deal be contemplated, either by intention or invitation? Alongside these objectives should be matched the considerations − especially costs − which follow this section. It may be that the chairman likes village cricket − as happened with a certain whisky sponsorship − but is that a sound commercial reason for spending a lot of money? The whims of chairmen have certainly resulted in certain sponsorships, but it can be an expensive luxury. If the public relations manager or consultant wishes to recommend sponsorship, the homework needs to have been done. The idea needs to be substantiated by acceptable reasons supported by an estimate of total costs and likely results. Let us therefore examine some practical reasons for engaging in sponsorship.

Corporate image

We will start with this one because it is often talked about rather glibly as the main reason for sponsorship, but usually there are more hard-fisted practical ones. However, one of the benefits of sponsorship is to establish what a company is and does. Canon, *inter alia* wanted to be seen as a maker of office machines as well as cameras, and also to distinguish itself from makers of cookers, steel, rubber products and an insurance company with a similar name. However, its primary objective was to establish itself as number one among office machine manufacturers, which it did by sponsoring the Football League for three years.

Corporate identity

By means of sponsorship a company can make familiar its logo, house colour, typography, livery and other physical representations to intensify recognition of its corporate identity. This can then relate to many commercial activities such as correspondence, sales literature, advertising, packaging, vehicles and so on.

Name familiarization

Sponsorship offers intensive repetition of a company or brand name, which may be necessary with a new or foreign name, or to make sure that a well-established name continues to be remembered. Moreover, people tend to trust a name they know. Sponsorship may be a way of penetrating foreign markets where the name is unfamiliar, and where traditional advertising methods would be slow and costly, or not even possible in some parts of the world. It is significant that throughout the world Japanese companies (whose promotions are always more name than product-benefit conscious) have used sponsorships as a means of establishing themselves in foreign markets. They sponsor a large number of sports in Britain. Sponsorship exploits that elementary form of advertising, repetition.

Even so, it can be a slow process for companies to penetrate foreign markets. Continental Europe is notoriously stubborn in favouring its own products, such as makes of motorcar, German, French and Italian motorcars dominating their home markets unlike the situation in Britain. McCann-Erickson Europe published a report in February 1993 which showed that few Japanese brands had captured European consumer consciousness. Out of 20 brands, only Sony and Toyota gained a place as a top brand.

Goodwill

The Japanese have excelled here too, using the goodwill created by sponsorships to overcome prejudices in countries which they either occupied or fought during the Second World War. This has been no mean achievement, especially in countries such as Hong Kong, Indonesia, Malaysia and Singapore where hardly a British motorcar is to be seen today whereas Japanese vehicles of all kinds dominate the roads. The Japanese, like the Scandinavian and Dutch economies, depend on exports.

The sponsor and the sponsored subject are not the only beneficiaries of sponsorship: it is enjoyed by thousands, perhaps millions of people, as with the Olympic Games, who attend, watch, view, listen to or read about it. Pleasure and gratitude can generate goodwill towards the provider of enjoyment.

Goodwill can also be created when a company provides a service for its customers by funding events, as the Midland Bank has done with promenade ballets and operas among other cultural events.

Understanding

We should not forget the basic purpose of public relations, which is to create understanding, and implicit in the four previous objectives is the over-riding one of creating understanding of an organization and its products or services. This is worth repeating as a separate yet unifying objective. An interesting example of this was the way in which Yamaha emphasized that its sponsorship of snooker was on behalf of its organs, not its motorcycles.

Dealer relations

Another aim may be to strengthen dealer relations by engaging in sponsorships which help the stockist to promote products. Window displays may be organized with the sponsorship, especially when the sponsor has been successful in winning an event, or the product, e.g. a tyre, has been used by a successful participant. Special showcards or posters can be supplied to dealers so that they may arrange topical displays. A winning safari car, still spattered with mud, can make a dramatic display. Sponsorships can also be featured in external house journals distributed to dealers, or provide news items for the trade press.

Staff relations

Employers may well take pride in the sponsorship activities of their company and may be able to participate in them. Cornhill discovered that their support for test match cricket enjoyed the spin-off of being a morale booster for their staff. Sponsors of race horses and show jumpers have taken parties of employees to events to see the horses perform. Sponsorships can also feature in staff house journals.

Video records

Sponsorships can be recorded on video and the video used for a variety of public relations purposes. One of the most exciting videos ever made was of the Cameroon Mountain Race, involving the ascent and descent of a mountain in West Africa, sponsored by Guinness Cameroon. The video was made from edited television coverage, and has been shown by Guinness all over the world. Thus, sponsorship provides the opportunity to produce a video which can be shown to many audiences on numerous occasions. It can also be circulated to overseas staff in a multi-national company.

Media interest

The sponsor may have suffered from meagre interest in the past, but sponsorship could make them extremely newsworthy, and so awaken media interest which could be sustained in the future. When sports or leagues are sponsored they are so named by the media – it is the Whitbread Gold Cup horse race, the Ever Ready Derby, the Coca-Cola football cup final, the Barclays football league, the Vauxhall International athletics, the Silk Cut Rugby League Challenge Cup, the Royal Bank of Scotland hockey cup, and the Benson and Hedges Masters snooker tournament. These credits are given in press, radio and TV reports, in the listing magazines and by commentators.

Even where there is no direct coverage on TV it is possible to produce a video news release and supply it for news bulletin coverage, as occurred for instance with the Atlantic crossing of the *Sea Cat* catamaran ferry.

Hospitality

An excellent public relations purpose for sponsorship is to provide an opportunity to play host to one's business friends and clients. This can range from organizing parties of visitors to an event, such as a show-jumping evening, to the provision of free tickets to football matches. With 92 football teams in the Football League, the latter provides hospitality opportunities every week for nine months, an aspect which Canon exploited to the full during their three-year sponsorship. They also organized product displays at stadiums, and invited customers to see these as well as watch the local match.

Essential considerations

When investing in sponsorship for marketing, advertising or public relations reasons, and often it is a combination of these, it is necessary to determine whether a proposed sponsorship merits the expenditure and promises the desired results. Sometimes the expectations are clearly defined, but they may be obscure and of doubtful fulfilment. There are, for example, many feats and expeditions which require supplies. No one is likely to know of their provision and they are best regarded as charitable gifts not to be confused with commercial sponsorship.

The prospective sponsor must choose carefully, for he or she will be invited to fund a hundred-and-one ventures whose organizers regard business as a treasure house to be plundered. It is very easy to waste money on dubious sponsorships which are no better than buying advertisement space in charity programmes and magazines. The modern sponsor is rarely interested in giving money away, but is intent on receiving a good return for an investment. Both sides should benefit from a sponsorship.

Media coverage

A primary consideration is either the volume or the kind of media coverage that may be expected. Not all the media will credit the sponsor (as has been seen with some round-the-world yacht races), but this reticence is disappearing, as mentioned above in the section on 'Media interest' and commentators on radio and television, and press journalists, will now identify more readily the event or prize with the sponsor's name.

But it may be necessary to augment and reinforce the sponsor's name by some visible means which cannot be avoided or ignored. Names will be blazoned on players' or participants' clothing, or on vehicles or equipment which may be used, on the saddle cloths of show jumpers and, in the case of the Derby, on the huge saddle cloth which is spread over the back of the winning horse. Racing cars usually bear the names of several co-sponsors. Additionally, arena advertising boards may be hired in sports stadiums, large poster sites may be erected beside a race track, and banners may feature prominently at motor racing circuits.

Media coverage is not limited to the actual happening, but can extend before and after an event, as occurs with much talked about events such as the Grand National steeplechase, the Derby and the London marathon.

The cost

The full extent of the cost has to be reckoned very carefully, and a prospective sponsor may have to understand that costs are likely to exceed the initial one of supporting the object of the sponsorship, such as provision of prize money or a trophy. It could be double that. There can be many add-on costs, ranging from advertising to hospitality, which the sponsor has to meet.

Team maintenance

The cost of sponsoring a racehorse or show jumper means that it has to be fed, stabled, trained, transported and ridden, and the rider may or may not be sponsored too. There can also be veterinary fees, and entry fees for events. Racehorses, show jumpers and riders are sponsored as well as the races or events in which they run or jump. A yacht or powerboat has to be maintained, serviced, crewed and moored. A motor racing team is a very expensive unit with cars, spares, drivers and mechanics, and transport, all of which has to be financed, including the cost of travel and accommodation abroad.

Hospitality

As already mentioned above, the sponsor may feel obliged, or may wish, to provide entertainment and refreshments while the event is taking place. It could be 'a day at the races' for company guests, or lunch-boxes for the journalists in the commentators' box, be they sports writers or radio and TV commentators. This latter courtesy is much appreciated. There may be still more hospitality needs or opportunities, such as refreshment tents, meals while participants are travelling and overnight accommodation for them. Some of these catering items may be covered by co-sponsors, as when drinks are provided for marathon runners.

However, over-generous hospitality can have a boomerang effect, and some famous companies have been criticized by journalists for the obviously lavish provision of free drinks at events such as Conservative and Labour Party Annual Conferences.

Publications and print

Posters, leaflets, brochures, souvenirs, rule books, fixture lists, timetables, programmes, score cards and so on may be necessary or desirable for use by participants or the public. For instance, all those involved in the scheme may need a manual explaining what is required by everyone or how the benefits of the scheme are distributed. Posters and banners may be required for events, as when a newspaper sponsors a boxing match. The *Daily Mirror* and *Sunday Mirror* have usually sponsored Chris Eubank fights. Programmes may be needed for theatre and concert audiences, catalogues for visitors to an art exhibition. Admission or invitation tickets may have to be printed. The print bill could be substantial and must not be overlooked. Some publications such as catalogues, programmes and souvenir books may be sold.

Provision of clothing, equipment and supplies

Part of the sponsorship contract may be the supply of company products, but in what quantity, when and how often are supplies required, and when and where are they to be delivered? Again, considerable costs may be involved which are unlikely to stop at the goods themselves but may involve production, staffing, packaging, transportation and possibly actual provision at venues at home and abroad.

Each sponsorship will have its own individual supply problems concerning clothing, working equipment, food and drinks and manpower. Shirts for footballers, shoes for athletes, tennis racquets and cricket balls for players, golf balls for golfers, saddle-cloths for horses, overalls for mechanics, tyres for cars, all kinds of spare parts and repair and maintenance services; all manner of provisions, catering and catering services may be required. These are the sort of logistics which will justify the use of specialist consultancies such as those listed in the *Hollis Sponsorship and Donations Yearbook*.

Advertising

Participation in the event may need to be advertised, or included in current product advertising as is seen in poster advertising which carries a notice (such as a special strip pasted on the poster) drawing attention to, say, a Grand Prix event in which the advertiser's motorcar is racing. It may be necessary to advertise the event itself if the sponsor is the organizer, in order to attract an attendance. When events are televised, sponsors may buy space in the *Radio Times* or *TV Times*, or on the sports pages of newspapers. Advertisement space may also be bought in programmes published by the promoters and sold to members of the public. Arena boards, placards, beside-the-track signs, bunting, banners and flags may also be used, and inevitably these are picked up by the television cameras. Motor racing circuits, for instance, are festooned with the banners of sponsors such as Marlboro cigarettes, but as was seen in 1992 this led to the French authorities banning Grand Prix racing from French television.

Creative work

For some sponsorships a new logo may be devised, linking the company to the sponsored event, and this may even be adopted as the company's permanent logo. It is not easy to create something original, distinctive, characteristic and memorable, and it will usually be a complete corporate identity scheme including symbol, colour and typography. This will usually require the services of a specialist corporate identity expert such as SampsonTyrrell.

Photography is bound to play an important part. Many print items will need illustrations. Pictures will be needed for the media. The event may be the subject of later print work, not forgetting the annual report and possibly a calendar.

Sponsorship can be exploited in many ways in the future, or this future exploitation may be part of the sponsorship design. Either way, the costs have to be budgeted prior to taking up the sponsorship. Another popular creative item has been the video, which can be shown on numerous future occasions to employees, stockists, various publics and at press receptions and on exhibition stands.

Fees and salaries

The budget must also include the cost of hiring specialist consultants to negotiate possible contracts, and to administer the sponsorship. As can be seen from the foregoing, this can be a complex and highly skilled business. The sponsor will also need to allocate in-house staff to collaborate with the consultant. Where such work is an on-going affair it may be necessary to engage a sponsorship manager, as Lloyds Bank do, and this person may be totally responsible for sponsorship work or will liaise to a larger or lesser extent with an outside consultant. Either way, there is a manpower cost to budget.

Research

Finally, the sponsor should seek an evaluation. This may consist of a calculation of media coverage, and there are firms such as Sportscan and Research Services Ltd which monitor the press, radio and TV coverage achieved by sponsorships. Meticulous reports can be compiled of days, times and programmes of broadcast coverage, together with details of dates, media and volume of press coverage. The ITV Association publishes reports on the results of sponsored programmes, e.g. an extensive one on the Sony sponsorship of the Rugby World Cup.[7]

International Sponsorship Research of London offers a world-wide research and evaluation service, specializing in TV and media evaluation, and manages international research programmes for the Olympic Games, World Cup Soccer and World Championship Athletics. Sponsortrack, conducted by the British Market Research Bureau of Ealing, uses the Target Group Index database of 24,000 adults, targets samples to select minority samples, uses qualitative research, and also targets the business community and conducts international studies.

The European Sponsorship Consultants Association Guide to Sponsorship Practice

Produced on behalf of the ESCA by its honorary legal advisor, Stephen Townley, this 25-page guide[8] is published to help a potential client choose the right consultant. The services available from ESCA are of two kinds: those of ESCA members, representing the interests of the buyers of sponsorship rights or opportunities, and those of the interests of sellers of such opportunities, i.e. event or rights owners. Prospective members of the ESCA, which was founded in 1990, have 'to conform to criteria with regard to financial stability, track record, numbers of staff and length of experience'. They are also required in their dealings to abide by a Code of Professional Conduct designed to protect interests of their clients. Breach of the Code can lead to expulsion of the member.

The contents of the Guide include: Why ESCA?; Examples of Services; Engaging an ESCA Member; Specific Issues on Engagement; Consultant Checklist; Services Checklist; ESCA Policy on Programme Sponsorship; and ESCA Code of Conduct.

Sponsored broadcasting

When commercial broadcasting was first permitted in Britain just over 40 years ago, it was protected from the excesses of American broadcasting where the original soap operas were literally whole radio programmes sponsored by soap and other companies. In the 1980s we saw some relaxation of the rules, especially with BBC television programmes such as British Gas cathedral concerts and the Lloyds Bank Young Musician of the Year contest.

The Broadcasting Act 1990 brought about fundamental changes. The Independent Broadcasting Authority (covering both ITV and ILR) was replaced by the Independent Television Commission with responsibility for awarding regional commercial TV franchises, and the Radio Authority responsible for awarding both local and national commercial radio franchises. As a result of the auction of franchises some established stations such as Thames and Southern were replaced by Carlton and Meridian, and TV-am lost to Good Morning TV. The first national radio stations were Classic FM (which earned fame by popularizing the Polish Henryk Gorecki's 3rd Symphony, outselling Madonna in the Top Ten) and Virgin Radio.

Under the Act, commercial TV and radio programmes may now be sponsored, although the sponsor has no control over the programme and their products must not be featured. Instead, in the case of ITV programmes, there may be brief commercials in trailers, at the beginning and end of programmes, where there are breaks, these commercials being known as bumper breaks.

Doubtless, recession did not encourage a wild rush to exploit this new opportunity, but in 1992 £12m was spent on such sponsorship, and in 1993 £25m. Except for long-running sponsorships such as PowerGen's funding of the national weather forecast, the sponsorships of drama series cost around £500,000.

Two interesting things may be observed. Some of these sponsorships are well-matched to the product, e.g. Croft Port and *Rumpole of the Bailey*, Kronenbourg the French beer and *Inspector Maigret*, Beamish stout and *Inspector Morse*, and Legal and General's coloured umbrella logo and the weather forecast on London Weekend TV. The second point of interest is the ingenuity of creative effects in these very brief commercials or bumper breaks, several being devised by Media Dimensions.

Other sponsorships have been *Wish You Were Here* (Barclaycard), *Poirot* (AEG), Soccer World Cup (National Power), *It's A Dog's Life* (Pedigree Petfoods), *Prime Suspect* (Peugeot 106) and *Darling Buds of May* (Tetley Tea).

Is the sponsorship of television programmes a form of advertising or of public relations, or maybe a blend of each? In an article in *PR Week*, 'Switching On to TV' by Amanda Hall, Robin Courage of the Rowland Company was quoted as saying 'Programme sponsorship links a brand with the inherent values of the programme so that it takes on the qualities of that programme. A lot of people in advertising don't understand that. There are examples of deals that involve straight-forward buying of credits, but generally programme sponsorship is not an advertising buy.'[9] He suggests that one reason why broadcast sponsorship has not taken off is because it is being sold as airtime by the TV companies.

Commercial radio sponsorships take a slightly different form, with the presenter introducing the programme by declaring that it is broad-cast 'in association' with a funder followed by a brief statement or slogan. Sometimes these are long-running sponsorships, such as Nescafé's eight-year sponsorship of the Network Chart Show, or Rowntree-Mackintosh's Kit–Kat rock magazine series. They may be networked to many ILR stations or be limited to one station, such as the sponsorship of 'flying eye' traffic reports on Capital Radio.

The Network Chart Show is worth about £1m a year. From 1 August 1993 it was taken over by Pepsi. It is a three-hour package networked to 60 ILR stations, and has been broadened to include charts representing other musical tastes.

References

1   The Sports Business Survey, *The Economist*, London, 25 July 1992
2   Jefkins, Frank, *Public Relations*, 4th edn, Pitman, M&E Handbook, London, 1992
3   *Hollis Sponsorship and Donations Yearbook*, Hollis Directories, Sunbury-on-Thames, 1993
4   Jefkins, Frank, *Advertising*, 2nd edn, Pitman, M&E Handbooks, London, 1991

5   *Sponsorship News*, editorial, Wokingham, May 1986

6   Annual Report, National Trust, London, 1992

7   *ITV Rugby World Cup Sponsorship Research*, ITV Association, London, 31 January 1992

8   *European Sponsorship Consultants Association Guide to Sponsorship Practice*, ESCA, Chesham, 1990

9   Hall, Amanda, article, 'Switching On to TV', *PR Week*, 17 March 1992

34

Corporate and issue advertising

When we have sought to distinguish public relations from advertising, why does public relations, and especially public affairs, resort to advertising?

In planning public relations campaigns it is necessary to choose the best media for transmitting the message most effectively. When it is necessary to control the content of the message, and when, where and how it is to appear, the answer is advertising. Thus advertising is used:

1 To establish a corporate image.
2 To announce financial results.
3 To contest political policies, e.g. nationalization (as used to happen under Labour governments).
4 To contest or support a takeover bid.
5 To position a company regarding issues of the day.

Points 2 and 4 really belong to financial advertising, and point 3 verges on propaganda. So this chapter will be devoted to image and issue advertising.

Image advertising

Following the aggressive and knocking advertising used in certain takeover battles the Takeover Panel of the London Stock Exchange issued restrictions which took effect on 7 April 1986. These restrictions apply to advertisements about takeover offers and defences against them, but exclude 'product or corporate image advertisements not bearing on an offer or potential offer'.

A number of companies have become the prey of predators simply because shareholders and financial institutions did not know how good they were, and because their share prices had fallen due to lack of confidence in the money market. Their financial public relations had been neglected, and probably they had done no corporate advertising until it was too late. Then, in desperation, they indulged in expensive and usually useless last-ditch defensive advertising.

Corporate advertising is therefore a way of augmenting financial public relations. It has the advantage of making a company very visible and better understood. It may be very necessary when the full extent of a company's activities are not fully or widely known.

Corporate advertising also reflects on consumer attitudes to products, especially if they are not long-established household names. As Robert Worcester of MORI said in an article in *Campaign*:

> Two Britons in three believe that 'a company that has a good reputation would not sell poor quality products' and this figure has remained stable for the fifteen years or so that MORI has been measuring it. The bottom line is that people are most likely to try a new product from a company they regard highly than from a faceless conglomerate. They're also more likely to apply to a familiar firm for a job, buy its shares, believe its pronouncements and read its ads if they feel they know the company well and have a high regard for it.[1]

However this may be achieved, a corporate image is derived from knowledge and experience. Corporate advertising can contribute to this image-building by presenting information in attractive advertising. The quality of the advertising, e.g. the various Shell campaigns over the years, can enhance the corporate image. Image advertising can, for instance, show that a company is socially responsible, or employs high quality staff (as in IBM campaigns) as well as that it is a successful business. The latter can be achieved by using the narrative style to claim credit for achievement. Its presence in prestigious media can also help.

It is an expensive form of public relations, which means it is likely to be indulged in only by large companies, but then they are the ones most likely to be 'faceless conglomerates', prone to takeover bids or to want to take others over.

Many of these image advertisements appear in business journals such as *The Economist* and *Fortune*. Campaigns should not be short-lived, and the leading exponents of corporate advertising maintain series over the years. This persistence alone can exude confidence for it indicates that a company is consistently proud of its record. The following Bayer advertisement[2] is a good example:

Bayer: Expertise with Responsibility
Genetic research
paves the way for
medical progress.
It's our responsibility
to keep it on the
straight and narrow.

Gene technology has opened the way to totally new medical discoveries. It is helping us to find the origins of previously incurable diseases and so understand their causes and find cures.

Such knowledge is needed urgently, for there are still over twenty thousand illnesses for which there are at present no available remedies. They include cancers, AIDS, multiple sclerosis and rheumatism.

But if molecular research opens up new horizons, it gives us a duty to act responsibly. That is why it is Bayer's declared policy not to engage in developments that pose ethical problems, such as genetic experiments on the human germ line.

If you would like more information on our research write to:
Bayer plc, Department A, Newbury, Berks, RG13 IJA.
Bayer

Issue advertising

Here we have something different, and it is sometimes called 'advocacy' advertising. While a comparative stranger in Britain, it has been adopted quite widely in the USA, particularly during the past two decades.

One of the most dramatic uses of issue advertising has been that of Mobil Oil's 'op-eds', which first appeared on 19 October 1970. They came about when the *New York Times* introduced a second editorial page facing the original one and offered a quarter of the new page as space for image advertisements. Mobil converted this into issue advertising on all manner of topics not necessarily to do with the company or the oil industry. Similar 'op-eds' were inserted in other newspapers all over the USA.

These commentaries on public issues might seem irrelevant to the corporate image and yet in a Harris survey in 1976 on how the American public regarded forty major corporations, including seven oil companies, Mobil came out well and was seen to be the industry's pacesetter on nineteen out of twenty-one issues set out in the survey. Mobil continued to run these ads into the 1980s and many are reproduced in the book written by Herb Schmertz, vice-president for public affairs at Mobil.[3]

The objective of much issue advertising is to position a company in relation to the main policy issues of the day. Mobil uses issue advertising as a form of creative confrontation because the company has been treated unfairly by the media.

Large corporations are apt to be the victims of 'big is bad' prejudices by press, radio and TV journalists who seem to have a common left-wing or intellectual hatred of big business. Such critics fail to realize that big companies can only become big because they are popular and successful, because people like what they sell and they are well managed. Green seems to be the favourite colour of journalists, who bear the same grudge against public relations.

References

1   Worcester, Robert, 'Why corporate advertising is the key to public goodwill', *Campaign*, 16 May 1986
2   Bayer advertisement, *The Economist*, 24 October 1992
3   Schmertz, Herb (with Novak, William), *Goodbye to the Low Profile*, Mercury Books, London, 1986

35

Political and parliamentary public relations

Lobbying defined

This sphere of public relations is a practical example of public relations being two-way communication. It involves business and other organizations being made aware of Parliamentary procedures and activities which are of concern to them, and individual organizations and pressure groups putting their case to legislators. The latter is known as lobbying, and a 'lobby' represents a particular interest. In Europe, this type of public relations activity stretches beyond national politics to those of the EC in Brussels, Luxembourg and Strasbourg.

The expression 'lobbying' (as discussed in this chapter) should not be confused with those political journalists known as lobby correspondents. In a rather general sense, the word lobby refers to the large corridor where people meet in the House of Commons. Lobby correspondents, as distinct from the political journalists who report proceedings from the Press Gallery, are limited to journalists accredited by the Sargeant at Arms who are allowed access to certain parts of the Palace of Westminster, and lobby terms refer to non-attributable information given to journalists by ministers. In 1986 *The Guardian* and *The Independent* refused to supply lobby correspondents because they objected to non-attributable political attacks issued by the No. 10 press office.

It is sometimes said that only those with enough money can indulge in political lobbying. On the other hand, democracy works best when the government can discuss its proposals with a representative group. When the original national health scheme was introduced it was possible for the government to negotiate with the medical profession, but there was no one to represent the patients. It is possible to discuss an annual review of farm prices with the National Farmers Union, or even – as we have seen in recent years – for the government to engage in protracted negotiations with dissatisfied teachers' trade unions. There have been successful lobbyings, such as that for lead-free petrol, a feature of which was the weakness of the motor industry lobby. Prior to agreement between the British and French governments for the building of the Eurotunnel, the promoters of competing schemes conducted very extensive and costly lobbying tactics.

In the USA, where numerous committees sit on the issues of the day, Washington is a hot-bed of lobbying. There are also Political Action Committees (PACs) representing numerous interests, to which corporations subscribe funds.

An organization may conduct political and parliamentary public relations in the following ways:

1 A specialist parliamentary liaison consultancy can be engaged, either permanently or as need arises.
2 Some of the larger public relations consultancies offer political services, and they may have an MP as a director or adviser.
3 A Member of Parliament may be paid a fee to give advice on political matters of importance to an organization.
4 The in-house public relations manager may handle political lobbying direct.
5 A trade association may lobby on behalf of members, e.g. the NFU, BMA or Brewers Society.

It should be remembered that political and parliamentary public relations is a very broad term, and it could embrace local government, quasi-autonomous non-governmental organizations (quangos), civil service chiefs, members of the government (some 100 people), MPs of all parties, the local MP/MPs, members of the House of Lords, MEPs of all EC countries at the European Parliament in Strasbourg, Ministers at Luxembourg, Commissioners and others at Brussels, and even MPs and Ministers in other countries. However, in spite of this galaxy of political figures, it is possible to lobby and work with one sympathetic politician who is prepared to take up one's cause. This has happened in the case of the British Medical Association, whose public relations manager has worked directly with an individual MP. Later in this chapter the case is recorded of the British MP who championed CPC's case with European governments. At the end of the chapter it is shown that the media can also be a lobbying tool.

Parliamentary liaison

The term 'Parliamentary liaison' is sometimes confused to mean attempts by the government to present its case to the public, but the opposite is true. It may consist of using a specialist public relations consultancy to learn what is happening in Parliament. The expression 'Parliament' is a broad one. It can mean the business of the house such as Question Time when the Prime Minister is asked questions (for which there are prepared answers) and supplementary questions, debates, and the reading of bills. Much occurs outside the chambers of the Commons and the Lords. Various committees and commissions are sitting, to which evidence can be presented by interested parties.

A political public relations consultancy can provide clients with services such as advice on when various issues have been awarded Parliamentary time for discussion or debate, and they can also supply clients with copies of Hansard, White Papers, Green Papers, Bills and other publications, with interpretations and advice as necessary. More general consultancies, such as Hill & Knowlton, also employ MPs. A number of experienced politicians (such as dismissed ministers, who were plentiful during the Thatcher regime) work for public consultancies, to mention only Francis Maude, John Marples and John Maude. Of these, Francis Maude, lost his seat in the 1992 General Election.

Many interests, such as farming, medicine and motoring, have groups of MPs who are particularly qualified or interested in them, while there are always the MPs who represent constituencies in which businesses have their premises or plants. An MP representing a constituency which is a fishing port, or a centre of agriculture, or contains a nuclear power station is likely to be sympathetic to the special problems of such industries.

Political public relations does not mean bribing MPs to speak on behalf of an issue, and fortunately in British politics cases of bribery and corruption are extremely rare. This may be because our politicians seem to be more interested in power than money. If they do speak on a subject with which they are financially connected they are expected to declare their interest, and there is a register of MPs' outside interests. Members of Parliament often do have outside sources of income such as journalism, broadcasting, directorships and legal practices. Some are directors of public relations consultancies, or receive retainers from public relations consultancies and companies for advisory services only. Both the Institute of Public Relations and the Public Relations Consultants Association maintain a register, publicly available, of member MPs so engaged.

Criticism is sometimes made of MPs who receive substantial fees for consultancy services, on the grounds that they are paid salaries to serve as MPs and should not receive other payments. This is a false criticism since any MP may well have other income as a farmer, lawyer, journalist, public speaker or company director, provided he or she is not a member of the government, when any conflicting interests would have to be renounced.

Lobbying

As an indication of the breadth of Parliamentary liaison and especially lobbying, the following list of topics was set out in a mail shot to promote *Effective Lobbying*,[1] a monthly publication from Stonehart Publications.

- What legislation that may affect your organization is in the works – what is planned, what is rumoured.
- Which key personnel, government committees and quangos are involved.
- What the special pressure points are, and how to exploit them.
- When to expect Green Papers, White Papers, Second Readings etc.
- How best to present your case at each stage in the process.
- Which politicians and officials may champion your particular cause, and what their standing is.
- How ministers and civil servants are likely to react to your proposals.

Effective Lobbying also offered information on:

- How the consultative process really works, and how to influence it.
- How to persuade a select committee to listen to you.
- How to cultivate civil services and understand their language.
- Where and how to apply indirect pressure: third-party endorsements, the local press, opinion polls.
- How to get key words changed in a piece of legislation.
- When the House of Lords can help, and how to approach peers.

From the above it will be seen that civil servants – senior ones mostly – are also important. This may sound like shades of *Yes, Minister*, but ministers do have to take advice from civil servants.

The penultimate item could be crucial to a company. A feature of the Common Market has been harmonization of legislation so that laws are made common to all EC countries. Difficulties can occur due to words having different interpretations in different languages. A major public relations exercise occurred in Europe where CPC Europe was prevented from marketing foods containing starch, which is a common ingredient of baking powder, soups and mayonnaise. But in certain European countries starch (derived from corn) was listed as a drug and not a food! By employing an expert dietician to make representations to the governments in each country, the wording of the regulation was changed, resulting in millions of pounds of new business in EC countries. This affected the sales of products as famous as Knorr soups.

Nature of politicians

They may be representatives of the electorate, but MPs are rarely typical of them, and they seldom have any business or industrial experience. They are mostly drawn from teachers, trade unionists, journalists and, especially, lawyers. They have to deal with a great array of subjects about which they know very little. Inevitably, they represent the four negative states of hostility, prejudice, apathy and ignorance which public relations has to set about changing. Consequently, Parliamentary liaison and lobbying is an important public relations activity.

Writing in *Campaign*,[2] Dorothy Drake, chairman of Profile Public Relations, which specializes in government affairs, said:

> Lobbying is a perfectly legitimate activity. Indeed, the right to lobby is enshrined in Magna Carta. Many groups and individuals have organized themselves to make their views known and to press for changes – and have been successful in doing so. Without the pressure brought to bear by the consumer movement in the late '60s and early '70s it is unlikely that either the Office of Fair Trading or the Consumer Council would have been set up. Business, too, is learning to argue its case effectively.

Sometimes this lobbying covers many sides of society, each of which may be making pressure in different ways, such as by writing to MPs. It means that the government of the day is not allowed to steamroller new laws, particularly if members of the ruling party disagree with them. We saw this in early 1986 when the government wanted to allow shops to open on Sundays, but opposition from many sections of society, from trade unions to churches, was so intense that many members of the Conservative Party were persuaded to vote against the Sunday Trading Bill, and it was lost.

Although Sunday trading was illegal, it depended on legal proceedings being taken by local authorities. Some did, some refused. Eventually, in 1992, most of the supermarket chains and the big stores on out-of-town shopping complexes, defied the law. The government retreated with the excuse that they were waiting for a decision of the European Court of Justice on the subject.

The public relations manager, needing to be involved in political public relations has to decide whether he or she has the expertise, money and manpower to handle it alone. Of course, if the company is constantly involved in political matters, a full-time in-house service will be justified. But many companies engage in political public relations only occasionally, or only when a special issue arises. It may then pay to use either the regular advisory or the *ad hoc* services of a political relations consultancy. For example, if a company is being investigated by the Monopolies and Mergers Commission, a consultancy could be called in.

Yet another way of lobbying is through a trade association or professional body of which one is a member. A member may approach such a society, or the society may itself initiate matters as a pressure group on behalf of its members. For instance, the Advertising Association has negotiated with the European Commission over attempts to lay down rules about advertising which were offensive to British practice, and out of line with the British Code of Advertising Practice. Some of the EC proposals were absurd, and these included outlandish interpretations of what may be considered misleading in an advertisement. The British Medical Association has lobbied on a number of medical subjects, and not just on behalf of doctors. In such a case it is far better for the spokesperson of the industry to do the lobbying.

The subject of lobbying was explored at great length in *Marketing Week*, and the following is quoted from the supporting leader article:

> Industries that make the least noise haven't necessarily got something to hide, but they often warrant a closer look. The UK lobbying industry, with its elusive but crucial powers of influence is one . . . Such is the stuff of Jeffrey Archer novels but not, we are assured, the stuff of reality. In practice, lobbying is about the painstaking cultivation of contacts who may, or may not, be in a position to put a word in if the need arises. The basic communications nature of the task means marketers are increasingly finding themselves involved . . .
>
> The Proprietary Association of Great Britain, lobbying on behalf of the country's pharmaceutical firms, effected a change to the EC directive on drugs classification that saved the manufacturers a claimed £100m. PAGB members, including Smith Kline Beecham and Brookes Healthcare, contribute £1m a year to a joint lobbying fund . . . Lobbying has a role in developing freer business practice, not in ensuring that Might is Right.[3]

Unfortunately, the article that prompted the leader, written by Tom O'Sullivan,[4] got the wrong end of the stick about Shell Select shops at Shell garages, giving the false impression that Shell UK was about to indulge in a massive lobbying campaign to sell alcohol at these premises.

Two stories got confused, demonstrating how the media can create an anti public-relations situation. By 1996 Shell plans to convert half of its 3000 forecourt shops into franchised retail outlets, as part of a £250m rebuilding programme. An addition of 1988 to the 1964 Licensing laws forbids an outlet that 'primarily' sells petrol to also sell alcohol.

There are strong cases for and against the selling of alcohol at petrol stations. The Select shop has, in some areas, to compete with super-markets which also sell petrol and usually cheap petrol at that. However, the argument is that whereas the supermarket shopper may primarily buy a quantity of goods, and may then buy petrol on leaving, the motorist calls at a garage primarily to buy petrol and could also buy alcohol to consume on the road. It is not Shell UK which will be lobbying, but the individual Select franchiser who will lobby the local authority.

In his article Tom O'Sullivan did refer to lobbying, which he rather mischievously termed 'political PR' as distinct from the more diplomatic kind. This was no doubt a journalist's distinction, and he reserved his 'political PR' lobbying to expensive junketing 'designed to enable a company director or chief executive to mix with politicians − the type of limited-effect lobbying that went on at both the Labour and Con-servative annual conferences when an estimated £1.5m was spent by companies ranging from Kingfisher and Mercury Communications to the Courage Brewery'. Such costly extravagences deserve the contempt they incur, but these remarks were attributed by the feature writer to Nigel Clarke, director of GJW, the lobbying company.

In the following week's edition of *Marketing Week* some valid points were made in a letter from Lesley Abdela.[5] She said:

> The most important point to keep in mind when dealing with elected representatives is that their position rests in the hands of their constitu-ents. Meanwhile, their chances of promotion rest with the media as well as their ability to impress their party in the debating Chamber, on select committees and standing committees at conferences.
>
> So getting positive and effective publicity for an MP is a very definite plus . . . When I founded the all-party 300 Group for Women in Politics and Public Life I knew 'Fleet Street' would be an essential estate, a vital part of the lobbying game . . .
>
> If the national press, from tabloid to broadsheet, had not immediately and wholeheartedly realized that we needed more women in our national legislatures, I do not believe the cause would have advanced so far. In a decade, the number of women MPs has gone from 19 to 60.

Lesley Abdela, experienced in working in the Chief Whip's office at Westminster, has seen it all, but the above is a timely reminder that not all lobbying is diplomatic stuff behind closed doors, but can benefit from the glare of media coverage.

When Pamela Taylor, now director of public affairs at the BBC and president of the IPR in 1993, was head of public relations at the British Medical Association, she declared[6] that in her lobbying work for the BMA she never bought an MP a meal or a drink.

The duty free case

The complications of European politics were brought out in an article by Mark Leverton and Douglas Smith, well-known lobbyists of Political Communication, which appeared in *Public Relations*.[7] With the authors' permission, the following is a paraphrase with quotations.

Tax-free dairy products — mostly butter — were being sold on ships which made day trips from North German ports, sailing outside territorial waters but never actually landing at a foreign port. They earned the name of 'butterboats'. The legality of these tax-free ships was challenged by a German supermarket chain called Rewe. Duty free allowances are governed by the EC. In July 1981 the European Court of Justice upheld the challenge and ruled that the butterboats were illegal. 'It declared that the "butterboats" were in contravention of the EC regulations and that duty free sales of goods manufactured outside the European Community were against the law.'

Political Communications, as advisers to the British Airports Authority, were asked to study the situation and make recommendations. A large part of the profits of BAA is earned from duty free airports, which include Heathrow and Gatwick.

'The Commission, which is responsible for interpreting and implementing Court decisions, declared that member states must collect customs duty from third country goods sold in duty free shops. They also laid down that Germany must abolish its "butterboats" within a set period of time.' The German government refused, although the BAA accepted the ruling. The situation was further complicated by legislation introduced by the Commission in 1980 to abolish duty free allowances, but subsequently withdrawn under pressure from member states. Nevertheless, there was a school of thought which still maintained that duty free allowances contradicted the purpose of a common market within a customs union. The legal situation had become a quagmire. BAA's profitable duty free shops were at risk.

Political Communication's job was two-fold. 'First, to make the EC institutions, the member governments and the public fully aware of the threat and the consequences of abolition. Second, to press for the introduction of legislation to remove the legal ambiguity forever and preserve the allowances.' A first step was to have a discussion with the responsible Commissioner who was sympathetic but pessimistic.

European correspondents were invited to a press conference in Brussels at which the rumour that abolition of duty free was on the Commission's agenda was scotched.

Then the lobby was broadened to include other interested parties such as other airports, airlines, sea ferries and suppliers to duty free shops, and they were asked to lobby governments and politicians. Members of the European Parliament from all countries were briefed. Their re-election could depend on this issue!

The British government was persuaded to intervene in the Court in the Commission's case against Germany, since such intervention is permissible where a member state has a direct interest. Germany was a key to the problem. A study was commissioned showing the social grades who use airports in Germany, and how often they patronized duty free shops. The results gained wide coverage in the German press.

As a result, the issue was raised by politicians, in private, in debates and in Question Time in the European Parliament. In March 1983, after saying such legislation was impossible, the Commission passed a draft directive to make duty free allowances, and this went before the Council of Ministers for adoption.

Several lessons emerge from the campaign which apply to lobbying more generally. The first is never to be daunted by initial pessimism and statements by governments or officials, that 'we have made up our minds and it will never happen'. Clearly it is always better to work with politicians rather than against them but, ultimately, elected politicians rule the roost. They can always be swung by grassroots arguments, especially if an election is pending.

The second is to make full use of the media to buttress the lobbying case. Marshall the arguments by all means and present them privately without clamour. But often they will be more fully studied and considered if there is a backing of newspaper, magazine, radio and television coverage . . . and support. In this case, on an emotive issue affecting millions of travellers, general media sympathy was assured.

Finally, try to push the issue to a conclusion. If one simply 'scares off' government and its officials, they could well return to fight another day, using greater subtlety next time round. Pressure, once monitored with success behind it, can be sustained to ensure that the problem is resolved once and for all.

The above is a good example of how a fairly large organization with its own public relations department found it valuable to use a highly-experienced specialist public relations consultancy.

One last word from Dorothy Drake's article:

> A particularly inadequate way of dealing with parliamentary relations is for a company simply to have an MP on its board, or to retain an MP in an advisory capacity. However good an individual MP may be, he represents only one party, whereas effective parliamentary relations should be an all-party affair.

Such retainers can be very expensive, judging by the figures which were revealed during the controversy over MPs' earnings outside parliament.

Party and government public relations

There is a difference between political party propaganda and political party public relations which needs to be distinguished. All political parties issue propaganda to present their case and to seek supporters and, in elections, votes. But there can also be legitimate public relations to explain policy and to make a party understood for what it is so that a clear image is established. Similarly, a government may indulge in propaganda on behalf of its country, and this is especially true in wartime when propaganda is issued to boost the morale of the civilian population, or to undermine the enemy. But there can also be legitimate public relations to explain the services provided by government departments and agencies. Indeed, some of the earlier forms of public relations in Britain occurred before and after the First World War when old age pensions and housing schemes were introduced.

Thus we could have the party of the government in power using propaganda to boost its fortunes, but government public relations to help the electorate to understand its policies, legislation and public services. For the latter purpose, government departments have their chief information officers and their public relations staff.

Pertinent to this discussion is the PRCA Guidance Paper, *Lobbying in the British Parliament*,[8] which the PRCA published in 1986. It covers General Principles, Information Base, All-Party Groups and Trade Associations, Approaching MPs, 'The other Place' (House of Lords), The Media in Lobbying and Hazards and Pitfalls. It therefore augments this chapter with much valuable advice from its experienced authors, Arthur Butler and Douglas Smith.

However, this was a contentious topic during the Thatcher regime when the No. 10 press office annoyed journalists by trying to blend government information with Conservative Party propaganda. The two are quite different. Parties conduct publicity on behalf of themselves, but State PROs need to be impartial and so capable of serving any government. Mrs Thatcher and her spokesman Bernard Ingham disagreed with this view.

The subject of lobbying was investigated for three years by an all-party committee of MPs which sought to decide whether tighter controls were necessary. A tepid report came out in September 1991, recommending that professional lobbyists should be forced to register. But what makes anyone a 'professional' lobbyist? There is no monopoly, and lobbyists are not like Lobby correspondents who have to be approved, giving them the privilege of advance copies of Parliamentary documents. So, the recommendations have, up to the time of writing, remained dormant. Similarly, there have been abortive investigations by the European parliament, and with intensive lobbying against tighter controls. The advocates of controls on lobbying are inevitably socialists who see lobbying as a stick with which to beat their opponents.

Political correctness is a comparatively new phenomenon, quoted by Smythe, Dorward and Reback in their book *Corporate Reputation*,[9] which has spread from American university campuses to the business world. To quote the authors, 'The movement . . . is championing a social exorcism of "Politically Incorrect" behaviour like drinking, smoking and holding the "wrong" views. At one level this can be seen as people harnessing a well-organized style of lobbying. But it can also be seen as the start of a process which allows one social group to dominate and even suppress another.

> Whether PC is a fad or not, it has already taught more benign lobby groups to marshall their cases more effectively against organizations and the state . . . . Corporations need to learn about what drives the decisions of their customers. They have to take into account what these groups expect of them, and decide whether their own behaviour is good enough to guarantee their future.

Local government public relations

In the early to mid-1990s local government public relations took on new communication responsibilities which required public relations services. Three areas in particular were the further reorganization of local authorities, replacement of the hated Community Charge or poll tax by the Council Tax, and the implications of the Citizens Charter.

Central government continued to impose itself on local government.

Increased public rights and expectations are envisaged under the Citizens Charter, and local authorities are required to communicate better with their customers. This invites local councils to declare their corporate aims and their customer contract regarding the delivery of services.

The scheme includes the award of charter marks for recognized excellence, and in 1992, 36 awards were made by Prime Minister John Major, 11 of them going to local government. There were 300 applications in the first year of the awards.

Local government PROs will be engaged in information services about the proposals and decisions of the individual council, and about the services and amenities provided to local residents, who are all people of all ages, irrespective of who actually pays the Council Tax, which will normally be the property owner. Various authorities have different things to provide information about and they can include public transport, car parking, entertainments, markets, libraries, art galleries and museums, parks and recreation grounds, street and shopping centre replanning, industrial estates, and in some cases special subjects such as exhibition centres, holiday attractions, airports and seaports. Local authorities are often trading enterprises that require constant public relations support.

Central government public relations

The government is not only Britain's largest advertiser but its ministries, departments, quangos and the Prime Minister's office at No. 10 have information officers who keep the media informed about policies and services. Again, this is not limited to the electorate but to everyone living in the country, such as children, immigrants and foreign visitors. It covers numerous campaigns such as that on road safety, and about AIDS, social benefits and drug addiction.

The Central Office of Information provides creative services for the ministries, departments and government agencies, or arranges for the appointment of advertising agencies, and this is carefully costed so that the COI pays its way. At one time the COI provided exporters with many free services through the overseas distribution (via High Commissions abroad) of news stories, photographs and films. Today, the COI has to operate more cost-effectively, and most overseas information work is conducted by the COI as commissioned by the Department of Trade and Industry, which has its own export publicity unit.

References

1　*Effective Lobbying*, monthly, Stonehart Publications Ltd, London
2　Drake, Dorothy, 'The Rules of the House', *Campaign*, 1 May 1986
3　*Marketing Week*, Leader, 'Seeing the dark side of lobbying', 25 October 1992
4　O'Sullivan, Tom, *Marketing Week*, Feature, 'Reform Clubs', 23 October 1992
5　Abdela, Lesley (Eyecatcher Associates), Letter, 'Fleet Street − useful in the lobby game', *Marketing Week*, 6 November 1992
6　Taylor, Pamela, Political Lobbying, Address at the 13th annual Summer School, Frank Jefkins School of Public Relations, London, 27 July 1992
7　Leverton, Mark and Smith, Douglas, 'Duty Free', *Public Relations*, Summer 1985
8　Butler, Arthur and Smith, Douglas, *Lobbying in the British Parliament*, PRCA Guidance Paper, Public Relations Consultants Association, 1986
9　Smythe, John, Dorward, Collette and Reback, Jerome, *Corporate Reputation*, Century Business, London, 1992

36

Pre-selling through market education

The case for market education

In Chapter 28 a section was devoted to market education and pre-selling as one of the elements of the marketing mix to which public relations techniques could be applied. It is an area of marketing communications which is really public relations, and what we decide to call it is a matter of semantics between marketing and public relations practitioners. It does not matter what it is called so long as it is done, and lack of it can be, and has been, disastrous.

At the Marketing Education Group annual conference at Plymouth Polytechnic in July 1986, which was attended by marketing lecturers from universities, polytechnics and colleges of higher education, the author presented the following paper. It was published in the official proceedings, and is reproduced here by courtesy of MEG.[1] This paper has been reproduced again in this edition because it demonstrates two things: the successful application of public relations techniques to marketing problems during the past 40 years, and the role of public relations as a problem solving process.

This paper looks at some examples of product launches which were initially failures, the reasons for these failures and how they were remedied. After this, some successful uses of market education are quoted. Then the paper considers some of the practical techniques which may be applied to prepare the market for the successful introduction of a new product or service.

Introduction

Unless the product is a highly competitive FMCG such as a new chocolate bar, or one where great secrecy has to be maintained before the launch, it can be foolish to depend on weight of advertising to break down sales resistance and secure a successful launch. Even test marketing can be inadequate, and A. C. Nielsen have admitted that 50 per cent of products test marketed prove to be failures when placed on the national market. The proposition presented in this paper is that, given a good product or service, there can be a successful launch if a pre-selling market education programme is conducted well in advance. According to the nature of the subject, this action may be necessary six to eighteen months in advance, something which is foreign to some marketing strategies.

The reasons why pre-selling action is desirable are four-fold, and they concern both distributors and final buyers. Four negative attitudes may have to be overcome and converted into positive ones. These are: hostility, prejudice, apathy and ignorance. If we take some current attitudes: people are hostile to the Eurotunnel, airships and nuclear power; prejudiced about holidays in certain countries or wines from untraditional wine-growing countries (e.g. Canada); apathetic about home security, eating health foods, or protecting woodwork; and they are ignorant about countless things in our complex society. To launch something new which is subject to one or more of these four dis-advantages is a suicidal gamble.

Definition

Pre-selling is that area of marketing communications which aims at creating a favourable marketing situation in advance of selling, distribution, advertising and sales promotion.

The case for pre-selling (1)

To justify the hypothesis that pre-selling can contribute handsomely to the success of a marketing strategy let us look at some disaster situations which could have been avoided had there been market education, or which were overcome when the market was subsequently educated. These examples span a number of years, but some have become classics of their kind.

In the 1950s an exceptionally good British summer resulted in the cancellation of supplies of mutton from New Zealand. The New Zealand Meat Producers Board was faced with the dilemma of how and where to sell their excess mutton. An apparently obvious solution seemed to be to exploit the nearby wealthy Japanese market which had never previously imported mutton. But when they set about mounting a marketing campaign the Board found itself confronted by the four negative attitudes stated in the Introduction above. The Japanese ate fish, not meat, and did not have ovens for cooking joints. Meat suited neither their traditional diets nor their culinary habits, and there were no butcher's shops. There was, however, a new kind of liberated modern Japanese woman, and there were huge stores in city centres. It was possible to educate both potential customer and potential distributor.

Eventually Japan became a great importer of New Zealand mutton and lamb, and advertisements and signs for the King of Meats became familiar. But it took a long educational programme which involved selling mutton for school meals, using a pop group on TV cookery programmes, and producing recipe books which explained how mutton could be cooked by traditional Japanese methods. Retail sales began in a supermarket close to the Tokyo metro where thousands of passengers were able to see the signs.

The first non-drip one-coat paint was Berger's Magicote. One Easter an advertising campaign was addressed to DIY enthusiasts listing the addresses of stockists. But when would-be buyers enquired at the shops counter assistants scoffed at the idea of not using an undercoat. It then took 18 months of public relations activity ranging from trade press receptions and demonstrations, to a dealer magazine circulated to the trade to retrieve the situation. After that, advertising did work, the trade was convinced, the product sold well, and ICI had to bring out its own version. Today such paints are commonplace.

When Thoresen first brought drive-on-drive-off ferries to Britain he tried to operate them from Southampton to Cherbourg, the advertising not only failed but the concepts of the new kind of ferry and the new route to France were not understood by travel agents. A novel solution was adopted on the basis that no travel agent is more than 150 miles from some parts of the British coast. At the end of the first season one of the ferries did a round-Britain voyage, stopping at ports to which coachloads of travel agents were taken to inspect the vessel. Next year, travel agents were well-informed and able to recommend the ferry and the route to their customers. Today, there are numerous such ferries plying to and from British and Irish or continental European ports.

The UK franchise for a Hungarian electro-osmotic damp proofing system was obtained by Rentokil, and was about to be launched when a Building Research Station report was published by the Stationery Office stating that the method did not work. It had actually been mis-used by another company. For 18 months Rentokil carried out free treatments at Gloucester Cathedral and on National Trust properties. This proof was published in articles in the building and architectural press, and made known through presentations and demonstrations.

Today the system is used successfully by both Rentokil and rival companies worldwide.

A successful engineering company bought the rights to a teaching machine, set up a factory, appointed a sales manager and engaged a consultant to organize trade promotions at the Festival Hall, London. But the consultant recognized that the machine was incompatible with teaching programmes and insisted that teaching establishments be researched. As a result of this survey, the machine was never made, the factory was closed, and the sales manager was dismissed.

A similar situation occurred when the British subsidiary of a large American chemical company was about to launch a cool box for food, but it was made of expanded polystyrene which gave it a peculiar smell. A consultant was engaged to promote it, but he advised that it was not marketable, and the product was never made. But for this advice the manufacturer would have plunged into advertising. In these last two cases no amount of pre-selling would have helped, but they indicate how far well-known companies will go along a blind route.

Let us take two more recent examples. First, the tobacco industry, which is strong on advertising, attempted to launch cigarettes that were not made of tobacco and were thought to be the answer to the smoking and cancer scare. The shops were stocked up and millions were spent on full-page advertisements for NSM (New Smoking Mixture), but the product failed and stocks had to be removed from the shops and destroyed. The public did not understand the product and raised other objections. The mistake was made of believing that because half the population did not smoke they would smoke NSM. But it is possible that had a pre-selling programme been operated so that smokers would have welcomed a safe cigarette, NSM could today be a big seller.

One of the most disastrous product launches was that of Sir Clive Sinclair's C5 electric tricycle. Its concept was so different from the public's anticipation of an electric car, that it was highly criticized and scorned. Had there been preparatory market education, either acceptance might have been won or the product could have been modified to satisfy the market. There could even have been a different market use for it, as one American buyer has since suggested. In this case secrecy led to disappointment and failure.

The case for pre-selling (2)

Now let us look at some examples where clever pre-selling won the day.

The manufacturer of industrial dishwashers produced a larger version which would wash cooking utensils. Its advantages were ones of hygiene, labour saving, and undamaged utensils. A prototype was operated for a year at the London Hospital. The success of its operation was described in a trade press article which coincided with an exhibition at which the machine was sold to schools, hotels, holiday camps and other hospitals.

For some three years BL's Metro was openly discussed and the publicity led to a number of modifications so that when it was finally launched the car was what the market wanted. The Maestro followed a similar pattern, and although the Montego was handled more secretively it gained from the halo effect of the previous two launches.

When Kleinwort Benson decided to promote unit trusts they advertised a free video which educated prospective clients about the merits of unit trust investment. They did not just advertise unit trusts which might not have been understood by those who had never bought them.

Privatization has seen some extensive market education. Charles Barker Lyons spent a year preparing the market for the British Aerospace flotation, using a very successful financial press relations campaign. The British Telecom sale incurred several pre-selling operations, first to convince the City of the viability of the operation and then with a double operation preceding the actual issue. Because the government wished to widen share ownership and it was the biggest share issue ever mounted, this larger market had to be educated not only about the BT offer, but about the whole process of share buying. Dewe Rogerson, public relations consultants, handled this.

Thomson Holidays had an interesting problem when they decided to offer cheap weekend holidays in mid-winter in Moscow of all places. The four negative situations of hostility, prejudice, apathy and ignorance were present very strongly. All four were overcome very successfully − they now run such holidays to Outer Mongolia! − by taking a planeload of travel journalists on a sample weekend. The result was extensive press coverage in papers as diverse as the *Sunday Times* and the *Reading Post*, with a *Better Red Than Med* headline in the *Sunday Times*. After that, and ever since, their advertising has worked.

About 18 months ago one could read about the Sony Camcorder which made video filming less of a chore than with the older heavy equipment. The market was well prepared for the eventual product launch. Anticipation was created among people who had been sceptical about the bulky earlier video cameras. When the product arrived in the shops the market was ready for it.

Techniques which can be applied

Whether we call it 'marketing communication' or 'public relations' is unimportant, except that the opportunity does exist to demonstrate that public relations is not merely an optional extra which can be added to advertising and sales promotion and at that late stage as a form of publicity under the promotional 'P'.

Its more valuable and proper role of educating and informing and in this case of educating the market, can now be seen as a form of communication which can enhance the success of the marketing strategy. But it does need to come into play early in the marketing strategy, and it can impinge on a number of elements of the marketing mix such as familiarizing the name, building good trade relations and distribution, and selecting the right market segment. A reason for failure in marketing new, technical or unfamiliar products and services is that public relations methods were never applied either at all, or sufficiently early, to make eventual promotion economic and effective. Sometimes, needlessly heavy expenditures on heavyweight advertising have been incurred which would not have been necessary had a favourable marketing situation been created in advance so that more modest advertising would have been adequate.

The following are some of the pre-selling techniques which can be applied:

1 Press relations including feature articles.
2 Audio visuals – slides, videos.
3 Private exhibitions, including mobile or portable ones.
4 Educational literature and print including explanatory posters.
5 Technical seminars and trade presentations.
6 TV and radio coverage, e.g. *Tomorrow's World*.
7 External house journals to the trade and consumers/users.
8 Testing of prototypes by typical users, with published reports.
9 Advance use, testing by appropriate personalities.
10 Advance use, testing by appropriate journalists.

Reference

1 Pre-selling through Market Education, paper presented at Marketing Education Group Chartered Institute of Marketing, Plymouth Polytechnic, July 1986

Appendix 1

CAM Diploma syllabuses

Management and Strategy (compulsory)

Aim

The aim of this module is to give candidates an in-depth knowledge of business management, practice and strategy, and to allow them to consider its specific application in the communication and related industries.

On completion of this module candidates will have a knowledge of the organization and structure of all types of enterprises, the financing of them and management procedures and practice. They will also be able to analyse situations, develop the appropriate strategies in pursuance of organizational objectives and be able to apply the practice of management to the communication industry.

Objectives

On completion of this module candidates should know how:
- To describe and examine the different forms of organizational structure
- To examine the sources of finance available to organizations
- To examine the process of management at corporate and business unit level
- To analyse situations and develop appropriate strategies consistent with corporate goals
- To describe the functions, duties and techniques of management
- To develop management skills for all types of organizations, commercial and non-commercial

- To apply the above to the communication and related industries

1 Organizational structures
- Single-owner firms, partnerships and co-partnerships
- Public and private companies, interlocking and holding companies, amalgamations, mergers, monopolies and cartels
- Cooperative undertakings
- Professional institutions and trade associations
- Central and local government, public bodies, charities and membership organizations
- Alternative corporate structures: matrix, pyramid etc.
- Line and staff management
- Entrepreneurs and intrapreneurs
- Global, multi-national, international

2 Financing of organizations
- Sources of capital, internal and external
- Financing of enterprises
- Capital market: domestic and international
- Venture capital
- Government and private subsidies and grants

3 Management – the planning process
This section covers the process of planning including situation analysis,

strategy option generation,
implementation and implications for the
communication and marketing mix.
- Organizational objectives –
  corporate, strategic, tactical
- Defining the business
- The Strategic Audit – Strengths,
  Weaknesses, Opportunities and
  Threats (SWOT)
- Integration of objectives: corporate,
  institutional, business, marketing
  operational, communications and
  other functional
- Portfolio analysis/use of matrices:
  Boston Consulting Group Matrix
  Market growth (brand share)
  Market attractiveness
  Market maturity/competitive
  strength
- Profit impact of marketing strategy
- Creative approaches, e.g. Porter,
  organic, changing rules of the
  competitive game
- Resource allocation
- Competitive analysis – product life
  cycles and experience curve effects
- Audience segmentation/target market
  opportunities
- Corporate and product positioning/
  brand mapping
- Uses of primary and secondary
  market/marketing research
- Search for profit in declining markets
- Legal/voluntary/ethical constraints
- Implementation: marketing mix
  planning, sources of competitive
  advantage, the role of communication
  in achieving strategic goals

4   Management – practice

- Management functions, techniques,
  duties and responsibilities
- Managing personnel, change, conflict
  and developments in organizations,
  the importance of interpersonal skills
  and interface skills relationship
  within and between organizations'
  departments
- Planning, control and evaluating
  performance/resources including
  human resources
  - performance criteria, control and
    evaluation
  - forecasting, budgetary, costing and
    statistical controls
  - financial analysis – DCF, cashflow,
    break-even

- human resource analyses,
  recruitment procedures, control,
  evaluation
- uses of marketing audit, marketing
  and audience research and
  operational research techniques
- awareness of legal/voluntary/
  ethical constraints, e.g. Trades
  Union legislation

5   Management – communication industry applications

- The role of in-house and external
  services and their interrelationships
- Management, organization and
  structure of advertising agencies,
  media independents, PR and PR
  consultancies, sales promotion
  houses, direct marketing, market
  research agencies etc.
- Specific management problem areas
  in the above

Public Relations Management

Introduction

Public relations is a function or a task of
management which presents a particular
set of demands to those having
responsibility for managing the function
and integrating it effectively into the
overall management of an organization.

This paper requires an understanding of
the principles of public relations
management in organizations in the
public, private, non-profit and other
sectors, and of public relations programme
management in consultancy settings.

Aim

The syllabus for this paper is designed to
provide a basis for assessing the
candidates' knowledge of principles of
public relations management, their
application to public relations programme
development and activities in
organizations, and their application in the
integration of public relations into overall
management planning and decision-
making.

Objectives

On completion of this module candidates should be able:
- To describe and examine public relations as a function and/or task of management in and for organizations in the public, private, non-profit and other sectors. Organizations in each of these sectors include:

Public sector

- Government and government agencies – national, local and international
- Quangos: quasi-autonomous non-governmental organizations
- Public utilities
- Education bodies, authorities; trusts
- Broadcasting authorities

Private sector

- Corporations
- Business organizations
- Professional partnerships
- Financial institutions

Non-profit

- Charities
- Community, youth and voluntary organizations
- Other organizations; membership associations
- Professional bodies
- Trade associations
- Campaigning organizations – pressure and minority interest groups
- Religious groups and organizations
- Political parties
- Trade unions

- To examine the opportunities and constraints for public relations management presented by organizations in each of these sectors, whether the public relations resource is internal, external, or a combination of the two.
- To examine public relations' contribution to overall management planning and decision-making, to financial, personnel and marketing management, and to internal communication, employee relations and organizational development.
- To examine candidates' knowledge of

other organizations and key publics and their likely impact on the organization and its public relations activities, for example government agencies at local, national and international levels including the EEC, other regulatory bodies, the Charities Commission, the media, special interest groups and the local community.

- To examine knowledge of specific topics in public relations management including:

- The use of research, auditing, scanning and monitoring techniques in issues management, programme planning and evaluation
- Strategic planning
- Planning processes and techniques
- Communication programme planning, budgeting and implementation
- Crisis management and crisis communication
- Issues management
- Legal issues
- Staffing public relations positions
- Structuring and managing the public relations department
- Managing external services and creative staff
- Public relations programme management in consultancy settings
- The role of the public relations practitioner as a consultant and phases in the consultation process
- Establishing the way to balance the use of internal and external resources to best effect

Public Relations Practice

Introduction

Public relations management depends on knowledge of, and skill in applying, a number of techniques drawn from general management and from public relations practice.

This paper will seek to show, on a case study basis, that candidates understand how the techniques of public relations management are applied within organizations, in public, private and non-profit sectors, and in consultancy settings.

Aim

This paper is intended to test candidates' ability to apply in practice the principles and techniques of public relations and public relations management to problems and opportunities faced by organizations.

Objectives

- To provide opportunities, through the use of case studies, for candidates to demonstrate that they understand how the principles and techniques of public relations and public relations management may be applied to the exploitation of opportunities and to the solution of problems faced in practice.
- To test candidates' knowledge of commercial, marketing, city and financial applications
- To test candidates' knowledge of the application, in the case studies presented, of consulting techniques and specific techniques such as:
  - Social, market and communication research techniques
- Trend analysis
- Management by objectives, programme evaluation and review techniques (PERT), and critical path methods of programme planning
- Strategic planning
- Programme budgeting
- Communication programme planning, budgeting and implementation
- To test cadidates' abilities to make decisions regarding approaches to staff selection, personnel and project management, delegation of tasks and control of activities
- To examine candidates' knowledge of the use and effectiveness of currently available communications techniques, including those depending on the use of communication technology.

Case study practice

Students should keep abreast of current news items and regularly read the financial and political pages of the press. Case studies are likely to be related to current events.

Appendix 2

CAM Diploma past examination papers and case studies in public relations practice and public relations management

---

Examination in
MANAGEMENT & STRATEGY
JUNE 1992

Time allowed: THREE HOURS.

The paper is divided into four sections. All candidates are required to answer FOUR QUESTIONS. Questions must be selected from at least THREE of the four sections.

All questions carry a maximum of 25 marks.

Candidates are advised that the examiners will be seeking evidence of ability to translate knowledge of facts and techniques into appropriate practical applications.

The examiners will also be impressed by legibility and clarity of expression.

Rough work should be included in the answer book(s) and ruled through, but it will not be accepted as part of the candidate's answers.

SECTION A
Question One
Small firms find it difficult to survive in some industries, particularly in manufacturing; yet in others, for example retailing, they trade side by side with large companies. Some industries – and particularly service industries – are dominated by small and medium sized enterprises.

Explain why there are such differences between industries (50%) and why firms of all sizes operate successfully in the marketing and advertising services fields (50%).

Question Two
You are managing director of a sizeable and profitable subsidiary of a publicly quoted but ailing communications group. Your board is considering undertaking a management buyout. (a) What are the chief considerations in attempting the buyout? How could it be financed and structured? What possible personal and corporate risks and rewards would be entailed? (50%). (b) What are the possible sources of finance and their relative merits? (50%).

SECTION B
Question Three
UK charities find themselves in an ever more competitive environment. There are many new fund raising ideas involving concerts, television and many relief initiatives such as Red Nose Day. Many large charities have appointed marketing directors to maximise their revenue opportunities.

Consider one of these listed charities and identify the key elements of a marketing plan with the objective of increasing income:

Oxfam
Royal National Lifeboat Institution
Royal Society for the Prevention of Cruelty to Animals
Battersea Dogs' Home
Greenpeace

Imagine that you are the new Marketing Director and that you are writing an outline presentation to the Management Board.

Question Four
In the 90s a competitive edge will be gained by many companies working in close partnership with major customers in the development of new products and services. For example, FMCG companies might gain by a close developmental relationship with powerful multiple retail groups; similarly manufacturers of hi-tec components might succeed by working very closely with major customers for those components.

What factors of your customers' businesses would you need to take into account? (40%). What difficulties are likely to be encountered in implementation? (30%). How can the process be facilitated? (30%).

SECTION C
Question Five
British companies seeking to expand and trade in Europe would be greatly aided by a rapid movement to a single market. Construct a S.W.O.T. analysis

for any company with which you are familiar on the basis of a single (EEC) market for their products/services over the next decade.

Question Six
You are the Chief Executive of a large PR company with six divisions addressing different marketplaces — Corporate, Pharmaceuticals, Hi-Technology, Financial Services, Consumer Products and Property & Construction. The Pharmaceutical Division is a star performer in terms of profitability and growth. It is becoming increasingly impatient with 'under- performers' — the other divisions — and is developing its own way of doing things.

These tensions are becoming a major pre-occupation within the company. As Chief Executive you decide to draw up a programme to encourage the company to break down the barriers between the divisions and develop a stronger cohesion. What areas might this address? (40%). What options might you have to deal with this situation? (40%) Are there any ways of implementing any proposed change which will increase the likelihood of its acceptance and success? (20%).

SECTION D
Question Seven
You are the Marketing Research Manager of a manufacturing company that puts all market research out to external market research agencies. Write a report which demonstrates how your department adds value to your company's operation.

Question Eight
Within a company marketing business products, the Director of Marketing Services has been asked by the Board for increased efficiencies. Major expenditure is concentrated on external PR consultancies and on a wide range of sales literature.

What major issues would need to be considered? (50%). What are the practical considerations surrounding any change of suppliers? (50%).

Case study

Aggro plc, a UK-based public company quoted on the London Stock Exchange, manufactures agricultural fertilisers. The domestic market accounts for 10% of its turnover with 80% from exports to other EC countries. One of the company's major specialisations is in support of beet cultivation — a crop which farmers are increasingly turning to and on which Aggro is pinning hopes for its own future. Over the past five years the company has spent £25 million on a research programme to develop a fertiliser to increase yields of beet by at least 50%. The outcome is Beetup — planned for launch in six months.

The European Commission announced yesterday its intention to introduce a draft directive which would ban the use of Notix — a substance widely used in the agrochemicals industry and considered by some EC scientists to be carcinogenic. Notix is also a key ingredient of Beetup. It is expected that the draft directive will be enforced within two years.

The Aggro directors have decided to delay the launch of Beetup for one year so that research can identify a non-carcinogenic substitute for Notix. In addition, the Board has ordered, as a matter of urgency, a review of all its products to ascertain the extent of current use of Notix and the effect of a ban on Aggro's markets. Simultaneously a full-scale internal environmental audit has been implemented.

Examination in
PUBLIC RELATIONS MANAGEMENT
JUNE 1992

Time allowed THREE HOURS.

All candidates are required to answer QUESTION ONE and ONE OTHER QUESTION.

Question One carries 75% of the marks and the other question 25%.

Rough work should be included in the answer book(s) and ruled through, but it will not be accepted as part of the candidate's answers.

Question One (Mandatory, based on the Case Study)
You are the chief executive of Worldwide PR Inc, which advises Aggro on corporate and marketing communications. The Chairman of Aggro has asked you to provide him with a memo presenting an overview of the current and potential strategic issues which the company is likely to face as a result of the EC announcement. An outline of how these issues might be addressed, giving due attention to timescale and budgetary considerations, is also required.

You should write this memo and include five factors which, in your view, must receive priority. Bear in mind that you are addressing the Chairman as one senior businessman to another and at this stage he does not require details of how your recommendations will be implemented. However, pay attention to communications aspects, publics and commercial implications which might not have occurred to him, so as to ensure that the memo is coherent and a clear statement of the company's position from which decisions on public relations action can be made.

Question Two
The Cutie Cake Company plc was founded in 1912 to manufacture biscuits, pies, cakes and pastries and by 1970 had become one of the top three players in the biscuits market. It is publicly quoted and the head office is in Stockport, Cheshire where the business was started.

The company added ranges of frozen foods, savoury ready meals and snacks in 1982 and also introduced artificial ingredients and additives (sweeteners and colourings) to some of the best-selling lines. However consumers considered that this compromised the CCC's reputation for quality and some activist groups began to pinpoint the dangers associated with additives.

Sales began to decline in 1990 and, last year, a number of crises faced the company including the death of a child following an allergic reaction to an additive used in one product. A court case is pending on this issue.

Last week, the CCC board decided to examine the possibility of stopping the use of artificial ingredients in favour of natural products, some of which would have to be sourced from abroad.

Your Managing Director has asked you, as Public Relations Manager of CCC, to write a memo on the communications impact of the various options open to the board.

Question Three
The Blue Star charity was founded over 100 years ago to assist people at home and abroad. Its work covers all aspects of care and the relief of human suffering. It is involved in disaster relief and refugee support in Third World countries through to the operation of day care centres for the elderly and provision of volunteer medical services in the UK.

There are some 100,000 volunteer supporters in the UK who are organised in a branch structure based on large towns and cities. They include individuals who are trained in emergency medical support as well as fundraisers and welfare workers who help out in day care centres. Apart from those fund-raising activities which are the traditional hallmark of charitable giving in the UK, there is a file of 150,000 regular donors, both individuals and companies. Blue Star used to be the UK's leading charity but it has rather faded from prominence and has been overtaken by newer, more dynamic organisations. It is now 15th on the Charities Aid Foundation list which ranks charities according to donated income.

Although Blue Star has not always used aggressive marketing techniques, the trustees have agreed to spend £2 million over three years to increase the charity's profile and to boost funds needed for its caring work. From this budget, £500,000 has been allocated for public relations.

Your brief is to draw up a programme which addresses the key objective of progressively increasing and extending media coverage and the perception of the charity as a vibrant and progressive organisation. Write a paper for the trustees setting out the creative strategy on which this programme will be based.

Case study
You work for an engineering company WIDGETS which makes specialist parts for the aeroplane industry. The company employs 3,500 people in

the UK of whom 85% are men. There are no women in senior management positions.

As technology has progressed the skills required in the workforce have become increasingly electronics orientated.

The current demographic situation offers WIDGETS fewer graduates with the necessary scientific background you want. Of these graduates 55% are women. However the 'male' orientation of the company means that few female graduates perceive your company to be an attractive place to work. Also those already employed find the environment unwelcoming and unrewarding with few career opportunities for pregnant women or returnees and as such you are losing a valuable resource in whom the company has an investment.

The chairman and the board of the company have decreed that WIDGETS as a company must change its culture to make itself more attractive to female graduates and women employees.

The human resources department has now completed extensive research to establish what actions should be taken to achieve cultural change. They have an action plan which includes a review of the physical environment to ensure it meets women's requirements, intensive regular appraisals seeking to identify women who can be promoted, job share in selective instances, a creche for shift workers, career breaks for up to five years for female employees with young families, paternity leave and a childcare location service. They have also recommended that the normal working day should be from 8 am–6 pm and that meetings should be held within this time-frame if at all possible.

Examination in
PUBLIC RELATIONS PRACTICE
JUNE 1992

Time allowed: THREE HOURS.

All candidates are required to answer QUESTION ONE and ONE OTHER QUESTION.

Question One carries 75% of the marks and the other question 25%.

Rough work should be included in the answer book(s) and ruled through, but it will not be accepted as part of the candidate's answers.

Question One (Mandatory, based on the Case Study)
You have been asked to recommend a communications programme to accelerate this cultural change internally and externally. Please list your key target audiences, outline your message, suggest five high priority vehicles by which to communicate and make a recommendation as to how to measure your communications' success. (A budget and timetable are not required at this stage).

Question Two

A southeast harbour board is concerned about the impact the opening of the Channel Tunnel will have on cross channel ferry traffic. The board is worried that jobs will be lost, and that the number of visitors to the town will be severely curtailed. Having lost the battle against the construction of the Tunnel, the harbour board is concerned to learn that a vigorous campaign has been launched to abolish duty free goods. This would have a further negative impact on business. The campaign argues that 'duty free' runs contrary to the dismantling of trade and tariff barriers required under the Single European Act. It also charges that 'duty free' gives an unfair competitive advantage to the ferries and airlines over the Tunnel.

While acknowledging the 'duty free' will eventually have to go, the British Government is prepared to seek derogation of powers from The Community to retain 'duty free' for a transitional period. Given the harbour board's limited public relations resources, outline your strategy for stiffening the Government's resolve in trying to secure as generous a transition period as possible.

Identify the clear message which you want to get across, your key target audiences and suggest some effective methods for generating public and political support for your case.

Question Three

You are the corporate affairs manager of Harrisons — a company which is fully listed on the London Stock Exchange. In recent years, there have been a number of management changes at board level that created considerable media attention, not least because of the size of the 'golden handshakes'. However, life has become easier during the past twelve months as a new management team has got on quietly with running the business and improving profitability.

You receive a phone call at home from the Chairman who explains that the Chief Executive (Bob Jones), brought in from another major company last year, was leaving the company forthwith. Following an investigation by the Stock Exchange, there was evidence that he had been involved in insider dealing whilst at his previous company.

Jones strongly denied the charges but had felt obliged to inform the Chairman since he was likely to be arrested and charged shortly. The Chairman had insisted upon his resignation which Jones had refused to provide, claiming that the company should stand behind him. After taking legal advice, the Chairman terminated his contract and escorted him from the building.

(a) Identify the key audiences.
(b) Draft a 'bullet-point' outline of the announcement which will form the press release that would be issued in the morning.
(c) Draft a timetable of actions during the following day.
(d) Describe the tactics you would employ in handling the announcement, bearing in mind the requirement that price sensitive information is released simultaneously.

Appendix 3

Bibliography

Magazines and periodicals

Adline, Adline Publishing Ltd, Adline House, 361−363 Moseley Road, Birmingham, B12 9DE. Monthly.

BAIE News (Journal of the BAIE), 3 Locks Yard, High Street, Sevenoaks, Kent, TN13 1LT. Monthly.

Campaign, Haymarket Marketing Publications Ltd, 22 Lancaster Gate, London, W2 2LY. Weekly.

Communication World (Journal of the IABC), One Hallidie Plaza, Suite 600, San Francisco, CA 95102, USA. Monthly.

Conferences, Exhibitions & Incentives International, Haymarket Management Magazines, 30 Lancaster Gate, London, W2 3LP. Monthly.

Exhibition Bulletin, London Bureau, 266−272 Kirkdale, Sydenham, London, SE26 4RZ. Monthly.

Exhibitor, The, Conference & Travel Publications Ltd. Media House, The Square, Forest Row, East Sussex. Quarterly.

International Public Relations Review (Journal of IPRA), P.O. Box 9588, Washington DC 20016, USA. Quarterly.

Marketing, Haymarket Marketing Publications Ltd, 22 Lancaster Gate, London, W2 3LP. Weekly.

Marketing Business (Journal of the CIM), Headway, Home and Law Publishing Group Ltd, Greater London House, Hampstead Road, London, NW1 7QQ. Monthly.

Marketing Week, Centaur Publications Ltd, St Giles House, 50 Poland Street, London, WIV 4AX. Weekly.

Overseas Trade, Overseas Trade Services, Room 802, Bridge Place, 88−89 Eccleston Square, London, SWIV 1PT. Monthly.

PR Week, Haymarket Business Publications Ltd, 22 Lancaster Gate, London, W2 3LP. Weekly.

Public Relations Journal (Journal of the IPR), The Institute of Public Relations, 4th Floor, The Old Trading House, 15 Northburgh Street, London, ECIV OPR. Eight times a year.

Sponsorship News, Charterhouse Business Publications, P.O. Box 66, Wokingham, Berks, RG11 4RQ. Monthly.

Televisual, Centaur Publications Ltd, St Giles House, 50 Poland Street, London, W1V 4AX. Monthly.

UK Press Gazette, Maclean Hunter House, Chalk Lane, Cockfosters Road, Barnet, Herts, EN4 OBU. Weekly.

Directories and works of reference

Advance (monthly loose-leaf information about press features), Themetree Ltd, 2 Prebendal Court, Oxford Road, Aylesbury, Bucks, HP19 3EY.

Advertisers Annual, Reed Information Services Ltd, Windsor Court, East Grinstead House, East Grinstead, West Sussex, RH19 1XA. Vol. 1. Agencies & Advertisers, Vol. 2. UK Media, Vol. 3. Overseas Media.

Benn's Media Directory, Benn Business Information Services Ltd, P.O. Box 20, Sovereign Way, Tonbridge, Kent, TN9

IRQ, Annual. Vol. 1. UK, Vol. 2. Europe, Vol. 3. World.

Blue Book of British Broadcasting, Tellex Monitors Ltd, Communications House, 210 Old Street, London EC1V 9UN. Annual.

Editors, Media Directories Ltd, 9–10 Great Sutton Street, London, EC1V OBX. Six volume media directory.

Europe Information Pocket Book, NTC Publications Ltd, Farm Road, Henley-on-Thames, Oxfordshire, RG9 1ES. Annual.

European Marketing Pocket Book, NTC Publications Ltd, Farm Road, Henley-on-Thames, Oxfordshire, RG9 1ES. Annual.

Guide to European Business Media, Business Communications, Swallows Farm, Thaxted Road, Wimblish, Essex, CB10 2XP. Three times a year.

Hollis Press and Public Relations Annual, Hollis Directories, Contact House, Lower Hampton Road, Sunbury-on-Thames, Middx, TW16 5HG.

Hollis Europe, Hollis Directories, Contact House, Lower Hampton Road, Sunbury-on-Thames, Middx, TW16 5HG. Annual.

Hollis Sponsorship and Donations Yearbook, Hollis Directories, Contact House, Lower Hampton Road, Sunbury-on-Thames, Middx, TW16 5HG. Annual.

Institute of Public Relations Handbook (IPR membership list and year book), Kogan Page Ltd, 120 Pentonville Road, London, N1 9JN.

Marketing Pocket Book, NTC Publications Ltd, Farm Road, Henley-on-Thames, Oxfordshire, RG9 1ES. Annual.

Media Pocket Book, NTC Publications Ltd, Farm Road, Henley-on-Thames, Oxfordshire, RG9 1ES. Annual.

PIMS Directories, PIMS House Mildmay Avenue, London N1 4RS. Media, Townslist, European (Trade and Newspapers), Financial, USA (Trade, Newspapers, Consumer) directories.

PR Planner-Europe and *PR Planner-UK*, Hale House, 290–296 Green Lanes, London, N13 5TP. Updated looseleaf.

Printing Reproduction Pocket Pal, R. Prior, 277 Torbay Road, Harrow, HA2 9QE.

Public Relations Consultancy (Public Relations Yearbook), (PRCA), Financial Times Business Information, 50–64 Broadway, London, SW1H ODB.

Royal Mail International Business Travel Guide, Royal Mail International, 52 Grosvenor Gardens, London, SW1W 0AA.

Willings Press Guide, Reed Information Services Ltd, Windsor Court, East Grinstead House, East Grinstead, West Sussex, RH19 1BR. Vol. 1. UK, Vol. 2. Overseas.

Writers and Artists Yearbook, A & C Black (Publishers) Ltd, 35 Bedford Road, London, WCIR 4JH. Annual.

Books

All About Public Relations, 2nd edn, Haywood, Roger, McGraw-Hill, Maidenhead, 1991.

Company Image and Reality, Bernstein, David, Cassell, London, 1984.

Complete Spokesperson, The, Coulson-Thomas, Colin and Bartram, Peter, Kogan Page, London, 1991.

Communications in Industrialising Countries, Jefkins, Frank and Ugboajah, Frank, Macmillan, London, 1989.

Corporate Culture, Hampden-Turner, Charles, The Economist Books, London, 1991.

Corporate Image, Ind, Nicholas, Kogan Page, London, 1990.

Effective Employee Communications, Bland, Michael and Jackson, Peter, Kogan Page, London, 1990.

Handbook of Public Relations & Communications, 4th edn, Lesley, Philip, Amacon, New York, 1991.

How To Manage Public Relations, Stone, Norman, McGraw-Hill, Maidenhead, 1991.

International Public Relations in Practice, Ed. Nally, Margaret, Kogan Page, London, 1991.

Mission & Business Philosophy, Campbell, Andrew and Tawadey, Kiran, Butterworth-Heinemann, Oxford, 1991.

Modern Marketing Communications, Jefkins, Frank, Blackie, Glasgow, 1990.

PR Business, The, Bell, Quentin, Kogan Page, London, 1991.

Practice of Public Relations, The, 3rd edn, Ed. Howard, Wilfred, Butterworth-Heinemann, Oxford, 1988.

Public Relations, 4th edn, Jefkins, Frank, Pitman, London, 1992.

Public Relations Casebook, Capper, Alan and Cunard, Peter, Kogan Page, London, 1990.

Public Relations for Your Business, Jefkins, Frank, Pfeiffer–Mercury Books (W.H. Allen), London, 1987.

Public Relations in Practice, Ed. Moss, Danny Routledge, London, 1991.

Public Relations Techniques, 2nd edn, Jefkins, Frank, Butterworth-Heinemann, Oxford, 1993.

Sense of Mission, A, Campbell, Andrew, Devine, Marion and Young, David of Ashridge. Hutchinson Business Books, London, 1990.

Sponsorship, Sleight, Steve, McGraw-Hill, Maidenhead, 1989.

Appendix 4

Addresses of societies and educational organizations

British Association of Industrial Editors, 3 Locks Yard, High Street, Sevenoaks, Kent TN13 1LT; (01732) 459331. Membership: Editors of house journals. Entry by examination. *BAIE News.*

Communication, Advertising and Marketing Education Foundation (CAM), Abford House, 15 Wilton Road, SW1V 1NJ; 0171–828 7506. Certificate and Diploma examinations. Vocational examinations for those working in British communications industry. Holders of CIM Diploma exempt from certificate, except PR, if they wish to take CAM Diploma in PR.

Institute of Public Relations, The Old Trading House, 15 Northburgh Street, London, ECIV OPR 0172–253–5151. Membership by age and experience plus CAM Diploma or its equivalent. Journal *Public Relations.* Annual Sword of Excellence awards.

International Association of Business Communicators, One Hallidie Plaza, Suite 600, San Francisco, CA 94102, USA. Membersip, Accredited Membership (by exam). *IABC News,* *Communication World.* Annual Gold Quill awards. Chapters in UK and other countries.

International Public Relations Asociation. Case Postale 126, CH-1211 Geneva 20, Switzerland. Has members in 70 countries. Membership by election according to international PR experience, *IPRA Newsletter, International Public Relations Review,* international conferences.

The London Chamber of Commerce and Industry, Examinations Board. Marlowe House, Station Road, Sidcup, Kent DA15 7BJ; 0171–302 0261. Third Level certificate Examinations in advertising, Marketing, Public Relations, Selling and Sales Management (with Diplomas for passes in three or four subjects taken at the same time). Diploma in Management Studies if three subjects passed at different times.

Public Relations Consultants Association. Willow House, Willow Place, Victoria, London, SWIP 1JM; 0171–233 6026. Corporate Membership. *PRCA News.*

Appendix 5

Services

BBC World Service, Bush House, P.O. Box 76, Strand, London, WC2B 4PH.
British Council, 10 Spring Gardens, London, SW1A 2BN.
Central Office of Information, Hercules Road, London SE1 7DU.
EIBIS International, Chancery House, 53– 64 Chancery Lane, London, WC2A 1QU
PIMS, Pims House, Mildmay Avenue, London, N1 4RS.
Two-Ten Communications (incorporating UNS/PNA), Communication House, 210 Old Street, London, EC1V 9UN.

Appendix 6

Institute of Public Relations
Code of Professional Conduct

Guidelines for members

Introduction

The Code of Professional Conduct has been drawn up by the Institute of Public Relations to set down standards which will, it is hoped, make for good relationships and, reputable business dealing by public relations practitioners. There are other, internationally adopted, Codes of Conduct which have the support of the Institute.

The Code is binding on members of the Institute and is under constant review. The latest revisions were approved by the Annual General Meeting in 1992. These Guidelines should be used in conjunction with other Guidelines and Recommended Practice Papers issued by the Institute from time to time (see end). They are intended to assist members in interpreting the Code, but it must be emphasised that they cannot be all-embracing. Circumstances vary and it is up to members to measure their conduct against the standards set by the Code.

Complaints about breaches of the Code, which may come from any individual or organisation, are investigated by the Institute's Professional Practices Committee which, if considered appropriate, may refer the matter to the Disciplinary Committee for action. The Code is in no way a substitute for the law of the land, and anyone seeking redress against a member should do so through the normal legal processes.

Arbitration over a dispute is not part of the function of the Professional Practices Committee, but the Committee can sometimes appoint three senior Fellows of the Institute to act as arbitrators, provided all the parties connected with the dispute agree, in advance, to be bound by the outcome.

Nor does the Committee comment on the amount of fees charged by a member, since these are conditioned by many factors outside the Institute's control. Terms of business are usually negotiated in advance and should be adhered to.

While the Committee will consider complaints about members from non-members, it is not usually able to consider complaints from members about non-members.

Conduct concerning the practice of public relations

A member shall:

1.1   Have a positive duty to observe the highest standards in the practice of public relations and to deal fairly and honestly with employers and clients (past and present), fellow members and professionals, the public relations profession, other professions, suppliers, intermediaries, the media of communications, employees and the public.

This clause emphasises the fact that the Code applies to a member's relationships with many different 'publics'. The list may not be comprehensive.

1.2   Be aware of, understand and observe this Code, any amendment to it, and any other codes which shall be incorporated into it; remain up to date with the content and recommendations of any guidance or practice papers issued by IPR; and have a duty to conform to good practice as expressed in such guidance or practice papers.

The Code is not a piece of window dressing; members have a positive duty to observe the Code, follow any changes that may be made to it and conform to any guidance or interpretation that may from time to time be agreed by the Institute's Council and promulgated to members.

1.3   Uphold this Code and co-operate with fellow members to enforce decisions on any matter arising from its application. A member who knowingly causes or allows his or her staff to act in a manner inconsistent with this Code is party to such action and shall be deemed to be in breach of this Code. Staff employed by a member who act in a manner inconsistent with this Code should be disciplined by the member.

Responsibility for upholding the Code and the principles it embodies does not apply solely to members' own behaviour, but also to the extent to which they can exercise influence over others, especially members of their staff and fellow members.

A member shall not:

1.4   Engage in any practice nor be seen to conduct him or her self in any manner detrimental to the reputation of the Institute or the reputation and interest of the public relations profession.

This is a 'catch-all' clause. If, for example, a member is seen to be drunk or found to be dishonest, such behaviour may be detrimental to the Institute or the public relations profession. Whether such behaviour is actually in breach of this clause would have to be judged on the particular circumstances of the case.

Conduct concerning the public, the media and other professionals

A member shall:

2.1 Conduct his or her professional activities with proper regard to the public interest.

Emphasises the importance of responsible behaviour by public relations practitioners. The public interest is not easy to define; a product may be in the interests of one section of the public but contrary to the interests of another. The Code calls for a responsible attitude to all sections of the public.

2.2 Have a positive duty at all times to respect the truth and shall not disseminate false or misleading information knowingly or recklessly, and take proper care to check all information prior to its dissemination.

It is worth emphasising that this clause applies whether the member is an employer or an employee.

2.3 Have a duty to ensure that the actual interest of any organisation with which he or she may be professionally concerned is adequately declared.

A member representing a client or employer must make the client's interest known when making representations and in a manner which is straightforward and does not mislead. The use of a 'front' organisation or name suggesting an objective different from that of a member's client or employer is not permitted. (e.g. a hypothetical 'Paint Advisory Service' whose title would suggest the availability of 'neutral' advice on any paint problem, but whose ultimate objective is the sale of a particular make of paint.)

2.4 When working in association with other professionals, identify and respect the codes of those professions.

Public relations work is not done in isolation as is the case with some professions. A member may be working closely with, for example, a journalist, accountant or lawyer and must take care that they or their profession are in no way compromised.

2.5 Respect any statutory or regulatory codes laid down by any other authorities which are relevant to the actions of his or her employer or client, or taken on behalf of an employer or client.

This is a warning about the many regulations or codes, voluntary and statutory that may be relevant to an intended course of action. Where appropriate, members should familiarise themselves with these regulations and not only avoid offending against them, but should warn their employer or client against so doing.

2.6 Ensure that the names of all directors, executives, and retained advisers of his or her employers or company who hold public office, are members of either House of Parliament, Local Authorities or of any statutory organisation or body, are recorded in the IPR Register.

Members have a positive duty to declare, in the register, any public office-holder retained by them or their employers. The register is maintained by the Institute and is available to members or non-members on request.

2.7 Honour confidences received or given in the course of professional activity.

Members can only work effectively if they have the confidence of their client or employer. This clause emphasises that respecting such confidence is a professional duty and applies even if the connection with that employer or client has ended.

2.8 Neither propose nor undertake, or cause an employer or client to propose or undertake, any action which would be an improper influence on government, legislation, holders of public office or members of any statutory body or organisation, or the media of communication.

The purpose of public relations is to promote better mutual understanding and this should be the keynote in trying to impress on the media or on representatives of the government, local authorities or other organisations, any need to effect changes in the law or the rules laid down by such organisations.

It is for individual members to judge whether payments, gifts or other 'inducements' given to holders of public office other than those declared under 2.6, are in contravention of this clause. Though, in the event of a complaint, such judgement would fall to the Professional Practices Committee.

Conduct concerning employers and clients

A member shall:

3.1 Safeguard the confidences of both present and former employers or clients: shall not disclose or use these confidences to the disadvantage or prejudice of such employers or clients, or to the financial advantage of the member (unless the employer or client has released such information for public use, or has given specific permission for disclosure), except upon the order of a court of law.

This is an extension to clause 2.7, applying specifically to confidential information gained from past or present clients or employers. For example: a member may not give confidential information about one client to a competitor of the client, or provide information about a client to a third party in return for some sort of reward. There are various other ways in which this clause could be contravened, but the clause could be over-ruled by a Court of Law.

3.2 Inform an employer or client of any shareholding or financial interest held by that member or any staff employed by that member in any company or person whose services he or she recommends.

This safeguards employers or clients from possible undisclosed interests a member may have when recommending the use of a third party.

3.3 Be free to accept fees, commissions or other valuable considerations from persons other than an employer or client, if such considerations are disclosed to the employer or client.

This permits, for example, a percentage of printing costs being taken by a member, but only if this is disclosed to the client or employer. Although not specifically stated, it is implied in the Code that this disclosure should be at the time fees are agreed.

3.4 Be free to negotiate, or renegotiate, with an employer or client terms that are a fair reflection of demands of the work involved and take into account factors other than hours worked and the experience involved. These special factors, which are also applied by other professional advisers, shall have regard to all the circumstances of the specific situation and in particular to:

(a) The complexity of the issue, case, problem or assignment, and the difficulties associated with its completion.
(b) The professional or specialised skills required and the degree of responsibility involved.
(c) The amount of documentation necessary to be perused or prepared, and its importance.
(d) The place and circumstances where the work is carried out, in whole or in part.
(e) The scope, scale and value of the task and its importance as an activity, issue or project to the employer or client.

Public relations work varies greatly in complexity and this clause sets out five factors to be taken into account in negotiating fee or salary. There may well be others. If, during the course of an assignment circumstances change a renegotiation could be in order.

A member shall not:

3.5 Misuse information regarding his or her employer's or client's business for financial or other gain.

This clause refers to the misuse of any information about an employer's or client's business, to a member's advantage whether or not the information is confidential.

3.6 Use inside information for gain. Nor may a member of staff managed or employed by a member directly trade in his or her employer's or client's securities without the prior written permission of the employer or client and of the member's chief executive or chief financial officer or compliance officer.

'Inside information' is information about an employer or client obtained during the course of a member's employment which would not be fully available to outsiders. The clause applies particularly to information concerning the financial status of the company concerned. Statutory and regulatory provisions place strict conditions on the conduct of financial communications and on trading in the company's shares or other securities as required by the Stock Exchange's listing requirements.

3.7 Serve an employer or client under terms or conditions which might impair his or her independence, objectivity or integrity.

This clause is designed to protect members from unfair conditions being imposed that might impair their judgement or compromise their integrity. For example, members should not accept a condition seeking to cause them to publish false information, thus breaching clause 2.2.

3.8 Represent conflicting interests but may represent competing interests with the express consent of the parties concerned.

Example: It would be a breach to represent both Coca Cola and Pepsi Cola, but provided both parties agreed, a member might represent one of them and also a brewer or a retailer. If a member is in doubt about the possibility of two clients being in conflict, the client's views should be sought before agreeing to represent them.

3.9 Guarantee the achievement of results which are beyond the member's direct capacity to achieve or prevent.

In most of the campaigns which a public relations practitioner undertakes, the outcome is influenced by a number of factors only partially or not at all under the control of the practitioner. For example, a member acting for a company making a hostile bid for another would be quite wrong to guarantee success. Similarly it would be wrong to guarantee a specific amount of favourable press coverage.

Conduct concerning colleagues

A member shall:

4.1 Adhere to the highest standards of accuracy and truth, avoiding extravagant claims or unfair comparisons and giving credit for ideas and words borrowed from others.

All public relations work is concerned with ideas, which may come from various sources. Practitioners naturally want to lay claim to their successes, but must stick to the truth in doing so, give credit where it is due and not plagiarise other people's ideas.

4.2 Be free to represent his or her capabilities and service to any potential employer or client, either on his or her own initiative or at the behest of any client, provided in so doing he or she does not seek to break any existing contract or detract from the reputation or capabilities of any member already serving that employer or client.

A member is, of course, free to seek new clients or a new employer, but in doing so must not in any way denigrate another member, who may be already working for the prospective client or employer. If a member is making a presentation to a prospective client it is usual and courteous to inform any existing member concerned, or at least to ask the 'prospect' to ignore the approach where PR needs are already being satisfactorily met.

A member shall not:

4.3 Injure the professional reputation or practice of another member.

This clause scarcely calls for further comment. It is not difficult to damage a person's or a corporation's professional reputation. To do so where a fellow member is concerned would contravene the Code if not the libel laws.

Interpreting the Code

5.1 In the interpretation of this code, the Laws of the Land shall apply.

Even the IPR Code is not above the law.

Other Guidelines and Recommended Practice Papers issued by, and available from the Institute are:

Public Relations and the Law; Public Relations Practice: Its Role and Parameters; Resolving the Advertising/Editorial Conflict; The Use, Misuse and Abuse of Embargoes; Fees and Methods of Charging for Public Relations Services; The News Release; Photographs Accompanying News Releases; Press Kits.

Dealing ·ith complaints

The following extracts from the Institute's Memorandum and Articles of Association describe the procedure used to deal with complaints regarding breaches of the Code of Professional Conduct and the subsequent disciplinary process. This procedure was revised in 1986 and adopted by special resolution at the Annual General Meeting of the Institute of Public Relations on 8 April 1987.

Amended Articles 12–18

Disciplinary powers

12 The Council shall be empowered to reprimand a member or suspend a member from membership for a period not exceeding two years or terminate the membership of a member who acts or conducts himself in such a manner that the council shall deem him to have:

(i) violated any such standards of professional conduct as may be established or prescribed under the provisions of the Memorandum; or
(ii) acted in breach of any rule of the Memorandum and Articles or any regulation made by the Council under the provisions of these Articles; or
(iii) brought or been likely to bring public relations practice, public relations practitioners or the Institute into disrepute.

13 When disciplinary action is taken this should be in accordance with the disciplinary proceedings rules set out in Appendix B.

14 Subject to the provisions of these Articles the Council may make rules for regulating the consideration and complaints by the Professional Practices Committee and subsequent reference of complaints to the Disciplinary Committee and the hearing and adjudication by the Disciplinary Committee of complaints or applications. If a member wishes to resign his membership of the Institute when a complaint against him has been referred to the Disciplinary Committee his resignation shall not become effective until such complaint has been disposed of.

15 The Disciplinary Committee shall, as soon as possible following its hearing, report its findings and decisions to the Council. If the Committee finds that the complaint has been substantiated it shall also instruct the Council as to how the Council's powers under Article 12 should be exercised.

16 The Council shall accept the findings and decision of the Disciplinary Committee and shall forthwith exercise its powers under Article 12 accordingly. Any decision by the Council to reprimand, suspend or terminate the member-ship of a member shall automatically disqualify for five years the member concerned from holding any office or committee membership within the Institute (including offices or committee membership within regional or vocational groups recognised by the Council of the Institute). Such disqualifi-cation may nevertheless be withdrawn at any time after the expiry of two years from its commencement at the discretion of the Council upon application by the member concerned.

17 The decision of the Disciplinary Committee shall be final subject to Article 18 and binding on all parties and shall be communicated to them as soon as possible following the exercise by the Council of its powers. The decision shall also be published to members at the earliest opportunity by inclusion in an official publication of the Institute of particulars of the complaint with the findings and any order of the Council thereupon. At its discretion the Council may cause wider publication of such information and the Disciplinary Committee may make recommendations to the Council in this respect.

18 Any reprimand or suspension or termination of membership under these Articles may at any time be revoked or modified by the Council subject to such terms and conditions as the Council shall think fit and provided that the resolution revoking or modifying the reprimand, suspension or termination be passed at a meeting of the Council convened with notice of the resolution, at which meeting the quorum shall be two-thirds of the membership of the Council and for which resolution not less than three-quarters of those present shall vote.

Appendix B — disciplinary proceedings rules

1   Definitions
For the purpose of these rules 'Complaint' means a complaint against a member of the Institute made in accordance with Articles 12−18 (Disciplinary Powers), 'Complainant' means the originator of such a complaint; and 'defendant' means the member against whom the complaint is being lodged.

2   The complaint
A complaint may be originated by any individual, whether a member of the Institute or not, or by any organisation, or by any committee of the Council (other than the Disciplinary Committee) or by the Council itself.

3   On receipt of a formal complaint the Secretary shall if necessary correspond with the Complainant in order to clarity (sic) any matters of uncertainty and identify the specific clause or clauses of the Code of Professional Conduct referred to in the complaint. The Secretary must also inform the Complainant in writing of the Institute's Disciplinary Procedure and in particular explain that the Defendant will be notified of the complaint in order than he may exercise his right to reply. The Secretary shall then send details of the complaint to the Defendant and invite him to submit written observations which will be placed before the Professional Practices Committee.

4   Any complaint must be placed by the Secretary before the Professional Practices Committee as soon as possible but no longer than eight weeks after the complaint was received except by agreement of both parties.

5   Hearing the complaint
The Professional Practices Committee shall consider the complaint together with any written comments or observations offered by the Complainant and the Defendant.

6   The Professional Practices Committee may instruct the Secretary to seek further details from the parties concerned or additional information from any appropriate source and will inform the parties concerned of their rights to attend. No party may be represented before the Professional Practices Committee by any other person without leave of the Committee and such leave will be granted only in exceptional circumstances. In the event however of the Complainant being the Council or a committee thereof the Complainant may nominate one of its members for the purpose of attending on its behalf before the Professional Practices Committee.

7   Decision by Professional Practices Committee
If, in the opinion of the Professional Practices Committee, the complaint has no substance or for any other reason should not be referred to the Disciplinary Committee the papers will be returned to the Secretary who will advise the

Complainant and the member complained of accordingly. At the same time the Chairman of the Professional Practices Committee may write to the member complained of and while reporting that the matter would not be referred to the Disciplinary Committee may draw attention to any relevant matter in the Institute's Code of Professional Conduct. The dispatch of such a letter will be at the Chairman's discretion and no reference to the existence of such a letter will ever be made in any other subsequent Disciplinary Proceedings.

8 If, in the opinion of the Professional Practices Committee, a prima facie case within the terms of Articles 12(i), (ii) or (iii) has been established, the Professional Practices Committee may refer the case to the Disciplinary Committee and the Secretary shall notify the Complainant and the person complained about of this fact forthwith. The person complained about shall be informed of his right to appear before the Disciplinary Committee in person and/or by legal or other representative and to submit evidence.

9 The Professional Practices Committee shall not report upon the facts of the case to the Council but merely report that the matter has been referred to the Disciplinary Committee for a hearing. The Secretary shall also notify the Complainant and the person complained about of the decision of the Professional Practices Committee.

10 Date for hearing

The Disciplinary Committee shall fix a day for hearing, which shall be no later than eight weeks from the date of the reference by the Professional Practices Committee unless by agreement of the parties and then only in exceptional circumstances.

11 Notice of the date of hearing shall be issued to all parties at least 21 days before that date.

12 The notice of hearing shall require the party to whom it is addressed to furnish to the Secretary and to any other party at least 14 days before the day fixed for hearing a list of all documents on which the party to whom it is addressed intends to reply.

13 Parties to a complaint

The parties to a complaint laid before the Disciplinary Committee by the Professional Practices Committee shall be the Professional Practices Committee and the Defendant or Defendants. The Professional Practices Committee will normally delegate its Chairman or another member to be responsible for the conduct of the case on its behalf.

14 Statement of offences

As soon as possible, and not later than 21 days before the day fixed for hearing, the Professional Practices Committee, after referring a case to the Disciplinary Committee shall supply to the Disciplinary Committee and to the

Defendant or Defendants a full statement of the offence or offences alleged, specifying the sub-section or sub-sections of Article 12 and/or the article or articles of the Code of Professional Conduct alleged to have been infringed.

15 Further evidence

The Professional Practices Committee may after referring a case to the Disciplinary Committee require the Complainant to supply such further information and documents relating to the complaint as they think fit. They may instruct the Secretary to make such enquiries and assemble such evidence as seems to them necessary, and may instruct solicitors and/or Counsel if they consider it to be desirable in the interests of justice.

16 Documents

Any party may inspect the documents included in the list furnished by any other party. A copy of any document mentioned in the list furnished by a party shall on application and on payment of reasonable charges therefore by the party requiring it, be furnished to that party by any other within seven days of receipt of such application.

17 (i) Any party may by notice in writing at any time not later than nine days before the day fixed for the hearing call upon any other party to admit any document saving all just exceptions and if such other party desires to challenge the authenticity of the document, he shall within six days after service of such notice, give notice that he does not admit the document and requires it to be proved at the hearing.

(ii) If such other party refuses or neglects to give notice of non-admission within the time prescribed in the last preceding paragraph he shall be deemed to have admitted the document unless otherwise ordered by the Disciplinary Committee.

18 Appearance at hearing

If any party fails to appear at the hearing the Disciplinary Committee may, upon proof of service on such party of the notice of the hearing, proceed to hear and determine the complaint in his absence. If they have heard and determined the complaint in the absence of that party and they are afterwards satisfied that such absence was unavoidable they may at their discretion re-hear the case.

19 Evidence by affidavit

The Disciplinary Committee may, in their discretion, either as to the whole case or as to any particular fact or facts proceed and act upon evidence given by affidavit, provided that any party to the proceedings may request the attendance of any such deponent to any such affidavit for the purpose of giving oral evidence, unless the Committee are satisfied that the affidavit is purely formal and that the requirement of the attendance of the deponent is made with the sole object of causing delay.

20   Hearing to be private

The proceedings of the Disciplinary Committee shall be held in private, unless otherwise agreed by all parties.

21   Withdrawal of complaint

No complaint shall be withdrawn after it has been referred to the Disciplinary Committee, unless that Committee directs otherwise.

22   Adjournment of hearing

The Disciplinary Committee may of their own notion or upon the application of any party adjourn the hearing upon such terms as the Committee shall think fit.

23   Multiple cases

In the case of a complaint in respect of a member's employee, who is also a member, the Disciplinary Committee may on the application of any party or on their own motion order that any such complaint shall be heard prior to, in the course of, concurrently with, or subsequent to the hearing of a complaint in respect of the employing member.

24   Subsequent allegations

If upon the hearing it shall appear to the Disciplinary Committee that the allegations require to be amended, or added to, the Committee may permit such amendment or addition, or if in the opinion of the Committee such amendment or addition is not within the scope of the complaint, may require the same to be embodied in a further complaint provided that if such amendment or addition shall be such as to take any party by surprise or prejudice the conduct of his case, the Committee shall grant an adjournment of the hearing upon such terms as the Committee shall think fit.

25   Records of proceedings

At the request of either party on application in writing to the Secretary 14 days prior to the date fixed for the proceedings before the Disciplinary Committee or on the instruction of the Chairman of the Disciplinary Committee, the Secretary shall arrange that a record of the proceedings shall be taken by a person approved by the Committee, provided that if such arrangement is made at the request of a party that party shall undertake to meet the costs of the attendance of such person and the making of such records. Such a person appointed to take a record of the proceedings shall be required to supply to the Committee, to each party to the proceedings, but to no other person, a copy or copies of the transcript of such notes or extracts therefrom on payment of his transcribing and copying charges. The transcribing charge shall be paid as to one third each by the complainant and the defendant and one third by the Institute. The charges for copies shall be apportioned pro rata among those receiving them.

26   Service documents

Service of any notice or document may be effected under these Rules to any party or to his solicitor by recorded delivery or registered post addressed to the last known place of business or abode of the person on whom the notice or document is to be served, and such service shall be deemed to be effected at the time when the letter would be delivered in the ordinary course of post.

27   Filing of documents

All papers and documents relating to proceedings before the Disciplinary Committee shall be filed and kept by the Secretary.

28   Quorum of Professional Practices Committee and of Disciplinary Committee

The quorum of the Professional Practices Committee and that of the Disciplinary Committee for all purposes shall respectively be four and three.

29   Legal assessors

The Disciplinary Committee may appoint legally qualified assessors and in appropriate cases instruct one or more to sit and act as non-voting members of Disciplinary Committee to ensure that the proceedings are conducted in accordance with the principles of natural justice and the law. The Disciplinary Committee shall not be bound by the legal rules of evidence.

30   Date of Disciplinary Committee's decision

The Secretary shall give notice to the parties of the date when the decision of the Disciplinary Committee will be pronounced.

31   The Disciplinary Committee will report to the Council the result of the hearing and the decision of the Committee concerning the action to be taken.

April 1992

Index